WORLD YEARBOOK
OF EDUCATION 1995

World Yearbook of Education 1982/83
Computers and Education
Edited by Jacquetta Megarry, David R F Walker,
Stanley Nisbet and Eric Hoyle

World Yearbook of Education 1984
Women and Education
Edited by Sandra Acker, Jacquetta Megarry,
Stanley Nisbet and Eric Hoyle

World Yearbook of Education 1985
Research, Policy and Practice
Edited by John Nisbet, Jacquetta Megarry and Stanley Nisbet

World Yearbook of Education 1986
The Management of Schools
Edited by Eric Hoyle and Agnes McMahon

World Yearbook of Education 1987
Vocational Education
Edited by John Twining, Stanley Nisbet and Jacquetta Megarry

World Yearbook of Education 1988
Education for the New Technologies
Edited by Duncan Harris (Series Editor)

World Yearbook of Education 1989
Health Education
Edited by Chris James, John Balding and Duncan Harris (Series Editor)

World Yearbook of Education 1990
Assessment and Evaluation
Edited by Chris Bell and Duncan Harris (Series Editor)

World Yearbook of Education 1991
International Schools and International Education
Edited by Patricia L. Jonietz (Guest Editor) and Duncan Harris (Series Editor)

World Yearbook of Education 1992
Urban Education
Edited by David Coulby, Crispin Jones and Duncan Harris (Series Editor)

World Yearbook of Education 1993
Special Needs Education
Edited by Peter Mittler
Ron Brouillette and Duncan Harris (Series Editor)

World Yearbook of Education 1994
The Gender Gap in Higher Education
Edited by Suzanne Stiver Lie, Lynda Malik and Duncan Harris (Series Editor)

WORLD YEARBOOK OF EDUCATION 1995

YOUTH, EDUCATION AND WORK

Edited by Leslie Bash and Andy Green
Series Editors: David Coulby and Crispin Jones

KOGAN PAGE

London ● Philadelphia

First published in 1995

Kogan Page Limited
120 Pentonville Road
London N1 9JN

British Library Cataloguing in Publication Data
A CIP record for this book is available from the British Library.

ISBN 0 7494 1419 7
ISSN 0084–2508

Typeset by BookEns Ltd, Royston, Herts.
Printed and bound in Great Britain by Biddles Ltd, Guildford and King's Lynn.

Contents

List of contributors   vii

Preface   viii

Part 1: Political and economic contexts

Introduction, *Leslie Bash*   3

1. Education, work and global economic change *Bruce Wilson and
   Roger Woock*   5

2. Post-Fordist possibilities: education, training and national development
   Phillip Brown and Hugh Lauder   19

3. Education and training in the New Europe: economic and political
   contexts
   Martin Mclean   33

4. Education, work and the restructuring of Central-Eastern and Eastern
   Europe *J J Tomiak*   49

Part 2: Education, training and labour market change

Introduction *Andy Green*   65

5. Work, labour markets and vocational preparation: Anglo-German
   comparisons of training in intermediate skills *David Marsden and
   Paul Ryan*   67

6. Gender and the school–work transition in Canada and the USA
   Jane Gaskell   80

7. The role of the state and the social partners in VET systems
   Andy Green   92

8. Youth training for a changing economy in Holland *Eva Voncken and
   Jeroen Onstenk*   109

9. Educating and training youth for the world of work in Malaysia and
   Singapore *Elwyn Thomas*   119

Part 3: Curriculum and qualification reform in post-compulsory education and training

Introduction *Andy Green*   135

10. Vocational qualifications in Europe: The emergence of common assessment *Alison Wolf*   137

11. Strategies for reforming post-compulsory education and training in the Australian states *Jack Keating*   149

12. Education as a foundation for work? The efficiency and problems of the Japanese upper-secondary school *Akio Inui and Tsuneo Hosogane*   162

13. Human resource development in post-apartheid South Africa: some initial observations *Elaine Unterhalter and Michael Young*   173

14. From education to work: the case of technical schools *Gary McCulloch*   188

Part 4: Youth, society and citizenship

Introduction *Leslie Bash*   201

15. Youth transitions in the European Union *Lynne Chisholm*   203

16. Careers guidance systems in the European Community *A G Watts*   218

17. Risky futures for the daughters of the Nordic welfare state *Anja Heikkinen*   230

18. Teacher–student estrangement and the schooling of urban youth for citizenship *William B Thomas and Kevin J Moran*   243

19. The integration of young people into UK society with particular reference to the Jewish community *Leslie Bash*   258

Biographical notes on contributors   268

Bibliography   272

Index   285

List of contributors

Leslie Bash, Anglia Polytechnic University   *Chapter 19*
Phillip Brown, University of Kent   *Chapter 2*
Lynne Chisholm, University of Marburg   *Chapter 15*
Jane Gaskell, University of British Columbia   *Chapter 6*
Andy Green, Institute of Education, University of London   *Chapter 7*
Tsuneo Hosogane, Waseda University   *Chapter 12*
Akio Inui, Hosei University   *Chapter 12*
Jack Keating, Curriculum Corporation, Melbourne   *Chapter 11*
Hugh Lauder, Victoria University of Wellington   *Chapter 2*
Gary McCulloch, Sheffield University   *Chapter 14*
Martin McLean, Institute of Education, University of London   *Chapter 3*
David Marsden, London School of Economics and Political Science   *Chapter 5*
Kevin J Moran, University of Pittsburgh   *Chapter 18*
Jeroen Onstenk, University of Amsterdam   *Chapter 8*
Paul Ryan, King's College, University of Cambridge   *Chapter 5*
Elwyn Thomas, Institute of Education, University of London   *Chapter 9*
William B Thomas, University of Pittsburgh   *Chapter 18*
J J Tomiak, University of London (retd)   *Chapter 4*
Elaine Unterhalter, Institute of Education, University of London   *Chapter 13*
Eva Voncken, University of Amsterdam   *Chapter 8*
A G Watts, National Institute for Careers Education and
    Counselling, Cambridge   *Chapter 16*
Bruce Wilson, Union Research Centre on Organisation and
    Technology, Australia   *Chapter 1*
Alison Wolf, Institute of Education, University of London   *Chapter 10*
Roger R Woock, University of Melbourne   *Chapter 1*
Michael Young, Institute of Education, University of London   *Chapter 13*

Preface

This edition of the *World Yearbook of Education* addresses themes related to the transition from childhood to adulthood. Entry into employment and other areas of social life which are symbolic of maturity and the attainment of full citizenship differs from society to society and, importantly, is contingent upon appropriate political and economic factors.

As such, the volume draws upon a diversity of approaches and tries to reflect the experiences of different regions of the world. It has, like previous editions, been only partially successful in this; inevitably, there is something of a Eurocentric bias. Even so, besides North America and Australasia, there are chapters which examine crucial aspects of youth and work in countries such as Malaysia and South Africa.

The 1995 *World Yearbook* came to fruition after a lengthy period of development in which a number of eminent scholars specializing in the theme of youth, education and work were approached as possible contributors. As editors, we were very pleased at the positive response and we are certain that the volume as a whole reflects a commitment to this aspect of the educational process.

We are, of course, grateful for the help given to us by the series editors, Crispin Jones and David Coulby, and we must also thank various colleagues, partners and others who have given support when it was needed.

Leslie Bash
Andy Green

Part 1: Political and economic contexts

Introduction

Leslie Bash

No analysis of youth, education and work can be undertaken without reference to political formations and structures of economic relations. While the final years of the twentieth century have seen developments in political and economic cooperation between nation-states, the most resounding impact upon consciousness has been in relation to processes of disintegration. This was exemplified by the destruction of the communist regimes in Eastern Europe but also by an accompanying resurgence of nationalism. On the other hand, there has been the development of an ever-expanding European Union, fundamental changes in the productive technological base with the corollary of restructured employment, and an increasing globalization of the economy. This latter phenomenon has, of course, involved the further uncoupling of consumption from production, as manufacturing capacity locks in with low-cost labour wherever it is located in the world.

The ramifications for young people and their entry into the productive sphere have been recognized across nation-states. The old assumptions regarding prospects for employment have long been challenged by changing economic fortunes, but with the decline of statism in both East and West the market has begun to bite in a fairly severe manner. The chapters in this section consider some of these important changes. The first, by Wilson and Woock, looks at global economic change and its implications for work and education, focusing in a critical manner upon Australia as a case study. In the chapter, economic theories about education are examined, while the model of a crudely utilitarian approach to education and industrial restructuring is subject to critique. The chapter by Brown and Lauder assumes a neo-Fordist/post-Fordist structure of global industrial activity. Post-Fordism, based on customized production and multi-skilled workers, suggests a new educational paradigm centred upon the development of a 'collective intelligence'. McLean's chapter deals with the 'New Europe', describing the interaction of economic change and the historic tradition of training, while Tomiak concludes the section with an examination of the political and economic factors influencing educational and employment policies in contemporary Central-Eastern and Eastern Europe. These last two chapters point to the dangers of cross-national transfer where policy-making and successful policy implementation are contingent upon the cultural contexts in which they originally occurred.

1. Education, work and global economic change

Bruce Wilson and Roger R Woock

International pressures

After the Second World War, the industrialized countries of the northern hemisphere enjoyed a lengthy period of economic growth. This boom came to an end in the early 1970s, prompted partly by the growing incapacity of the United States economy to finance the war in Vietnam, and by the sudden increase in energy costs sparked by the OPEC countries' decision to increase the price of oil significantly. The international economic instability which resulted has presaged a much more complex transition in international capitalism.

> [T]he long postwar boom, from 1945 to 1973, was built upon a certain set of labour control practices, technological mixes, consumption habits, and configurations of political-economic power... The break up of this system since 1973 has inaugurated a period of rapid change, flux and uncertainty... [T]he contrasts between the present political-economic practices and those of the postwar boom period are sufficiently strong to make the hypothesis of a shift from Fordism to what might be called a 'flexible' regime of accumulation a telling way to characterise recent history. (Harvey, 1989, p 124)

While there has been extensive debate over the nature of the changes that have occurred during the past 20 years, there seems to be little doubt that significant problems in international capitalism had resulted from a crisis of overaccumulation, and excessive rigidities in the developed world in capital investment, production processes, labour relations and markets. This situation was complicated by the steady industrialization of the developing countries: Brazil, and the 'mini-dragons' of Asia.

> [C]orporations found themselves with a lot of unusable capacity (chiefly idle plant and equipment) under conditions of intensifying competition ... Technological change, automation, the search for new product lines and market niches, geographical dispersal to zones of easier labour control, mergers, and steps to accelerate the turnover

5

time of their capital surged to the fore of corporate strategies for survival under general conditions of deflation. (Harvey, 1989, p 145)

Economies of scope and flexibility in manufacturing, targeting at sophisticated niche markets, have resulted in considerable profitability, while the prices of primary commodities have declined steadily. 'Flexible accumulation' has become increasingly evident in production processes, patterns of consumption and in labour markets. Finance services and the finance sector have been fundamentally reorganized and become much more central to the operation of the international economy. New forms of organization and technological innovation have become crucial to maintaining rates of corporate profitability. The undermining of traditional labour relations has had serious consequences for trade unions, which have had to reflect carefully on the changes occurring in the organization of capital, if they are to do any more than react post hoc to corporate initiatives. The resurgence of 'informal' economies in developed countries, as well as in Asia, Africa and South America, has made disadvantaged workers even more vulnerable, leading to a growth in patriarchal family businesses and homeworking.

Global change in social and technological context

For four decades, social commentators have remarked on the significance of the transformations occurring in the advanced industrial (and capitalist) nations. As their forebears did with the formative years of the Industrial Revolution, these commentators have attempted often to encapsulate the core of the transformation in a specific concept. Some of the concepts, reflected in labels such as 'organizational revolution', 'knowledge economy', 'scientific-technological revolution', 'information society', 'service society', and 'post-industrial society', have emphasized the changes in the economic basis of society. Other analysts, more concerned with the political character of change, have referred to the 'post-capitalist society', 'managerial capitalism', 'post-collectivist', or 'post-modern' society.

There is little doubt that while each of these concepts, and the many others introduced into this debate, add something to the understanding of contemporary change, very little is yet agreed about its nature or scale, or its longer-term implications for the economic and social futures of human communities throughout the world. The one insight on which most analysts are now agreed is that the successful implementation of technological innovations depends on complex interactions between social, technical and economic forces. Many of the predictions made in the 1960s and 1970s about the impact of computers and other new technologies ('electronic cottages', 'paperless, one-person offices', 'robot-run factories', and productivity improvements) have simply not occurred, because of inadequate understanding of the implications of these contextual complexities.

Beyond this, there is very little agreement about whether the contemporary process of change constitutes a radical break with the past, such that the very fabric of society is being transformed, or whether the new technologies, radical though they may be, represent more of a transition from one type of industrial society to another (see Harvey, 1989). The debate on this issue is a matter not only of dispassionate analysis, but also of political interests. Beniger (1986), for example, has argued that the rapid expansion in the use of information technology is essentially a continuing reflection of the priority placed by capitalist management on control of their employees; Touraine (1989), however, suggests that the coincidence of technological advances with the diminishing authority of the state and the increasing importance of social movements, offers the possibility that democratic processes can be enhanced in new ways.

> Today it is even more true that society is the totality of states of social conflicts. Because industrial societies have increased their ability to intervene in their own structures ... the field of conflicts has been broadened and at the same time separated more clearly from political struggles in the strict sense, ie, those that have to do with the conquest of state power. The real centre of social life is the general and permanent debate about the utilization of new technologies, new instruments for the transformation of personal and collective life ... From nuclear industry to genetic engineering, from the media to the universities – in all those domains we see the development of discussion and of currents of opinion which all relate to the same central question: under what conditions can our technological potential be used to enhance the liberty and security of every individual, instead of subordinating individuals and groups to a technocratic power? (Touraine, 1989, p 17)

The issues have been particularly pertinent not only to debates about the transformation of civil life, but also to developments in workplace organization.

New technologies in the workplace

Until recent years, much of the debate about the economic impact of new technologies was limited by a conceptualization of 'productivity' in terms of the value of output per worker. Analyses were made of the aggregate benefits of capital investment in new technology, and in education, the production of human capital. Whilst these analyses suggested that increased education levels produced greater productivity and, hence, profitability, little attention was given to analysing the precise nature of this relationship, or to how the worker's knowledge and skill actually enhanced the value of the output. As early as 1975, Thurow had argued that increase in a company's productivity was related to the organization of, and skills required in, particular jobs, rather than of individual workers and their qualifications (Thurow, 1975).

In the 1980s, however, a more sophisticated approach has focused not on the contributions of individual workers, but on the trends in demands for specific occupations and the relationship between investment in new technologies, workplace organization, occupational restructuring, skill availability and development, productivity and output. As the OECD has noted, deriving the maximum benefit from technological innovation depends on taking into account 'the key sets of interrelationships that affect technology decisions and outcomes' (OECD, 1988, p 29).

Important among these is the character of the technical attributes of workers and, perhaps even more importantly, how they are deployed within and between particular enterprises. Developments in the institutionalized arrangements for addressing skills formation have very significant implications for the effectiveness of organizations in achieving the objective of becoming internationally competitive in the new era of 'flexible accumulation'. Before discussing the new emphases in this area, it is important to consider different theoretical approaches to educational provision.

Economic theories about education

Economic theories about education can be classified in ways which will suggest something about the relationship between the economy and education in almost all nations of the world. Two broad categories of economic theories about education can be identified: human capital theory and economic rationalism.

Human capital theory

Having its origin in slavery, a very clear definition of human capital, the modern origin of the theory was identified by Adam Smith in *The Wealth of Nations*:

> the acquired and useful abilities of all the inhabitants or members of this society. The acquisition of such talents by the maintenance of the acquirer during his education study or apprenticeship, always costs a real expense, which is a capital fixed and realised, as it were, in his person. Those talents, as they make a part of his fortune, so do they likewise to that of the society to which he belongs. The improved dexterity of a workman may be considered in the same light as a machine or instrument of trade which facilitates and abridges labour in which, though it costs a certain expense, repays that expense with a profit. (Smith, 1979, p 377)

Although John Stuart Mill reminded readers that human beings are the purpose for which wealth exists, it soon became common among economists to treat human beings themselves as capital and not the skills or knowledge which they possess. While this may seem a small difference it has led to a view of human beings as economic actors to the exclusion of other aspects of human life. This exclusion is important both in the new human capital theory and in economic rationalism.

Human capital theory attracted renewed interest in the 1960s in association with development policies in the Third World as well as economic policies in the developed world. The argument was that the education and skills level of a nation was crucial for its economic development and for it moving from a client state to a full participant in the world economy. This simple formula of expenditure on education in developing countries equalling growth still underlies many of the programmes of education and training fostered by international agencies working in developing nations. Sweden was looked to as a model of the development of human capital theory and much was made of Swedish budget presentation which listed the money spent on education under investment rather than expenditure.

During this phase of support for government expenditure to increase economic wellbeing there were questions raised because of the inability of human capital theorists to separate out in any convincing way the effect that education itself has on economic growth. Some economists of education including Sir John Vaizey (1962) and Mark Blaug (1976), insisted that the simple formula of investment leading to return could not be economically sustained. It is important to note that despite these questions it is still the case that many educational programmes in both developed and developing nations are based on the rather simple idea that educational investment leads to higher skills which lead to higher economic productivity.

After a period of eclipse in the 1970s a new or revised human capital theory emerged. Led by the OECD in the mid-80s, this revised version of human capital theory admitted to some of the errors and oversimplifications of the earlier period. While calling for an increase in the level of general education as well as higher and specialized education, the OECD did not argue that this increase necessarily justified an increase in public expenditure. The new analysis provided by the OECD and others argued that while public funding was necessary, an objective study of the private value received from education indicated that more private money in the form of fees and private tuition would be required, particularly at the higher or more specialized level of education and training. 'Broadening the resource base' was a phrase used in Australia and other countries to suggest that students themselves would be required to pay a proportion of the cost of their education.

Human capital theory in either its early or revised form still assumes some things which need to be questioned. The revised human capital theory, although focusing on private value, has still not demonstrated in any sensible way the connection between education, work and earnings. These theorists have not yet resolved the problem, as perceived by non-economists, of their identification of human beings as units of capital controlled by economic forces external to them and not reasonable self-determining knowledgeable members of a human community.

Economic rationalism

The rise of free market neo-classical economics applied to education and other areas of public policy is in one sense the story of this chapter and it is appropriate to conceive of revised human capital theory and economic rationalism as points on a continuum. Broadly speaking, economic rationalism makes three important assumptions. The first is that there is a need to get economic policy and economic objectives solved before other issues can addressed. This means that the main political issues in any society are in a fundamental sense economic: 'education is now seen as a branch of economic policy rather than a mix of social economic and cultural policy. To the extent that there is continuing concern about social policy in education it is mostly understood as labour market policy' (Marginson, 1993, p 56). The second assumption of economic rationalism is that the economic content of public policy is market oriented. The third assumption is that there must be a serious reform in the public service which emphasizes managerial efficiency at the expense of public service. The dominant style of administration has been christened 'corporate managerialism'. Bob Bessant (1992) identifies a number of features of corporate managerialism including strong central control in relation to devolved responsibility for operation, policy determination at the centre, focus on output using input/output models of production and emphasis on selling the product.

It is clear that this form of public administration fits well with the concept of market competition. Economic rationalists are totally opposed to government intervention and particularly to government planning. They are committed to reducing the role of politics and removing areas of policy from democratic control. The universal claim of the neo-classical economics underlying economic rationalism must be a worrying one for educationists because it suggests that the pursuit of private economic interest in the free market economies should be extended across the whole of social life and form the basis for judgement about people's worth. The economic rationalist model suggests that there can indeed be such a thing as too much education and educators who want to maximize intellectual, cultural and academic development of individuals will find that this objective is at some point incompatible with economic usefulness as defined by the economic rationalists.

The American economist, Paul Samuelson, made an important contribution to economic rationalist theory in 1954, namely the distinction between public and private goods. This distinction is used widely in national economic analysis, in many policy areas. While the concept of private goods is relatively simple to understand, the definition of public goods is more controversial. Samuelson used the term 'collective consumption goods' as a synonym for public goods. He argued that any public good had two characteristics: those of non-rivalry and non-exclusability. Non-rivalry means that any consumption of such a good leads to no lessening of any other individual's ability to consume that good. In that sense the air we breathe may be identified clearly as a public good. Non-exclusability means that it is impossible basically to exclude anyone from a benefit whether or not they pay to support it. National defence is clearly such a public good since it would be impossible to defend only certain individuals or, probably, only certain groups.

The first of these characteristics speaks to an absence of scarcity; that is, the difficulty of confining the good to particular individuals. The second refers to what economists call externalities; that is, benefits that could not be appropriated by individuals.

The question of externalities is important in the discussion of economic theories about education. Externalities may be defined as those benefits which accrue to the wider community and do not accrue to the individual holder of the skills or education in question. The health standards of an isolated community provided by a doctor might be a case of externalities or external value as opposed to the salary and/or fees received by her. The argument about externalities is central to the discussion in this section because under current economic thinking the only justification for public support of education at any level is through arguing for the significance of externalities. It is the serious disagreement about the extent and even the existence of such externalities that divide economists, political scientists and sociologists as they study economic theories about education today.

While existing nowhere in the world in its pure form, there is no question that the values which underlie economic rationalism and some of its policy implications, particularly the smaller role of government and the reduced expenditure required by government on education, have gained considerable support. Whether this support is for the theory or merely for some reduction in taxes is not at all clear. While the economic theories briefly identified above exist imperfectly they nevertheless have had an impact on the actual development and operation of educational and training programmes.

'Skill' and control

In the last decade, both of these theories have contributed to a tightening of the relationship between economic objectives and educational policy. With respect to the objective of hastening the diffusion and successful implementation of new technologies, considerable emphasis has been placed on the relationship between particular technologies and the skill levels of the workforce; this policy development has been confounded, however, by some debate about the nature of management control required to maximize efficiency. With respect to education and training policies, this distinction between skill and efficiency is important, as the identification of necessary 'skills' has often been made problematic by the (sometimes deliberate) confusion of 'skill' and control requirements, leading to an emphasis on behaviour and compliance rather than technical capacity (see Bates et al, 1984).

A key issue is the approach to the organization of production. A CERI (Centre for Eductional Research and Innovation) study has indicated that organizational choices have a profound effect on how particular technologies will alter the educational requirements for specific jobs. It also emphasized the importance of considering the people involved as much as the technology itself.

> The trend towards teamwork puts a premium upon broadening the competence profile of the individual worker. Increased emphasis on education and training is being directed towards communication and social skills and the need to complement necessary technical skills with a more holistic view. (OECD, 1985, p 2)

Dix, the managing director of Ford Australia, has observed that,

> The most significant advances will be gained from the return on investment in human resources, the energies and intelligence of its people ... harnessing the human factor in the quality and productivity challenge today calls for a radical new approach to human relationships in business. (Dix, quoted in ACTU/TDC, 1987, p 6)

Dix's observation is supported in a general review of the literature.

> In summary, there is considerable evidence that supports the view that the potential allocative contribution of workers to productive efficiency requires work organizations that create challenges for workers and encourage their participation in decision-making at appropriate levels. That is, the organization of the firm will determine to a large degree whether the capabilities of educated workers to contribute to higher output will be realized. (Levin, 1984, p 14)

Recent trends in award restructuring in Australia will lead to a fundamental transformation in the way in which these issues are conceptualized and to the kinds of approaches adopted to technological change and production. As Mathews has observed, 'skills' will be central to the definition of jobs whereas the restructuring of work, associated with new technologies, will be crucial in 'the definition of skills' (Mathews, 1989, p 123). How does the current provision for formal education and training arrangements in Australia reflect these trends?

Australian government policy

Two sets of decisions by the Australian (federal) government in 1987–8 demonstrated their view of the relationship that should exist between education, training and economic expansion, and set the tone for the development of education policy in subsequent years:

a) the 1987–8 budget allocations for education reflected perceived fiscal pressures, on the one hand, and a narrow determination of priorities on the other. In subsequent years, education initiatives have concentrated resources according to economic priorities and have sought to increase the level of private funding for both teaching and research; and

b) the abolition of the Commonwealth Tertiary and Schools

Commissions in favour of a National Board of Employment, Education and Training which placed control of education policy in the hands of business, unions and politicians, rather than teachers, parents or other educators. While some educators have continued to play a significant role in national advisory positions, the influence of industry has been much more pronounced.

The key decisions in 1987 set the policy and resource context within which educators at tertiary, secondary and even primary levels were to operate. The two decisions were interrelated: the education system was perceived as a major cost on government resources which had not delivered the results which the government had desired. The National Board was established to expedite the efficient restructuring of the system. The underlying philosophy was set out in Budget Related Paper No. 9 (1987), entitled 'Skills For Australia' and circulated by John Dawkins as Minister for Employment, Education and Training. In part it stated:

> The adjustments required in the structure of the economy, and improvements in Australia's international competitiveness, will make heavy demands on our human resources and labour force skills. Our skills formation and training arrangements are not yet adequate to meet those demands.

> The world's most successful economies over the last two decades have given high priority to education, skills and competence at work as vital factors in economic performance, and have supported their skills development policies accordingly. Now we must do likewise.

> Specifically action is required to:

> - increase the total level of participation in education and training, and expand the national training capacity;
> - improve the quality and flexibility of our education and training systems, and hence the quality, breadth and adaptability of skills acquired;
> - improve the distribution and balance of the national education and training effort, to better meet the long-term needs of the economy and labour market;
> - raise the level of private sector investment in training and skills formation;
> - improve the employment and training opportunities available to the unemployed and otherwise disadvantaged members of the community (including measures to reduce the high degree of occupational segregation in the labour market and to improve training opportunities for women); and
> - increase the productivity of our education and training resources and evaluate the outputs from the use of those resources. (p iii)

The rhetoric of this statement might be regarded as optimistic, and indeed, there were initiatives designed to realize the positive intentions. However, the blunt reality was that the government either could not, or was not prepared to, commit the resources necessary to achieve their objectives properly. Funding for tertiary programmes was reduced in real terms. Growth in student numbers was financed at less than the full cost, and funds for research were removed subsequently from universities and redistributed from a central fund. The increases in assistance to the disadvantaged and the expansion of training arrangements overall were financed by reductions in the public and private sector programmes intended to provide work experience for unemployed people.

More seriously, perhaps, the primary focus of government policy on macroeconomic issues seems to have limited the attention given to the actual interaction between particular strategies of education and training, workplace relationships and improved productivity. In 1985, the Kirby Committee of Inquiry into Labour Market Programs had commented that,

> ... Australians favour jobs which involve participation in decision-making, which require the use of human capacity, and which provide fulfilment and satisfaction. If such aspirations are to be met, the production mix will require more highly skilled workers. If organisations choose the alternative approach of using lower skilled workers for perceived technical efficiency, that efficiency may in fact be constrained by increasing worker dissatisfaction and alienation. The best work systems take into account both technical and human resources. (Kirby, 1985, p 59)

The underlying argument of the Kirby Report was that economic growth depended on the interaction between a skilled society, innovation, new technology, and a commitment to enterprise and individual productivity. Subsequently endorsed by the OECD (1988), this approach implied a planned development of investment in appropriate technology, arrangements for research and innovation, and the development of management practices to take advantage of the broad improvement in the skills and flexibility of the workforce. The integration of policy initiatives has not been addressed by government, other than in relation to specific industry sectors such as motor vehicle manufacture and textiles, clothing and footwear.

Education and training arrangements

Does the government's preferred education and training paradigm reflect a narrow focus on economic priorities and the inculcation of 'skills', or a more comprehensive approach which would explore the social and personal dimensions of the nature and organization of work? Technical 'skills' have, in the past, been taught in Australia mostly in a relatively discrete and specific manner. Some recent curriculum initiatives have attempted to provide an opportunity for students to learn about social and economic contexts, alongside the more specific focus on technical skills.

The success of these initiatives will depend on a fundamental change in the underlying culture of technical training in Australia. Historically, 'skill' has been used to refer not only to certain technical attributes or specialized masteries but also to more general habits and attitudes. The relationship between the technical and social aspects of a 'skill' have not always been clearly defined. The exercise of skill requires both mental coordination and manual dexterity, and there is substantial variation in the use of relatively similar technical competences across different occupations and companies, even those in the same industry.

Second, the Australian industrial training system has depended on a formal apprenticeship system. For a substantial period, it provided a successful and structured means of meeting Australian industrial training needs. However, it also produced a close link between skill definitions and privileged, government-sponsored training arrangements which managed not only the supply, but also the price of specific skills. These particular definitions of skill had more to do with maintaining divisions between workers, especially male and female workers, than with their actual contribution, real or potential, to the production or process (O'Donnell, 1984). Hence, the concept of 'skill' referred not simply to particular knowledges and associated techniques for application, but also implies the particular set of social relations within which they are embedded (Game and Pringle, 1983).

In recent years, the process of award restructuring has attempted to reconceptualize the traditional training paradigm in terms of 'skills formation'. Hence, the new awards have tried to link performance of duties with regular training opportunities. In conjunction with other initiatives for workplace and training reform, it was intended that decisions about workforce deployment and training should be integrated with organizational review and technological change; rather than the technology driving the production process, decisions about investment in technologies should reflect a coordinated approach to the use of all the resources available in an enterprise. An OECD study of Sweden's Volvo operations highlighted management's concern to have new technology designed to fit the organization's preferred method of work organization. By contrast, a failure to address these interrelationships has led to increasing problems of technology down-time in Australian industry (see Ford, 1986, p 123).

Although some Australian enterprises have established training centres they are few in number. This has led to the isolation of formal training arrangements in tertiary and TAFE (Technical and Further Education) institutions, away from organizational life.

In 1991, the Australian government introduced the Training Guarantee Scheme, as one initiative designed to overcome some of this isolation. Employers with an annual payroll of more than A$200,000 were required to spend at least 1 per cent of that payroll on 'structured training' to enhance the productivity and flexibility of the Australian workforce. Individual enterprises have considerable flexibility to use the levy in whichever manner they consider appropriate, including specific negotiations with TAFE colleges for specific courses to be provided. It is clear that ultimately this may lead to fundamental changes in the character of technical training in Australia. It is not so clear that it will facilitate the kind of skills formation programme that is considered necessary. Indeed, its implementation demonstrates a fundamental flaw in the overall approach of the federal government to industry restructuring in Australia: no attempt has been made to coordinate the kinds of activities which enterprises initiate, either with other enterprises or industries, or with government programmes. The Australian Taxation Office has the responsibility for implementing the scheme.

A cultural revolution?

Technological and organizational transformations have consequences that go well beyond the workplace. The transition in the sense of time and place that information and communications technologies make possible contributes to the rise of 'cultural specificities' (Touraine, 1989) on the one hand, and to the reality of the global village on the other. It is the demand for national autonomy by the Lithuanians, or the Basques, or the Bosnians which can almost instantaneously become news, broadcast on television, on the other side of the world.

Another approach to industry restructuring, identified by the Australian Economic Planning Advisory Council, has emphasized the cultural dimension. In commenting on a comparative study of education and training in West Germany, Japan and the United States, undertaken for the Institute of Manpower Studies in the United Kingdom, EPAC emphasized the importance in those countries of a culturally based desire to succeed.

> To differing degrees their cultural values were assessed to be major factors in their propensity for entrepreneurship and risk taking at the national, corporate and individual level. These values and propensities in turn were reflected in, and reinforced by: their approaches to education and training, including retraining and continuing education; their approach to research and development, and product and service differentiation and specialization; and their approach to the design and organization of work. (EPAC, 1986, p 10)

Significant priority has been placed by governments in Australia on the importance of education and training in facilitating not only technological invention, but also the institutional and labour market adaptation necessary for successful implementation of new technologies.

There is no particular formula which summarizes skill formation processes. The important principle is that learning, research and development should be seen not as discrete functions but as part of an organizational plan which places primary emphasis on individual and organizational learning. Against the human capital proposition that investment in education is important preeminently for economic purposes, it is important to assert that human learning, whether by individuals or in groups, has important social benefits including the economic. Insofar as economic restructuring provides new opportunities for people to participate in democratic decision-making about matters which are central to their lives, so there might be expected to be some coincidence in contribution of human learning to both social and economic outcomes.

With respect to broader education policies, various government reports (eg, the Commonwealth Schools Commission's report in 1987, 'In the

National Interest') have emphasized that the education system will remain responsible for ensuring that all entrants to the labour market will have the necessary communication, mathematic, technical and interpersonal capacities. They have identified also the additional major responsibility for the system of fostering a society which is more creative, respectful of innovation and more entrepreneurial. Various reports have outlined the importance of new arrangements for continuous or lifelong education and for encouraging educational institutions to become more involved with their local community.

Without a broadly based education that emphasizes the issues of work organization, industrial democracy and decision-making, it is possible that some forms of technological change will provide new efficiencies and expanded access to communication services, but also increase unemployment, the deskilling of many jobs, and polarization of the labour market. So far, governments have focused much more on developing unified national systems, both secondary and tertiary, than they have on encouraging teachers and students to be creative, cooperative and engaged in problem solving.

Conclusion

The development of education and training policies and programmes to assist in meeting the overall goals of industry restructuring has been severely limited by a lack of resources, and of appropriate understanding of the relationship between education, new technologies and workplace organization. The evidence outlined above suggests that a reliance on a narrowly construed field of science, technology and business studies, currently favoured in higher education policy, is not likely to assure successful diffusion of technology or the implementation of efficient production arrangements. If one adds to this the claim that education and training must contribute to social outcomes such as good citizenship or creative use of leisure time then a narrowly construed technical and economic rationalist approach is totally inadequate since it has no way of including the social within its intellectual compass.

References

ACTU/Trade Development Council (1987) *Australia Reconstructed*, Melbourne.
Bates, I, Cohen, P, Finn, D and Willis, P (1984) *Schooling for the Dole? The New Vocationalism*, London: Macmillan.
Beniger, J (1986) *The Control Revolution: Technological and Economic Origins of the Information Society*, Cambridge, MA: HUP.
Bessant, B (1992) 'Managerialism, economic rationalism and higher education', paper delivered at a conference on The Governance and Funding of Australian Education, Federalism Research Centre, Research School of Social Sciences, Australian National University, February.
Blaug, M (1976) 'The empirical status of human capital theory: a slightly jaundiced survey', *Journal of Economic Literature*, **14**, 827–55.
Economic Planning Advisory Council (1986) *Human Capital and Productivity Growth*, Council Paper 15, Canberra.

Finn, B (Chair) (1991) *Young People's Participation in Postcompulsory Education and Training*, report of the AEC Review Committee, Canberra: AGPS.

Ford, Bill (1986) 'Learning from Japan: the concept of skill formation', *Australian Bulletin of Labor*, **12**, 2.

Game, A and Pringle, R (1983) *Gender at Work*, Sydney/Boston: Allen & Unwin.

Garibaldo, F (1989) 'The crisis of the "demanding model" and the search for an alternative in the experiences of the metal workers union in Emilia Romagna', paper delivered at meeting at Bielefeld University.

Harvey, D, (1989) *The Conditions of Postmodernity*, Oxford: Blackwell.

Kirby, P (Chair) (1985) *Report of the Committee of Inquiry into Labour Market Programs*, Canberra: Australian Government Printing Service.

Levin, H (1984) 'Improving productivity through education and technology', working paper, Stanford University.

Marginson, S (1993) *Education and Education Policy in Australia*, Cambridge: Cambridge University Press.

Mathews, J (1989) *Tools for Change: New Technology and the Democratisation of Work*, Sydney: Pluto.

O'Donnell, C (1984) *The Basis of the Bargain*, Sydney: Allen & Unwin.

OECD (1985) 'Changes in work patterns: implications for education', *Innovation in Education*, Paris: OECD.

OECD (1988) *New technologies in the 1990s: a socio-economic strategy*, Paris: OECD.

Samuelson, P (1954) 'The Pure Theory of Public Expenditure', *Review of Economics and Statistics*, **36**, 4, 387–9.

Smith, A (1979) [1776] *The Wealth of Nations*, Harmondsworth: Penguin.

Thurow, L (1975) *Generating Inequality*, New York: Basic Books.

Touraine, A (1989) 'Is sociology still the study of society?', *Thesis Eleven* **23**.

Vaizey, J (1962) *The Economics of Education*, London: Faber and Faber.

2. Post-Fordist possibilities: education, training and national development

Phillip Brown and Hugh Lauder

At the end of the twentieth century the social and economic world is being transformed in many significant ways. The globalization of markets for goods and services facilitated by GATT, technological innovation and cheaper transportation costs has led to an intensification of economic competition between firms, regions and nation states (Dicken, 1992). Advances in information technology have contributed to increased levels of productivity and to the development of flexible forms of accumulation offering the opportunity of high-value, low-volume manufacturing in place of the mass production of standardized products. In Western Europe and North America the threat of global competition has led to the creation of regional trading blocs to enhance economic growth and cooperation. Such changes have led to considerable speculation about the enduring significance of new forms of social and economic organization. However, there is little agreement as to whether the emergence of more 'flexible' modes of capitalist accumulation represents a shift in surface appearance or signs of some entirely new post-industrial, post-Fordist or post-modern society (Harvey, 1989).

Notwithstanding such disputes, there is increasing agreement that the descriptive value of terms such as 'industrial' or 'Fordist' are inappropriate when applied to the advanced economies in the 1990s. Indeed, it has been argued that the declining economic hegemony of Western nations is due to a failure to modernize production in ways which overcome the debilitating consequences of 'Fordism' (Piore and Sabel, 1984). This is because the Fordist inheritance has been identified as a source of inefficiency in uncertain and rapidly changing market conditions. It is suggested that organizations now need to apply 'entrepreneurial principles to the traditional corporation, creating a marriage between entrepreneurial creativity and corporate discipline, cooperation, and team-work' (Kanter, 1989, pp 9–10). A broader version of this debate turns on the claim that bureaucratic organizations are no longer appropriate to the conditions of the late twentieth century:

> Bureaucracy thrived in a highly competitive, undifferentiated, and stable environment, such as the climate of its youth, the Industrial

Revolution. A pyramidal structure of authority, with power concentrated in the hands of few with the knowledge and resources to control an entire enterprise was, and is, an eminently suitable social arrangement for routinised tasks. However, the environment has changed in just those ways which make the mechanism most problematic. Stability has vanished. (Bennis, 1972, p 111)

In this chapter we will assume that 'Fordism' is being undermined in Western capitalist societies, although its global significance has remained undiminished as the mass production of standardized goods and services is transplanted in the newly industrializing nations (NICs), especially in Asia and South America (Dicken, 1992). We also believe that a massive process of organizational restructuring is occurring in Western economies in an attempt to break down the rigidities of bureaucratic and Fordist paradigms. The same process of restructuring can be seen in public as well as private sector organizations, and in medium as well as large enterprises. There is no doubt, for instance, that the introduction of new technologies has expanded the range of strategic choice available to employers and managers. However, this has exposed increasing differences, rather than similarities, in organizational cultures, job design and training regimes (Lane, 1989; Green and Steedman, 1993). There are few guarantees that employers will successfully exploit the potential for 'efficiency', precisely because they may fail to break free of conventional assumptions about the role of management and workers, and cling to the established hierarchy of authority, status and power.

This should alert us to the fact that the shift towards 'flexible accumulation' does not necessarily lead to changes in the nature of skills and involvement which are required in order to compete in 'high value' production. The interests of employers seeking to maximize profits and workers seeking to enhance the quality of working life and wages remain an important source of cleavage given that it is still possible for companies to 'profit' from low-tech, low-wage operations. Therefore, it is more appropriate to talk in terms of *post-Fordist possibilities* which recognize that some of the key elements of Fordism are being transformed in Western economies without prejudging the direction of these changes which must remain a question for detailed empirical investigation (see Block, 1990).

For analytical purposes it is possible to distinguish two 'ideal typical' models of national economic development in terms of *neo-Fordism* and *post-Fordism*. Neo-Fordism can be characterized in terms of a shift to flexible accumulation based on the creation of a flexible workforce engaged in low-skill, low-wage, temporary and often part-time employment. Alternatively, post-Fordism is based on a shift to 'high-value' customized production and services using multi-skilled and high-waged workers.

Given the concerns addressed in this chapter, these 'models' will be linked to different interpretations of the economic 'crisis' in the advanced Western economies, and will be considered in terms of their implications for education and training policies. At the same time it is important to recognize that in the 'real' world the relationship between education and economic development reveals examples of contradiction as much as correspondence. Moreover, although it is true to say that countries such as Germany, Japan and Singapore come closer to the model of post-Fordism, and the USA and Britain approximate neo-Fordist solutions, we should not ignore clear examples of 'uneven' and contradictory developments within the same region or country. It also highlights the fact that there are important differences in the way nation-states may move towards a post-Fordist economy with far-reaching implications for democracy and social justice.

The importance of these debates to an understanding of education and training systems is difficult to exaggerate. It is not only of theoretical importance given that debates within the sociology of education have been premised on 'industrial' models of capitalism or state socialism, but equally as Block (1990) has recognized:

> Those educational reformers who succeeded in linking their proposals to widely shared views of the direction in which the society was moving tended to be more successful than those who were unable to connect their reform proposals to the master concepts of social science. (Block, 1990, p 8)

All Western nations, in their domestic economies and foreign affairs, have had to look to their own social institutions and human resources to meet the global challenges they confront (OECD, 1989). Their diminished power to control economic competition has forced them to stake out a policy framework for the 'new competition' in terms of the *global knowledge wars*. Lessons learnt from Japan and the Asian 'Tigers' suggest that the 'human side of enterprise' is now a crucial factor in winning a competitive advantage in the global economy. Advantage is therefore seen to depend upon raising the quality and productivity of human capital. Knowledge, learning, information, and technical competence are the new raw materials of international commerce:

> Knowledge itself, therefore, turns out to be not only the source of the highest-quality power, but also the most important ingredient of force and wealth. Put differently, knowledge has gone from being an adjunct of money power and muscle power, to being their very essence. It is, in fact, the ultimate amplifier. This is the key to the power shift that lies ahead, and it explains why the battle for control of knowledge and the means of communication is heating up all over the world. (Toffler, 1990, p 18)

Although such statements greatly exaggerate the importance of knowledge in advanced capitalist economies, without exception, national governments of all political persuasions have declared that it is the quality of their education and training systems which will decisively shape the international division of labour and national prosperity. In *A Nation at Risk*, The National Commission on Excellence in Education in the USA (1983) asserted:

> History is not kind to idlers ... We live among determined, well-educated, and strongly motivated competitors ... America's position

in the world may once have been reasonably secure with only a few exceptionally well-trained men and women. It is no longer. (NCEA, 1983, p 6)

But how the problem of human resources is understood and what education and training policies are to be pursued is subject to contestation and political struggle. In what remains of this chapter we will argue that those nation-states which have adopted New Right 'market' reforms in education, training and the labour market, gravitate towards the neo-Fordist route to national development, whereas the shift towards post-Fordism will require a fundamentally different response based on the struggle for collective intelligence.

Fordism and national development

Fordist mass production is based on the standardization of products and their component parts. Many of the tasks previously undertaken by skilled artisans, such as making door panels or parts of the car's engine 'by hand', can be mechanized by designing jigs, presses and machines able to perform the same operations hundreds, if not thousands of times a day, with the use of a semi-skilled operative. The Fordist production line is also characterized by a moving assembly line, where the product passes the workers along a conveyer, rather than the worker having to move to the product as in nodal production.

A further feature of 'Fordism' is a detailed division of labour, within which the job tasks of shopfloor workers are reduced to their most elementary form in order to maximize both efficiency and managerial control over the labour process. Hence, Fordism is based on many of the principles of 'scientific management' outlined by Frederick Taylor in his analysis of pig-iron handling in 1911. In this work, Taylor suggests that it would be possible to train an intelligent gorilla to become a more efficient pig-iron handler than a human (quoted in Gramsci, 1971, p 302). The importance of Taylor's ideas in the development of Fordism was that he offered a 'scientific' justification for the separation of *conception* from *execution*, where managers monopolized knowledge of the labour process, and controlled every step of production.

Fordism, bureaucracy and education

The rise of mass schooling has never resembled a simple *correspondence* to the requirements of the economy (Green, 1990). The education system throughout the twentieth century has been shaped less by Fordist production techniques than by the principles of bureaucratic organization which Weber described in terms of a

form of organization that emphasises precision, speed, clarity, regularity, reliability, and efficiency achieved through the creation of a fixed division of tasks, hierarchical supervision, and detailed rules and regulations. (Morgan, 1986, pp 24–5)

As well as providing a social technology which can create a set of predictable outcomes, bureaucracy is intimately related to the idea of a 'meritocracy' because it treats individuals according to 'objective' achievement criteria. In education, individuals are treated according to ability rather than on the basis of ascribed characteristics such as social class, gender or race. The organization of formal educational systems according to bureaucratic criteria therefore provided a rational means of social selection for expanding public administrations and capitalist corporations. School and college credentials provide a useful screening device for employers who are concerned that future employees should be inculcated into the appropriate forms of rule-following behaviour, as well as having the appropriate knowledge and skills for their place in the technostructure. However, given the demand for large numbers of low-skilled workers with little room for individual autonomy, the educational system has had to confront the problem of offering greater equality of opportunity whilst limiting the aspirations and ambitions of the majority by defining them as academic failures. This contradiction at the heart of bureaucratic education – of seeking to promote a 'talented' few while attempting to 'cool out' the majority – has consistently presented a problem of legitimation and resulted in various forms of working-class resistance (Brown and Lauder, 1992).

The demise of the bureaucratic/Fordist paradigms of organizational efficiency and their implications for education and training systems, can not be explained in 'technocratic' terms. There is no internal 'logic of industrialism' or 'logic of capitalism' which has set Western nations on the path to either neo-Fordism or post-Fordism. The direction of change will crucially depend upon the outcome of political struggle, which in most Western economies currently centres on the role of the nation-state and the free market.

Market reform and political interests

The New Right interpretation of the Fordist 'crisis' is based on what we will call the *welfare shackle thesis*. In the nineteenth century it was the aristocracy and the old regime in Europe who were blamed for 'shackling' the market and free enterprise. In the late twentieth century it is the welfare state. The New Right argue that Western societies have run into trouble because of the extensive and unwarranted interference by the state. Inflation, high unemployment, economic recession and urban unrest all stem from the legacy of Fordist/Keynesian economics and an egalitarian ideology which promoted economic redistribution, equality of opportunity and welfare rights for all. Hence, the overriding problem confronting Western capitalist nations is to reimpose the disciplines of the market.

According to the New Right, the route to national salvation in the context of global knowledge wars is through the survival of the fittest, based on an extension of parental choice in a market of competing schools, colleges and universities (Ball, 1990). In the case of education, where funding, at least during the compulsory school years, will come from the public purse, the idea is to create a quasi-market within which schools will compete (Lauder, 1987). This approximation to the operation of a market is achieved by seeking to create a variety of schools in a mixed economy of public and private institutions. In some cases they will aim at different client groups such as the ethnic minorities, religious sects, or 'high flyers'. This 'variety' it is argued will provide parents with a genuine choice of different products (Boyd and Cibulka, 1989; Halstead, 1994). Choice of product (type of school) is seen to be sufficient to raise the standards for all, because if schools cannot sell enough deskspace to be economically viable, they risk going out of business. Moreover, the economic needs of the nation will be met through the market, because when people have to pay for education they are more likely to make investment decisions which will realize an economic return. This will lead consumers to pick subjects and courses where there is a demand for labour, subsequently overcoming the problem of skill shortages. Equally, there will be a tendency for employment training to be 'demand led' in response to changing market conditions (Deakin and Wilkinson, 1991).

Critics of the marketization of education argue that the introduction of choice and competition provides a mechanism by which the middle classes can gain an advantage in the competition for credentials. This is because not all social groups come to an educational market as equals (Collins, 1979). Cultural and material capital are distributed unequally among classes and among ethnic groups. In particular, it is the middle classes which are more likely to have the cultural capital to make educational choices which best advantage their children (Brown, 1990; Brown and Lauder, 1992). In consequence, the introduction of parental choice and competition among schools will amount to a covert system of educational selection according to social class as middle-class children exit schools with significant numbers of working-class children. The consequence will be that the school system will become polarized in terms of social class and ethnic segregation and in terms of resources. As middle-class students exit from schools with working-class children they will also take much-needed resources from those schools and effectively add to already well-off middle-class schools.

What evidence there is about the workings of educational markets suggests that they are far more complex than critics suggest (Lauder et al, 1994). Nevertheless, the evidence so far confirms the prediction that choice and competition tend to lead to social class and ethnic polarization in schools (Willms and Echols, 1992; Lauder et al, 1994). In nations like the UK, the net result will again be a massive wastage of talent as able working-class students again find themselves trapped in schools which do not give them the opportunity of going to university (Halsey et al, 1980). If this is the overall effect then it can be argued that the marketization of education, while appearing to offer efficiency and flexibility of the kind demanded in the post-Fordist era, will in fact school the majority of children for a neo-Fordist economy which requires a low level of talent and skill.

The impact of this on the ability of nation-states to compete in the 'global auction' for inward investment and jobs may be highly significant. Although multinational organizations are always on the lookout to reduce their overheads, including labour costs, investment in 'high-value' products and services crucially depends upon the quality, commitment and insights of the workforce, for which they are prepared to pay high salaries. The problem that nation-states now confront is one of how to balance commercial pressures to reduce labour costs and other overheads whilst mobilizing an educated labour force, and maintaining a sophisticated social, financial and communications infrastructure. This problem has been exacerbated by the fact that the low-skill, high-wage jobs associated with Fordism in North America and Europe are either being transplanted to the NICs, where labour costs are much lower, or are leading to a significant deterioration in working conditions and wages in the West.

In the context of the global auction, the market reforms in education are likely to leave a large majority of the future working population without the human resources to flourish in the global economy. Here the link between market reforms and neo-Fordism is barely disguised in countries with New Right governments such as the UK. The principal objective of economic policy is to improve the competitiveness of workers by increasing labour market flexibility by restricting the power of trade unions, especially in order to bring wages into line with their 'market' value. The Social Chapter of the Maastrict Treaty was rejected by the British Conservative government because it was argued that the introduction of a minimum wage and protective legislation relating to working conditions would undermine the UK's competitiveness in terms of inward investment from global corporations, despite the low wages and inferior working conditions which this inflicts on employees.

In contradistinction, market reforms in education and the economy have ensured the conditions in which highly paid middle-class professionals and elite groups are able to give their children an 'excellent' education in preparation for their bid to join the ranks of the 'symbolic analysts'.

A different critique, albeit coming to the same conclusion, can be mounted against the introduction of market mechanisms in post-compulsory education and training. A key area of the post-compulsory sector for a post-Fordist economy is that which is concerned with the education of skilled tradespeople and technicians (Streeck, 1989). The New Right has argued that the introduction of market mechanisms into this area will ensure a closer matching of supply and demand for trained labour and hence greater efficiency in the allocation of skilled labour. The argument rests on the assumptions that individuals and employers should bear the cost and responsibility for training. It is assumed that individuals gain most of the benefits from such training and that they should therefore bear much of the cost (Lauder, 1987). Moreover, since they are paying substantially for their training they will choose to train in an area in which there is market demand. Insofar as employers should help bear the cost of training and the responsibility for the type of training offered, it is argued that employers are in the best position to assess the numbers of skilled workers required and the kind of skills they should possess. Underlying this observation is an appreciation of employers' interests. Given the assumption that they 'know best' what levels and nature of skilled labour there should be, it follows that they will be reluctant to pay taxes or levies for training undertaken by a third party, such as the state.

While this view, as with other New Right views, is plausible, it has come in for sustained criticism. One of the most cogent is that of Streeck (1989, 1992). He argues that under a free labour contract of the kind found in liberal capitalist societies which gives workers the right to move from one firm to another, skills become a collective good in the eyes of employers. This is because the rewards of training individuals can easily be 'socialized' by the expedient of trained workers moving to another job while the costs of training remain with the original employer. Since employers face a clear risk in losing their investment they are unlikely to invest heavily in training. Streeck argues that, as a result, Western economies are likely to face a chronic skill shortage unless the state intervenes to ensure adequate training occurs.

Moreover, unless there is state intervention employers will reduce the training programmes they do have when placed under intense competitive pressure and/or during a recession. Streeck (1989) notes that in the prolonged economic crisis of the seventies, Western economies, with the exception of Germany, reduced their apprenticeship programmes. In Germany government and trade union pressure ensured that the apprenticeship programme was extended. Two consequences followed: the apprenticeship system helped to alleviate youth unemployment and it contributed to the technical and economic advantage enjoyed by German industry in the early eighties.

There are further criticisms that can be made of a market-determined training system. From the standpoint of the individual, it is unlikely that those who would potentially enter a skilled trade or technical training, usually working-class and lower-middle-class school leavers, could either afford the costs of such training or take the risks involved. The risks are twofold: first, given the time lag between entering a training programme and completing it, market demand for a particular type of training may have changed with a resulting lack of jobs. In the competitive global market, such an outcome is all too likely. If the training received were of a sufficiently general nature to produce a flexible worker that may be less of a problem. However, in an employer-led training system the pressure will always exist for training to meet employers' specific and immediate needs. The consequence is that such a training system is likely to be too narrowly focused to meet rapidly changing demand conditions. A second point follows from this, namely that the industries of today are likely to be tomorrow's dinosaurs. As a result, employer-led training schemes may not contain the vision and practice required in order to maintain the high skill base necessary for a post-Fordist economy. Clearly the structure of Germany's training system offers an example of an alternative which can begin to meet the requirements of a post-Fordist economy. This, as Streeck (1992) notes, involves a partnership between the state, employers and trade unions. It is a system which ensures that employers' immediate interests are subsumed within a system concerned with medium- and longer-term outcomes.

Towards an education system for a post-Fordist economy

The question of whether the state or the market should fund and provide education and training is not just a technical question of weighing up the merits of the two types of delivery. Rather what is at stake is the question of whether the political interests which have been unleashed by the creation of the new global economy can be sufficiently reconciled to create an educational settlement which reflects the national interest rather than the sectarian interests of the middle class and social elites. In what follows we will argue that the development of 'collective intelligence' will need to be an integral feature of a post-Fordist society.

Collective intelligence, education and the economy

We have argued that the education systems in most industrial societies have been based on the bureaucracy paradigm. This includes the idea that there is a limited 'pool of talent' in a sea of mediocrity and ignores the important ways in which intelligence is collectively structured by the form of production (Kohn and Schooler, 1983). Moreover, the low-discretion and low-skill work roles which confront large numbers of workers in Fordist organizations have generated low trust responses including worker resistance, minimum level of commitment, high rates of absenteeism, wildcat strikes, etc (Fox, 1974). These responses have traditionally been interpreted by management as a manifestation of the feckless irresponsible nature of most workers. Indeed, managers have typically recognized these responses as a justification for the use of surveillance and the threat of sanctions in the control of the workforce.

Our conception of collective intelligence involves a fundamental reevaluation of these ideas which is outlined in Figure 2.1.

There is an urgent need to jack-up the normal curve of human intelligence. Given the right motivation (which is socially determined), at least 80 per cent of the population are capable of achieving the intellectual standards required to obtain a university degree in adult life. This view is supported by comparative evidence which shows significant differences in the proportion of students from different advanced industrial societies participating in higher education. Such differences need to be explained in terms of the social, cultural and institutional differences between nation-states rather than in terms of the distribution of individual intelligence. What we are suggesting is that the vast wealth of talent has not been harnessed by current systems of education and training, and that it is nonsense to suggest that current levels of 'academic' performance are a reasonable reflection of individual and collective capability.

The creation of a post-Fordist economy will need to continue to structure opportunity on the basis of individual effort and ability, but the 'ideology of meritocracy' will have to be strongly reinforced. There is strong evidence to suggest that education and training systems must be organized on the premise that all rather than a few are capable of significant practical and academic achievements; of creative thought and

Fordism	Post-Fordism
Intelligence is a scarce resource, but can be 'scientifically' identified among children at an early age	Unfolding of human capacity limited by social hierarchy and cultural attitudes
The organization of education and employment corresponds to the normal distribution of talent	The capacity to exercise imagination, ingenuity, creativity, etc is widely distributed in the population
The average human being has a dislike of 'work' and will avoid it if possible	The expenditure of physical and mental effort in 'work' is as natural as play or rest
People must be coerced, controlled, directed, threatened with punishment to fulfil organizational goals	People will exercise self-direction and self-control to fulfil aims to which they are committed
Most people avoid responsibility, have relatively little ambition, and above all want security	Under the right conditions most people will both accept and seek responsibility

Figure 2.1 *Human ability and motivation*

skill; and of taking responsibility for making informed judgements. The role of education in this context must become one of nurturing this wealth of talent. We will need to redirect our attention away from the attributes of individual students as the cause of low ability systems of education, to the institutional context in which the learning process takes place. Instead of pointing to the fact that their 'failing' students are usually working class or black, teachers, trainers and employers would be forced to examine the institutional context and their professional practices for explanations of trained incapacity. This strategy would certainly help to generate a more integrated system of education and training involving teachers, students, parents, trade unionists and employers.

From individual to collective intelligence

Developing collective intelligence means more than simply increasing the pool of knowledgeable and technically competent people. It also needs to be understood as a measure of our ability to face up to the problems that confront us collectively and to develop collective solutions (Lacey, 1988, p 94). Therefore, an education which does not examine the issues of the day, or help students to make connections between different aspects of their studies, renders the latter less intelligent than they need be. A state, for example, which denies its youth the opportunity to examine issues concerning the causes and consequences of environmental pollution, the nature of HIV and AIDS, or fails to offer political education is also likely to be a low-trust and low-ability society.

Equally, a new division of learning will be needed to support a new division of labour. Zuboff (1988), for instance, in her account of technological innovation in the USA, distinguished technology which *automates* from that which *informates*. Automation simply involves the replacement of the human body with a technology that enables the same processes to be performed with more continuity and control. In other words, it conforms to the principles of Fordism. Rather than decrease the dependence on human skills, technology which has the capacity to informate can enlarge job tasks and the room for individual discretion given that activities, events and objects are translated into and made visible by information:

> ... an informated organization is structured to promote the possibility of useful learning among all members and thus presupposes relations of equality ... In the traditional organization, the division of learning lent credibility to the legitimacy of imperative control. In an informated organization, the new division of learning produces experiences that encourage a synthesis of members' interest, and the flow of value-adding knowledge helps legitimate the organization as a learning community. (Zuboff, 1988, p 394)

In terms of education and training this raises important issues about the way employers and managers deploy new technology in the workplace, and the need to break down low-trust and low-discretion relations which often existed in the past and which many managers seek to preserve (Scase and Goffee, 1989).

If we are to shape the future in ways which will facilitate social progress, formal systems of education and training will need to prepare a much larger proportion of worker/citizens to contribute to the decision-making process and to be more self-directed. Moreover, as Kanter (1984) has noted, single-skilled people are unable to function in the kinds of cross disciplinary teams that produce innovation, and are less adaptable when circumstances change. The potential blurring or breakdown of the rigid classification and framing (Bernstein, 1975) of knowledge, skill, and job tasks, will require a more integrated approach to education and training; increasing emphasis on collective as well as individual roles and achievement; and the provision of lifelong programmes of formal learning (Ashton *et al.*, 1990).

In search of excellence

In our view, excellence in education is best achieved through a state-provided comprehensive system. The fact is that education differentiated according to privilege and status would militate against the promotion of collective intelligence. Recent evidence would lead us to suggest that the better the social mix of schools the better the performance of the majority of students (Lauder and Hughes, 1990). In other words, far from a proliferation of school types in competition, what is required is a well maintained comprehensive state system. Parents would have some choice of school, but the general thrust of policy would be to generate high trust relations between teachers and parents, given that schools would truly become a community resource, used daily by people of all ages. In general, selection for the various routes into employment would be delayed as long as possible in order to provide the greatest opportunity for students' intelligence and creativity to flourish. There should be open access to all forms of tertiary education and training, which are increasingly part of a lifelong learning process.

Underlying these principles is the aim of developing a common educational culture. If a general aim of educating for a post-Fordist economy is to foster teamwork and cooperation, then just as the hierarchies and differential cultures distinctive of Fordist production would have to be discarded, so would the differential cultures which undermine contemporary schooling. This can only be achieved by breaking down the class, gender and racial barriers within systems of education and training.

If we are genuinely concerned to produce the labour force of the future, the educational and training systems must break down sexist (and racist) practices which operate against both girls and boys and foster the development of narrow gender-specific occupational preferences and skills by, among other things, reinforcing the processes through which boys enter metalwork, woodwork and technical design courses, and the girls are channelled into home economics, childcare and office practice.

Similarly, the divisions between academic and vocational education will need to be broken down. Although there is nothing inherently superior about receiving a narrow and intensive 'academic' education, it is favoured because it has the most 'cultural capital' and 'exchange value' in the school and labour market. It is for this reason that virtually all programmes of vocational education have failed to provide a 'parity of esteem' because they deny access to the real vocational prizes (Watts, 1983; Kantor and Tyack, 1982). There are consequently strong social and educational grounds for developing a broad based curriculum of academic, technical and practical study for all students, at least during the compulsory school years.

There is also a need to stop thinking about excellence in elitist terms. Excellence should be defined in terms of the collective skills, knowledge and know-how which can be deployed within a society as a whole. To achieve the latter, it is necessary to end our obsession with the 'great man' and 'token woman' view of history. Sustainable economic growth will increasingly depend on the collective efforts of executives, managers, researchers, teachers, child carers, shopfloor workers, etc, because significant technological advances are rarely the result of the efforts and insights of any one person. It is, therefore, equally important to challenge the excessive individualism which is endemic in Western countries, such as the USA and the UK, which among other things leads employers to be more concerned with poaching skilled labour from each other than developing a mutual social obligation to train.

Conclusion

This chapter has argued that the transformation of the global economy is having profound implications for Western systems of education and training. We have attempted to describe these changes against a backdrop of bureaucratic/Fordist organizational principles. Out of the Fordist crisis have emerged *post-Fordist possibilities* for more democratic industrial relations and more interesting and fulfilling working lives. However, the realization of this potential appears remote in nations which have pursued free-market policies as a route to economic salvation. Such reforms conform to a neo-Fordist strategy which will lead to increasing social and economic polarization in education, training and the labour market.

If post-Fordist possibilities are to stand any chance of being brought to fruition, an altogether different political agenda will need to be defined. In the final section of this chapter we have been able to do no more than outline one aspect of this New Left agenda focusing on the struggle for 'collective intelligence'. What is already clear, however, is that the way nation-states are responding to these new challenges will determine the nature of their economic survival in the twenty-first century.

References

Ashton, D N, Maguire, M and Spilsbury, M (1990) *Restructuring the Labour Market: The Implications for Youth*, London: Macmillan.
Ball, S (1990) *Education, Inequality and School Reform: Values in Crisis*, inaugural lecture, Centre for Educational Studies, King's College, London.
Bennis, W (1972) 'The decline of bureaucracy and organisations of the future', in Shepard, J M (ed) *Organizational Issues in Industrial Society*, Englewood Cliffs: Prentice-Hall.
Bernstein, B (1975) *Class, Codes and Control*, Vol 3, London: Routledge.
Block, F (1990) *Postindustrial Possibilities: A Critique of Economic Discourse*, Berkeley: University of California Press.
Boyd, W and Cibulka, J (eds) (1989) *Private Schools and Public Policy*, London: Falmer.
Brown, P (1990) 'The "Third Wave": education and the ideology of parentocracy', *British Journal of Sociology of Education*, **11**, 65–85.
Brown, P and Lauder, H (1992) 'Education, economy and society: an introduction to a new agenda', in Brown, P and Lauder, H (eds) *Education for Economic Survival: From Fordism to Post-Fordism?* London: Routledge.
Brown, P and Scase, R (1994) *Higher Education and Corporate Realities*, London: UCL Press.
Collins, R (1979) *The Credential Society*, New York: Academic Press.
Deakin, S and Wilkinson, F (1991) 'Social policy and economic efficiency: the deregulation of the labour market in Britain', *Critical Social Policy* **11**, 3, 40–61.
Dicken, P (1992) *Global Shift: The Internationalisation of Economic Activity*, London: Paul Chapman.
Fox, A (1974) *Beyond Contract: Work, Politics and Trust Relations*, London: Faber & Faber.
Gramsci, A (1971) *Selections from Prison Notebooks*, London: Lawrence and Wishart.
Green, A (1990) *Education and State Formation*, London: Macmillan.
Green, A and Steedman, H (1993) *Education Provision, Educational Attainment and the Needs of Identity: A Review of Research for Germany, France, Japan, the USA and Britain*, London: NIESR.
Halsey, A.H, Heath, A and Ridge, J (1980) *Origins and Destinations*, Oxford: Clarendon.
Halstead, M (ed) (1994) *Parental Choice and Education*, London: Kogan Page.
Harvey, D (1989) *The Conditions of Postmodernity*, Oxford: Blackwell.
Kanter, R (1984) *The Change Masters*, London: Unwin.
Kanter, R (1989) *When Giants Learn to Dance*, London: Unwin.

Kantor, H and Tyack, D (eds) (1982) *Youth, Work and Schooling*, Stanford: Stanford University Press.

Kohn, M and Schooler, C (1983) *Work and Personality: An Inquiry into the Impact of Social Stratification*, New Jersey: Ablex.

Lacey, C (1988) 'The idea of a socialist education', in Lauder, H and Brown, P (eds) *Education in Search of a Future*, Lewes: Falmer.

Lane, C (1989) *Management and Labour in Europe*, Aldershot: Edward Elgar.

Lauder, H (1987) 'The New Right and educational policy in New Zealand', *New Zealand Journal of Educational Studies*, **22**, 3–23.

Lauder, H and Hughes, D (1990) 'Social inequalities and differences in school outcomes', *New Zealand Journal of Educational Studies*, **23**, 37–60.

Lauder, H et al (1994) *The Creation of Market Competition for Education in New Zealand*, Wellington: Ministry of Education.

Morgan, G (1986) *Images of Organisations*, London: Sage.

National Commission on Excellence in Education (NCEA) (1983) *A Nation at Risk: The Imperative for Educational Reform*, Washington, DC: US Government Printing Office.

OECD (1989) *Education and the Economy in a Changing World*, Paris: OECD.

Piore, M and Sabel, C (1984) *The Second Industrial Divide: Possibilities for Prosperity*, New York: Basic Books.

Reich, R (1991) *The Work of Nations*, London: Simon and Schuster.

Sabel, C F (1982) *Work and Politics*, Cambridge: Cambridge University Press.

Scase, R and Goffee, R (1989) *Reluctant Managers*, London: Unwin Hyman.

Streeck, W (1989) 'Skills and the limits of neo-liberalism: the enterprise of the future as a place of learning', *Work, Employment and Society*, **3** (1), 89–104.

Streeck, W (1992) *Social Institutions and Economic Performance*, London: Sage.

Toffler, A (1990) *Powershift*, New York: Bantam.

Watts, A (1983) *Education, Unemployment and the Future of Work*, Milton Keynes: Open University Press.

Willms, J and Echols, F (1992) 'Alert and inert clients: the Scottish experience of parental choice of schools', *Economics of Education Review*, **11**, 339–50.

Zuboff, S (1988) *In the Age of the Smart Machine: The Future of Work and Power*, New York: Basic Books.

3. Education and training in the New Europe: economic and political contexts

Martin McLean

Cross-national comparisons may refine general concepts by testing against a wide range of examples or they may explore abiding variations between national cultures. Too frequently they are driven by selective enthusiasm for foreign practices. Comparative studies of vocational education in Britain since the early 1980s (Prais, 1981; NEDO/MSC, 1984) have outgrown uncritical borrowing. They have still to reach their full maturity.

So, from a universalist standpoint, description of the global economy may help in understanding of the pressures for an international convergence in vocational education. From a culture-specific orientation, the differences in vocational training between countries which derive from deeply embedded values of work, education and politics need to be explored.

Both approaches suggest caution about cross-national transplants. Those national systems of vocational education which are currently admired may be the product of a felicitous but ephemeral coincidence of historic traditions and current economic-occupational demands. Each country may be advised to seek its own unique blend of old and new.

This chapter describes the interaction of international economic change and historic traditions of training across Europe. A putative conception of a global economy may indicate common pressures. The culturally specific aspects may be delineated across the continent through a distinction between state-school and work-employer strategies of vocational education. The focus is largely upon France and Germany but as a means to constructing a wider European pattern.

What kind of economy and what kind of work?

Three questions are central. Does a global economy require each state to compete internationally in the training of its workers? Does it stratify labour forces across countries along a continuum from high-technology innovation to low-skill production with major implications for living standards? What kinds of attributes do workers need at the advanced end of a high-technology international economy?

Global or national economies?

'Globalization' has been associated with multinational companies from North America, Europe and the Pacific Rim which have been able to take advantage of financial liberalization and telecommunications to disperse their operations across the world (Chesnais, 1993; Dunning 1988, 1993). Globalization challenges training policies because companies can shift, quite rapidly, their centres of production across national boundaries according to perceptions of, among other factors, the cost and quality of labour. High-skill management and research and development can be located in one country and low-skill production in another.

The new can be hypnotic. Competition for world markets among national enterprises has occurred for centuries and labour efficiency has always been a factor in international industrial competitiveness. What has changed is the advanced level of competence required by workers in high-technology enterprises. Globalization intensifies and accelerates the social consequences of success and failure in training highly adept workers.

In contrast, every country has simple service enterprises and older crafts which are less affected by internationalization except for cross-national labour migration which is relatively inelastic. Segmented labour markets are a feature of all national economies (Carnoy, Levin and King, 1980) but stratification can be more acute in some countries than others with differing outcomes in social fissures, alienation and injustices.

The standing of some occupations depends less on international competition than on national valuations, which may reflect historic forms of production which continue to influence contemporary attitudes to work and training. Claims that the decline of British economic supremacy in the late nineteenth century was a result of the survival of anti-industrial attitudes (Weiner, 1985), have been countered by arguments that Britain has always been a commercial rather than a manufacturing nation (Rubinstein, 1993). If this is the case, then comparison may be more appropriate with the Netherlands than with traditionally manufacturing economies such as Germany.

Similarly, an unskilled worker tradition persists in some countries, linked to events such as the eighteenth-century disappearance of independent small farmers in Britain which was not paralleled elsewhere in Europe, or traditions of migration to find work as found in Greece, Portugal, Ireland or southern Italy. The survival of preindustrial craft values in Germany has a different kind of contemporary impact. Within countries there may be powerful historic regional and local differences as in the nineteenth-century contrasts between the steel industry in Birmingham and Sheffield (Briggs, 1968).

These qualifications do not remove the need for study of the impact of international competitive pressures on all kinds of economic activity in every country. The Single European Market, by reducing tariff and other trade, investment and employment barriers since 1957, encourages such competition. The outcomes may be stratification between winners and losers with major social consequences for populations of the unsuccessful zones.

If the division in Europe between core and peripheral economies, high-technology and primitive production, the economically competitive and the ineffective, derives as much from historic as contemporary conditions, what are these differences and why do they have a continued impact as processes of production change? These questions underlie the comparison of training systems.

Work and skill

The major conceptual hurdle for the comparative study of training is how to link analysis of economies with examination of vocational education. Economies are both international and national/local in character. Vocational education more firmly is the outcome of national historic conditions.

The analyses of the relationship between education and the economy through manpower planning techniques matched labels on jobs with corresponding labels on educational courses (Youdi and Hinchcliffe, 1985). The widening technology gap between various kinds of production has led, instead, to a focus upon the kinds of aptitudes needed by workers and the ways in which vocational education can develop these attributes.

Taxonomies of skill have dangers, despite their popularity, notably that they may become simply lists of platitudes that are not capable of consistent interpretation or application. But behind these lists are conceptions of changing patterns of work. In a preindustrial economy, independent farmers and craftspeople individually plan their tasks, manage their own time and acquire skill in a familial environment without needing to extend substantially the capacities learnt in youth. An early industrial economy needs low-skill workers who accept externally imposed disciplines of effort and consistency.

Workers in high-technology manufacture are expected to have high initial competence in rational thinking and literary/numerical/spatial communication. Over time, there may then be greater need for individual creativity; flexible definitions of skills, competences and even basic occupations; or ability to work cooperatively in small teams.

Each of these sets of characteristics may be unequally distributed among cultures, countries, regions or social groups. Changes in production at a global level may give a new importance to older types of nationally predominant worker skill. Investment may circulate according to historic strengths of national labour forces rather than because of relative efficiency in carrying out a standardized and homogeneous set of tasks.

The practical and policy purpose of comparison is to be able to identify the special characteristics of the labour force of each country and region, which includes vocational education, and to assess the strengths and weaknesses of each system in relation to contemporary developments in the global economy. The target for each country is to be able to determine how far their own system of training can be developed within its own traditions to exploit these differences.

What kind of vocational education?

One strategy of vocational education for the whole European continent is unlikely since no approach will be consistent with the traditions of all countries. On the other hand, continuance of choices based on idiosyncratic local traditions may simply exacerbate inequalities by failing to provide external stimuli for improvement in the loser regions.

Vocational education is affected by government, employers and by the system of general education. One comparative distinction is between state controlled/school located and industry controlled/work located systems of vocational training. This separation has underpinned recent comparative studies of British vocational education, especially where France is taken as the exemplar of the state-school model and Germany of the industry-work approach.

How far does this institutional distinction reflect differences of political systems and values? How does it relate to differences between educational valuations of skill, knowledge, attainment and opportunity? How far does it arise from differing occupational structures between countries? How far does the state-school and industry-work distinction help description not simply in France and Germany but across all countries in Europe?

Within each type, specific differences in kinds of vocational school, forms of selection, approaches to assessment of competence and expectations of teaching and learning may be explored. Broadly, differences may be explained by reference to diverging political cultures in the various countries.

State-school vocational education

State predominance in the provision of vocational training is accompanied by a tradition of state economic planning; by articulation of the content of general and vocational education; and by state manipulation of vocational education to meet the social consequences of industrial production.

While this strategy reached its apogee in war-dominated economies – especially the five-year plans of Stalin's Soviet Union or the post-1945 urge in Western Europe to maintain the planning imperatives of autarkic economies – its history can be traced, especially in France, to the Enlightened Despotism of the seventeenth century. Its values persisted through initial industrialization.

Vocational educational provision is determined first of all by state planning objectives. French five-year plans since 1945 have identified future labour needs, based on projections of anticipated changes in production. The plans are created by interministerial teams and are then given to ministries such as education to form a central element in policy. Vocational schools and courses are financed by reference to these priorities, even when the outcome is the provision of unused places. The difficulties of economic forecasting and the problems of reconciling employer needs and student demand are not necessarily overcome. At least a coherent and continuous process of educational provision is maintained (Paul, 1985; Hacham, 1992).

Vocational and general education are unified in ways that company based schemes can rarely achieve. Sweden from 1968 created single upper secondary institutions to unite general education and vocational courses (Marklund, 1987). The partial integration of general and technical *lycées* after 1971 in France provided ladders between general courses leading to the *baccalauréat* and a range of technological options. General courses from the 1980s were also tied to occupational possibilities (Prost, 1992).These measures were intended to reduce the obstacles to social opportunity associated with separate vocational upper secondary institutions. They did not necessarily succeed but they could provide training for low-achieving over-16s.

National plans had social as well as simply economic dimensions. The ladders in France linked, through a series of stages, the high status general *baccalauréat* and the catch-all skilled worker qualification of the *Certificat d'Aptitude Professionnel* (CAP). This system may be more effective than the UK's in engaging educational low attainers in training and maintaining their opportunities (Wolf and Rapiau, 1993). Their success depended on their harmony with established traditions – notably the residual political-administrative values and surviving concepts of worthwhile knowledge and learning.

Political-administrative cultures

Corporatist regimes deal with vocational education in line with their political traditions as much as in response to economic imperatives. The essence of collectivist political culture is that all public services are under the aegis of the state. The state can take decisions about vocational education which in other countries would be considered the responsibility of employers or semi-autonomous educational authorities. The political-administrative framework of vocational education in France was the 1919 Astier Law. Government provided vocational education in state educational institutions and required employers to finance it through a levy (Charmasson *et al*, 1987, p 470).

The Astier Law had precedents. The elite *grandes écoles*, most dating from the 1789 Revolution, were run by a variety of government ministries. The selective examinations ensured them an exclusivity denied to relatively open access universities. They train students in most cases in branches of engineering. The expectation was that graduates would work in the ministry which controlled the *grande école* they attended. In practice, the students moved into private enterprise – usually large corporations. Their career paths took them in and out of government and private enterprise (Ardagh, 1973, pp 487–95). The consequence is a bureau-cratization of French industrial management and links with the state administrative culture (Crozier, 1964).

The manual vocational educational institutions in France after 1919 were based on a model of industrial subordination to the state. It was not difficult for employers or workers to accept that even the practical vocational elements of training should be provided in state institutions. It was entirely consistent with the political culture that every level of vocational education qualification – lack of possession of which disbarred workers from legally practising their crafts – was issued by the state. Every other kind of licence to work as well as every general education qualification had a similar imprimatur.

There are limits to the extent to which state planning can challenge economic interests or social aspirations. Some courses and qualifications have not had enthusiastic support from employers in France when they do not correspond to niches in the labour market. The value of the first diploma of higher education – introduced in the early 1970s as a way of reducing excessive drop-outs and failures in higher education – was not accepted by employers. Changes in the labour market can also affect the standing of state controlled courses. It has been claimed more recently that employers want more flexibility and practical experience from recruits than a *grande école* education provides (Fauconnier, 1992, pp 14–28).

Vocational courses can be rejected when they are the product of political-social goals rather than responses to real economic needs. Craft courses are unpopular and their association with educational failure is reinforced by the creation of centres preparing for the CAP for 16-year-olds who did not complete the four-year lower secondary course because of grade repetition. The technical *baccalauréat* is highly regarded because of rigorous intellectual standards yet its 'business studies' branch is seen to be for low aspirers. The *baccalauréat professionnel*, set up after 1985, was deemed by all to be inferior to other *baccalauréats* because it was seen as a mechanism by government to raise educational participation rates. There is a dilemma about the CAP because its status is partly based on high failure rates (sixty per cent or more) which are a disincentive to potential students and a mark of inefficiency. There are also differing perceptions of mid-career workers. Technicians have more positive views of their training than craft workers (Tanguy, 1991, pp 138–42).

There are limits to the administrative/managerial capacity of centralized administration to construct and operate vocational courses. 'Manpower' planning originated in economies with labour shortages and major nationalized industries. Since 1986, planning in France has become less ambitious and *dirigiste*, partly because state finance for investment has been restricted. There has been both the devolution of power to regional administrations in general education (decisions about resources for schooling, inspection) and in economic development policy.

French vocational education based on a corporatist-statist political culture has been successful when judged against world standards. Italy, Spain, Portugal and Greece have state-directed, school-based vocational education systems with a broad rationale of planning and provision not dissimilar to France. The outcomes have been different in other corporatist cultures.

Of the four countries above, Italy has the highest proportion of school leavers entering vocational schools both at craft (vocational institutes) and technician (technical institutes) preparation levels (Meijer, 1991). A central government with residual ambitions of total planning lacks both the capacity and legitimacy to make these ambitions effective. Localities develop their own technical schools and vocational schools which feed sufficiently well into the labour market for them to attract students. A school-based system of vocational education works because of vibrant local cultures and commitments rather than because of any central planning.

In the other three countries, despite relatively high levels of economic growth in the 1980s, corporatist states have failed to overcome popular disdain for vocational education. In Spain and Greece, a large majority of students completing lower secondary education go on to general upper secondary education and thence compete to enter the oversubscribed higher education system. In both countries, vocational education is seen clearly as a dead-end for those who fail to enter general upper secondary education. Together with Portugal, access to upper secondary education in these states has been widened only recently. It is difficult to build a school-based, state-directed system of vocational education upon this weak foundation of general education.

The school-based, state-directed model, even within Europe, clearly requires the diffusion of certain values about education and the socio-economic development function of the state for it to be successful. A fundamental base of general education may also be a precondition of success.

Educational cultures

The state-school strategy may depend not only on a corporatist political culture but also on the relationship between views of knowledge underpinning the content of general and vocational education. A rational-materialist culture of knowledge in Southern and, formerly, Eastern Europe reduces the gap between humanist education and practical training which applies in the UK (and to a certain degree in Germany and the Netherlands). I have elaborated these epistemological traditions elsewhere (McLean, 1990, pp 13–38).

In summary, the distinction is that rational-encyclopedic conceptions of knowledge emphasize understanding of the material world rather than of the human spirit. There is stress on understanding abstract patterns and a status for subjects which best give that theoretical understanding and which also give opportunity to develop rational capacities among students (notably mathematics and physical sciences). There is a requirement that all valid subjects should be studied for as long as possible by as many students as possible. Humanist conceptions of knowledge emphasize understanding of the moral spring of human action, insight into human feeling and action. There is status for subjects which allow this kind of study – notably literature and history.

Onto these two major views, historically expressed in elite education, can be added, local, individual or community constructions which include conceptions of the individual for whom tangible, concrete and emotional experience is as important as the intellectual. There are also the views that learning is about communities of people coming to terms with the practical (including vocational) world and employing knowledge for its use rather than for its own sake, a formulation known best in the pragmatism and progressivism of John Dewey but which also has strong European roots.

Different forms of encyclopedism, like humanism and naturalism, are found in various European cultures. The action orientation and inductionism-experientialism in the English conception of humanism is not found in its equivalents elsewhere in Europe; nor is the strong vein of public utility in the encyclopedic formulation in France replicated in other West European countries – though it was paralleled by the Marxist–Leninist conception of polytechnicalism which was adopted (but not necessarily implemented) in East and Central Europe. The encyclopedic-humanist distinction also works best in a confrontation of Britain and France. In Germany and the Netherlands, there are differing combinations of humanism and encyclopedism which have other outcomes.

Despite these reservations, this scheme has implications for the relationship between general and vocational education. The dominance of encyclopedism in France and other Southern European countries has ensured on the one hand that mathematics and physical sciences have a high status in general upper secondary schooling and that this preparation is linked to a high status for engineering studies in higher education in France and in Spain. Vocational studies leading to high level professional qualifications have a high status – not only in the elite *grandes écoles* in France but also in the university institutes of technology offering first level higher education since 1968. The unification of general and vocational studies at lower levels is accepted as natural. Mathematics and physical sciences are central in vocational certificate courses leading both to qualifications giving higher education entrance and to those assuring skilled-worker standing. Practical studies are seen to be based upon theoretical conceptions – a link derived from a deep epistemological culture.

This link does not produce a great demand and status for skilled manual worker courses. Students aspire to higher level theoretical studies leading to prestigious professional preparation. For this reason there is an equation between entry to lower level vocational courses and general educational failure in France and Southern Europe as in Britain. But the epistemological gulf between general and vocational education is not as great.

Work-employer based vocational education

Vocational preparation occurs mainly in work and is controlled by employers rather than by state educational institutions. The approach most fully characterizes vocational education in Germany and contrasts with most other countries of Europe which are closer to France. The many studies of German vocational education in Britain in recent years reflect its similarity with historic British practice. A wider comparison might highlight the peculiarity of the German system even in relation to Britain.

The dual system of Germany is workplace centred and employer dominated. Apprentices, taken on by companies at the ages of 16, 17 or

18, are given a formal training within the firm in practical skills and knowledge under the direction of a qualified skilled worker — the *Meister*. The apprentice is recognized as a skilled worker when he or she succeeds in an examination organized primarily by employer associations and based largely on skills and knowledge acquired within the company.

Apprenticeships cover a very wide range of occupations so that fewer than 10 per cent of school leavers enter work outside the apprenticeship system. Private enterprises have succeeded therefore in providing training for the vast majority of those who do not proceed in general education. The qualifications they provide are also recognized throughout the country.

The role of the state school system is minor. By federal law since 1938, which followed laws of states such as Bavaria since the turn of the century, apprentices must be given release to attend state schools for one or two days a week. The content of this education is largely general — German, social studies, religion as well as some theoretical technical subjects — and the schools have the subsidiary place in the assessment of students.

The role of employers in training is not the product of an unrestrained free enterprise culture. There is a partnership between state and employers in which trade unions have also played a part. The legislative requirement of universal education for young workers up to the age of 18 reinforced historic obligations of employers to provide work-based training. Full-time vocational training in state educational institutions has developed at both upper secondary and higher education level since the 1960s (*Berufs-fachschulen* and *Fachhochschulen*). State-educational initiatives to give a work-experience element to general education programmes within secondary schools — notably the *Arbeitslehre* — have been taken at the behest of educational authorities rather than employers.

The commitment of employers both to provide work-based training and to cooperate with the state education system has different roots from parallels which have operated in, for instance, the USA, Japan or the UK. Accordingly, the broader political-economic culture needs examination.

Political-social cultures of work and education

Three themes may be explored. First has been the peculiar concordat between state, industry and workers which developed in Germany especially through Otto von Bismarck's policies of the 1880s. Second has been the historic conception of work and craft. Third is the relationship between humanist general education and an expanded conception of vocational education.

Centralism, localism and pluralism conflict in German political traditions. The political culture is more corporatist than that of Britain, the USA or even the Netherlands. The provincial autonomy of independent states existed for a thousand years prior to unification in 1871 and to the return to a federal system after 1945. Centralist authoritarian traditions derive from seventeenth-century Prussia which expanded into the unified Germany of 1871 to 1945.

Education for most of German history has been a provincial affair, though state governments both before and after 1871 could regard schools and universities as institutions which served state needs. Business, especially after mid-nineteenth-century industrialization, largely escaped provincial control. It had an ambivalent relationship with central government after 1871 — partially autonomous and partly subservient. The dual system of training has reflected this tension.

The corporatist function of general education in Germany has deep historical roots. Entry to traditional state occupations depended upon possession of state educational qualifications. The academic upper secondary *Gymnasium* and the obscurantist university were defended by Wilhelm von Humboldt, in his reform of Prussian education in the early nineteenth century, as the appropriate preparation for officials of state. This tradition has survived in the twentieth century with *Land* control over schools and higher education, including prescriptive state teaching programmes, state award of certificates and the civil servant status of teachers at both school and higher education levels.

Industry in the nineteenth century grew from a local to national scale even before the nation was created, especially through the internal free trade area of the Zollverein of 1834. After unification, massive industrial enterprises, especially the cartels, developed which were unparalleled in Britain or even the USA. German industrialists, unlike their British counterparts, became a powerful class which kept a social arm's length from the relatively impoverished aristocracy. They were denied political power but maintained paternalist relations with their workers.

Bismarck's unified state in the 1880s, legitimated by the traditional power of Prussian landowners, treated both businesses and workers as alien political entities. Employers were to provide the welfare measures for workers that political stability — faced with an increasingly militant Marxist workers' party — required (Pinson, 1966, 240–6). The state expected employers to provide training and job stability for workers. Yet the overall framework was a conservative and partly pluralist political culture which contrasted with the unitary, radical and egalitarian politics of post-1789 France.

Preindustrial practice survived in the training schemes of German manufacturing. Bismarck, in a series of laws between 1878 and 1886, protected the monopoly of the medieval guilds over the enrolment and training of apprentices (Clapham, 1961, p 334). Conservative government fossilized a medieval training system in modern manufacturing.

Profession and craft have been powerful indicators of social status and self-esteem in Germany. An individual is socially identified and professions (in the Anglo-American terminology) have been highly regarded socially and derive this status from links to medieval guilds. There may be a religious link with the association of commitment to craft with religious piety especially in Lutheran beliefs (though similar associations are found in Catholic areas of Germany). Furthermore, many more occupations in Germany than in, for instance, Britain are regarded as crafts requiring apprenticeship training.

The survival of a high status for craft occupations in Germany contrasted with early industrial Britain. In the latter, a much stronger culture of unskilled workers emerged whose supremacy was signalled by the victory of their unions over the skilled workers at the end of the nineteenth century. Popular and historical valuations of manual work in Germany drew upon traditions of craft stretching back to medieval guilds which were then incorporated in large, mass-production factories from the late nineteenth century.

However, this social-political culture had to respond to particular kinds of educational organization and values in Germany. Educational traditions were as important as the political-social in vocational education provision.

Educational cultures

The oddity of German vocational education, to foreign eyes, is that an envied craft and industrial training system is built upon archaic general education. Perhaps it is more accurate to depict German education as schizophrenically divided between the ethereal and the practical. Vocational education has been able to develop because it is firmly separated from German academic values rather than because it is linked to them as in France or, in different ways, in the USA.

German general education is antiquated both in differentiation of institutions and in the content of teaching. Secondary and higher education are stratified in ways that would be unacceptable in most other countries. Selection at the age of ten determines whether a child will enter an academic *Gymnasium* orientated towards university admission after a nine-year course, a terminal but selective *Realschule* for seven years or an unselective *Hauptschule* for six years. Despite the decline in *Hauptschule* numbers since the 1970s, they still take nearly 40 per cent of the age group. Comprehensive schools cater for only 10 per cent of the secondary school population and there is little political impetus to expand them, signalled in the replacement of comprehensive schools by bipartite and tripartite models in the former East German states after 1989.

Traditional universities still treat students as apprentice researchers who have great latitude of choice of subjects of study, supervisors and timing of examinations. As a result, students only enter universities at the age of 20 and take an average of almost seven years to complete their courses. Technical *Fachhochschulen* since the 1960s succeed in graduating higher education students in four years but they are institutionally separate as well as rigidly utilitarian in function. The apex of the system is irrelevant to industrial training as well as being inefficient and socially discriminatory.

The content of academic education has been backward looking. The German philosophy of curriculum was described by Joseph Lauwerys as concerned with the 'moral personality and with the inner freedom of the individual ... in the notion that there exists an inner reality and unity in the cosmos and that it can be apprehended in an almost mystical manner by a process of identification, ontological, metaphysical, spiritual' (Lauwerys, 1967, p 15).

This view applied particularly in the *Gymnasium* and traditional university. The grand ideals in practice have been associated with an academic education emphasizing philology – ancient and modern languages – and with higher education whose summit is grand philosophy.

Yet there are some aspects of German general education which have supported the vocational education system. While the *Gymnasium* remained a bastion of a humanist education, there was a shift towards a greater emphasis on mathematics and science branches in specific *Gymnasien* in the late nineteenth century. The *Realschulen*, which developed in the nineteenth century, combined highly regarded academic education with a general vocational preparation. Unlike the ill-fated technical secondary schools after 1944 in England and Wales the *Realschulen* flourished, taking about a third of the total age group and providing a general education with a clear commercial and industrial tinge.

The *Hauptschule* has maintained its vocational bent in recent years with practical subjects existing alongside the academic. Significantly, craft was reformed from the 1960s to provide a coherent pre-vocational education. The *Arbeitslehre* included not only making objects to a high enough standard to sell but systematic planning of their production from design and assessing demand to marketing. There were also work experience elements of the course together with careers guidance and study of the social-economic foundations of industrial society. Indeed, some have seen the *Arbeitslehre* as the truest application of the Marxist–Leninist ideal of polytechnicalism (Castles and Wustenberg, 1979, pp 147–66).

The diverse and contradictory character of German general education has been made functional to vocational education by employers who have clearly and stringently emphasized those aspects of general education which they consider appropriate. They have demanded that those whom they take on as apprentices should have passed the final examination of the *Hauptschule*. Employers thus put pressure on pupils in lower secondary education to perform effectively in general education as a precondition of employment and retained this demand even in periods of labour shortage. As participation in general education in schools has expanded, so employers have increasingly favoured those with higher level general education including university entrance qualifications in their recruitment of apprentices. The German separation of general and vocational education has still given a pivotal role for basic general education skills before employment.

The philosophical bases of German vocational education are also important. Georg Kerschensteiner had a key role. As Director of Education for Bavaria at the turn of the century, he in effect created the dual system of work and schooling which then spread to other states especially through the advocacy of Eduard Spranger. Kerschensteiner's justifications had a strong moral-religious and civic strain. For him 'education was occupation' and manual training was closely linked to both religious and citizenship education. It was an answer to what was seen to be the crisis in values produced by urbanization. To this prescription was added a commitment to reviving older craft cultures and pride, revealed in his commitment to the ideas of William Morris. The irony is that, with

Kerschensteiner's support, Morris's programme was more fully established in Germany than in its native Britain (Simons, 1966; Gonon, 1993).

The effectiveness of German vocational education derives from established traditions of both work and education. Both the strengths and the weaknesses of German general education allow vocational education to succeed. So possibilities of transfer to other countries need to be considered critically and sceptically. Furthermore, the German system of training has its own problems including the lack of flexibility of workers who identify with particular trades and the high cost of the generous training provision to employers. Indeed, the German system stands out as peculiar in Europe even though some elements of the culture that supports it do have echoes in other European countries.

Indeed, one of the main reasons for urging caution about adoption of German approaches is that they may be even more culturally unique and non-transferable than the French which do have some claims to universal relevance. It is difficult to identify major European countries which follow the German system apart from culturally associated systems of Austria and parts of Switzerland. Of the non-Germanic countries, only the Netherlands and, perhaps more marginally, Denmark, have parallels with German vocational education.

Indeed the Netherlands shares the educational anachronism of Germany. A differentiated secondary school system includes non-selective institutions with a pre-vocational bias (LBOs) which socialize children into entry to craft training and occupations yet which are able to insist on relatively high levels of student attainment (Prais and Beadle, 1991). There are also traditions of employer and trade union agreement on recruitment and training of apprentices. Both the stratification and consensual paternalism parallel German traditions. The higher education system has old, humanist universities, which are inefficient at graduating students, and also a larger sector of specialized vocational training institutions.

However, the Netherlands has not been able to secure the match between employers' demands and government-education controlled craft-technician training programmes which has succeeded in Germany. In effect the Netherlands may share some of the social-industrial values of Germany but has a state-school training system which appears to lack coherence and relevance to the labour market (Liebrand, 1991, pp 55–66).

Indeed, deeper comparisons suggest that the distinction between the state-school and employer-work patterns of vocational education only have relevance at certain levels. The historic value systems of politics, work and education also impinge on the effectiveness of both systems. The peculiarity of the French and German cultures of training and their anachronistic characteristics suggests that, if the point of comparison is, apart from to warn of inappropriate cultural borrowing, to identify a range of models for future reform, then attention may be directed as much outside Europe as within it.

Overview: extra-European perspectives

A comparative study of European vocational education systems is unlikely to throw up any universal solutions for future development. The study identifies, inevitably, the bases for past success or failure rather than future possibilities which depend on the nature of work, society and education in the immediate future. Its usefulness is confined to introducing caveats about cultural borrowing of institutions that are deeply embedded in national historical traditions.

There is a need for a wider comparative survey. A European analysis provides only a slice of such a project. The USA and Japan also repay study. The United States may no longer have a system of vocational education which attracts great attention, though questions remain about whether this neglect is a product of the relative industrial decline of the USA rather than of perceived weaknesses of its vocational education. The United States has offered historically a system which differs from any of those in Europe by more fully integrating vocational and general education not only in a single institution but also within the courses followed by individual students; and by having a tradition of local community employer involvement in general and vocational education.

The pragmatic tradition of valuing knowledge and skills for their use rather than their own sake, and consequently of dissolving boundaries between fields of knowledge, has had the weakness in recent years of not encouraging sufficiently high levels of attainment in basic intellectual skill. But it has the longer term value that it requires flexibility and adaptability among students in mastering all types of knowledge and in encouraging a positive dynamic view of learning. Pragmatism was the product of philistine small-town America of the nineteenth century. Its usefulness was overtaken by the growth of large corporations and high-technology production. It may have a future value in the capacity of those working within these values to combine social/cooperative, intellectual, practical and personal skills in the most effective way – a strategy which has not developed in Europe to any great extent.

The Japanese approach is also instructive. For those aspiring and destined for work in the large industrial corporations (thus excluding the 25 per cent of upper secondary students in vocational-general education), an intellectually demanding general secondary and often higher education has been followed by vocational training provided entirely within the company. Such a scheme has depended upon employee loyalty to the company and the assumption that company specific training could be appropriate for workers who had lifetime employment. If such conditions continue to prevail, this separation of general and vocational education is efficient. It produces workers with high levels of general education and broad intellectual skill and it gives them training which is highly relevant to their actual employment. It takes account of the company specific nature of training and the difficulty of providing generalized vocational education.

This Japanese scheme is, in many ways, becoming the world standard which at the same time is increasingly adopted in the USA. The difficulty, experienced in the USA, is how to produce high enough levels of general educational attainment among the majority of young people in a state-supported education system and how to induce employers to accept responsibility for providing thorough in-house training for all their employees. In conditions of high unemployment, economic enterprises widely varying in size and stability, and deeply segmented labour forces, this ideal may not be feasible and more flawed European schemes may continue to be necessary. In which case, these latter schemes still need to draw on subterranean springs of historic national traditions of work, education and state and employer responsibility.

References

Ardagh, J (1973) *The New France 1945–1973*, Harmondsworth: Penguin.

Briggs, A (1968) *Victorian Cities*, Harmondsworth: Penguin.

Carnoy, M, Levin, H M and King, K (1980) *Education, Work and Employment*, Vol 2, Paris: UNESCO.

Castles, S and Wustenberg, W (1979) *The Education of the Future*, London: Pluto.

Charmasson, T *et al* (1987) *L'Enseignement technique de la revolution à nos jours*, Vol 1, Paris: Economica.

Chesnais, F (1993) 'Globalisation, world oligopoly and some of their implications', in Humbert, M (ed) *The Impact of Globalisation on Europe's Firms and Industries*, London: Pinter.

Clapham, J H (1961) *The Economic Development of France and Germany 1815–1914*, Cambridge: Cambridge University Press.

Crozier, M (1964) *The Bureaucratic Phenomenon*, Chicago: University of Chicago Press.

Dunning, J H (1988) *Multinationals, Technology and Competitiveness*, London: Unwin Hyman.

Dunning, J H (1993) *The Globalisation of Business*, London: Routledge.

Fauconnier, P (1992) 'Les grandes écoles dans les collimateur', *Le Nouvelle Observateur*, **1437**, 24, 14–28.

Gonon, P (1993) Georg Kerschensteiner Lecture at the University of London Institute of Education, June.

Hacham, T F El (1992) *A quoi sert le plan? Un regard sur le system educatif*, Paris: Economica.

Lauwerys, J A (1967) 'Opening Address', in *General Education in a Changing World*, Berlin: CESE.

Liebrand, C G M (1991) 'Recent developments in the Dutch system of vocational qualifications', *European Journal of Education*, **26**, 1.

McLean, M (1990) *Britain and a Single Market Europe: Prospects for a Common School Curriculum*, London: Kogan Page.

Marklund, S (1987) 'Integration of school and the world of work in Sweden', in Lauglo, J and Lillis, K (eds) *Vocationalizing Education: an International Perspective*, Oxford: Pergamon, pp 181–6.

Meijer, K (1991) 'Reforms in vocational education and training in Italy, Spain and Portugal', *European Journal of Education*, **26**, 1, 13–27.

National Economic Development Office/Manpower Services Commission (1984) *Competence and Competition: Training and Education in the Federal Republic of Germany, the United States and Japan*, London: NEDO.

Paul, J-J (1985) 'Basic concepts and methods used in forecasting skilled manpower requirements in France', in Youdi, R V and Hinchcliffe, K (eds) *Forecasting Skilled Manpower Needs: The Experience of Eleven Countries*, Paris: UNESCO/IIEP, pp 35–56.

Pinson, K S (1966) *Modern Germany*, New York: Macmillan.

Prais, S J (1981) 'Some practical aspects of human capital investment: training standards in five occupations in Britain and Germany', *National Institute Economic Review*, **98**, 47–59.

Prais, S J and Beadle, E (1991) *Pre-vocational Schooling in Europe Today*, report series 1, London: National Institute of Economic and Social Research.

Prost, A (1992) *Education, societé et politiques: une histoire de l'enseignement en France de 1945 a nos jours*, Paris: Editions Seuil.

Rubinstein, W D (1993) *Capitalism, Culture and Decline in Britain 1750–1990*, London: Routledge.

Simons, D (1966) *Georg Kerschensteiner*, London: Methuen.

Tanguy, (1991) *L'Enseignement professionel en France: des ouvriers aux techniciens*, Paris: Presse Universitaires de France.

Wiener, M J (1985) *English Culture and the Decline of the Industrial Spirit 1850–1980*, Harmondsworth: Penguin.

Wolf, A and Rapiau, M T (1993) 'The academic achievement of craft apprentices in France and England: contrasting systems and common dilemmas', *Comparative Education*, **29**, 1, 29–43.

Youdi, R V and Hinchcliffe, K (eds) (1985) *Forecasting Skilled Manpower Needs: the Experience of Eleven Countries*, Paris: UNESCO/IIEP.

4 Education, work and the restructuring of Central-Eastern and Eastern Europe

J J Tomiak

The aim of this chapter is to examine the broader outlines of the political and economic contexts which directly influence the educational and employment policies in the countries of Central-Eastern and Eastern Europe today. However, the contexts themselves are parameters which are not constant, but tend to evolve through time faster than they do in respect of other regions and areas in the world. Hence, it is necessary to watch the Eastern European scene carefully all the time and to introduce the necessary corrective rectifications whenever the circumstances demand (Amann, 1994, pp 14–15; Brzezinski, 1993, pp 7–55 and 155–81; Motyl, 1993, pp 1–55; Tomiak, 1992c, pp 19–34).

It is also necessary to draw attention to the changing role and functions of post-compulsory education within the educational systems which are experiencing a fundamental transformation. Education is now universally seen as having a multi-purpose social function which meets distinct political, social, economic and cultural needs of the society as a whole as well as of its individual members. Post-compulsory education has to take into account all such needs, but is expected by its very nature to be in position to contribute to the economic growth of a country by providing skilled manpower of all kinds and at all levels and improving the competency and efficiency of the working population. This can be done under the conditions of relative political and economic stability and continuity of the productive forms of activity of different kinds, provided that the appropriate policies are pursued. Destabilization of the economy, uncertainty concerning the future, radical changes in the ownership of the means of production, inflation, the collapse of foreign markets or financial crises inevitably result in sudden major shifts in the existing industrial structures and, as a result, are bound to cause severe imbalances and problems, particularly in technical and vocational training. (*The Economist*, 1994b, pp 3–16; Karlov and Merkuriev, 1992, pp 1–3; Pipes, 1992, p 17).

The great divide: Central-Eastern and Eastern Europe since 1989/91

The countries of Central-Eastern Europe are normally considered to be Poland, the Czech Republic, Slovakia and Hungary. The countries of Eastern Europe are those which previously were parts of the Soviet Union, that is Belarus, Ukraine, Moldova, European Russia and the Baltic states of Lithuania, Latvia and Estonia. One should stress here the fact that they are all distinctive historical, cultural and political entities in their own right. However, in this case, the explicit intention is to consider the overall characteristics of that part of Europe as a whole and, in such circumstances, only the principal lines of recent developments can be taken into account. They reflect the difficulties and dilemmas generally created by the problems intimately connected with the fundamental political and socio-economic changes which inevitably affect education, especially post-compulsory education. In the text, the reader's attention is drawn to the most recent publications examining the situation in particular countries in greater detail. This is advisable, because although the principal trends such as the decline in industrial production, employment as well as in birth- and infant-mortality rates, life expectancy, health standards and confidence in the future are similar in all countries, the national differences are significant and cannot be ignored. Indeed, as time moves on, the contrast between Central-Eastern European countries and the former Soviet republics is becoming more and more pronounced (*The Economist*, 1992, 1993; Heyneman, 1991, pp 1–3; Mitter, 1992, pp 123–30; Tomiak, 1992b, pp 137–55).

The countries situated in this part of Europe had been for many decades the integral parts of the communist bloc and pursued educational and employment policies based upon clearly defined Marxist–Leninist principles. Between 1989 and 1991 all these countries abandoned such principles one by one, often in a dramatic and very categorical way, and embraced political liberalism and open market economics. Of the utmost importance were the speed of change and its direct consequences.

It must be accepted that the pressures for change were irrepressible (Brzezinski, 1989, pp 232–58; Gorbachev, 1987, pp 83–102; Stanglin *et al*, 1992, pp 40–9). One-party rule, over-rigorous and highly centralized planning, lack of proper incentives, not to mention the persisting memories of the ruthlessly oppressive character of the early years of communist domination in every Eastern and Central-Eastern European country made discontent and disapproval of the system prevailing up to 1989/91 increasingly widespread. Low productivity, inefficient management and the consequent economic stagnation resulted in open criticism of the party hierarchy in each country and opened up the way for unequivocal demands for a complete change of the political and economic structures. Yet, a change of that magnitude could not possibly be an easy one and it required a proper analysis of the actual way in which the transformation was to be accomplished.

The ultimate objectives of the envisaged transformation were clear: to create a civil society and a stable and viable economy. But that required many things which could not be attained in a short period of time. The creation of a stable and properly functioning political system demanded the establishment of several (but not too numerous) political parties with clearly defined programmes; the existence of an electorate which was fully conscious of its new civic obligations; honest and hard-working politicians; clearly defined spheres of responsibility of the legislative, executive and judicial powers in each country; properly functioning political channels for the pursuit of specific objectives by the different pressure groups.

Laying down firm foundations of a stable social order demanded, amongst many things, first of all a universal respect for law; the existence of a network of social institutions which would provide genuine opportunities for the expression of individual and group interests in a free, but orderly, manner; the acceptance of the principle that in all the controversies and disputes the voices of minorities must be clearly heard and never be suppressed by illegitimate means, but the voice of majority must ultimately prevail (Kicinski, 1993, pp 97–109; Lloyd, 1994, pp i and x; Tomiak, 1993, pp 393–6).

Creating a well functioning economic system which would match the awakened expectations of the population required that the system operated as it ought to do in an open society, that is in a way transparent to all the citizens; that serious efforts were made to provide employment for all who wanted to work; that the units of production were operating efficiently and all the financial institutions strictly observed the regulations specified by law; that the National Income was distributed fairly among all the social strata and all the occupational categories, but that individual efforts, hard work, inventiveness and efficiency received a proper reward; that the preparation of the younger generation for gainful employment in the agricultural, industrial and service sectors of the economy was adequate to meet the increasingly complex demands for highly skilled labour (Kopp, 1993, pp 85–91; Sachs, 1993, pp 1–34; Tomiak, 1988, pp 1018–20).

It is clear that requirements of that order could not be met in the short run as they amounted to nothing less than a complete restructuring of the Central-Eastern and Eastern European societies and economies. And yet, the demands for a rapid change tended to intensify. Nevertheless, realistically speaking, it was evident from the start that the process of transition was bound to be difficult and the final outcome uncertain (Hosking, 1993, p 17; Kaletsky, 1994, p 6; Keay, 1993, pp 6–9; OECD, 1992, pp 1–30).

The political upheaval: the end of one-party rule

The peculiar nature of the communist political system was based upon the principle of the communist party performing the role of the vanguard and exercising full control over the destiny of each nation. The internal party hierarchy, the concentration of the effective power in the hands of the politburos, in fact precluded the possibility of active participation in the political decision making process by the wider ranks of the population in each country. Civic obligations were reduced to following the political leadership unquestioningly and any criticism of it, overt or covert, was condemned as an unacceptable manifestation of a hostile attitude towards the system as a whole (Brzezinski, 1989, pp 13–50; Millard, 1994, pp 1–55).

The creation of the firm foundations of civil society is now a major task of the reformed educational systems and, in particular, of secondary and tertiary education. Hence, there now is a general conviction that post-compulsory education in ex-communist countries must necessarily include the political dimension. Its function should be to provide a reliable knowledge of democratic institutions and to promote positive attitudes towards the full exercise of civic rights and obligations by all citizens.

This task is not rendered easy by the prevailing climate of cynicism which is spread widely among the members of the younger generation. The young obviously find it difficult to trust and listen to the members of the older generation whom they accuse, very frequently not without reason, of egoism, indifference, lack of respect for the laws of the country, corruption and invidious practices of all kinds. The greater then is the need for an open and honest discussion concerning the very foundations of the society of the future. Not surprisingly, therefore, there are numerous educators in the Central-Eastern and Eastern European countries who firmly believe that the education of the older adolescents affords the best opportunity to prepare the younger generation for the responsibilities of democratic citizenship (Kicinski, 1993, pp 97–109; Eklof and Dneprov, 1993, pp 65–72). The new curricula for general secondary schools envisage everywhere courses in civics and social studies which explicitly orient themselves to exploit that opportunity. The challenge remains to make sure that this is also done in all post-compulsory educational establishments providing technical and vocational training, so that no members of the younger generation grow unaware of their civic right and obligations (UNESCO, 1983, pp 75–6).

Transforming the economy: shock therapy versus gradual transformation

At the time of the abandonment of the old system each Central-Eastern and Eastern European country faced a dilemma: whether to accomplish the transition to a market economy in a sudden and dramatic manner by liberalizing, privatizing and reorganizing the economic system in one 'big jump' forward or to attempt a gradual change extending over a considerably longer period of time.

There was no lack of advice from the West and clear-cut strategies were proposed by some Western economists favouring the sudden change. They came from scholars with considerable reputation who argued their case with great force and found eager supporters in a number of the countries concerned.

The example of Poland illustrates best the course of a rapid reform executed according to the strategy worked out in detail by Professor

Jeffrey Sachs of Harvard University and put into operation by the Polish finance minister Leszek Balcerowicz and hence known as the Balcerowicz Plan.

The main pillars of the big jump forward to the market economy were clearly identified. The first one was macroeconomic stabilization – to ensure that the rate of credit expansion was cut drastically and the value of the Polish zloty was fixed to allow stability of the exchange rates. The second pillar was liberalization – to allow for the free play of the market forces of demand and supply while, at the same time, a legal framework was created in order to provide a solid basis for the formation of private businesses and the enforcement of contracts. The third pillar was privatization. As privatizing and restructuring industry was expected to create considerable unemployment, a 'social safety net' to offer help to the unemployed was to be provided. Ample foreign credits were to be obtained from abroad to support the process of transformation. However, the last two aspects proved difficult to attain in practice. Unemployment rose rapidly and foreign credits which were granted were inadequate. Nevertheless this strategy produced some positive results in economic terms, although at the cost of creating social problems on a massive scale (Keay, 1992, pp 8–10; Levy, 1992, pp 13–17; Millard, 1994, pp 173–84; Sachs, 1993, pp 35–78).

The advantages and disadvantages of the rapid transformation strategy were thus delicately balanced and there were other economists and politicians who were active on the Central-Eastern and Eastern European scene who advocated gradual change. According to them, the 'big bang' risked the complete destruction of the existing set-up *before* the lasting foundations of the new one were securely laid. This, in their eyes, was bound to produce confusion and uncertainty with new opportunities for some people but hardship and adversity for many more. That could easily lead to new conflicts and confrontations. They advocated, therefore, gradual change, less drastic monetary and fiscal measures, a slower pace of economic liberalization, arguing that in this way sudden restructuring of industry and large-scale unemployment could be avoided.

The ultimate objectives of the two strategies were identical, the actual economic and social repercussions of them differed very significantly. The subsequent events demonstrated that the sudden rise in prices of goods and services as well as in unemployment associated with the 'big bang' approach caused massive social protest in the countries which had adopted it and very much weakened the original enthusiasm for open market economics (Amann, 1994, pp 14–15; Kampfner, 1994, p 10; Pipes, 1993, p 15).

The transition from central planning to open market economy

Creating a strong industrial infrastructure was always one of the main objectives of economic policy under the communist rule in every country, in Eastern and Central-Eastern Europe. This priority was also given a strong support by other undercurrents of opinion associated with nationalistic aspirations as it tended to reinforce national self-sufficiency and national prestige. Providing the expanding industry with the right kind of properly qualified labour force was a natural corollary. Each country, therefore, following the Soviet example dating back to the late 1920s, introduced central planning, defined as 'directive planning', which involved a detailed specification of manpower requirements for each branch of production. This meant that each higher education establishment, each vocational and technical school in every country, had to recruit and train a clearly identified number of technologists, engineers, technicians or skilled workers in order to meet the total demand for all the different categories of employees. The system was not very efficient and was increasingly becoming over-bureaucratized but it operated for many decades. A sudden dismantling of such an elaborate educational planning mechanism was bound to have far-reaching consequences (Millard, 1994, pp 194–5). Meanwhile, the creation of an open market exposed thousands of the existing units of production, both in public as well as in private hands (eg, in agriculture) to the full force of foreign competition. Many factories and businesses went bankrupt and had to close down.

Additional considerations must be taken into account. With the creation of the COMECON (the Council for Mutual Economic Assistance) in January 1949, a closely integrated pattern of regional specialization in industrial production brought the whole of the Eastern bloc together. It was designed to cement the industries of the communist countries into one system, serving the joint economic needs of the whole area, while at the same time allowing each country to concentrate on the production of what it was best suited for. The assumption was that this kind of arrangement would be a lasting one and would permit an appreciable increase in production in the bloc as a whole. The reality was rather different, as the envisaged integration began to experience numerous bottlenecks, delays and technical difficulties in production. The events of 1989/91 completely destroyed this strategy as each country freed itself from the outside control which had been forced upon it and began to orient itself to meeting the demands of the market. This reflected the consumers' preferences which for all intents and purposes were fundamentally different from the priorities determined earlier on by political and military imperatives arising out of the arms race and the cold war with the West. Industrial restructuring on a very large scale was unavoidable.

In addition, the Russian market for Central-European goods not only declined but simply collapsed in 1992 with the deteriorating situation in that country. This development caused enormous difficulties in several countries as exports in that direction ceased and no substitute markets for a large range of products could be found in the West or anywhere else. Productive activities in many fields thus ceased, leading to even greater unemployment in many regions, particularly in those that tended to rely chiefly upon just one kind of industry and could not offer alternative opportunities for work (*The Economist*, 1993, pp 10–15; 1994b, pp 83–7).

Economic restructuring and new opportunities for employment

The shift from state-sponsored demand to consumer-generated demand for goods and services was a phenomenon of great consequence and caused great turbulence in all the Eastern and Central-Eastern European economic systems. Its immediate impact was twofold. On the one hand, there was a sudden abundance of certain kinds of commodities for which there was, in the new situation, no or very limited demand at home or abroad, for example many kinds of capital equipment, arms and munitions, poor quality durable consumer goods. On the other hand, there were simultaneous high demand for many other goods which were available only in limited quantities. As a result, there were corresponding price changes to equate demand and supply of the particular commodities. That meant a sharp rise in the prices of many consumer goods. The withdrawal of state subsidies only added to the pressure to increase prices and caused widespread dissatisfaction.

The long-run consequences were even more serious. Capital and labour had to leave the fields of economic activity which had to contract and enter those which promised profits and, therefore, had to expand. This could not be done quickly. Manpower which had been trained for a particular job that was no longer in demand could not be expected to find employment right away in the new enterprises producing very different goods and using very different kinds of machines and equipment or in the service sector of the economy. That could only be possible if an elaborate and costly network of courses and facilities for retraining and learning new skills (sometimes mastering entirely new occupations) could be created. It also required labour to be geographically mobile, a condition which could not easily be satisfied, given the serious shortages of housing and accommodation prevailing in all countries.

Meanwhile, the service sectors of the economy began to expand in all countries. The growth in trade and commerce, banking and insurance and privately owned small-scale businesses created a strong demand for entirely new kinds of expertise and new skills. Yet for a full expansion of the labour market in each country a massive injection of capital was required for a speedy restructuring and modernization of industry. Capital resources at home were emphatically quite inadequate for this purpose and the only alternative was to try to obtain capital from abroad. Desperate efforts were therefore made by the newly established governments in Central-Eastern and Eastern Europe to attract foreign investors. Such efforts were only partially successful. There were two principal reasons for this. One was that foreign investors were not welcome everywhere. In some countries there was simply a fear that foreign capital would pour in on a large scale and come to dominate the national economy (Sachs, 1993, p 90). The other reason was that obtaining foreign credits was difficult in any case. International organizations such as the International Monetary Fund and the new European Bank for Reconstruction and Development did offer credits, but they were quite inadequate to meet the overall needs of the region. The commercial banks in the West which were still owed very large sums of money by many Central-Eastern and Eastern European

governments for loans contracted earlier on were very reluctant to grant
additional credit facilities, fearing even greater problems. The situation was
further aggravated by the unexpected depth and length of the recession in
the West, the end of which is still not in sight (Kitaev, 1992, pp 3–5).
Forced by the foreign creditors, the International Monetary Fund and the
World Bank to balance the budgets and avoid hyperinflation, most new
governments quickly abandoned their desire to support the collapsing
industries, risking loss of popularity and, ultimately, loss of power. Some
Eastern European governments, however, faced with the prospect of social
unrest on a large scale, capitulated and continued their support for the
troubled industries, saving them from extinction but, at the same time,
undermining the very foundations of stable economy (*The Economist*, 1993,
and 1994b).

Reforming and restructuring education

The determination to create a civil society, a state based upon a universal
respect for law and an efficiently functioning economy, was bound to
fundamentally affect the educational systems and educational processes
everywhere in Central-Eastern and Eastern Europe. To put it in a nutshell,
the educational systems were to be diversified, democratized, liberalized
and modernized (Eklof and Dneprov, 1993, pp 48–9; Mieszalski and
Kupisiewicz, 1992, pp 78–81; Prucha, 1992, pp 88–91; Razumovskij, 1992,
pp 59–68). Yet, inadequate attention was paid to the fact that changes of
that character and magnitude required critical and constructive thinking,
time and money. In fact, the countries of Central-Eastern and, particularly,
Eastern Europe were short of all three requirements, even if the situation
varied considerably from country to country (Mitter, 1993, pp 1–12;
Tjeldvoll, 1992, pp 29–38).

New laws and regulations concerning education and responding to the
new political and economic imperatives came slowly and piecemeal.
Expenditure on education began to decline, seriously undermining
prospects for modernization and improvement (Applebaum, 1994, p 7;
Gerschunskij, 1994, p 18). Vocational education lost the little prestige it
had in the past and became even less popular among the young people
(Ministry of Education of the Russian Federation, 1992, pp 43–5). The
state systems of education came to lag behind the economic and social
changes, starved of funds, burdened by the legacy of the past and
increasingly experiencing an exodus of the most talented and capable
teachers who were moving into more lucrative employment in the service
sectors of the different countries (Council of Europe, 1992, p 9; Hughes,
1992, p 23; Kitaev, 1992, pp 11–16; Zinberg, 1993, p 12).

Private enterprise entered the field of education. In all ex-communist
countries numerous private schools and other educational establishments
came into existence, charging fees – often very high fees – but all claiming
that they were responding to the needs of the market (Setenyi, 1993, pp
4–5). Today, private schools constitute a significant part of the educational
structures in all Central-Eastern and Eastern European countries (Eklof and

Dneprov, 1993, pp 74–6; Karakovsky, 1993, p 19; Ministry of Education of the Russian Federation, 1992, pp 17–18; Nagy, 1992, p 3; Prucha, 1992, pp 92–3; Tomiak, 1992a, pp 38–9). In such schools classes are small and instruction is given by well qualified teachers who, sometimes, are university lecturers or professors. Courses include, besides the full range of subjects normally taught in secondary schools, intensive studies in economics and business, several foreign languages, information technology, the use of computers and word processors.

Numerous private colleges concentrate their attention on teaching the above mentioned subjects at an advanced level with the help of experts possessing considerable experience in a given field and using the latest modern learning aids available. They also run courses in management and marketing. Despite the high fees, studies of this kind are in great demand and there is no shortage of applicants (Bathory, 1992, pp 27–8; Kornilov, 1992, pp 1–3; Mieszalski and Kupisiewicz, 1992, pp 76–80). The growth of international trade and in the number of joint ventures all over Central-Eastern and Eastern Europe makes such courses increasingly popular among the young and ambitious residents of larger towns and urbanized areas.

However, privatization has brought undesirable consequences insofar as industrial training in ex-communist countries is concerned. In the past, most large-scale units of production possessed big departments for training their future employees in all kinds of the relevant skills and specializations. Tens of thousands of young workers were then learning their future occupations that way every year. Now, the declining output in the traditional industries, difficulties in changing into any alternative forms of production, uncertainty concerning the future and, above all, shortage of funds have drastically cut and sometimes wiped out altogether the training schemes which provided the main means for training skilled workers in years gone by.

The relevance of the past: polytechnical education and preparation for work

A summary report of the international symposium on the transition from technical and vocational schools to work, published in 1983, stressed the fact that technical and vocational education ought to be understood as:

a) an integral part of general education;
b) a means of preparing for an occupational field;
c) an aspect of continuing education (UNESCO, p 76).

This observation makes it clear that post-compulsory education, being a part of the total educational process, should not be seen in isolation from the preceding stage of universal compulsory education. Polytechnical education was an important ingredient of that education under communism, although its origins are very much older and can be said to constitute a key element in the radical tradition in education (Skatkin, 1963, pp 17–33). As such it possessed cognitive, affective and conative aspects and it also embraced industrial practice. Admittedly, there were differences in respect of a successful linkage between theory and practice of polytechnical education among all the different Central-Eastern and Eastern European countries (Alyokhina, 1992, pp 2–3; Tomiak, 1986, pp 7–9). But the idea was that every adolescent's educational experience should include an introduction to modern industry and the world of technology, and the inculcation of respect for work, should be retained as one of the permanent features of compulsory education in modern times, despite the political change. This practice, though far from being followed in all countries, constituted a more meaningful form of pre-vocational awareness of the real diversity of the productive processes and provided an opportunity for developing initial vocational orientation. Combined with properly developed schemes of vocational guidance it could well continue, despite ongoing industrial restructuring, and take into account the increase in demand for more complex and more sophisticated skills in the future.

Concluding remarks

The process of economic, political and social restructuring of Central-Eastern and Eastern Europe is proving much more difficult and protracted than it was originally envisaged at the time of the disappearance of the iron curtain (Amann, 1994, p 14; Mitter, 1993, pp 1–3; Tomiak, 1992b, pp 145–52). The naive expectation that quick change was possible, based upon an inadequate analysis of the enormity of the task and the scale of the planned transformation, began to produce a counter-reaction in many Eastern and – to a considerable extent – also Central-Eastern European countries as early as 1992. Large scale unemployment has now developed into a permanent inability of the new systems to secure full employment for the workforce in every country of the region. The non-availability of long term credit on a larger scale has made industrial restructuring very problematic and the recession in the West has added greatly to future uncertainty. Social discontent has now turned into definite political opposition against further reforms along capitalistic lines in several countries (*The Economist*, 1994a).

Such developments have made educational reconstruction and renewal difficult and the modernization of post-compulsory education to meet the new requirements in that part of Europe a very tall order indeed. The different modes of vocational training suitable for economically fully developed countries such as Germany, Sweden or Japan (Lauglo, 1993, pp 70–5) cannot easily be borrowed by the Central-Eastern and Eastern European countries, as they correspond to a different kind of set-up, rooted in advanced industrial and technological culture.

The most powerful impetus for change and improvement always comes from the demand side. Total effective home demand in the countries of the area seems for the time being, however, quite inadequate to augur a change for the better. Without an injection of additional long-term credits from abroad and political integration of the two halves of Europe a more marked improvement seems impossible. Yet, without that, the renewal and modernization, post-compulsory education – and particularly technical and vocational training – in Europe's eastern half is bound to remain very problematic for several years yet.

References

Alyokhina, M (1992) 'Some practical aspects of transition to market economy', paper presented to the Educational Leadership International, held in Oslo in November, Moscow: MGPU, pp 1–12.

Amann, R (1994) 'What is to be done?', *Times Higher Education Supplement*, 11 February, pp 14–15.

Applebaum, D (1994) 'Education: unions fail to learn their lessons', *Financial Times*, 18 March, p 7.

Bathory, Z (1992) 'Some consequences of the change of regime in Hungarian public education', in Mitter *et al*, pp 27–39.

Brzezinski, Z (1989) *The Grand Failure: The Birth and Death of Communism in the Twentieth Century*, New York: Scribner.

Brzezinski Z (1993) *Out of Control: Global Turmoil on the Eve of the 21st Century*, New York: Scribner.

Council of Europe (1992) *Standing Conference on University Problems, Legislative Reform in Higher Education, Russia*, Strasbourg: Directorate of Education, Culture and Sport, pp 1–12.

The Economist (1992) 'A Survey of Russia', supplement, 5 December, pp 3–30.

The Economist (1993) 'A Survey of Eastern Europe', supplement, 13 March, pp 3–22.

The Economist (1994a) 'Russia: the road to ruin', 29 January, pp 27–9.

The Economist (1994b) 'Russia's bankruptcy bears', business section, 19 March, pp 83–7.

The Economist (1994c) 'Russian privatisation – not the real thing yet', 12 December, p 46.

Eklof, B and Dneprov, E (eds) (1993) *Democracy in the Russian School: The Reform Movement in Education Since 1984*, Boulder: Westview Press.

Gerschunskij, B (1994) 'Russland: Bildung und die Zukuft', in Mitter, W (ed) *Curricula in der Schule: Russland 1992*, Deutsches Institut fur Internationale Pedogogische Forschung, Cologne, Weimar, Vienna, Böhlau, pp 13–38.

Gorbachev, M (1987) *Perestroika: New Thinking for Our Country and the World*, London: Collins.

Heyneman, S (1991) 'Revolution in the East: the educational lessons', paper presented to the Oxford International Round Table on Educational Policy, 5 September, New York.

Hosking, G (1993) 'Watching the big brother', *Times Higher Education Supplement*, 19 November, p 17.

Hughes, J (1992) 'For sale – Russia's best brains', *Guardian*, 15 September, p 23.

Kaletsky, A (1994) 'Why Russians mustn't be slaves to the free market', *Sunday Telegraph*, 6 February, p 6.

Kampfner, J (1994) 'A farewell to Russia', *Daily Telegraph*, 10 January, p 10.

Karakovsky, V (1993) 'Russia's schools today and tomorrow', *Education in Russia, The Independent States and Eastern Europe*, Bulletin of the Study Group, **2**, 1, pp 18–24.

Karlov, M and Merkuriev, S (1992) *Education and the Economy in Russia*, Paris: OECD.

Keay, J (1992) 'Czechoslovakia – the art of falling apart', *Business Europa*, August/September, pp 7–12.

Keay, J (1993) 'Much pain, little gain', *Business Europa*, January/February, pp 6–9.

Kicinski, K (1993) *Wizjeszkoly w spoleczenstwiepost-totalitarnym (Visions of schools in a post-totalitarian society)*, Warsaw: OPEN.

Kitaev, I (1992) *Labour Markets and Educational Systems in the Former Soviet Union*, Paris: IIEP.

Kopp, B von (1993) 'Global changes and the context of education democracy and development in Eastern Europe', in Mitter and Schäfer, pp 85–98.

Kornilov, V (1992) 'Transition to market economy and its effect on the system of education in Russia', paper presented to the Educational Leadership International, held in Oslo in November. Moscow: MGPU, pp I–II.

Lauglo, J (1993) *Vocational Training: Analysis of Policy and Modes, Case Studies of Sweden, Germany and Japan,* Paris: IIEP.

Levy, M (1992) 'The Baltics: bridge over roubled waters', *Business Europa,* August/September, pp 13–17.

Lloyd, J (1994) 'Beware of the sickly Russian bear', *Financial Times,* 20 March, Section II, pp i and x.

Mieszalski, S and Kupisiewicz, C (1992) 'The present state and recent trends in Polish education', in Mitter *et al,* pp 69–81.

Millard, F (1994) *The Anatomy of the New Poland: Post-Communist Politics in its First Phase,* Aldershot: Edward Elgar.

Ministry of Education of the Russian Federation (1992) *Development of Education in Russia,* national report for the 43rd Session, International Conference on Education in Geneva. Moscow.

Mitter, W (1992) 'Education in Eastern Europe and the Soviet Union in a period of revolutionary change', Mitter *et al,* pp 121–36.

Mitter, W (1993) 'Education, democracy and development in a period of revolutionary change', Mitter, W and Schäfer, pp 1–2.

Mitter, W and Schäfer, U (eds) (1993) *Upheaval and Change in Education,* Frankfurt am Main: German Institute for International Educational Research.

Mitter, W *et al* (eds) (1992) *Recent Trends in Eastern European Education,* Frankfurt am Main: German Institute for International Educational Research.

Motyl, A (1993) *Dilemmas of Independence: Ukraine after Totalitarianism,* New York: Council of Foreign Relations Press.

Nagy, M (1992) 'A transition to market economy and changes in the education system in Hungary', paper presented to the Educational Leadership International, held in Oslo in November, Budapest: National Institute of Public Education.

OECD (1992) *Report on Education and Training in Poland during the Transformation of the Socio-Economic System,* Paris: OECD.

Pipes, R (1992) 'Starting from scratch', *Independent,* 19 August, p 17.

Pipes, R (1993) 'Yeltsin's move: the struggle to achieve stable and effective government in Russia', *Times Literary Supplement,* 18 October, p 15.

Prucha, J (1992) 'Trends in Czechoslovak education', in Mitter *et al,* pp 83–102.

Razumovskij, V (1992) 'Education in the Soviet school today and tomorrow', in Mitter *et al,* pp 57–68.

Sachs, J (1993) *Poland's Jump to the Market Economy,* Cambridge, MA, and London: MIT Press.

Setenyi, J (1993) 'Regional human resource development and the modernization of the non-university sector in Hungary', paper presented to the annual meeting of the Study Group on Education in Russia, the Independent States and Eastern Europe in November, 1993, in London, Budapest: Hungarian Institute for Educational Research.

Skatkin, M (1963) 'Marxist–Leninist ideas on polytechnical education', in Shapovalenko, S *Polytechnical Education in the USSR,* Paris: UNESCO.

Stanglin, D *et al* (1992) 'The wreck of Russia', *US News and World Report,* 7 December, pp 40–55.

Tjeldvoll, A (1992) 'Ideological changes and educational consequences – Eastern Europe after 1989', *Educational Leadership International Education in East/Central Europe, 1991,* report from a Seminar held in the University of Oslo, 28–30 November, 1991, University of Oslo, pp 29–38.

Tomiak, J (1986) 'Education and vocationalism in Eastern Europe', *Secondary Education Journal,* **16**, 2, pp 7–9.

Tomiak, J (1988) 'Poland', in Kurian, G (ed) *World Education Encyclopedia,* Vol 2, New York and Oxford: Facts on File, pp 1006–20.

Tomiak, J (1992a) 'Education in the Baltic States, Ukraine, Belarus and Russia', *Comparative Education,* **28**, 1, pp 33–44.

Tomiak, J (1992b) 'General trends in Eastern Europe in West European perspective', in Mitter *et al,* pp 137–55.

Tomiak, J (1992c) 'Implications of political change in Eastern Europe for educational policy development', *Journal of Educational Finance,* **17**, 3, pp 19–34.

Tomiak, J (1993) 'Erziehung, kulturelle Identität und nationale Loyalität. Die Fälle Ukraine und Belarus' (Education, cultural identity and national loyalty. The cases of Ukraine and

Belarus), *Bildung und Erziehung*, Cologne, Weimar, Vienna, Böhlau, **46**, 4, pp 393–409.
UNESCO (1983) 'The transition from technical and vocational schools to work', *Trends and Issues in Technical and Vocational Education*, **2**, Paris: UNESCO.
Zinberg, D (1993) 'Russia's hard frontier', *Times Higher Education Supplement*, London, p 12.

Part 2: Education, training and labour market change

Introduction

Andy Green

The purpose of initial vocational education and training is to prepare young people for entry into work and other societal roles. As this transition becomes more complex in many societies, so the nature of the connection between Vocational Education and Training (VET) systems and the labour markets they serve becomes an increasingly important concern.

In different countries we find various forms of articulation between systems of VET and the different segments of the labour market, functioning more or less harmoniously. Typically, in countries with strong internal labour markets, like Japan and France, we find a dominant pattern of general and broadly vocational upper secondary education, with occupational training provided in employment. Conversely, in countries with strong occupational labour markets, like Britain and Germany, there has been a tradition of apprenticeship training which provides the qualifications for labour market mobility. In reality, however, the patterns are more complex than this since most economies have complex mixes of internal and occupational structures, more or less well served by the dominant form of VET. Likewise, labour markets tend to involve high levels of gender segmentation which are more or less reinforced by the structures of VET.

Labour markets in many countries are also undergoing profound structural change. New technologies and the new work processes associated with them often reinforce internal labour markets and create new demands for higher level and flexible skills in core sectors. However, this is often accompanied by increasing labour market casualization at the periphery and higher levels of structural unemployment, particularly amongst youth, whose traditional labour markets have frequently atrophied.

National VET systems have often struggled to respond to these changes. They have been required to provide for an increasingly diverse mass of young people displaced from work; to offer a broad foundation of general and vocational education in preparation for fluid job roles and changing careers; and to respond to swift changes in technologies and skills requirements. As the pace of technological change accelerates – making lifelong learning a necessity – so the worlds of work and education become increasingly intermeshed. The need to deliver relevant and flexible

VET has raised the importance of effective collaboration between the social partners and the various stakeholders in education and training.

The five chapters in this section all look at the implications of these changes. The first three chapters take a broad and cross-national view.

Marsden and Ryan examine the relations between changing labour market structures and VET provision in the UK and Germany, analysing why labour market adjustments in one country have led to the consolidation of a relatively adaptive apprenticeship system, whilst in the other causing ongoing problems for skills training. Gaskell examines the relationship between a gender segmented labour market in the USA and Canada and the VET systems which sustain and reproduce it. Green makes an historical and comparative analysis of VET in England and continental Europe, showing how the different roles played by the state and the social partners in different countries have critically affected the quality and nature of provision.

The last two chapters examine in detail the same relations but in contrasting national contexts. Voncken and Onstenk analyse how youth training in the Netherlands is responding to the needs of flexible production and changing social aspirations. Thomas takes the argument to South East Asia, investigating the connections between youth, education and work in Malaysia and Singapore.

5. Work, labour markets and vocational preparation: Anglo-German comparisons of training in intermediate skills

David Marsden and Paul Ryan

In November 1993 the British government announced a Modern Apprenticeship initiative, involving greater public funding for employers who train young people in intermediate skills. Such craft and technician skills have been found central to economic performance by a range of studies. After nearly 15 years of 'malign neglect' of apprenticeship by government, a major change of course has been signalled. Similar developments can be seen in the USA (Finegold, 1993).

Why should such a policy change occur and what are its prospects? These questions are best approached from a comparative and historical perspective, considering the evolution of training for intermediate skills in Britain during the past half-century in comparison to that in Germany, and focusing on the links between vocational preparation and labour market structure. This chapter recapitulates and extends the argument made elsewhere (Marsden and Ryan, 1990; 1991) concerning training and labour market structures in the context of recent developments in technology, training methods and qualification systems. The first section reviews labour market structures and training methods. The second section discusses the implications for youth training in the two countries of contemporary changes in such structures and methods. A preliminary overview of Modern Apprenticeship is presented in the final section.

Labour market structures and training methods

Training for intermediate skills in both Britain and Germany has traditionally taken the form of apprenticeship training, where part-time vocational education is combined with on-the-job training and work experience. This common pattern has been associated historically with the predominance of occupational labour markets in both countries. However, since the 1960s, patterns of training have increasingly diverged. Whilst in Germany the apprenticeship system has been consolidated and strengthened, in Britain it has been subject to a secular decline.

Moreover, in Britain there has been a growing emphasis on deregulatory policies which have not been paralleled in Germany. These trends can be related not only to differences in government policies but also to the different relationships which are emerging between occupational, internal and secondary labour markets in the two countries.

Internal and occupational labour markets can be defined as structures which involve an inclusionary criterion which distinguishes insiders from those excluded from the 'market'. In occupational markets, the possession of a recognized occupational qualification provides the criterion; in internal markets, employee status with a particular employer provides the criterion.

Occupational markets encourage the mobility of qualified workers amongst employers but limit the movement of unqualified workers into the market. By contrast internal markets favour vertical mobility along job and promotion ladders within the firm, with movement from the external labour market into positions above entry level reduced in the extreme to zero. In both cases insiders enjoy greater economic security than do outsiders but the locus of their security is the occupation in the former case and the employer in the latter case. Membership of occupational and internal structures in the UK is exemplified by legal and medical professionals and Nissan employees respectively.

A third category must also be recognized: unstructured, or secondary, labour markets, in which pay and economic security both tend to be low, given the skills involved. Casual work in service occupations exemplifies such conditions. Although the importance of secondary employment has undoubtedly increased in Britain in recent years (Walsh, 1993), no such changes are apparent in Germany and this discussion concentrates on the mix of occupational and internal elements within the more structured parts of both countries' labour markets.

This characterization of labour market structure has involved ideal types. In practice mixed forms are found. One variant has internal, occupational and secondary structures functioning alongside each other in a particular plant. In chemicals and coal in the UK, for example, maintenance skills have typically been linked to occupational markets, process skills to internal markets and cleaning ones to secondary markets (Marsden, 1982). In a second variant, occupational and internal structures both affect individual workers. In the UK, graduate engineers and accountants working for large firms are involved in both occupational structures, through the professional status which makes them valuable to a range of employers, and internal structures, through the firm-specific career ladders via which many seek to progress (Mace, 1979).

Vocational preparation differs according to labour market structure. Occupational markets require that skills be developed and certified on broad occupational criteria, ideally involving vocational education as well as practical training. Training in internal markets is commonly geared to the requirements of the individual employer, resulting in informal, narrow, specific and uncertified skills. In occupational markets, vocational preparation often involves vocational education and practical training, whether conducted in succession, as in the professions, or side by side, as in apprenticeship. In internal markets vocational preparation relies heavily on on-the-job training delivered by the employer and experienced workers. The deficiencies of such vocational preparation can be – and in many countries are – compensated for in practice by vocational preparation in secondary education.

The UK and Germany have traditionally exhibited more marked occupational structures in their labour markets than have other large EU economies, not to mention the USA and Japan (Marsden and Ryan, 1990), and their training has been traditionally apprenticeship-based in contrast to the combinations of full-time schooling and job-based training which have prevailed in Sweden, France, Japan and the USA. (Marsden and Ryan, 1991). Low pay rates for apprentices relative to adults in the same occupation have encouraged employers to hire and train young people to a greater extent in Britain and Germany than elsewhere (Marsden and Ryan, 1991).

The quality of apprenticeship training improved considerably in both countries during the postwar period – in Germany, throughout the period, in association with a progressively elaborated system of tripartite regulation; in the UK, primarily during 1964–81, in association with the Industrial Training Boards (Streeck et al., 1987).

The quantity of training has, however, diverged strongly in the two countries. In West Germany the apprenticeship covered 72 per cent of the youth cohort by 1988 (GB HMI, 1991), whereas in the UK, where it was always biased towards male manual crafts in industry, it has declined yet more rapidly than that category of employment. Accurate data have become increasingly unavailable but it appears unlikely that apprentices (interpreted here as long-term young trainees sponsored by employers) amounted to more than 5 per cent of the youth cohort by 1990 (Dolton, 1993). In UK metalworking, traditionally apprenticeship's national stronghold, the scale of apprenticeship matched that in West German industry and commerce until the late 1960s but thereafter declined to less than 2 per cent after 1984 (See Figure 5.1).

Since 1983 a number of new training initiatives in the UK (the Youth Training Scheme, Youth Training, Youth Credits) have complicated the picture. The YTS was promoted by government as a deregulatory improvement upon apprenticeship, in which lower trainee payroll costs would encourage employers to provide more training and in which high quality, occupationally oriented, training would be promoted by design and public monitoring. The extension of YT programmes to two years in 1986 was intended to give them credibility as an alternative form of intermediate skills training which would overcome the problems of the apprenticeship.

By the late 1980s 16 per cent of the youth cohort were engaged in YT (Dolton, 1993) suggesting that significant progress had been made in narrowing the gap with German rates of apprentice training. However, the change was more apparent than real. These schemes have been oriented heavily towards low-cost training for lower-level skills; training quality has been highly dispersed, with a large low-quality segment marked by extensive trainee exploitation; employers have widely adapted them to provide longer periods of probationary screening for juvenile recruitment.

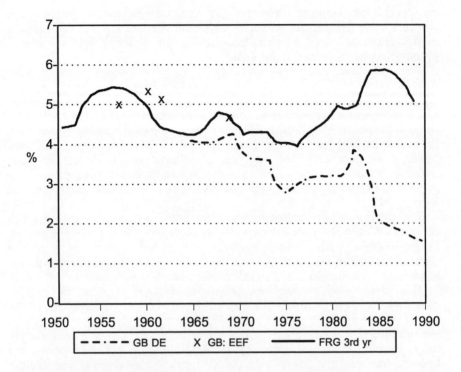

Note: British series before 1964 cover federated engineering employers only.
Sources: GB – Department of Employment estimates; EEF internal surveys; FRG – Bundesminster für Arbeit und Sozialordnung, *Arbeits- und Sozialstatistik*, various years.

Figure 5.1 *Apprentice numbers as a share of sectoral employment in Federal Republic of Germany (Industry and Commerce) and Britain (Engineering and Shipbuilding), 1950–89*

The poverty of the schemes' reputation among young people is illustrated by the actions of participants, the great majority of whom left their programmes well before completion, as well as implicitly by the Modern Apprenticeship initiative, for which there would be no need had these schemes succeeded in terms of intermediate skill development (Marsden and Ryan, 1991).

The traditional importance of occupational markets in both countries did not prevent in either a significant extension of internal labour markets during the postwar period. Common factors contributing to such developments include the growth of large firms, the increasing role of corporate personnel policy and the growing importance within those policies of long-term, career-oriented incentives to employees. Factors noteworthy in the West German context included the adoption of enterprise-based works councils, the value to large employers of selecting among their apprentices for long-term employment, the insistence of employers on the unilateral regulation of continuing training, and the institutional obstacles erected against layoffs.

If internal structures became more prominent in both countries during the postwar decades, occupational markets have also become more important in certain sectors, particularly in Germany. In German chemicals, steel and docks, employers supported the introduction of apprenticeships designed for their sector, consistent with the widespread perception that the job structures and training methods of internal labour markets were too narrowly focused for successful adjustment to industrial change (Drexel, 1980). Such employers had previously relied on ex-apprentices from the *Handwerk* sector to fill production jobs organized at semi-skilled levels.

In Germany these occupational structures have often coexisted more harmoniously with internal labour markets than in the UK and have been sustained by widespread support from employers and unions. This is manifest in many ways, not least in widespread support for pay structures which favour apprenticeship, in terms both of low trainee allowances and of industry-wide pay agreements which prevent individual employers from raising pay in order to poach skilled workers from other employers.

The success with which occupational and internal structures have been dovetailed in Germany is also illustrated by the hierarchy of qualifications to which skilled workers (*Facharbeiter*) may aspire, notably, master-craftworker (*Meister*), technician (*Techniker*) and professional grades. More than 90 per cent of technicians at work in the late 1980s had been promoted from the ranks of qualified skilled workers. Around a half of such promotees possessed only an apprenticeship qualification but a growing percentage – rising from 38 to 44 per cent between 1980 and 1989 – has acquired a technician diploma, often with the financial help from their employers (Géhin and Méhaut, 1993). Indeed, larger German firms seek to retain skilled workers, despite the transferability of their skills, by offering advancement into technician and intermediate level engineer jobs (Drexel, 1994). Yet despite the integration of their holders into long-term employment relationships and internal promotion in large firms, many of the additional skills obtained are certified by externally awarded diplomas, thereby ensuring high degrees of transparency and transfer-ability.

Britain has by contrast seen a progressive erosion of occupational structures by internal ones. Sectors in which occupational markets were most pronounced, primarily durable goods manufacturing, have undergone protracted decline. Employer associations have lost ground to individual employers as the vehicle for pay determination and sectoral regulation (Walsh, 1993). Larger employers have developed internal systems for pay, promotion and training. The progressive replacement since 1981 of Industrial Training Boards by voluntary Industry Training Organisations has removed what limited statutory support had been developed for apprenticeship training (Rainbird, 1991). Nor have burgeoning internal markets in Britain blended effectively with what remains of occupational structures. The locus of bargaining has indeed shifted widely from the employers' association to the individual employer but the flexible working agreements which seek to break down occupational demarcations in work organization have made only painful and limited progress in the face of customary practice (Millward, 1994).

Progress appears particularly slow in the development of vertical mobility for employees, normally encouraged within internal labour markets. Whilst internal upgrading appears to be common in new and foreign-owned plants and is increasingly pursued elsewhere through flexibility agreements, its overall growth during the last decade remains limited. As recently as 1983–4 fewer than 1 per cent of semi-skilled manual workers in Britain were upgraded to skilled jobs (Marsden, 1990). By comparison with the USA, Japan and Germany, upgrade training in UK internal markets appears weak and thus provides little compensation for the decline in apprenticeship training as a source of intermediate skills.

The decline of apprenticeship in the UK and its buoyancy in Germany have thus helped to erode and maintain occupational structures in the two countries respectively. As such, the causes of the divergence are of considerable importance. Divergent national trends in apprenticeship may be attributed partly to changes in pay structures, which shape incentives for employers to offer, and trainees to undertake, training. The payroll costs of trainees depend primarily on the gap between their earnings and their productivity during training, which depends inversely on the amount of training provided (Ryan, 1994b). Small pay differentials between trainee and qualified workers mean correspondingly high training costs to employers, as do long duration and high quality in training. High training costs encourage employers to acquire skilled labour through recruitment rather than training, particularly if unemployment is high.

In both countries training costs to employers increased during the postwar period in association with increased training quality resulting from the 1969 Vocational Training Act in West Germany and the 1964 Industrial Training Act in the UK. However, the UK employers also had to face the rising costs of apprentice wages which increased faster than in Germany. Apprentice incomes (relative to skilled worker pay) stood at broadly similar levels before the war and increased noticeably in the postwar years in both countries. The increase was, however, much smaller in Germany than in Britain. The gap between pay ratios for apprentices at similar stages in their training in the two countries rose from 22 to 42 percentage points over the four decades after 1950 in a leading metalworking region (see Figure 5.2). The contrast between the two national experiences remains similarly sharp if actual earnings are used instead of negotiated rates (Ryan, 1993).

Increases in apprentice relative pay in the UK are indeed spread out over a longer period than declines in training volumes, which occurred primarily after 1968. This discrepancy in timing casts some doubt on the putative role of relative pay, as opposed to the low levels of skill shortage and the high real interest rates which have been associated with depressed training levels throughout the 1980s (Stevens, 1994). Trainee pay, however, is only one side of the coin of payroll costs. The other is training quality, which appears to have risen rapidly after 1964, particularly in small and medium sized firms, as the Industrial Training

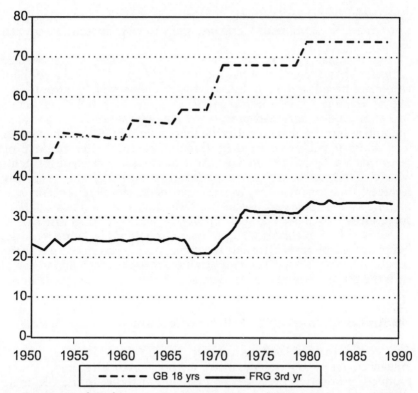

Sources: Department of Employment, *Time Rates of Wages and Hours of Labour*; Die Tariflöhne (Ecklöhne) in der Metallindustrie 1948–89: Facharbeiter, (unpublished worksheets) and *Abkommen uber die Lehrlingsvergutung*, annual (Nordrhein-Westfalen); IGM, Frankfurt.

Figure 5.2 *Negotiated pay (allowances) of apprentices as a percentage of adult craft rates, British and German engineering, 1950–89*

Boards began operations. Moreover, when the perspective is widened to bring in both the interwar period and postwar German trends, and when hourly earnings are considered as well as rates, the role of trainee payroll costs appears more prominent (Ryan, 1993).

The divergence in national pay structures reflects the collective bargaining which determined them in the industrial sectors of both countries and, within that, the bargaining goals of trade unions and apprentices, who in the postwar UK demanded increased apprentice relative pay with a frequency and urgency which lacked any counterpart in Germany (Ryan, 1993).

The resulting divergence in pay structures meant that UK employers faced a much sharper escalation in the payroll costs of training than did their German counterparts, with increasingly adverse effects on their willingness to offer training places. The three-way cost sharing between employers, trainees and the state which characterized German apprenticeship throughout the postwar period contrasts with a strong upward trend in the employer share in Britain. The casualty zone has accordingly proved to be the UK rather than Germany; the casualty, apprenticeship activity itself.

The national contrast is however not polarized. A succession of problems have faced German apprenticeship. The balance between workplace-based and school-based training was widely disputed in the 1960s, leading to the introduction of a year of full-time vocational education as a widespread precursor to an apprenticeship. The supply of apprenticeships became a matter of concern in the 1970s, when proposals for statutory collective funding through payroll levies made progress before falling to judicial review. Around the same time, discontent was widely expressed amongst apprentices concerning the emphasis on technical training relative to that on personal development in their training. The *Handwerk* sector, which trains a large proportion of apprentices, has been charged repeatedly with profiting from excessive amounts of low-quality training in inappropriate skills. More recently, the future appeal of apprenticeship to young people has become a matter of debate (Drexel, 1994). These difficulties, however, are minor compared with the problem of employer reluctance to take on apprentices in Britain.

Technical change and skill certification

The youth training systems of both the UK and Germany have been influenced lately by several other factors, notably technical change in products, production processes and training methods. In the UK, there has also been labour market deregulation and the abolition of the Training Boards, the decentralization of the delivery of public training programmes to Training and Enterprise Councils (TECs), the development of National Vocational Qualifications (NVQs) and, most recently, the Modern Apprenticeship initiative itself.

Technical change is a powerful and problematic influence on initial training. 'Lean production' has become associated with increased productivity and, as such, is widely pursued by many larger producers of sophisticated goods and services. It is associated with a greater emphasis on teamwork, with lower levels of immediate supervision and with skill-intensive work involving increased functional flexibility, in which employees perform a wider range of tasks than under the high subdivision of labour of postwar mass production.

The German approach to initial training is in many ways well suited to such implications. The traditional criticism that German apprentices are overtrained relative to their future job requirements is encountered less frequently nowadays, apart from enduring concerns over the downgrading experienced by the large number of ex-apprentices who work in an occupation other than that in which they qualified. Especially in larger firms, the breadth and depth of German apprenticeship, complementing more skill-intensive production methods, contrasts with the narrow and shallow vocational preparation of many British employees, which corresponds in turn to skill-economizing production techniques. The difference in initial training and skill mixes has been associated with the more successful performance of German than of comparable British enterprises (eg, Prais *et al*, 1991) – evidence which has in turn promoted the recent revival of government interest in apprenticeship in the UK.

German training has certainly reacted to technical change. Many larger employers have set up training workshops with the equipment, facilities and instruction required for training in new technologies. Joint training centres have been established in a variety of sectors to allow smaller employers to offer training to national occupational standards (Streeck *et al*, 1987). At the same time, technical change poses some problems for German apprenticeship. Training quality is ensured in Germany by a complex multi-level system of tripartite regulation, centring upon the set of recognized training occupations and the associated training schedules promulgated by the Federal Vocational Training Institute. The adaptation of these to technical change can be slow, as instanced by the full decade which it took after 1975 to arrange an overall reduction to 378 in the number of recognized occupations by increasing the content of individual ones (Streeck *et al*, 1987). Similarly, the revision of the job and pay classification agreements of the steel and engineering industries to increase work flexibility and recognize contextual skills has also proved a protracted affair (Huber and Lang, 1993). The educational component of German apprenticeship, ensured by the statutory requirement for enrolment in part-time further education, is also slow to respond to innovations in teaching technology and methods. The curricula and teaching methods of *Berufsschule* courses tend to the stagnant and uncreative respectively (GB HMI, 1991).

Contemporary technical change also favours internalization, as employers seek to adjust teamwork to their own requirements. A more variegated organization of work reduces the standardization of job classifications across firms, weakening one prop for occupational markets. Such changes also threaten promotion paths out of skilled manual work by reducing the number of supervisory positions and increasing the technical demands on technicians.

These difficulties do not, however, detract greatly from the enduring strengths of German initial training. Apprentice-based occupational skills – suitably updated through revised classification agreements – still provide German employers and young people with a broadly effective basis for dealing with changes in technology and work organization.

In the UK, the weakness of collective regulation rules out such comforting conclusions. The Industrial Training Boards which covered engineering, construction and road transport had by and large managed by 1979 to raise training standards in intermediate skills to levels close to their German counterparts (Prais and Wagner, 1983), even if they had made little headway elsewhere and had lost the battle for training volumes. The demise during 1981–91 of all but the Construction Board has effectively ended statutory and tripartite elements in the regulation of apprenticeship.

The non-statutory Industry Training Organisations with which the ITBs have been replaced continue much of the advisory work but lack their regulatory powers. Large companies have consequently extended the scope which they won in the later years of the ITBs to choose their own training methods. A variety of training initiatives has also emerged from the locally based Training and Enterprise Councils charged with promoting training as well as delivering specific public programmes such as YT, as YTS was relabelled in 1990.

Some interesting innovations have resulted from these deregulatory and decentralizing trends. ICI, British Steel and Shell have set up independent training companies in both Teesside and Merseyside from which they and other employers purchase the first two years of apprenticeship-type training. Both of these training companies have redesigned their training curricula to respond to the demands of their employer customers for greater emphasis on creativity, teamworking and multi-skilling (Pickard, 1994). BMW (GB) now contracts with six further education colleges around Britain to provide off-the-job instruction to its dealers' apprentices, providing the colleges in turn with BMW-specific equipment, vehicles and training (BMW, 1993). Some TECs have even developed well-funded programmes to support apprenticeship.

The creativity evident in such initiatives has also been encouraged by the development of National Vocational Qualifications (NVQs). In contrast to the reliance of German apprenticeship upon nationally negotiated training criteria, NVQs are explicitly slanted towards current employer practice as the criterion of occupational skill. Such skills are to be assessed primarily through workplace-based assessments of employee competence. In principle, therefore, NVQs are capable of keeping abreast of technical change in a flexible and low-key way. By enabling the constituent competences of NVQs to be built up progressively, they also provide a stepping stone by which semi-skilled workers with no qualifications can aspire to more highly skilled work – which could in turn counteract the longstanding weakness of internal upgrading in British employment.

The proponents of the NVQ emphasize these advantages relative to what is readily depicted as an inflexible German counterpart (Jessup, 1991). The issue is however more complex. The NVQ approach underestimates what it takes for such assessments of occupational competence to signal validly and reliably the attainment of high levels of skill. Even employers and training experts broadly sympathetic to the NVQ approach expect NVQs to show basic deficiencies, even at intermediate levels (3 and 4).

The first problem is low validity in relation to occupational competence. Despite the claims of NVQ to assess underpinning knowledge as well as practical skills, workplace-based assessment is an intrinsically limited way of determining the former. Employers therefore enjoy considerable scope to discard the educational component of apprenticeship (Steedman, 1992). Second, even practical skills are unlikely to be assessed reliably. NVQs' adherence to written statements of competence standards leaves many workplace assessors uncertain about what standards should be required, resulting in an unnecessarily high rate of assessment errors (Wolf, 1993).

Third, incentive problems are likely to lower NVQ validity overall. NVQs can be expected to certify substandard skill learning when the evaluation is performed by the supervisor/trainer without effective external verification and when economic rewards to the employer and the trainee hinge on a favourable outcome. The problem is becoming acute in government-supported training as it shifts towards 'output-related funding', ie, paying training grants for NVQs achieved by trainees rather than time spent in training (Green *et al*, 1993; Prais *et al*, 1991; Ryan, 1994a; 1994b). Finally, the problem can be expected to arise in employer-sponsored training as well. While increased skills transferability based on effective NVQ certification would provide a welcome boost to occupational structures in Britain, the threat posed by poaching to the individual employer's investment in training would simultaneously be increased (Katz and Ziderman, 1990). Employers will then either offer still fewer training places or use their scope to undermine the transparency and transferability of NVQs themselves (Marsden, 1994).

Any superiority for Britain relative to Germany in terms of the flexibility of training and qualification in the face of technical change is therefore likely to be achieved only at the expense of training quality. Young people in the UK can all too easily qualify at craft and technician level after vocational preparation deficient in both educational and practical content. Indeed, deregulation and the limitations of NVQs together increase the scope for such outcomes relative even to that in the recent past, where the problem for intermediate skills was one more of inadequate numbers than of inadequate quality. Now problems can be expected on both counts.

Modern Apprenticeship

The decline of apprenticeship and occupational labour markets in Britain stands out sharply relative both to previous history and to contemporary Germany. The adverse effects of the decline have thus far been offset only weakly and unevenly by the development of vocational education and informal upgrade training in internal labour markets.

A new factor has recently appeared on the UK horizon, in the shape of the Modern Apprenticeship initiative, the first policy in fifteen years to address these problems directly. The initiative has as yet been delineated only in general terms. It is to be geared to youth training in intermediate skills at NVQ levels 3–4; to extend apprenticeship into previously untouched occupations and sectors; to require written apprenticeship compacts between employer and trainee; and to expect that the great majority of trainees will acquire employee status at some time during training (GB DE, 1994).

The initiative is a welcome, if overdue, response to the secular decline of apprenticeship. It will require the trainee to achieve NVQ3 or NVQ4 if the employer is to claim a public training grant. It will increase the scope within youth programmes for the longer training periods and higher public subsidies – relative to pre-1990 YTS format – which are required for training to intermediate levels.

There are, however, two main areas of concern for Modern

Apprenticeship. The first concerns quality assurance, specifically the qualification system against which training results are to be measured and to which its funding is to be tied. As NVQs do not on their own inspire confidence in either respect, there is a clear case for developing both other forms of certification and better quality control within NVQs. Apprentices should be required to acquire vocational educational qualifications as well as NVQs. ITB-type statutory powers to require training programmes to comply with the wider set of attributes (eg, presence of qualified trainers) which are required in Germany could also counter the limitations of NVQs. Without such measures, a low-quality tail can be expected to flourish, which is liable to cause damage not only to the trainees but also to the initiative's wider reputation.

The second matter of concern involves training volumes, which brings up Modern Apprenticeship's potential for correcting the contrastingly lopsided incentives which characterize YT/YC and traditional apprenticeship. The initiative might well explore the middle ground between the low income, insecure contracts offered under YTS/YT, where most 16-year-olds still start at only £29.50 per week, and the high income, secure contracts associated with contemporary apprenticeship, where a select few start at rates commonly exceeding £100 per week. The incentives to trainees to persevere with employer-based training need to be improved relative to those under Youth Training, but not so strongly as to prevent a major increase in the incentives to employers to take on trainees relative to those under contemporary apprenticeship contracts.

The initiative appeared initially to have missed the point here in preferring employee status for the great majority of participants. Employee status certainly improves the incentive to young people to complete training. But by bringing with it high trainee payroll costs and indefinite contracts it deters employers from offering apprenticeships in the first place. A more attractive option would be to provide all participants (a) with apprentice rather than trainee or employee status; (b) with training allowances which start at around £50 rather than £30 or £100 per week; and (c) with fixed-term (3–4 year) rather than indefinite contracts. Such are the attributes of German apprenticeship. They offer a clear option to draw on international comparisons in the design of UK training policy. Modern Apprenticeship may yet move in that direction despite the reluctance of employers and unions to address the issue of trainee pay.

Even were such requirements inserted into Modern Apprenticeship, its task of increasing employer interest in delivering apprenticeship to consistently high standards of certified skill could be expected to prove a slow and arduous one. Without them, its prospects are at most mixed and the postwar divergence in apprenticeship in the UK and Germany will remain largely unaltered.

References

BMW (1993) *Apprentice Training for the 90s*, Bracknell: BMW (GB) Technicians' Institute.
Dolton, P J (1993) 'The economics of youth training in Britain', *Economic Journal*, **420** (September), 1261–78.

Drexel, I (1980) 'Die Krise der Anlernung im Arbeitsprozess', Soziale Welt, 31, 3, 368–95.
Drexel, I (1994) 'The relationship between education and employment as seen by German Industriesoziologie', paper presented to CNRS Colloquium on Education and Work, Paris, March.
Finegold, D (1993) 'Making Apprenticeships Work', RAND issue paper, Santa Monica: RAND Corporation.
GB DE (1994) Modern Apprenticeship, Sheffield: Department of Employment.
GB HMI (1991) (Her Majesty's Inspectorate), Aspects of Vocational Education and Training in the Federal Republic of Germany, London: HMSO.
Géhin J-P, and Méhaut, P (1993) Apprentissage ou formation continue? Stratégies éducatives des entreprises en Allemagne et en France, Paris: L'Hartmann.
Green, A, Mace, J and Steedman, H (1993) Training for Work Funding Pilots Study: Internation Comparisons, report to Employment Department, London: National Institute of Economic and Social Research.
Huber, B and Lang, K (1993) 'Tarifreform 2000: Forderungskonzepte und Verhandlungs-stande im Bereich der Metalindustrie', WSI Mitteilungen, 12, 789–97.
Jessup, G (1991) Outcomes, Lewes: Falmer.
Katz, E and Ziderman, A (1990) 'Investment in training: the role of information and labour mobility', Economic Journal, December, 100, 1147–58.
Mace, J (1979) 'Internal labour markets for engineers in British industry', British Journal of Industrial Relations, 17, 1, 50–63.
Marsden, D W (1982) 'Career structures and training in internal labour markets in Britain and West Germany', Manpower Studies, 4, Spring, 10–17.
Marsden, D W (1990) 'Institutions and labour mobility: occupational and internal labour markets in Britain, France, Italy and West Germany', in Brunetta, R and Dell'Arringa, C (eds) Labour Relations and Economic Performance, London: Macmillan, 414-38.
Marsden, D W (1994) 'Industrial change, "competencies", and labour markets'. Vocational Training (forthcoming).
Marsden, D W and Ryan, P (1990) 'Institutional aspects of youth employment and training policy in Britain', British Journal of Industrial Relations, 28, 3, 351–70.
Marsden, D W and Ryan, P (1991) 'Initial training, labour market structure and public policy: intermediate skills in British and German industry', in Ryan, pp 251–85.
Millward, N (1994) The New Industrial Relations? London: Policy Studies Institute.
Pickard, J (1994) 'The future of apprenticeships', Personnel Management Plus, February, 24–5.
Prais, S J, Jarvis, V and Wagner, K (1991) 'Productivity and vocational skills in services in Britain and Germany', in Ryan, pp 119-45.
Prais, S J, and Wagner, K (1983) 'Some practical aspects of human capital investment: training standards in five occupations in Britain and Germany', National Institute Economic Review, 105, August, 46–65.
Rainbird, H (1991) Training Matters, Oxford: Blackwell.
Ryan, P (1993) 'Pay structures, collective bargaining and apprenticeship training in postwar British and German metalworking industry', presented to CEPR workshop on human capital and postwar European economic growth, Dublin.
Ryan, P (1994a) 'Training quality and trainee exploitation', in Layard, R, Mayhew, K and Owen, G (eds) Britain's Training Deficit, Aldershot: Avebury.
Ryan, P (1944b) 'Adult learning and work: finance, incentives and certification', in Hirsch, D and Wagner, D (eds) What Makes Workers Learn? The Role of Incentives in Adult Education and Training, Cresskill, NJ: Hampton.
Steedman, H (1992) 'Mathematics in vocational youth training for the building trades in Britain, France and Germany', discussion paper 9, London: National Institute of Economic and Social Research.
Stevens, M (1994) 'An investment model for the supply of training by employers', Economic Journal, May, 104, 556–70.
Streeck, W, Hilber, J, van Kevalaer, K, Maier, F and Weber, H (1987) The Role of the Social Partners in Vocational Education and Training in the FRG, Berlin: CEDEFOP.
Walsh, J (1993) 'Internalisation v. decentralisation: an analysis of recent developments in pay bargaining', British Journal of Industrial Relations, 31, 3, 409–32.
Wolf, A (1993) Assessment Issues and Problems in a Criterion-Based System, London: Further Education Unit.

6. Gender and the school–work transition in Canada and the USA

Jane Gaskell

The transition from school to work has been conceived in the academic world as the moment when a young person leaves school and enters into another world, the world of paid work. This change in status is dramatic and critical for adult life. It represents the move from dependence to independence, from unpaid to paid, from youth to adulthood (Willis, 1977). But such a conception is based on the experience of dominant groups under industrial capitalism; it is far from universal. Many never achieve a position in the paid labour force, and the whole idea avoids the unemployed, as well as the domestic, subsistence and informal economies. Even within dominant Western modes, it fails to come to terms with the experience of women, who have always had a more fluid relation to learning and paid work, moving in and out of the labour market as their domestic responsibilities and financial needs shift, learning the tasks necessary for adulthood in formal and informal ways. This kind of experience has disadvantaged women, or perhaps been a sign of their disadvantaged status.

Recent research on the transition from school to work has pointed to the many ways in which this transition no longer applies for most young people. There is no single moment in time when young people leave school. Many workers attend educational programmes on the job, and many return to school after spending some time in the paid labour force. There is no single moment when they begin paid work. In many communities, working at fast-food outlets is a defining mark of adolescence, while unemployment as well as work outside the paid labour force are experienced by adults. The dichotomizing of life into school (early on) and paid work (as an adult), which has always misrepresented the experience of most women, now misrepresents the experience of most people. What can we learn from the analysis of gender difference that helps us understand new ways of conceiving the transition from school to work? What policy directions might equalize women's chances at school and at work?

This chapter concentrates on the analysis of gender as it affects the transition from school to work in North America. The study of how gendered processes are involved in the school to work transition has been

80

part of a feminist tradition of scholarship, calling attention to the ways in which academic and policy analysis, as well as education and work, have omitted and devalued the contributions of women. Developing a new analysis in which women are visible is part of the project of struggling towards and helping to create a more equitable set of arrangements.

As gender intersects with and is shaped by social class, race, ethnicity and so on, it has no single meaning across North American labour markets and cultures. When women as a group are compared with men as a group, the analysis risks forgetting differences among women and concealing particular pockets of disadvantage or advantage, while claiming to represent the experience of all women. Feminist gender analysis has been criticized for advocating programmes like pay equity or affirmative action which have worked mainly to the advantage of professional, white women, while claiming to help all women (Cohen, 1991). It is clear that analysis of 'women's' or 'men's' experience at work is best carried out in relation to specific groups, in specific job categories, and that it is particularly important to look at the experience of the large majority of those who do not hold professional jobs. However, gender differences are pronounced at work and at school and gender categories continue to matter in personal and professional lives. Developing analyses that take them into account can be a first step in a much more differentiated look at programmes and practices at school and work.

The analysis in this chapter looks at two processes that account for differences in how men and women have experienced the transition from school to work. First, the segmentation of labour markets and educational systems is central to the analysis of gender processes. Women and men work in different jobs, and women's jobs bring fewer economic rewards. Schools and vocational programmes stream students into different programmes and document different levels of achievement in order better to feed them into the labour market. The fact that men and women tend to be located in different jobs, and to follow different courses through the educational system, means there are important gender differences in 'the transition'. Equalizing opportunities for women includes attempts to decrease the amount of gender segmentation at school and work, and to move women into higher paying areas.

Second, the study of gender has called attention to the organization and the content of vocational programmes in occupations filled primarily by men and in those filled primarily by women. The forms of training and credentialling required for women's jobs are organized differently from those required for the jobs in which men have tended to work. Women's jobs on average require more general pre-entry education, but provide less on-the-job training. The more social and interactive processes associated with much of women's work are less likely to be taught and credentialled than the more technical skills associated with much of men's work. Rethinking the skills and training associated with work involves a fundamental reassessment of the assumptions about value and skill in which inequalities in the workplace are based.

Segmentation: gender issues in the distribution of work and learning

The segregation of women's work and men's work is pronounced and is fundamental to gender inequality. Men earn more and are more likely to work in high paying jobs. Women earn less, and are more likely to be in low paying jobs. Women comprise 80 per cent of clerical workers, but only 2 per cent of construction workers; most of the nurses, but few of the lawyers. The fact that men and women so often work in different kinds of jobs explains a good deal of their differential experience at work. The attempt to get more women into traditionally male jobs and therefore into traditionally male job training programmes has been a large part of the feminist agenda in relation to education and work in North America.

The differences in men's and women's jobs and wages have been attributed to differences in both the level and the kind of education and training that men and women have. Human capital theory suggests that wages are related to the marginal productivity of workers, and that marginal productivity is related to education. More education should lead to higher wages.

However, since the turn of the century in North America, women have been more likely than men to graduate from elementary school and from high school. In the early twentieth century, most young men left school early to work on the farm or to learn their jobs through various forms of apprenticeship and on-the-job experience. As paid employment was considered inappropriate for many middle-class women, they stayed in school until marriage (Clifford, 1982), picking up vocationally relevant knowledge and skills along the way. At the turn of the century, educators were worrying about the 'feminization' of the school and trying desperately to think of ways to make schooling relevant for boys (Rosenberg, 1982). Young women stayed in the more protective environment of the school, where they got the education necessary to qualify for properly female, middle-class jobs in teaching, or clerical work, where pre-entry training was required, and little education was offered on the job.

Women in North America are still somewhat more likely to have completed secondary school than men, although men are somewhat more likely to have completed post-secondary schooling. As a small percentage of the population has gone on to post-secondary education until recently (just under 20 per cent of the adult population has completed a college degree), women's years of educational attainment have been virtually the same as men's. Both men and women with more education are more likely to participate in the labour force, but women's participation increases with education more than men's. The result is that the educational attainment of women in the labour force is higher than the educational attainment of men in the labour force.

Current enrolment data provide a picture of what is happening today, and what will happen to the labour force in the future. More young women than young men are presently enrolled in and are graduating from universities and colleges. It is projected that by 2001, 42 per cent of men and 40 per cent of women in Canada will have post-secondary education, and by 2021, slightly more women than men will have university degrees (Economic Council of Canada, 1990). Women still earn fewer graduate degrees than men, but the numbers are small in relation to the population at large and here again the difference is decreasing.

On average, then, women's educational attainment is not less than men's. In the few high status areas – graduate and professional programmes, BAs and BScs – where women have in the past attained less, the difference is gone or rapidly decreasing. And if men and women in the labour force are compared, women have more years of education than men. So women's lack of schooling cannot explain their lower wages. Women with the same education as men are paid about two-thirds of what men are paid for full-time work (Harlan and Steinberg, 1989, p 28). If one simply enters education into an equation in an attempt to explain the differential between women's wages and men's wages, the differential becomes more inexplicable, not less (England, 1982).

This suggests it is the kind of education, not the quantity of education that matters for women in the labour force. There is a great deal of difference in what men and women study, and where they study it. Young women spend as many years in school as young men, but they spend them studying in different programmes, with different economic and personal consequences. There is some evidence that segregation is beginning to decrease in the school and in vocational education, as it is in the labour market, but the problem remains a substantial one. In universities, the progress towards equality has been much faster than in secondary schools, community colleges and vocational training programmes.

Despite coeducational elementary schools, by the time students get to secondary schools, male and female students migrate to different elective courses which set them on different trajectories into the labour market. More young women 'choose' business education, home economics and languages. More young men 'choose' industrial education, the physical sciences and mathematics.

Enrolment of females in mathematics and physical science courses has been a particular concern (Science Council of Canada, 1982). There are relatively fewer female enrolments in physics, advanced mathematics and computer science. There are higher enrolments of females in business education and home economics, courses clearly related to women's traditional work. Business courses in the secondary schools have emphasized clerical and secretarial training, and been populated with young women going directly into these jobs (Gaskell, 1992).

At the level of the community college and the university, differences are again closely linked to vocational trajectories into segregated labour markets. At the colleges, more women take business programmes, and programmes in health, education and community service areas. Men are more likely to be enrolled in the trades, sciences and technologies.

At the university, women have made major strides in previously male dominated professional faculties like commerce, medicine and law. They have also increased their enrolment in the traditionally female areas of education, arts and social work. Men continue to dominate in the science faculty, in engineering and dentistry. Within the arts and science faculties, differences by department are often substantial. There are more women in English than economics, in zoology than in physics.

In trades' training, vocational programmes, government sponsored courses and on-the-job training, clear sex differences in enrolments persist. Women are less likely to be enrolled in courses where they must be sponsored by their employer. They are more likely to be in adult education courses that are not related to their work. Women are concentrated in clerical training. Few women are enrolled in apprenticeships as apprenticeships are mainly available in the unionized male trades. In the USA, the military is a significant source of vocational training, and about 10 per cent of the trainees are women. Women are also underrepresented in government sponsored skill upgrading programmes which require students to be already employed in areas of critical skill shortages. In some language training programmes, regulations require participation in the labour market, and exclude women who immigrate to Canada or the USA as dependents.

There has been legislation requiring more gender equity in job training, and particular programmes have been developed specifically to help women in need and to break down barriers to job entry in non-traditional areas. The Job Training Partnership programme in the USA targeted women receiving aid for dependent children, and in Canada, the Job Entry Programme targeted women returning to work, and encouraged the enrolment of women on welfare, native women and visible minority women in all programmes. However, progress is slow, as occupational and educational differences are embedded in the gendered lives of men and women today.

Women face many barriers in entering training programmes as adults, but the greatest are money and childcare. Women lack the resources to give up their jobs to enter full time training programmes. Employers are less likely to sponsor women than they are to sponsor men in training courses (Devereaux, 1984). The lack of affordable childcare is a major barrier to retraining for many women. About 90 per cent of all single-parent families are headed by women, and half of them live below the poverty line. The poverty of female single-parent households is both a cause of low participation in training, and an outcome, at least partially, of this lack of training.

Why do enrolment differences persist? The answer lies in the interaction between the socialization and aspirations of young women and young men and the organization of schooling, work and credentialling. Although young women are aspiring to more participation in the labour force, and in more diverse areas, there are still large differences between the aspirations of young women and young men (Labour Canada, 1986; Canadian Advisory Committee on the Status of Women, 1985; Gilligan et al, 1990). Young women are more likely to want and expect jobs in the traditionally female labour market, as nurses, teachers, service and clerical workers. Young women are more concerned about family and relationships, and their domestic and personal aspirations shape and constrain their aspirations for paid work. A recent study by the Canadian Teachers'

Federation concluded that the young women they talked to 'reflected deep resentment towards their male peers, their apparently carefree lives and their violence' (CTF, 1990, p 21). Young women choose remarkably few occupations when they are asked about their occupational aspirations. The crowding of women into a few, usually low paid, fields, prevents them from expressing the diversity of their interests, aptitudes and enthusiasms, and keeps wages low.

All of these factors are related to the way women enrol in programmes of study (Gaskell, 1992). They avoid courses that are overwhelmingly male because of the sexual harassment that can be involved, and the awkwardness that can be entailed. They take courses which they think will prepare them for the traditionally female labour market, where they think they can find jobs, will not be discriminated against and will feel comfortable. While they believe in equal opportunity, they try to be realistic about what the world offers, and this leads them to a fairly conservative assessment of their chances, especially if they are not academic high flyers or from privileged families. Gilligan *et al* (1990) conclude that adolescent girls need to be encouraged to take risks, to speak out, to have the confidence to assert themselves.

The aspirations and beliefs of young women arise in the context of families, schools and social services. Families support and constrain their daughters, reflecting culture, social class and individual experiences. Schools and social service agencies reinforce tradition or help young women to try out new options and to realize more equality. New career educational programmes, job-shadowing programmes and vocational alternatives in schools sometimes reproduce existing patterns of job segregation and sometimes introduce young women to options they may not have considered.

Some programmes are designed to break down gender segregation in education and training. After-school classes to encourage girls in non-traditional areas, non-sexist career education, career conferences focused on breaking down stereotypes, visiting women scientists, maths anxiety clinics, and in-service programmes for teachers focused on gender equity have been tried successfully by some school districts (Becker, 1987). The adoption of equal opportunities policies which encourage discussion of gender issues also makes a difference (Burton, 1986).

The structure of vocational programmes and their admission require-ments have an important impact on how young women's preferences are translated into course enrolments. To take a simple example, if a programme requires senior mathematics for entrance, the fact that girls are more likely to drop maths will reduce female enrolment. If the requirement is dropped, more girls are eligible. There are many other examples. Medical schools have changed their admissions requirements to admit arts as well as science graduates, making many more young women eligible to apply. Redesigning programmes so that sex-segregated options are not available and/or not vocationally necessary reduces sexual segregation in schooling and opens up the job market. The question becomes what skills and knowledge are really necessary, as jobs change, and which ones have merely been traditional.

Attracting women into traditionally male areas has meant attempts to rethink the curriculum in male dominated areas, and to revalue those areas of knowledge and practice where women have predominated. Concern for ending segmentation leads to concern for redesigning work and school, rethinking skill and knowledge. It also leads to concern about getting women into men's areas of work, as well as revaluing women's traditional areas of work. If women successfully compete for the higher status programmes and the higher paying jobs, who will remain in the fields of teaching and nursing and clerical work and childcare? As options for women open, rethinking and reevaluating their traditional areas of study and work is part of the economic and educational readjustment that is involved in rethinking gender relations.

Rethinking skill: gender issues in the structure and content of vocational programmes

Women and men have tended to do different kinds of tasks, in the labour force, in the home, and in informal settings. The previous section examined the differences this has entailed in vocational preparation. But the attempt to integrate men and women in the same programmes opens the question of how preparation for male and female jobs has been different, and what equality in this sphere would look like.

The economic roles women perform are varied, changing and often not well understood. We do not adequately measure the unpaid economic contribution women make to society. Common measures of a country's productivity and of the extent of economic participation, like the GNP and the 'labour force', ignore women's domestic labour. Important notions like skill and human capital have been defined in ways that eclipse the strengths women bring to their work. The wages women earn for their economic contribution also underestimate in many ways the value of this contribution, for it has historically been possible for employers to pay women less than men for work of equal value. Feminist analysis has been an attempt to rethink the contributions women have made, as well as pointing to the ways women have been marginalized and kept from positions of power.

For women's work is fundamental to how things get done. Somehow people must learn to do it, and there must be enough rewards attached to it that people want to perform it. As North American women argue for their right to move into male spheres of work, they resist performing their traditional work roles for free or for pocket money. Moreover, in a changing society, they often fail to learn informally from their mothers and friends. This poses a new challenge for education and for the economy.

The concept of skill is central to our understanding of how education and work are related. Education and vocational training teach the skills that are necessary on the job. But how do we decide what those skills are and how they will be learned? Although, as Ronnie Steinberg (1990) points out, 'sociologists and political economists have tended to agree more than they disagree about what constitutes skilled work,' notions of skill are constructed through social conventions and ideologies and the discourse of skill is a discourse of power. The specification of skills is always and everywhere a judgemental process that involves reducing a varied set of activities to a few definable and rankable capacities. 'Classifications of workers are neither "natural" nor self evident, nor is the degree of skill a self evident quality which can simply be read from the labels given to various classifications' (Braverman, 1974, p 428). As Phillips and Taylor, (1980, p 79) put it: 'far from being an objective economic fact, skill is often an ideological category imposed on certain types of work by virtue of the sex and power of the workers who perform it.'

Any version of skill requirements is partial and interested. Some workers have had more power to insist on the skilled nature of their jobs than other workers. Skill designations are used to give status and importance to some kinds of work, and to take it away from others. They are also used to justify and specify the length and type of educational requirements. As this is recognized, they have been challenged by pay equity legislation, and become the arena for political negotiation over gender equity.

Constructing work as 'unskilled' keeps the price down. Women's work has tended to be paid poorly and to require little on-the-job training. Employers were unwilling to invest in on-the-job training of women, as women were never considered long-term employees. Women themselves did not have the economic power to insist that employers provide on-the-job training. However, this does not mean women's work is unskilled. Training has been done in public educational institutions where women as we have seen get as much education as men, and it has been done informally, at home and at work. An analysis of clerical and secretarial tasks, quintessentially women's work, provides an example of how varied are the intellectual and social competences they require and how long it takes to learn them well.

Clerical and secretarial work involves a wide variety of types of jobs and activities. There is a huge range of kinds of work labelled generally 'clerical' or 'secretarial'. Typing, bookkeeping, formatting documents, filing and spelling are commonly part of what the work involves. But many analyses of secretaries and clerical workers emphasize their role as office 'wives', as helpmates in whatever task needs to be done, as the smiling, cooperative and decorative women, answering the phone, receiving the public, making the coffee, anticipating the needs of the boss, calming furious customers, pleasing everyone in the office, remembering birthdays and listening to personal stories. Standard job descriptions, when they are available, underrepresent the variety and the social nature of many of the tasks that are done (Benet, 1972). The specific technical skills required are inextricably entwined with interpersonal competences.

While these interpersonal demands are particularly obvious in the work and the image of the secretary, they are present in many of the jobs women do: teacher, waitress, librarian, salesperson, nurse, domestic worker. The jobs filled predominantly by women involve more social and verbal tasks than jobs filled predominantly by men (England et al, 1988). The sex segregation of jobs reinforces 'the association of masculinity with mechanical and technical skills and the association of femininity with patience and selfless dedication to repetitive tasks' (Acker, 1988, p 482). 'Caretaking' is often a part of the work women do and it is rarely given the respect and rewards it deserves.

The interpersonal work women do is rarely recognized as skill or rewarded in salaries or status. It is treated as an aspect of femininity or perhaps a personality attribute of the woman doing it. To judge the skills involved in work is to engage in evaluations and political judgements that have never counted what women do seriously. Our commonsense notions of skill arise in the context of male crafts, for these were the workers that had the power to regulate and define their work. Women were excluded from the skilled trades, at least by the late nineteenth century in Europe and North America. Women worked in their own trades as well as in the home. They were less often organized, less often explicitly trained for their work, and their skills, instead of being mysterious and esoteric, became the skills of 'everywoman.' Skilled workers were craft workers who had gone through an apprenticeship. The census defined skilled workers as those who learned to work with machinery (Braverman, 1974).

Vocational curriculum buys into this technical and industrial discourse, emphasizing technical skills, downplaying the social. Vocational education became part of the school curriculum in North America in the context of technological change and industrialization in the early twentieth century. Its justification drew on the technical and industrial skills that workers needed to cope with these changes (Jackson and Gaskell, 1987). Today, the rhetoric of vocational education is still about the specification of skills of a technical nature, skills that can be defined clearly, graded 'objectively' and traded profitably in the labour market. The education of clerical workers is forced into this mould.

The interpersonal dimensions of women's work are central to the Western stereotype of the feminine. It is not surprising that women have an ambivalent relation to this interpersonal work, sometimes seeing it as an aspect of femininity which must be left behind in order to attain equality with men, and sometimes taking pride and pleasure in its accomplishment. Many important strands of feminist theory have tried to reclaim the interpersonal, the reproductive, the nurturant, the caring, not just for the sake of increasing the recognition due to women, but also because of its importance for all of us (Martin, 1985). The public world depends on the domestic, as Jane Roland Martin points out. Men have only been able to marginalize the domestic and the reproductive because they can take for granted that women will do it. But it is not just the domestic world that depends on women's interpersonal work. The workplace has been run on the backs of women who get the coffee, look after the emotional needs of clients and workers, share personal stories, create a sense of community, smile and handle complaints. Not all women do it, or do it well, but it is a critical part of getting work done. It is not something women do 'naturally'. It is learned, stressful, difficult.

There are strands of feminist scholarship which are uneasy with the link between women and nurturing and caring, pointing to the culturally limited basis of these images as well as to the way they are used to limit, control and exploit women's labour. Not all women are or want to be nurturing and warm. The association of women with interpersonal, relational work has always been used to limit their access to positions of power, and to reinforce their association with the domestic realm. It can be argued that it is Western, white, middle-class images of the mother that underlie a feminism dedicated to reclaiming caring in the name of the women's movement (Hooks, 1984). In the workplace, these representations have been used to identify particular tasks – secretary, nurse, primary school teacher – with women, and to trivialize them. It is not surprising that women want a break from the relational and the interpersonal work they have been held responsible for, and that unions of clerical workers have fought for clear technical job descriptions and hiring policies that make 'personality' and 'attitude' illegitimate bases to judge the work or the worker. It is an attempt to combat the devaluation of the work that is a consequence of its association with women.

Understandable, but ultimately self defeating. This kind of work has got to be done in universities, offices and factories as well as at home. No one functions outside a human community that must be sustained by lots of interpersonal work. Clearly men as well as women should do it, but the low status of the work is self perpetuating. Recognizing and valuing it is necessary to produce equality for women, to get men to share in it, and to increase the wellbeing of everyone in the domestic sphere as well as in the workplace.

Pay equity schemes have been one mechanism for putting the discussion of skill back on the table, and trying to revalue the things women do (Gaskell, 1992). There is an increasing amount of work on the invisible skills of women at work, which emphasizes the social (MacKeracher, 1990). But vocational educators, themselves low in status in the school hierarchy, have been reluctant to take on board the interpersonal, the female, the low status. Reforms to vocational education have been aimed at bolstering its status by attaching it to high status images and attracting material and symbolic resources (Goodson and Dowbiggan, 1991). Taking on the social realm seems to promise neither. Vocational education has been valued for its technical tasks, its machines, its scarce skills, and criticized for its lack of 'serious' content, its emphasis on the 'hidden' curriculum, ie, social expectations. Increasing the number of specific technical skills required has been a way of demonstrating the status and importance of the work and of the instruction.

But, recognizing all this, vocational education has much to gain by expanding its understanding of what is necessary for work, what can be taught and how. Social skills can be reclaimed as 'real' skills, ones that involve moral judgement and sophisticated emotional and intellectual work. They can be taught and learned, recognized and evaluated.

Conclusions

In this chapter I have set out two arguments about how training programmes for women's work fail to produce equality. First, vocational education has tended to reproduce the segmentation of the labour market, and channel women into lower paying and traditionally female jobs. Second, the organization of vocational training has tended to reproduce our notions of skilled and unskilled work. Increasingly all jobs require interpersonal sensitivity and understanding of social relations, neither of which are recognized in existing training programmes.

Gender is implicated not just in the overt messages young women receive about how to be feminine and dress appropriately, but in the ways they come to conceive of what is involved in 'women's work'. For the problem women have had in the workplace is not that they do not have skills and knowledge, but that their skills have not been counted when they move from school to work. This is at the centre of gender inequality and must always be interrogated as we study how the transitions take place.

References

Acker, J (1988) 'Class, gender and the relations of distribution', *Signs*, **13**, 3, 473–97.

Becker, J R (1987) 'Sex equity programs which work', *School Science and Mathematics*, **87**, 3, 223–32.

Benet, M K (1972) *Secretarial Ghetto*, New York: McGraw Hill.

Braverman, H (1974) *Labour and Monopoly Capitalism*, New York: Monthly Review Press.

Burton, L (ed) (1986) *Girls into Maths Can Go*, London: Holt, Rinehart & Winston.

Canadian Advisory Committee on the Status of Women (1985) *What Will Tomorrow Bring? A Study of the Aspirations of Adolescent Women*, Ottawa: Government Printer.

Canadian Teachers' Federation (CTF) (1990) *A Capella: A Report of the Realities, Concerns, Expectations and Barriers Experienced by Adolescent Women in Canada*, Ottawa: Canadian Teachers' Federation.

Clifford, G (1982) 'Marry, stitch, die, or do worse: educating women for work', in Kantor, H and Tyack, D (eds) *Work, Youth and Schooling: Historical Perspectives on Vocationalism in American Education*, Stanford: Stanford University Press.

Cohen, M (1991) 'Restructuring of women's employment opportunities: policy implications for feminist organizing', occasional paper, Toronto: OISE.

Devereaux, M S (1984) *One in Every Five: A Survey of Adult Education in Canada*, Ottawa: Supply and Services Canada.

Dewey, J (1916) *Democracy and Education*, New York: Free Press.

Economic Council of Canada (1990) *Good Jobs, Bad Jobs*, Ottawa: Economic Council.

England, P (1982) 'The failure of human capital theory to explain occupational sex segregation', *Journal of Human Resources*, **17**, 4, 358–70.

England, P G, Farkas, B, Kilbourne, B, and Dau, T (1988) 'Explaining sex segregation and wages: findings from a model with fixed effects', *American Sociological Review*, **53**, 4, 544–58.

Gaskell, J (1992) *Gender Matters from School to Work*, Milton Keynes: Open University Press.

Gilligan, C, Lyons, N, and Hanmer, T (1990) *Making Connections: The Relational Worlds of Adolescent Girls at Emma Willard School*, Cambridge, MA: Harvard University Press.

Goodson, I and Dowbiggan, I (1991) 'Subject status and curriculum change: commercial education in London, Ontario 1920–1940', *Paedagogia Historia*, **29**, 2.

Harlan, S and Steinberg, R (1989) *Job Training for Women: The Promise and Limits of Public Policies*, Philadelphia: Temple University Press.

Hooks, B (1984) *Feminist Theory: From Margin to Center*, Boston: South End Press.

Jackson, N and Gaskell, J (1987) 'White collar vocationalism: the rise of commercial education in Ontario and BC', *Curriculum Inquiry*, **17**, 2, 77–201.

Labour Canada (1986) *When I grow up ... Career Expectations and Aspirations of Canadian School Children*, Ottawa: Labour Canada.

MacKeracher, D (1990) *Women's On the Job Procedural Knowing*, Victoria: Proceedings of the Canadian Association for the Study of Adult Education.

Martin, J R (1985) *Reclaiming a Conversation*, New Haven: Yale University Press.

Phillips, A and Taylor, B (1980) 'Sex and skill: notes toward a feminist economics', *Feminist Review*, **79**, 79–88.

Rosenberg, R (1982) *Beyond Separate Spheres: Intellectual Roots of Modern Feminism*, New Haven: Yale University Press.

Science Council of Canada (1982) *Who turns the wheel?* Ottawa: proceedings of a workshop on the science education of women in Canada.

Steinberg, R (1990) 'Social construction of skill: gender power and comparable worth', in *Work and Occupations*, Beverley Hills: Sage.

Willis, P (1977) *Learning to Labour*, Farnborough: Saxon House.

7. The role of the state and the social partners in VET Systems

Andy Green

The historic demise of the centralized, command economies of the communist world has prompted ideologists in the West to proclaim the 'end of history' and the secular evolutionary ascendancy of the liberal, market system as a means of organizing societies and economies (Fukuyama, 1992). However, closer examination of the different trajectories of the Western capitalist states suggests more discriminating judgements, for while the recent Anglo-American experiments in free-market economics have proved unsustainable, and have merely consolidated the relative decline of Britain and the USA as world powers, the neo-corporatist, social-market policies of the continental European Union (EU) states have, in many cases, proved to be comparatively successful, providing the basis for continued economic innovation and growth through a combination of market dynamism and state regulation. Moreover, whereas advocates of the free market have often explicitly abandoned equity and fair distribution as political goals and have been prepared to see the decline of public services as a necessary cost of rejuvenating private enterprise, elsewhere social justice has at least remained on the political agenda and the effective provision of public services has been seen as a precondition of economic prosperity. The fundamental political debate in industrialized countries appears now to revolve around the relative merits of free-market economies versus socialized mixed economies and, while this is by no means yet resolved, the case for variations on the 'third way' remains powerful.

Education and training policy, in all advanced economies, occupies a central position in this debate. Not only does it bear critically on questions of both social justice and economic efficiency but it is also subject to very contrary 'solutions' which well illustrate the still marked ideological cleavages within Western politics. Whilst all governments appear to recognize the importance of a wide distribution of education and training throughout their populations, especially in the current context of rapid technological advance and intensified global economic competition, the policies they have adopted to achieve this have varied widely.

Typically, the UK and the USA, and some other English-speaking countries like New Zealand, have attempted to raise participation and achievement in education and training systems through institutional reforms that attempt to install market mechanisms, fostering greater competition and efficiency. In Britain this has been accompanied by measures that greatly increase central state control in education as regards curricula and qualifications, whilst reducing the powers of local education authorities and minimizing the decision-making roles of educationalists and trade unions.

In continental EU states the trends have been somewhat different. Centralized control has generally been reduced by attempts to devolve decision-making to the lowest effective level (the subsidiarity principle). This has generally meant giving more powers to the regions and encouraging the social partners to play increasingly prominent roles at national, regional, local and enterprise levels. The Social Chapter of the Maastricht Treaty, endorsed by all member states except the UK, makes social partnership and subsidiarity the cornerstones of its vocational training policy (CEDEFOP, 1992). However, this devolution, which diffuses control in both vertical and horizontal directions, occurs within the overall context of regulation by the central state, which determines both the roles and responsibilities of the different actors. Neo-liberal policies, involving unfettered control by the markets, have found little favour in systems where the principle remains that public authorities bear ultimate responsibility for collective services.

The different roles played by the state and other social partners in the determination and implementation of policies constitutes one of the most significant variables between different national systems of education and training. This chapter focuses on one particular area of the policy debate – vocational education and training (VET). Its main objective is to offer a preliminary analysis of the roles played by the state and other social partners in different areas of VET within a number of different national systems and to point to some of the effects of such differences. Reference will be made mainly to the systems of VET in England and western Germany.

Vocational education and training in England and Wales

VET in England is frequently seen as one of the weakest areas of the education system, traditionally suffering from a lack of prestige and coherent planning and organization (Ball, 1991; Green, 1991; Royal Society, 1991; Sanderson, 1994). Currently, despite widespread recent reforms, rates of participation in post-compulsory education and training are still much lower in Britain than most other EU countries and levels of qualification, particularly in vocational areas, likewise (Green and Steedman, 1993). The reasons for this are various and complex but much of the explanation arguably hinges on historical traditions of *laissez-faire*.

The liberal legacy

The UK was one of the last major European countries in the nineteenth century to create a national education system and, contrary to the pattern in continental Europe, the state was particularly slow to intervene in promoting technical education. This was partly due to a general complacency about the importance of technical education that was one of the legacies of an early, successful industrial revolution that appeared to owe little to formal education. It was also partly due to the fact that manufacturers were reluctant to lose child labour to the education system, particularly if they had to pay for it through their taxes, and particularly if it involved training in trade schools that might endanger their trade secrets. Most importantly, however, it was the inevitable consequence of a dominant liberal, *laissez-faire* philosophy that discouraged state intervention in anything unless it was absolutely unavoidable (Green, 1990).

The result of this voluntarist policy was that, with the exception of the evening classes provided by the mechanics institutes and the Department of Science and Art, there was no technical education to speak of before 1880 except that provided on the job. France by the mid-century had a wide range of vocational schools at different levels. These included over 85 elementary trade and agricultural schools; various intermediate vocational schools like the *écoles des arts et métiers* and the École Centrale; and a number of higher vocational school and *grandes écoles* like the celebrated École Polytechnique. England had few comparable full-time vocational schools which could impart both the theory and practice of different vocations. Nor, until the higher grade schools were developed, did it have much to compare with the vocationally oriented post-elementary schools on the Continent like the German *Realschulen* and the French *écoles primaires supérieurs* which numbered 700 by 1887 (Grew and Harrigan, 1991; Day, 1987; Weiss, 1982).

In the absence of these institutions, England relied largely on the apprenticeship. This was stoutly defended as the most effective way of imparting practical skills but few apprentices received the grounding in scientific principles or indeed basic education which was necessary for the skilled worker promoted to higher supervisory levels at the time when new technology and more complex processes began to make more demands on the scientific and technical knowledge of engineers and managers. Sylvanus Thompson, a contemporary critic of the apprentice system and a supporter of the French trade schools, referred to the apprentice as a 'common drudge, set to execute all kinds of miscellaneous jobs', of whom six years of apprenticeship failed to make anything except a 'bad, unintelligent, unskilful machine' (Thompson, 1879).

During the last two decades of the nineteenth century the situation did begin to change as the political climate became more conducive to state intervention and as the threat of foreign competition pressed home the importance of improving education and training. However, despite the achievements of the technical education movement in promoting the development of technical colleges and the civic universities, English technical education and training by the end of the century were still significantly underdeveloped by comparison with what had been achieved in many continental states (Barnett, 1986). It was still not widespread and what there was of it was generally still anti-theoretical, low in status and marginalized from mainstream education.

Throughout the first half of the twentieth century, vocational education and training continued to lag behind and, until the late 1950s, remained largely on a voluntary footing. Part-time enrolments at technical colleges grew steadily, if unspectacularly, but post-compulsory technical schooling remained a minority experience. Though twice enacted, in 1918 and 1944, compulsory continuation schooling was never implemented and most young people left school without receiving any further education or training. Sporadic attempts were made to develop technical secondary schooling with the pre-World War Two junior technical schools and the post-1944 secondary technical schools, but neither initiative gained much momentum or broke the status monopoly of academic secondary schooling, as recent studies by Gary McCulloch (1989) and Michael Sanderson (1994) have shown. By 1937 only around 30,000 pupils attended junior technical schools and attendance at secondary technical schools never grew beyond 4 per cent of the age cohort (Bailey, 1990).

The apprenticeship remained the main vehicle of vocational training throughout the period and was usually completed without any parallel off-the-job general or technical education. For all its strengths as a means for imparting job-specific vocational skills the apprenticeship system was never an adequate vehicle for meeting the skills needs of the economy. The craft unions tended to see the apprentice system as a means by which they could protect their skill status and differentials through restricting entry into tightly demarcated trades, whilst employers often valued the system as a way of gaining cheap labour without statutory obligations to provide expensive investment in training to given standards (Rainbird, 1990). Both sides of industry agreed on limiting the numbers of apprentices so that there were repeated skills shortage crises not only before and during the world wars but also increasingly during the expansionary post-1945 period. Not only did the apprentice system provide an inadequate supply of skilled workers but it was deficient in many other ways as the 1958 Carr Report made plain (Perry, 1976). It involved unduly lengthy periods of time-serving, failed to train to any specified standards, and was over-narrow in the skills it imparted and impoverished in terms of general education and theory; most damagingly, it ignored the training needs of semi-skilled workers and severely limited access to many groups, most notably women (Sheldrake and Vickerstaff, 1987).

Numerous reports (including the government's own 1956 White Paper on Technical Instruction) pointed to the relative deficiencies of UK training and the 1945 Ince Report called for the creation of a national training scheme (see Ainley and Corney, 1990). However, no government action was forthcoming. In 1952 the Ministry of Labour and National Service was still upholding the traditional government line that 'employers bear the major responsibility for the training of their own employees' (quoted in Sheldrake and Vickerstaff, 1987, p 27). The laissez-faire era in UK training policy thus continued until the beginning of the 1960s when renewed skills shortages, the challenge of Soviet technology, and the bulging youth cohort finally convinced government that policies on vocational training had to change.

Since 1964 and the Industrial Training Act, which marked the first major departure from the traditional *laissez-faire* approach, government policy on training has undergone repeated shifts but only to arrive in the 1990s very much where it started. The period can be divided into three main parts characterized by different forms of state control and social partnership.

The 1964–73 period, defined by the terms of the Industrial Training Act, saw training organized through a devolved form of social partnership between employers and industry with relatively light central state intervention. The period from 1974 to 1979 was the era of the Manpower Services Commission (MSC) under a Labour government, characterized by a more centralized form of social partnership through a highly interventionist government agency. The period from 1979 to 1988 was a transitional period during which central government intervened ever more directly through the MSC to shape training policy whilst simultaneously dismantling the apparatuses of social partnership in both education and training fields. Since 1988 there has been a return to the voluntarist model and this time with one of the social partners, the trade unions, largely removed from influence and control. Although numerous initiatives have been tried and despite the fact that vocational education and training has been higher on the political agenda than ever before, the policies of these periods have had limited success in reversing the historic backwardness of UK vocational education and training. It is important to see why.

The era of the Industrial Training Boards, 1964–73

The 1964 Act inaugurated the tripartite Industrial Training Boards (ITBs) to promote and coordinate training in the different sectors and empowered them to redistribute the costs of training among employers by means of the levy-grant system. Being organized by industrial sectors but without achieving full coverage, this was never quite a national apprenticeship system, still less a national training system for all grades of employees. However, it was as near as the country had come to such a thing in its history. During the ten years whilst the system was in operation the volume of training did marginally increase (up by 15 per cent in those areas of manufacturing covered by the ITBs between 1964 and 1969) and notable advances were made in improving the quality of training (Sheldrake and Vickerstaff, 1987). Day-release became common in many apprentice schemes; group training schemes proliferated, helping smaller firms to participate in formal training programmes; and the engineering ITB's modular training systems paved the way for greater flexibility and breadth in apprentice training (Perry, 1976). However, the system was far from achieving its objectives.

The quantitative gains in training provision were limited to skilled areas and were, in any case, soon wiped out by the secular decline in apprentice places which followed the onset of the recession in 1973. The ITBs failed to open up access to apprenticeships for previously excluded groups and did little to change the old practices of time-serving and age entry restrictions. Most seriously, little headway was made in the setting and monitoring of standards in training.

These shortcomings were not attributable to the principle of social partnership in training and nor do they undermine the argument for government intervention. What they did show was that a national training system could not be created on the basis of devolved sectoral organization and that the social partners in the different sectors could not be induced to act in a coordinated way to create a national system of training to standards without a strong central body to coordinate them. Unlike in Germany, the UK's national federations and 'peak bodies' for employers and unions (including the Confederation of British Industry and the Trades Union Congress) lacked binding powers over their members and the local chambers of commerce never attained great influence. The Central Training Council, as the TUC frequently complained, never had adequate powers to compensate for this and to ensure that the system fulfilled its objectives in meeting those long-term skills needs of the national economy which individual employers were always prone to ignore (Perry, 1976; Ainley and Corney, 1990).

The era of MSC tripartism, 1973–79

The next phase of training policy was inaugurated by the 1973 Employment and Training Act, which created the Manpower Services Commission, and can be said to have lasted until the Conservative government was elected in 1979 with a new economic agenda. The tripartite composition of the MSC suggested that the principle of social partnership was still to govern training but this time it was to be coordinated through a much more powerful central government agency with considerable public funds at its disposal. The TUC had, it appeared, finally got the Swedish-style central labour planning body which it had long sought and in its early years the MSC indeed seemed determined to provide the strategic labour planning and to facilitate the comprehensive national training system which had so long been lacking. In some areas it was remarkably successful. The Training Opportunities Programmes provided a new and viable form of publicly funded accelerated skills training for adults on 6–12 month courses. Numerous other initiatives, although not markedly successful in themselves, did also raise the profile of vocational training to a level not seen before.

However, two factors decisively undermined the MSC's efforts to revolutionize the UK's VET. The first concerned the limited nature of the social partnership which it represented. The MSC, which never gave equal representation to educational interests, soon managed to antagonize the powers in the education sector who viewed it, not without reason as it turned out, as a body that would be used by governments hostile to the education system to force changes on that system from without. The MSC, in its relations with education, thus soon came to exacerbate that longstanding historical division between education and training which it was part of its proclaimed mission to eradicate. The split deepened and the possibility of creating an integrated system of post-compulsory education and training receded. The second factor, which lay outside the MSC's control, was the state of the economy. With the deep recession which followed the oil price rises, and the massive increases in youth and adult unemployment which resulted, government training priorities swiftly changed. The MSC was pressed into service to provide emergency unemployment schemes and soon lost sight of its original goal of creating comprehensive and high quality skills training for the long-term needs of the national economy. The MSC was in effect blown off course by economic events. As Ainley and Corney have argued, by 1976 it had all but abandoned its original mission of comprehensive labour planning and now played a kind of fire-fighting role, dealing with the social consequences of youth unemployment (Ainley and Corney, 1990).

Training in transition, 1979–87

The third phase in recent training policy covered the years of the first two Thatcher governments and represented something of a transitional phase. Despite early signs that the new government would wind up the Commission in line with its general policy of 'rolling back the frontiers of the state', the MSC remained and even expanded, partly no doubt because the new recession of 1980–1 caused rocketing unemployment and a summer of urban riots which made the MSC's fire-fighting role ever more important. However, the MSC was to become a different kind of body with a different mission; a shift that was decisively signalled by the government's decision to appoint David Young to replace the existing Director, Geoffrey Holland (Ainley and Vickerstaff, 1993). Government took increasingly direct control of the MSC, using it now in a more interventionist and authoritarian fashion to impose new forms of vocationalism on the education system and to transform the apprentice-ship system, ridding it of time-serving and restrictive trade union controls. The notion of partnership was quickly abandoned. The 1981 Employment Training Act abolished 17 out of the 24 ITBs and replaced them with non-statutory Industry Training Organizations. These rarely included union representatives and the unions were thus deprived of an important forum for representing their views on training. Educational bodies also saw their influence diminished as government initiatives in education increasingly bypassed the DES (as with TVEI, the technical and vocational education initiative) and the local authorities. Relations between the latter and the MSC reached an all-time low in 1985 when government announced its intention to hand over control of a large slice of LEA funding for non-advanced further education to the MSC.

Central government intervention in VET during this phase was probably more intensive than in any other period this century and yet at the end of it UK training seems to be lagging as far behind other countries as ever. What went wrong? The simple answer is that government directed its interventions to the wrong ends. The policies were misconceived. The Youth Training Scheme was set up in a blaze of publicity which proclaimed that this was the first ever comprehensive national training scheme aimed at high quality training for both the employed and the unemployed. In fact it was cobbled together at breakneck speed without many of the preconditions for high quality training. The schemes were designed in such a way that they inevitably involved much routine work experience but little supervised training or education. The pressure to provide places to meet government targets was such that schemes were accepted even where there was little likelihood that training would be of a high standard and this was rarely monitored with any rigour. The removal of statutory grant-levy system meant that employers were actually investing less in training than before. Between 1979 and 1987 apprenticeships in manufacture declined from 155,000 to 58,000 only to be replaced by often lower quality Youth Training Schemes paid for by the state (Vickerstaff, 1992). The qualification system was not reformed to provide suitable certification for trainees and consequently fewer than a third came out with any recognized qualification (Green and Steedman, 1993). Without the prospect of a useful qualification or any guaranteed employment afterwards trainees inevitably tended to have little motivation on the schemes. In short the Youth Training Scheme never managed to throw off the reputation for low quality training which had dogged all previous MSC training schemes (Ainley and Corney, 1990).

The return to voluntarism, 1987–

Since 1988 training policy has undergone another radical shift which has involved the final abandonment of social partnership and a return to the voluntarist principles of the pre-1964 period. A third election victory in 1987, followed by the short-lived 'Lawson' economic boom, encouraged the government to apply in the training field the market-led policies it had been pursuing so vigorously in education. The long dispute with the unions over the Employment Training Initiative proved the decisive catalyst for the decision to return to a demand-led, employer-controlled training system. The Youth Training Scheme was substantially deregulated and relaunched as Youth Training, the MSC was abolished and the control of training was handed over to the new, employer-dominated, local Training and Enterprise Councils (TECs). This, according to the Employment Department's 1988 White Paper, 'Employment for the 1990s', would 'give leadership of the training system to employers, where it belongs'. Since then further measures have been adopted to place increased responsibility for training on individuals and employers and to replace the corporatist control over training with a new training market.

TECs have been promoted by government as 'one of the most radical and important initiatives ever undertaken in this country' (Shephard, 1992). Originally modelled on the US Private Industry Councils (PICs), the

TECs were designed as an entrepreneurial and strategic local mechanism for reversing the UK's skills deficit. They would make training responsive to local economic needs, inject a bottom-line, businesslike approach to programme management and use their influence in commerce and industry to persuade employers to take the initiative in solving their own training problems. Unlike the PICs in the USA, they would be responsible not just for training programmes for the disadvantaged but for a range of measures to stimulate all kinds of training and to promote local economic development. Their ability to provide strategic local leadership was seen as a key catalyst for solving the UK's skills problems and for restoring economic competitiveness.

Since 1990 TECs have been formed in 82 areas in England and Wales and there are a further 22 Local Enterprise Companies in Scotland. Their boards, of whom two-thirds must be local business leaders, and the civil servants who service them, manage budgets which average around £18m each and which accounted for a total national budget of £2.3 billion in 1993/4. Originally responsible for training programmes for unemployed youth and adults (Youth Training Programme and Employment Training Programme) and for a range of schemes to help local business (Business Growth Training; Enterprise Allowance Scheme and Small Firms Service), their responsibilities have been systematically increased during the past four years. They now have a significant role in the finance and governance of further education colleges, play the major part in a range of Education–Business Partnerships and Compacts, and are increasingly involved in the running of local careers services (Bennett *et al*, 1994). As the role of the local education authorities has declined in relation to secondary schools, colleges and training, so the TECs' importance has increased. They are now *de facto* amongst the most important agencies of planning in local education and training.

TECs are also centrally involved in several further initiatives designed to shift responsibility for training to employers and individuals. First, employers have been exhorted to take more responsibility for training through the promotion of targets for National Vocational Qualifications in firms and through the award of 'Investors in People' kitemarks to companies with demonstrated standards of human resource development. Second, individuals have been encouraged to take more responsibility through schemes like 'Gateway to Learning' and 'Skills Choice', which have sought to improve the range of careers guidance opportunities available to young people and adults, and also through the introduction of Training Credits (Felstead, 1993).

Training Credits are vouchers which can be used to purchase education and training from a range of accredited providers including colleges, training agencies and employers. Young people are counselled on how to 'spend' the vouchers through a process of Individual Action Planning which identifies suitable career/training progression paths and providers of suitable education or training. When the providers have received the Training Credits from the individual, payments are made through the TECs to providers by instalments and on the attainment of the target outcome (Outcome-Related Funding). The idea of the initiative is to encourage young people to see themselves as consumers making discriminating choices in the training market. According to the Employment Department (1992) 'this will put buying power into the hands of young people so that they can choose the training and training provider which best meets their needs'. The recent White Paper, 'Competitiveness: Helping Business to Win' (HM Government, 1994) proposes extending the system to the funding of all post-compulsory education and training.

The limits of voluntarism

There is some evidence that these and other measures have helped to stimulate a more robust training culture in some UK firms. Some half a million people have now attained National Vocational Qualifications, many within employment; over 800 firms have won the 'Investors in People' awards with 6000 more working towards them; and the general level of in-company training activity appears to have improved over the past decade (HM Government, 1994, p 812).

However, the TECs are still far from fulfilling their mission of creating world class levels of training and skills (Coffield, 1992; Bennett et al, 1994). The vast majority of firms are still not training their employees to NVQ levels; two-thirds of graduates from Youth Training schemes do not attain NVQs; and only 37 per cent of young people gain qualifications at A-level or NVQ/GNVQ level 3 standard, compared with over 55 per cent in France and Germany (Green and Steedman, 1993). The demand-led or voluntarist approach has still not delivered the UK's long-awaited skills revolution.

The current UK government policy on training has been described as the triumph of ideology over experience (Coffield, 1992). Two overarching sets of problems still bedevil Britain's approach to training and these both relate to the historical preference for *laissez-faire* or voluntarist policies. First, there is still no concerted national approach to training underpinned by the necessary statutory framework governing the roles, rights and responsibilities of different parties. Second, there is a marked and growing absence of effective collaboration between social partners and of institutional arrangements to promote this.

There are still no legal obligations on employers to train, to provide paid leave for training, or to contribute funds towards external training. While in other countries employers are bound to pay training taxes or to belong to employer organizations which exert pressure on them to invest in training, this option is still rejected in the UK. In the absence of these requirements and without the restraints of sectoral agreements on wages, it is still relatively easy for employers to avoid training by paying a wage premium to poach trained employees from other firms.

TECs have limited means for dealing with these problems. They only have at their disposal the power of persuasion backed up by their control over the allocation of public funds for training. However, these funds represent only a small proportion of the total costs of training in companies and thus do not necessarily provide great leverage (Meager, 1990).

As far as young people themselves are concerned there are no statutory rights to receive training and, given the prevalence of unregulated occupations, fewer requirements to qualify to find employment than in other countries where the majority of jobs require specified qualifications for entry. Training credits will do little to improve the supply of training since providers are already funded on a per capita basis and the possession of a credit will do little to 'empower' young people. At the age of 16, they are not necessarily in a position to use it to negotiate effectively with future employers about training options, especially in a recessionary labour market (Felstead, 1993).

There is also a concern that the uptake of the new opportunities may be very uneven and that those who are least qualified and less able to make informed choices will fare worst in this kind of training market. Outcome-related funding of training schemes under the Job Training Partnership Act in the USA has often discriminated against the most disadvantaged as training providers have naturally tended to select trainees who are likely to meet the targets and thus ensure payment (Green and Mace, 1994). Unless great care is taken with the specification of performance measures in the UK the same distortions are likely to arise with Training Credits.

Lack of collaboration between the social partners has also become an increasing problem in UK training. TECs were specifically designed as business-led bodies, not as partnerships. They not only underrepresent unions and education; they also underrepresent small business, public sector employers and sectors without regional headquarters like retailing, finance and insurance (Meager, 1990). They are unelected, unrepresentative bodies which do not have to account to a local electorate or, even, to local business. Recent research suggests that the lack of a sense of ownership in TECs by small and medium-sized firms limits the influence exercised by the TECs and their capacity to provide strategic leadership in local economic development (Bennett *et al*, 1994).

Trade unions, meanwhile, have been largely removed from any effective role in determining and implementing training policy. They are only minimally represented on the TECs and the Industry Lead Bodies (ILBs) which set standards in training, and have only a minor impact on the examining and awarding bodies like BTEC and City and Guilds. Educational representation has been similarly curtailed with the TECs generally having few educational representatives and with the removal of LEA representation on college governing bodies.

This breakdown in social partnership may have serious consequences for VET provision. Effective training policy cannot be devised without the active collaboration of the unions, since training cannot be divorced from other issues where unions have legitimate bargaining rights, like the implementation of new technology and labour processes, the definition and grading of jobs and the determination of pay (Rainbird, 1990). Unions can play an essential part in persuading employers to provide more training opportunities and in monitoring the quality of training provided. Where their influence is restricted to the individual firm and to local bargaining this can only encourage the continuation of the historical pattern of uncoordinated and uneven provision (Winterton and Winterton, 1994).

Union representation is also important at the level of national standard setting for training. Without significant educational and employee representation the ILBs have frequently defined occupational competences in the narrowest fashion to meet the immediate needs of employers rather than the longer-term needs of individuals and the economy.

The state and the social partners in continental systems

Historically, the central state has played a much greater part in VET systems in continental Europe, both in terms of setting up and financing provider institutions and via the regulation of curricula and examinations. This continues to be the case today despite the trend towards devolution of power towards regional levels, and to bodies representing the social partners. Continental European and Scandinavian VET systems clearly vary considerably, from the relatively centralized school-based systems of France and Sweden, to the more pluralist, employment-based systems of the German-speaking countries. In each case, however, the social partners play important roles in the system, represented at national, regional and local levels and participating in policy formulation and implementation with respect to various functions, including finance, training delivery, standard-setting, quality monitoring, and assessment.

In Germany, France, Denmark and the Netherlands there are tripartite national standard-setting bodies where unions are fully represented, and a number of countries, including Denmark, France and Italy, impose statutory training taxes on firms. It is also common to see national sectoral agreements between employer and employee organizations which regulate pay levels, link grade levels to qualifications and which seek to distribute the costs of training among different firms. Typically, in all these countries, the state is ultimately responsible for regulating the system and for determining the precise roles and responsibilities of the different social actors in the system.

Germany

Unlike the French System, the system of initial VET in western Germany is relatively decentralized and predominantly work-based. However, as in France, the overall framework is tightly governed by federal legislation and the concept of social partnership underpins the entire system. Wolfgang Streeck (1989) characterizes its organization as 'neo-corporatist' to denote its typical mixture of market and public regulation and the intricate and subtle network of partnership bodies which determine policy and administer the system.

Initially based on the traditional apprenticeship model, the German Dual System has evolved into a highly organized national system of mass VET. The basic structure of the system is easily described. The majority of young people (over 60 per cent) enter an apprenticeship when they leave school which they do at ages varying between 15 and 19 depending on whether they have been studying at the *Hauptschule*, the *Realschule* or the *Gymnasium*. They sign an apprentice contract with a firm licensed to provide training and thereafter, for between two and four years, spend part of their week (usually three days) in work-based training under the guidance of trained instructors (*Meisters*) and part of their week in the *Berufsschule* studying general subjects and learning the theoretical aspects of their vocation. The vast majority of these (over 90 per cent) manage to obtain their certificates of vocational competence at the end of the training period and are then qualified to enter full employment either with their initial employer or elsewhere.

The system is administered through a variety of corporate bodies operating at national, regional and local levels. At the national level, the Federal Institute of Vocational Training (BIBB) advises the Federal Minister of Education and Science (BMBW), who has ultimate control over training. The BIBB is a public body authorized by the state, whose central board gives equal representation to unions, employers and the *Länder* (11 members each) and includes five federal representatives with 11 votes. The DGB, the German equivalent of the TUC, nominates the employee representatives and the KWB, which brings together the peak organizations of the main chambers of commerce and the main confederations of employers, nominates the employer representatives. At the regional level the main power lies with the chambers of commerce (*Kammern*) and the *Länder* governments. Under the 1969 Act all the chambers have established vocational training committees made up of six representatives for each of the social partners (employers, employees, instructors, colleges). All *Länder* have tripartite training committees representing employers, employees and instructors. At the local level, power lies with the works councils which must exist in all firms with over 200 employees and whose roles in VET are enshrined in the 1976 Works Constitution Act and the Co-Determination Act (CEDEFOP, 1987).

The social partners are involved in all of the main functions of the VET system at national, regional and local levels. These functions include: the setting of objectives, standards and regulations; finance; administration and monitoring and assessment.

Objectives, standards and regulations are determined largely at the national level. The main responsibility lies with the Federal Ministry which is advised by the BIBB. Most decisions require a consensus to be reached amongst the social partners represented on the BIBB's central board, although this is often only by a bare majority. Federal law frames the entire system, defining the roles and responsibilities of the different social partners; the obligation of firms to join chambers; the obligation of firms to train all their young employees according to the standard terms of the apprentice contract; the obligation of firms providing training to be licensed by the chambers and to employ *Meisters*; the qualification requirements for entry into classified jobs; and training regulations on the duration, content and minimum standards for different classified occupations. At the regional level the *Länder* committees are responsible for coordinating these training regulations with the regulations for vocational college provision which they control.

The responsibility for financing the system is also spread between the social partners. The state (federal and *Länder*) finances the vocational colleges and the employers finance the on-the-job training. Trainees make a contribution through their reduced apprentice earnings. Federal government also provides large sums in incentives for employers to train and for special training programmes. National agreements are also reached by the employers and unions in some sectors for training levies on firms. At the regional level the *Land* governments also provide financial incentives for employers to train. The chambers charge dues to their members and they often levy firms for funds for external training centres.

Administration, monitoring and assessment occur largely at the regional level. The chambers (under BIBB guidelines) are responsible for training instructors; operating external training sites; approving training firms and monitoring their performance; arbitrating in disputes between employers and trainees; and examination setting and assessment. Monitoring and assessment are conducted by specialist training counsellors employed by the chambers and expert juries comprising vocational instructors and others. At the local level the works councils play an important role in ensuring that training regulations are followed and that the company meets or exceeds the standards laid down. At the national level the performance of the training system is evaluated in the annual BMBW vocational training reports over which the social partners have been consulted through the BIBB. National employee and employer organizations also have training research departments which monitor training for their sectors (CEDEFOP, 1987).

The Dual System has a number of drawbacks, most of which are endemic to all work-based training systems. The training is relatively narrow and job-specific, particularly in the smaller firms which provide most of it (Casey, 1990), and this is arguably a disadvantage at a time when new technology and reorganized work processes in leading-edge enterprises increasingly require multi-skilled and flexible employees. It is also a system which divides students into different academic and vocational tracks. This reproduces within the vocational system the usual hierarchies of labour within which women and migrant workers are confined to disadvantageous positions. However, it is undeniably successful in ensuring that a very high proportion of young people receive training to reasonable standards and attain recognized national qualifications at the end.

A number of factors can be adduced as responsible for the relative success of the system, including the historical and cultural traditions in Germany which place great stress on the importance of education and training and which maintain the high social status of the skilled worker (Hayes, 1984; see also McLean, Chapter 3 this volume). However, roles played by the social partners are also key. Although unions and employers are frequently at odds about aspects of policy, there is a level of basic agreement over objectives which in part accounts for the relative prestige, stability and longevity of the system. The close involvement of employee and employer organizations in policy formulation and implementation undoubtedly increases the commitment of all parties to making the system work, whilst at the same time helping to ensure that no pool of expertise is lost to the system and that no interest group can manipulate it to its own exclusive advantage. Regulation through the collective actions of the social partners is also vital for ensuring the effective articulation of training and labour market policy which is critical to the working of the system. It is the national agreements reached between the partners which ensure that apprentice pay levels are set at a level which encourages employers to train, which discourages firms from using additional pay incentives to poach trained employees, and which ensures that the costs of training are fairly spread across a wide range of employers. Equally critical to the success of the operation is the strong regulative role played by the federal state in setting the overall framework and defining the roles of the different parties. The Dual System is a work-based model of training but it is definitively not a free-market one.

The importance of the social partnership model

The historical and comparative analyses pursued in this chapter suggest the fundamental importance of collaboration between the social partners in the effective provision of VET. Such collaboration can only be effective where the state, at national and regional levels, intervenes to coordinate the roles and responsibilities of the different partners. Voluntarist policies, which minimize such interventions, have not generally been successful. This is due to the underlying limits of the market as a means of regulating the supply and demand for training (Finegold and Soskice, 1988; Streeck, 1989).

Training is a collective public good from which all social actors benefit. Individual actors, however, may frequently make rational choices not to train. Employers often prefer to poach rather than to invest in training, especially, as in the UK, where there is no strong training culture and where employer associations lack the power to enforce a common code of practice. Furthermore, it is in the employers' interests to provide narrow, job-specific training to minimize the risk of losing their trainees and forfeiting their investment, even though this may not be in the best long-term interests of the firm, let alone the individual or the national economy. Employers tend to think short term about their training needs and consider training as a cost rather than an investment for the future and this tendency is exacerbated, as in the UK, where the structure of company ownership and the threat of mergers and takeovers puts a premium on showing short-term profit. The supply of training in a market system consequently tends to be insufficient both in quantity and in quality and the costs are not fairly distributed between employers.

There are reciprocal problems on the demand side. Employers may well not seek to employ well qualified people or pay the rates to attract them because they have grown used to a shortage in the supply of skills and have organized their labour processes accordingly. This is the vicious circle of the 'low-skills equilibrium' for which the market has no answer (Finegold and Soskice, 1988). Likewise, young people may decide not to train because they have insufficient information and life experience to see the long-term advantages (Streeck, 1989) or because they calculate that the pay rewards resulting from the acquisition of qualifications do not warrant the opportunity costs incurred during the process of training. Relatively high wage rates for unqualified young people and poor differentials for those with skills and qualifications thus provide a disincentive that perpetuates low levels of training in the UK. These and other manifestations of market failure will virtually guarantee the limited effectiveness of a voluntarist training policy.

The foregoing analysis does not provide arguments for the superiority of any particular system or for the advisability of any one country trying to adopt the system of another. What it does attempt to show is that any mass system of VET must have certain properties in order to be effective. These might be defined as coherence, transparency, multi-determination and multi-agency.

Coherence and transparency in institutional structures, curricula and qualification systems are essential in order to promote access and progression for users of training provision and to ensure a close articulation with the labour market. Multi-determination and multi-agency are essential because VET systems are complex organisms, charged with carrying out multiple functions which touch on the vital interests of many different parties and require the investment and expertise of various groups to operate with maximum efficiency.

Employers, unions and educationalists must all be intimately involved at all levels for VET to be successful. VET without employer input is bound to lose relevance to the world of work which defeats one of its objects. VET without educational inputs will be narrow and inflexible and dangerously divorced from other areas of education. Without the active involvement of the trade unions VET is unlikely to achieve high quality and will not achieve any functional fit with other aspects of labour market and employment policy relating to job entry requirements, job definition, wage determination, labour mobility and so on.

The pluralist representation of interest groups in the design and implementation of VET systems does not, however, obviate the need for strong central coordination and control. Systems based on the principle of social partnership only work when one of the partners, the state, defines the roles of the others and determines the shape of the system as a whole.

References

Ainley, P and Corney, M (1990) *Training for the Future; The Rise and Fall of the Manpower Services Commission*, London: Cassell.

Ainley, P and Vickerstaff, S (1993) 'Transitions from corporatism: the privatisation of policy failure', *Contemporary Record*, 7, 3, 541-56.

Bailey, B (1990) 'Technical education and secondary schooling, 1905–1945', in Summerfield, P and Evans, E (eds) *Technical Education and the State Since 1950*, Manchester: Manchester University Press.

Ball, C (1991) *Learning Pays*, London: Royal Society of Arts.

Barnett, C (1986) *The Audit of War*, London: Macmillan.

Bennett, R J, Wicks, P and McCoshan, A (1994) *Local Empowerment and Business Services:*

Britain's Experiment with Training and Enterprise Councils, London: UCL Press.

Casey, B (1990) *Recent Developments in West Germany's Apprenticeship System*, London: Policy Studies Institute.

CEDEFOP (1987) *The Role of the Social Partners in Vocational Training and Further Training in the Federal Republic of Germany*, Berlin: CEDEFOP.

CEDEFOP (1992) *The Role of the State and the Social Partners; Mechanisms and Spheres of Influence: Vocational Training*, **1**, Berlin: CEDEFOP.

Coffield, F (1992) 'Training and Enterprise Councils: The last throw of voluntarism', *Policy Studies*, **13**, 4, 11–31.

Day, C R (1987) *Education and the Industrial World: The École d'Arts et Métiers and the Rise of French Industrial Engineering*, Cambridge, MA: MIT Press.

Department of Employment (1988) *Employment for the 1990s*, London: HMSO.

Department of Employment (1992) *People, Jobs and Opportunity*, London: HMSO.

Felstead, A (1993) 'Putting individuals in charge, leaving skills behind? UK training policy in the 1990s', Discussion Paper in Sociology S93 (7) University of Leicester.

Finegold, D and Soskice, S (1988) 'The failure of training in Britain: analysis and prescription', *Oxford Review of Economic Policy*, **4**, 3, 21–53.

Fukuyama, F (1992) *The End of History and the Last Man*, London: Hamish Hamilton.

Green, A (1991) *Education and State Formation. The Rise of Education Systems in England, France and the USA*, London: Macmillan.

Green, A and Mace, J (1994) 'Funding training outcomes', Post-16 Education Centre working paper, London: Institute of Education.

Green, A and Steedman, H (1993) *Educational Provision, Educational Attainment and the Needs of Industry: A Review of the Research for Germany, France, Japan, the USA and Britain*, report series 5, London: National Institute of Economic and Social Research.

Grew, R and Harrigan, P (1991) *Schools, State and Society: The Growth of Elementary Schooling in the Nineteenth Century*, Ann Arbor: University of Michigan Press.

Hayes, C (1984) *Competence and Competition*, London: IMS/NEDO.

HM Government (1994) 'Competitiveness: helping business to win', Cm 2563 London: HMSO.

McCulloch, G (1989) *The Secondary Technical School. A Usable Past*, London: Falmer.

Meager, N (1990) 'TECs: a revolution in training and enterprise, or old wine in new bottles?' *Local Economy*, **6**, May.

Perry, P J C (1976) *The Evolution of British Manpower Policy*, London: BACIE.

Rainbird, H (1990) *Training Matters: Union Perspectives on Industrial Restructuring and Training*, Oxford: Blackwell.

Royal Society (1991) *Beyond GCSE*, London: Royal Society.

Sanderson, M (1994) *The Missing Stratum: Technical School Education in England, 1900–1990s*, London: The Athlone Press.

Sheldrake, J and Vickerstaff, S (1987) *The History of Industrial Training in Britain*, Aldershot: Avebury.

Shephard, J (1992) Speech to TEC Conference, Birmingham, July.

Streeck, W (1989) 'Skills and the limits of neo-liberalism: the enterprise of the future as a place of learning', *Work, Employment and Society*, **3**, 1, 89–104.

Thompson, S (1879) *Apprentice Schools in France*, London.

Vickerstaff, S (1992) 'Training for economic survival', in Brown, P and Lauder, H (eds) *Education for Economic Survival*, London: Routledge.

Weiss, J H (1982) *The Making of Technological Man: The Social Origins of French Engineering Education*, Cambridge, MA: MIT Press.

Winterton, J and Winterton, R (1994) *Collective Bargaining and Consultation over Continuing Vocational Training*, London: Employment Department.

8. Youth training for a changing economy in Holland

Eva Voncken and Jeroen Onstenk

After a long time of relative neglect, vocational education in the Netherlands has become a much debated issue. By the end of the seventies, discrepancies between the demands of the labour market and qualifications obtained in vocational education became apparent. Transition from education to the labour market became a matter of concern, just like the relevance of qualifications, the flexibility of the schools and the high rates of early school leavers. In the eighties, the economic situation in the Netherlands slightly improved. However, the number of unemployed and, among them, juvenile unemployed, remained high. At the same time, technological change, asking for higher qualifications, and demographic changes, leading to a decline in newcomers on the labour market, led to a growing concern about the possibilities for providing enough (future) qualified workers. This paradoxical situation led to policy efforts both to upgrade the workforce and the unemployed on the one hand, and to provide as many qualified school leavers as possible on the other.

Since the beginning of the eighties, government, companies and education have made efforts to offer all young people in Holland the opportunity to acquire a vocational qualification. Recently, new arrangements have been made in order to deliver a minimum vocational qualification for everybody, both school leavers and employees already working. In this chapter, the most important changes and developments in the vocational educational system are described against the background of the changing economy and new government policies.

Innovation in the Dutch economy

The Dutch labour market is rapidly changing as a result of changes in economic activities. Two basic processes determine these changes. Holland is on its way to a post-industrial society or service economy. Even before the current crisis in industrial firms like Philips, Daf, Fokker or Hoogovens, the relative weight of jobs in business services (banks, insurance, consultancy, but also cleaning companies) and personal services (restaurants, homes for the elderly, etc) had sharply risen. This does not only mean more jobs, but also a professionalization process of administrative, service and caring occupations. There is also a sharp increase of vocational education in this field.

Labour market perspectives for school leavers seem to be improving. There is a relatively strong need for school leavers in the retail trade, agriculture and horticulture, the wholesale trade, building, services, the health service, and the catering industry. This is, however, partly caused by the fact that many vacancies offer low qualified and badly paid jobs. School leavers are wanted for these jobs because their labour is cheaper. So the factual pattern is different. Most school leavers actually find a job in the public sector, the retail trade, hotel and catering industry or industry. Most girls go to work in service sectors, while boys are going to work more in the industrial sector. In 1991 the vacancies which were most difficult to fill were for jobs like plumber, bricklayer, welder, nurse, salesman, mechanic, etc. For most of these jobs, the apprenticeship is the most common training (MSZW, 1992). Therefore, technical courses on all levels hold a relatively strong position on the labour market. The same goes for health-service training at senior levels and retail training courses.

The other process has to do with changes in labour organization and the emergence of a new organizational model. Although this is by no means an unequivocal or non-contradictory process, we see in Holland the emergence of a post-Taylorist or transformed model of organization. There is a kind of socio-technic movement in Holland, which has not only developed concepts and undertaken some very interesting research, but has also resulted in actual workplace reforms.

Contrary to early expectations on deskilling, technological and organizational renewal led in many jobs to upgrading, at least in complexity. The new type of organization is characterized by key words such as 'flexibility', 'quality improvement', 'task integration', etc (Onstenk and Voncken, 1993). It is not easy to observe to what extent these new models have spread. It is probably more appropriate to consider this as a period of transition. Nevertheless, there is a growing awareness concerning the need for broadly applicable and transferable skills. The new organizational models require other skills and qualifications, such as transitional skills, key qualifications, problem solving, capacity to learn, etc.

The new models anticipate the permanent changes brought about by new quality demands, anticipation of changes in the market and product differentiation. It is noticeable that these new concepts tend to go together with reorganizations in companies and with the reduction of the number of employees.

As a result of rapid changes concerning required qualifications, training will gain a more and more permanent character. Although part of the training which used to be provided by companies is now provided by vocational schools, especially for healthcare and administrative jobs, companies do participate and engage in training more often. In-company training used only to be given to employees with (higher) vocational training. Problems in filling vacancies, and ongoing technological changes, have led companies to provide training for more diverse groups of employees (women, poorly educated and elderly). The role of companies in training will therefore further increase.

This inevitably leads to the question about what to learn in which setting. Training and learning on the job is gaining in interest, not least because of the limitations imposed by formal off-the-job training. But, what is more important, it raises once again the problem of harmonizing education with labour, on all levels.

Lack of supply regarding employees at senior vocational levels forces employers to consider alternatives, such as hiring employees with lower qualifications and providing them with in-company training. Employers in Holland have a choice between having pupils educated for the most part in schools or having them trained via the Dual System. But, higher entry demands are at least partly based on the expectancy that employees are capable of learning and are able to cope with (ongoing) changes.

Trends in educational participation

Until 1993 there was a wide variety of courses which pupils beyond the age of 12 could follow. The Dutch system of secondary education is now divided into two main streams – a general one and a vocational one – at both the second and the third level of education.

Full-time secondary education is compulsory until the age of 16. There are four types of school. After basic education (age 12), admission to secondary education is based on a school-achievement test, teachers' recommendation and preferences expressed by parents. Secondary education is hierarchically ordered (high to low): VWO (pre-university education, six years), HAVO (senior general secondary education, five years), MAVO (junior general secondary education, four years) and VBO (junior secondary vocational education, also four years). Most of these schools are part of larger school communities. School communities mostly provide a transition year in which the first grade is combined. After the lower stage of the second level, at the age of 16, pupils can choose a vocational or a general track.

The vocational track (MBO) is a full-time, three- to four-year course provided by large regional institutes. The general track (HAVO/VWO) is provided by the same schools that provide the lower stage. Next to the full-time vocational system, pupils may enter the dual/apprenticeship system. The dual courses consist of on-the-job training combined with theoretical courses for one or two days a week. At the third level, the choice is limited to two types: vocational college (HBO) and university (WO). Table 8.1 presents the participation rates of 16 to 20-year-olds, in secondary and tertiary education.

Women leave full-time education at an earlier age than men, although this difference has diminished over the years as far as 16 to 18-year-olds are concerned; so women seem to have overcome their disadvantages in this respect (De Bruijn, 1994). Where males are concerned, the table shows an inclination towards vocational education at an earlier age. Female participation rates decline after reaching the age of 19. This can be

Table 8.1 *Participation rates of male and female 16 to 20-year-olds, school year 1990/91 by percentage*

Stream m/f Age	General m/f	VBO m/f	MBO m/f	HBO m/f	WO m/f	Total enrolled fte* m/f	Total enrolled pte** m/f	No education m/f
16	48/55	29/19	13/16	0/0	0/0	93/92	6/5	1/3
17	33/37	14/7	29/31	1/2	0/0	79/78	13/8	8/13
18	17/16	4/2	34/33	5/7	4/4	65/64	16/10	19/27
19	6/4	1/0	27/23	10/12	8/7	51/46	15/9	34/45
20	1/1	0/0	17/10	14/14	9/8	42/33	13/8	45/59

Source: De Bruijn, 1994.
Notes: * full-time education
       ** part-time education (mostly apprenticeship)

explained by the duration of the courses in senior vocational education; courses for administration, trade, health and social services take about three years, whereas technical courses last for four years.

In 1993 the first stage of secondary education was reformed: all schools (VBO-VWO) will provide a common (nationally prescribed) curriculum during the first three years of secondary education. The attainment targets that have to be met will be equal for all pupils (De Bruijn, 1993). The moment at which a choice for further education has to be made will be postponed. At the same time, mergers between schools will be encouraged. The consequences for MAVO and VBO (both four years) are not yet clear.

Over the last 20 years there has been a rise in participation in education. Table 8.2 shows the participation in education among youngsters aged 15 to 18. The highest rise is to be seen amongst the 17 and 18-year-olds: between 1972 and 1985, their participation in full-time education more than doubled. Educational participation of Dutch girls has risen even more. One result of this process is an overall rise in levels of education. However, as a consequence, the gap between those youngsters who stay in education as opposed to those who do not becomes wider. Thus, compared to former times, pupils who fail to obtain an officially recognized qualification nowadays come off worse, because of the headstart of the majority.

Another change is the rise of vocational education as the final educational step before entering the labour market. (In the Dutch educational system, the transition from vocational to general education hardly occurs.) In the sixties, half of the qualified pupils left junior secondary education to get a job. In 1986 this percentage had dropped to about 4 per cent. After completing junior vocational education, 41 per cent of the male and 54 per cent of female students pursue vocational education at full-time senior level. Among boys, 42 per cent enter apprenticeship versus 21 per cent of the girls. Comparing these figures to the outflow of junior general education, males as well as females tend to enter senior full-time vocational education (respectively 77 per cent and 70 per cent). Only

Table 8.2 *Participation in education; 15–18-year-olds (percentage of the total generation)*

Full-time education	15-year-olds	16-year-olds	17-year-olds	18-year-olds
1972	84.5	63.4	43.9	30.1
1980	98.4	88.1	67.3	45.3
1985	99.1	92.0	77.4	60.5
1990	99.0	92.6	78.7	64.3
Part-time education				
1972	9.2	13.7	15.8	14.6
1980	0.5	8.4	11.8	10.4
1985	0.3	5.6	10.2	11.1
1990	0.4	5.1	11.0	12.9
No education				
1972	6.4	22.9	40.3	55.2
1980	1.1	3.5	20.9	44.3
1985	0.6	2.4	12.4	28.4
1990	0.5	2.3	10.2	22.6

Source: Netherlands Central Bureau of Statistics.

about 20 per cent pursue the general track. This development is also reflected by the increase in senior and vocational colleges as final stages before entering the labour market.

Participation in vocational education is growing. Since 1970 there has been an enormous increase in the number of students attending senior vocational education (MBO). In 1970, 77,000 pupils attended senior vocational courses (this is 12 per cent of the 16–18 age group); by 1980 this figure had doubled. In 1991 about 288,000 pupils – 48 per cent of the total 16–18 age group – enrolled in senior vocational education.

At the same time, a switch has taken place away from more technical subjects towards more economically related ones (Dronkers, 1992). The share of students taking courses on social services and healthcare has decreased, although in absolute figures it remained the same between 1970 and 1991.

Table 8.3 *Senior vocational education-graduates by percentage*

	1975	1985	1991
Technical training	22	25	25
Agricultural training	6	9	8
Economics and administration training and retail trade	10	25	39
Social services and healthcare	62	40	29
Total	32,000	51,000	57,000

Source: De Bruijn, 1994.

Although this switch is in accordance with the changes in the job structure, the significance of the increase in vocational training is not yet very clear. There is some doubt as to whether growing participation in economically related training at a senior level could be an answer to increasing job complexity, or merely an answer to educational inflation.

Larger participation in senior full-time education is caused by larger numbers of students in the administrative service and in the financial sector. However, participation in advanced apprenticeship training is also substantial. Therefore, it may be concluded that both tracks are alternative and equivalent routes. This is not the case with the industrial sector where participation in full-time courses is outnumbered by apprenticeships.

This tendency is strongly supported by the Dutch government. In response to skill shortages and changes regarding required qualifications, the official policy Holland has adopted is completion of the first level of apprenticeship as a minimum qualification. Therefore, in the Netherlands, efforts are being made to expand the apprenticeship system and to remove barriers for groups at risk (eg, pupils from non-Dutch backgrounds). Participation in full-time senior vocational education is still twice as high as participation in apprenticeship.

The educational achievements of the new Dutch working generations are not only rising, but also changing. In Holland, traditionally, there was a dominance of general education. This is diminishing. People not only stay longer in school, but they choose more often vocational education at secondary or higher level. It could be said that we are witnessing a process of vocationalization. As a consequence, more people enter the labour market with some kind of vocational qualification. This process is caused by different, partly contradicting, partly reinforcing processes. So it can be said that a process of *externalization* of skill formation has been accelerated in the last 15 years. Training that was taking place in the company, mostly on the job, has been transmitted to a school-based form of vocational education, outside the company (rather than specific learning sites within the company). This process started in industry (eg, mechanics), but also took place in training for administrative (eg, banking), service or nursing occupations. The background to this process is the disappearance of learning possibilities on the shopfloor (as a consequence of higher work pressure or damage risks) and changes in learning needs and required skills. Automation, for example, seems to demand a more theoretical kind of learning process. But in the economic recession of the sixties and seventies, a lot of Dutch companies shut down their company schools.

Some jobs really have been *upgraded*, as a consequence of the introduction of new technology, but also – and even more so – as a consequence of new organizational forms, commercial demands on flexibility and product quality: in short, the new type of organization.

There is also an independent process of longer participation in education, as a result of both emancipation and youth unemployment. Longer participation leads to higher (vocational) qualifications which are not always usable in the job: so some research shows *under-utilization* of skills.

Which tendency actually dominates is not easy to establish. There are considerable differences between sectors, and also over time. There seems to be a growing consensus in Holland that the level of education has been rising much faster than the level of occupations. But evaluation of this differs. Some see this high vocational level as a prerequisite and a driving force for economic renewal. As a consequence of a shrinking birthrate and rising levels of skills in a growing number of branches, and a growing number of jobs, the actual demands are matching or even exceeding available skill levels. So, at the same time, there is a waste of acquired skills in some places and a skill shortage in other places. Underutilization seems to occur more often in technical jobs than in administrative jobs, although this is possibly a consequence of historical development rather than 'objective' skill differences.

Early school leaving

In the Netherlands, in 1989, about 11 per cent of all young people left the educational system without any qualification (Bock and Hövels, 1991). This percentage is more or less the same as in other European Union countries. But we should bear in mind that because of differences existing in various educational systems, the implications and consequences of early leaving can be very different. For example, in the Netherlands, the lowest level of examination occurs several years earlier than in Britain.

Over the years, a gradual change has occurred in the way of looking at the problem of early school-leaving. Although youth unemployment was still high (in 1990, 15 per cent of the school leavers), the focus has moved from a merely social problem to a stronger link with the labour market. In Holland, the discussion concerning early leaving is traditionally linked with providing equal opportunities for education and work. This shift implies not only the involvement of the educational field (schools), but also that of labour market policy. Since the end of the eighties, this viewpoint has been translated into policy objectives that encourage output improvement in schools as well as obtaining a vocational qualification in order to enter the labour process. By adopting this criteria, the government labelled all groups that do not meet these standards as 'early leavers'. However, the group of youngsters that has not obtained any qualification at all remains the most critical, because of its poor position and prospects on the labour market.

Recently, the awareness of early learning as a problem has increased and has expanded to the second stage of secondary education; more specifically, to senior vocational training (MBO) and apprenticeship. On average, about 50 per cent of all pupils starting apprenticeship drop out during their courses or fail their exams. In senior vocational training, about 12 per cent of the pupils do not complete the courses. As more efforts are aimed at encouraging pupils to enter the second stage of secondary education, similarly, preventing early school leaving is expected to be given higher priority.

In order to deal with high rates of youth unemployment, the Youth Work Plan has been developed. It is an attempt to create better opportunities for young people aged 16 and older, who have not been able to get a job, by offering them opportunities for work experience and training (training is not compulsory).

Perspectives for vocational education

The number of participants in senior vocational education, both senior vocational colleges and apprenticeship, has strongly increased in the last ten years. The period young people attend school has become longer. Moreover, more people enter the labour market after having completed a vocational course instead of general education. This process has had repercussions on the position of junior vocational education, which has lost its position as a final educational step. This is even expressed in its name, which has changed from 'junior vocational education' to 'pre-vocational education'. The main reason for this altered position is the preference expressed by parents for general education in the second stage (as high as possible). After general education, the educational career is completed with vocational training at second level or higher (Dronkers, 1992). As the term 'pre-vocational' denotes, this level of education is no longer intended as final, but merely as a springboard to further vocational education. Because of these developments, junior vocational training has also lost its links with senior vocational training. The number of junior vocational students pursuing their education in senior full-time vocational schools has declined. The majority of the pupils continue their training in the apprenticeship system. This aspect, supported also by the merger of VBO schools with the schools in the 'general track', has put the VBO schools at the bottom of the hierarchy and turned them into schools for pupils who fail in general education or groups of pupils with educational disadvantages (such as many non-Dutch pupils).

The introduction of a common curriculum in the first years of secondary education will take place in all schools in the lower stage of secondary education. However, schools themselves will have more room to set a course plan: in pre-vocational schools the first two years will be more oriented towards basic schooling, while in the upper secondary classes subjects will be more vocationally oriented. The difference between the general and the vocational track will, therefore, grow smaller in the lower stage of secondary education. Learning to learn is one of the main goals. For VBO pupils it will be possible to obtain certificates, in order to facilitate the way to apprenticeship. For youth at risk of drop-out, combined pathways with more accent on vocational subjects are permitted.

From the second half of the eighties onwards, the Dutch government has been restructuring the system of vocational education. The different branches of vocational education (in short: school-based secondary vocational education and the Dual System) are becoming more integrated in the new vocational 'sector school', which offers both long and short vocational courses. The government has also tried to involve companies more in the development of the curriculum and also in the actual educational process itself, by the proposed dualization of the vocational educational system. Structures are being decentralized, giving schools more independence in establishing relationships with industry. They also have more opportunities to offer company-oriented courses for employees.

In the nineties, vocational education and training are being radically restructured. Advisory boards have played an important role in this respect. The branches of vocational education are now being integrated in new vocational sector schools. The main branches, each directed at one particular sector of the labour market, are as follows: agriculture, social work and healthcare, administration, commerce and retailing as well as the technical sector. These new regional schools run both long and short full-time vocational courses as well as dual courses. The main objective of this reform is providing a coherent and flexible qualification structure through integrating different disciplines in large schools. Within a couple of years, all schools for vocational education and training as well as part-time education for adults and all apprenticeship courses will be combined in one system of legal regulations. Because of this, the vocational and general track will become more separated at the higher stage of secondary education. As a result, many schools have merged: in 1991 there were 142 MBO-schools as a result of mergers between 400 schools (De Bruijn, 1993). Furthermore, efforts have been made to involve companies more intensely in the system of vocational education. As a result of the recommendations offered by the Education Labour-market commission, an agreement has been reached between the government and its market partners. Central topics are the improvement of the transition between education and the labour market as well as decentralization.

Traditionally, the involvement of companies in full-time education was limited to practical training periods. Now the government has attempted to involve companies in the development of the curriculum as well, for instance in creating vocational (training) profiles, or by means of dualization. Dualization is aimed at improving the transition from education to work by achieving more interaction between vocational education and vocational practice. In this way, dualization has contributed to upgrading quality and educational output. The form in which dualization will be achieved is still unclear and so is the amount of time that will be allocated for this purpose in schools or in companies. These matters are to be decided at branch level. A condition in this respect is, however, that the dual and full-time tracks must provide final attainments of similar quality. Companies will be responsible for the practical component, which represents a considerable change for senior vocational schools. In the present arrangements, the schools themselves are responsible for quality control.

Another policy agreement between government and its social partners is a guaranteed right to acquiring a so-called 'primary vocational qualification' for everyone. This is not only guiding educational policy in that nobody should leave initial education without at least minimal vocational qualifications, but also identifies a new training target for companies, to deliver this level to workers who have not yet reached this vocational qualification (in Holland some 400,000 workers).

Conclusions

Over time, the systems of education and labour market, schools and companies have occupied different relative positions. Years ago, the collaboration within vocational education had a self-evident character, this leading, for instance, to training in the apprenticeship system. Later on, a separation occurred between educational institutions as well as between education and labour. Since the eighties, understanding of the need for a greater harmonization and mutual collaboration seems at last to have penetrated the educational field as well as all political parties and the social partners.

For youngsters this means that they can no longer confine themselves to the traditional sequence education – work. Learning to learn, the sequence labour–education, as well as learning to work have become just as self-evident in the new system of education.

References

Bock, B and Hövels, B (1991) *Zonder Beroepskwalificatie uit het Onderwijs: Deel 1: Een Kwantitatief Beeld van de Groep Voortijdig Schoolverlaters*, Nijmegen: Instituut voor Toegepast Sociale Wetenschappen.

De Bruijn, E (1993) *Equivalence of General and Vocational Education in the Netherlands*, Wissenschaftsforum Bildung und gesellschaft ev.

De Bruijn, E (1994) *Changing Pathways and Participation in Dutch Vocational and Technical Education and Training* (draft), Amsterdam: SCO-Kohnstamm Instituut.

Dronkers, J (1992) 'The precarious balance between general and vocational education in the Netherlands', paper for seminar hosted by the International Centre for Research on Assessment, Institute of Education, University of London, November.

Ministerie van Sociale Zaken en Werkgelegenheid (MSZW) (1992) *Schoolverlatersbrief 1992*, Rijswijk, Directoraat voor de Arbeidsvoorziening.

Onstenk, J H A M and Voncken, E (1993) *Labour Market, Vocational Education and Company Training Policies in the Netherlands*, Berlin: CEDEFOP.

9. Educating and training youth for the world of work in Malaysia and Singapore

Elwyn Thomas

This chapter examines aspects of the educational policies put forward from two of the most progressive and dynamic economies in South East Asia, namely Malaysia and Singapore, to meet the challenges of educating and training its youth for the world of work in the 1990s and into the next millennium. The leaders of both countries aspire to have 'developed' country status by the early part of the next century and therefore put particular stress on the education and training for youth employment to achieve this goal.

The Malaysian and Singapore governments have long recognized the necessity for a realistic policy to meet the pervasive issues which underpin many of the problems of youth employment, and the school work transition. However, the meritocratic nature of the education systems in both countries highlights the problem the two governments have in selling alternatives to an academic university education to school leavers and their parents. It is commonly recognized that students and parents in these countries express aspirations which are orientated towards credentialism, favouring a professional career rather than seeking a vocation in manufacturing, technology, commerce or the service industries.

Recent initiatives in Malaysia and Singapore, which are mainly reflective of official policy, have sought to provide opportunities for the anticipated and unrealized aspirations and expectations of many young school leavers. These opportunities take several forms. They include a secondary school curriculum with a repertoire covering both technical and academic subjects; a system of polytechnical education which has close links with industry for full time-students; apprenticeships with 'earn and learn' as a strong feature built into the work training arrangement for part-time students. These and other initiatives aim to prepare youth for the world of work by providing the necessary training in essential skills required for on-the-job performance, while improving the further education and training for the young school leaver.

This chapter will deal principally with the young people who do not find themselves entering tertiary academic education, although reference will be made to the role tertiary education plays in the transition process. This group of young people will form the bulk of the future working population. It is therefore from this section of the population that the major challenges will arise for policy-makers in the next decade.

It is argued here, that in spite of the vigour and enthusiasm typical of current plans for youth employment education in Malaysia and Singapore, the current provision of education and training for young people entering the job market appears to be rather narrow and restricted. This is particularly so in the apparent paucity of innovative and creative ideas in curriculum development. New and imaginative strategies are required to stimulate the youth of these countries, to respond to the challenging new world of technology, the danger of unemployment, environmental and global concerns such as pollution, the misuse and over exploitation of natural resources, the potential dangers of new health problems like AIDS, as well as an accumulation of social and emotional problems arising from economic success. Any programme of education and training for youth employment that does not address these issues as part of general education for all school leavers, will be failing this generation over the next decade. Therefore, the thesis of the present chapter is that there is a need for more flexible and forward looking policies to account for changes likely to affect the transition from school to work; furthermore that these policies will only be realized if education and training taps the potential of all school leavers to adapt and cope with change.

For the purposes of the present chapter, the concept of youth embraces a period in a school leaver's life where the young person is receiving full-time further education and training as a preparation for employment. The concept will also be extended to those school leavers who are in work, but are pursuing further education and training which is a hybridization of the school–work transition period. Following on from this, transition is understood to be the end of formal schooling and the onset of gainful employment, in which apprenticeship, a probationary period or work orientation is being served.

The distinction between education and training which is made here is one in which education is seen as the development of the individual in the knowledge, skills and attitudes which are required for personal survival within a social and societal context, and which may be related to a person's job. Training is viewed as the command of general and/or specific competences which are prescribed as part of a particular job description.

There are several key questions that are closely associated with the future of youth employment in Malaysia, Singapore and much of the South East Asian region. These questions appear below and their elaboration structures the remainder of the chapter.

First, to what extent is schooling an adequate preparation for the world of work? Second, how far is further education and training of school leavers an effective preparation for the world of work? Third, what are the issues that need to be tackled for the successful implementation of the education and training of school leavers? Finally, to what extent can the challenges of change in the workplace and in society be met by new ways of educating and training school leavers?

Schooling as preparation for the world of work

Malaysia and Singapore have built into their formal systems of schooling, alternative pathways for pupils to pursue their careers. In both systems there are possibilities for pupils to follow academic or technical and vocational pathways, depending on their performance in school and public examinations. However, at present, the meritocratic nature of both educational systems favours success in academic subjects over that in technical and vocational.

In Malaysia, after six years of primary schooling and three years of lower secondary school, pupils are either funnelled into four more years of academic secondary education with the hope of gaining access to university, or proceed, if they wish, to two years' vocational secondary education. The curriculum of these schools, apart from offering compulsory subjects like Bahasa Malaysia (the national language of Malaysia), mathematics and English, have the usual range of technical and vocational subjects such as technical drawing, commerce and business studies, and home economics. From here, they can proceed to a polytechnic provided they have the requisite qualifications. After two or three years they sit for a certificate or diploma in technical or vocational education. It is also possible for students from higher secondary schools to be admitted to polytechnics to take a certificate or diploma or have entry to a degree course in engineering.

In Singapore after six to eight years of primary schooling, pupils proceed to secondary school. There are two academic streams, special and express, each of four years' duration, and a normal stream of five years' duration. Those who are successful in the special and express streams can move on to junior college and after that to university.

The curriculum of the normal stream caters for less-academic students, and includes several technical and vocational subjects such as design, technology, commerce and accounting. Pupils who spend eight years in primary school in either the extended or monolingual stream may proceed to basic vocational training, where after three or four years they may be awarded a vocational and/or trade certificate. It is possible for a student, if successful, to be admitted to a polytechnic and thence to the Nanyang Technological University contingent on passing the requisite examinations.

Since January 1994, a new Normal Technical Course in secondary schools caters for pupils who are more likely to benefit from a technically oriented education than an academic one. The course in years one and two will provide tuition in English, mathematics, and mother tongue, in addition to computer applications, science, technical studies and home economics. In years three and four, there is an increase in the number of technical and vocational subjects offered to students and the contact time devoted to each. Students are prepared for the N-level (General Certificate of Education, 'Normal' level) examination after four years. More able students can stay on for an additional year to sit for O-level (GCE, 'Ordinary' level).

The school systems of both countries, although differing in a number of specific details such as assessment and streaming for Singapore, provide within their respective secondary school systems, opportunities for pupils to choose either an academic pathway or a more vocational and technical career path, provided they meet the specified assessment criteria. The problem, however, is that in both countries the preferred pathway is perceived by pupils, and especially parents, to be the academic one. There are several reasons for this. First, it has always been seen by most parents and teachers that the ultimate goal should be an award of a university degree, with the status and privilege associated with it (Leong et al, 1990). Second, there are deep-seated values which give a sanctity to the pursuit of knowledge. For the ethnic Malays, this is often manifested in the need to develop further their cultural, aesthetic and religious aspirations. For the Chinese and Indians, scientific knowledge, technology and law are highly prized (Chew et al, 1990). Third, although a growing number of students, teachers and parents are beginning to realize that there are attractive opportunities in computer technology, business, management and advertising, the message is not getting through sufficiently quickly.

There has to be a change of attitude towards the world of work, in which jobs in technology, manufacturing and commerce are prized alongside professional careers. In answer to the first of the four questions posed in this chapter, the school system in both countries, mainly at the secondary level, does make a start in preparing pupils for the world of work, and there is clear evidence that the curriculum is becoming responsive to the changing needs of the world of work. There are also clear signs that an adequate diversified curriculum exists, enabling pupil choice. The real problems are those of parental attitude and proper information dissemination. Parental attitudes towards a preference for an academic education for their children is still a strong factor (Thomas, 1990), with teachers bearing some responsibility for this too (Chew et al, 1990). This has a 'knock on' effect on children who then aspire towards a university education (Ungku et al, 1987; Chew et al, 1990). The lack of up-to-date information on wider job opportunities for young leavers is, it seems, another factor. The school has a responsibility to provide an effective and efficient level of career guidance for students, which could act as a springboard for educating parents as well.

Further education and training as preparation for the world of work

Post-secondary school education and training occupies a central position in the quest for school leavers to prepare themselves for work. The question raised here relates to the effectiveness of education and training in meeting the demands of the workplace, whatever and wherever that is. It will become clear from what will be discussed below, that in both countries the focus of education and training for a technical and vocational job is heavily skills based, making the training process the priority. This is to be expected and is of course necessary.

However, what becomes apparent when examining the curriculum provided by polytechnics and vocational training institutions, is that much education is being sacrificed to the need to train technicians and produce a skilled workforce. This trend is likely to intensify in the immediate future as the economies of Malaysia and Singapore grow. This means ever-increasing demands being made to increase and improve the quality of technical expertise. There is therefore a distinct danger that while an effective and efficient workforce may be created to meet the demands of the workplace, the emotional and social dimensions in the transition process will be neglected owing to an imbalance between training needs and the need for a general education.

Malaysia recognizes that polytechnical education has an important role to play in its success. The polytechnics are seen to be in the forefront of change as Malaysia enters its industrial and technological era, (MOE, 1992). It is envisaged that training secondary school leavers to be technicians, supervisors, middle and top management will help communication between staff and shopfloor workers in all sections of industry, and is a top priority for polytechnic education and training throughout Malaysia. It is envisaged that this will give the country a large and highly qualified pool of skilled workers well into the next century, so ensuring continued economic success and furthering the cause of national development.

However, future policy on technical and vocational education also emphasizes that students should be trained not only for specific industries, but have the opportunity to be exposed to general skills training. This would result in a more flexible workforce which would respond to changes in the labour market. To date, Malaysia has seven polytechnics, all of which closely collaborate with industry and commerce. A committee structure for each polytechnic ensures that it has representatives from various facets of manufacturing, commerce, technology and service industries. Emanating from this representation are opportunities for schools and polytechnics to have work attachments which promote vital 'hands on' experience for trainees and students.

The curriculum includes the usual technical and vocational subjects which are offered to both males and females. However, in certificate and diploma courses, core subjects like Bahasa Malaysia, English and religious studies are also taught, ensuring some balance between training and general education.

In Singapore, ever since self-government in 1959, there has been a recognition of the importance of technical and vocational education in the development of the country's economy. Vocational training started within the school system in the 1960s and this led eventually to an independent system of training under the charge of the Vocational and Industrial Training Board (VITB). There has been a complete restructuring of vocational education in Singapore in the last ten years to meet the demands of economic restructuring as well as to accommodate changes in the structure of the education system. (Law, 1984, 1985, 1990).

In 1992, the Institute of Technical Education (ITE) was set up to replace the VITB and has the functions of promoting, providing and administering technical education and training in the Republic (ITE, 1992). It is recognized by the Singapore government that school leavers are becoming better educated and better informed, and more discriminating in their choice of technical training and type of employment. On the other hand, employers are demanding not only a better educated workforce, but one which has broad based technical knowledge and skills. This is seen as especially important to meet the need for a flexible workforce for the next decade.

ITE also provides school leavers with the choice of full time training, or a hybrid type apprenticeship scheme with an initial off-the-job attendance at a technical institute. The ITE provides continuing education and training through the BEST, WISE and MOST programmes which are aimed at upgrading and retraining the more experienced and mature workforce. The ITE also renders consultancy services to industry and carries out research into technical skills training. The ITE has 15 training institutes with an enrolment of over 18,000 full-time students and a cumulative intake of over 52,000 placements in part-time education. The numbers for further education and training (BEST and WISE) attract an annual number of about 58,000 workers (Law, 1990). Apart from the usual technical and vocational subjects, all ITE trainees are required to take further education courses in English and mathematics and are taught 'good work attitudes' through physical education and club and society activities (ITE, 1992).

It is clear from the above that both Malaysia and Singapore mean business in their belief that technical and vocational education must be given top priority in the quest for improving economic success and therefore national development. There is clearly a strong emphasis on training and the development of skills for achieving excellence in the workplace. There is also an interesting underlying theme in the policies of both countries, not to become overspecialized by providing too much training for job-specific skills. The frequent mention of general skills training and the development of good work attitudes is perhaps a promising feature of the vision of a highly skilled but yet flexible and adaptable workforce for the next millennium. However, further education appears to be too narrowly focused in spite of some measures to include general skills training and some general education.

Tackling the issues for future success

The third question that was posed at the start of this chapter was concerned with how policies for the education and training of school leavers in Malaysia and Singapore could be effectively and successfully implemented. From recent discussions the author has had with researchers, educators, trainers, school leavers and representatives from industry and the world of commerce in Malaysia and Singapore, six key issues emerged, when plans for improving the provision and quality of education and training for school leavers were discussed. These are cited below.

a) The need for effective institutional linkages and networking.
b) The need for a higher quality of education and training for trainers.

c) More imaginative curriculum development.
d) The need for more and better career guidance and counselling.
e) Increased opportunities for research training and programme evaluation.
f) More training in organization, management and administration of technical and vocational education.

These issues deserve further discussion and analysis.

The need for effective institutional linkages and networking

A constant theme running through much of the literature on the school–work transition is the need for effective linkages to be made between training and the world of work (UNESCO, 1983). This is certainly borne out in recent developments in Malaysia and Singapore. The fact that there is a committee structure for most of the courses taught in the Malaysian polytechnics, which has substantive representation from industry and commerce, is testimony to this. Similarly in Singapore, the former VITB and now the ITE have always had strong bonds with manufacturing, technology, business and commerce. There are two aspects to the issue of improving institutional linkage that emerge from my observations in Malaysia and Singapore.

The first aspect relates to linkage between schools and the world of work, and the second between the provision of further and higher education for school leavers. In both countries there are opportunities for those in technical streams of the secondary school, who are contemplating a career in a technical or vocational field, to visit workplaces, and sometimes have some work experience. However, in Malaysia this is not as strong a feature as it might be. In Singapore, it appears there is a stronger liaison between school and the world of work, and this is likely to be strengthened with the new policy of having a technical stream at the secondary school level in 1994.

The second aspect of linkage refers to those who are either in full-time technical education and are released periodically for training, or those in apprenticeships who attend training institutes for further education and instruction. In Malaysia and Singapore, the link and collaboration between training and workplace practice is in most cases institutionalized. However, research in Singapore (Kwong et al, 1992), into factors affecting skills training of apprentices, showed that while the links between most institutional training and industry were found to be useful and productive, the quality of on-the-job and off-the-job training was not always sustained, especially when it came to the motivation and commitment of training instructors. It is one thing to have links and collaboration between training and work; but quite another to monitor and improve the quality and effectiveness of collaboration to the benefit of all parties. A major factor which arises from the Singapore research and from discussions with Malaysian technical educators is the poor level of instructor training, which many full-time and part-time students receive; this is especially the case for on-the-job trainers. In addition to linking between training institutions and industry there is a need to network schools, parent associations, chambers of trade, teacher organizations and the media so that there is more information about career opportunities for school leavers in fields other than the professions. The information prepared by the ITE and that for Malaysian Polytechnical Education should be more effectively distributed, especially to schools, so that what is on offer is widely publicized. From what has been discussed earlier in this chapter it is particularly important to target parents in any networking activity.

The need for a higher quality of education and training for trainers

This issue is closely related to some of the observations made earlier. There are several aspects to a discussion of the training of trainers; the first is related to finding out what constitutes an effective instructor of technical and vocational subjects. This, it seems, has yet to be carried out extensively. Another aspect is the need to improve the link between theory and practice, and how instructors can be trained to be better at communicating this to their students. There is, it seems, a crying need to improve pedagogical skills like use of more visual aids, better questioning and more feedback to trainees on task performance. 'On the job' trainers who play such an important role in the linkage between training and the workplace appear to lack motivation, show poor commitment to the job and feel they should be paid more for doing what they see as extra to their duties. Another feature is that all trainers need to feel they are part of the training process. This is apparently not the case. These attitudes were registered by trainers who took part in the Singapore Research by Kwong *et al* (1992) referenced above, but they are also attitudes expressed by many of their counterparts in Malaysia. The cry for upgrading and more professional contact through the setting up of alumni and instructor development centres (similar to teacher centres) to improve the quality of training, while at the same time contributing to staff development, may go some way to meeting these problems in both countries.

More imaginative curriculum development

In examining the range of subjects included in the various courses for technicians, business practice, computer technology and others, there appears to be, in general, a sensitivity to the changing needs of the world of work. The number of courses offered at polytechnics and technical institutes has increased significantly since the late 1970s in both countries. While the content appears therefore to be comprehensive, for the most part relevant and up to date, its design and delivery is less satisfactory. This is particularly the case in the unimaginative design of manuals for trainees and trainers, poor use and sequencing of audio-visual materials in teaching, and insufficient use being given to Computer Assisted Learning and instruction. The point made earlier in this section about the inability of many instructors to link theory to practice effectively may arise from poor design features of curriculum materials. These drawbacks have been highlighted by the SEAMEO Regional Centre of Vocational and Technical Education (VOCTECH) based in Brunei Darussalam. VOCTECH (1993) identified 41 areas of need which included curriculum design and development as a key problem for the region as a whole. VOCTECH, of which Malaysia and Singapore are members, has regular training programmes which try to address this and other issues discussed in this section. While the figures of training and administrative personnel in technical and vocational education needing upgrading is small for Singapore and Malaysia, compared with Indonesia and Thailand (VOCTECH, 1993), research in Malaysia and Singapore shows that a more innovative approach to curriculum development needs to be adopted.

The need for more and better quality career guidance and counselling

In the early 1980s, UNESCO identified ten problem areas relating to the question of school-work transition and among these was: '... a greater need for more effective teacher and counsellor training at industrial sites' (UNESCO, 1983).

This is still a major issue not only in Malaysia and Singapore but in the region as well (VOCTECH, 1993). There are really three levels here. One level is the pupil still in secondary school, intending to take up a career in industry or business after leaving school; the second is the school leaver who is in some form of apprenticeship, or on day release, and the third is at the staff level in training institutions and the workplace. At the school level it appears that there have been encouraging developments in the establishment of guidance and counselling as part of teacher training curricula in both countries, and its inclusion within job descriptions of certain teachers. However, according to the findings of the work of Leong *et al* (1990) in Malaysia, only 25 per cent of vocational and work-related objectives of the secondary school curriculum were attained. This has to be seen against the background of a secondary school population with a 93 per cent level of aspiration for university education coupled with substantial parental and teacher support. While the profile of career guidance and counselling in schools is considerably higher than it was in the late 1970s, the truth is that a meritocratic educational system with university education at the top of the agenda for pupils and parents means that plans for other jobs are viewed as second choice alternatives.

At the level of the school leavers either in work or in full-time further education, the issue is the lack of guidance and counselling on the industrial site, rather than in the training institution. There is a need for more induction programmes, and in-depth studies of how various apprenticeship schemes can lead to job options within a particular industry and in other sectors. Industry should act here, but so far there seems little evidence of it doing so.

At the staff level, guidance and counselling should be seen as part of staff development. It was found during the author's discussion in Malaysia and Singapore with administrators and teaching staff, that career pathways are not very clearly demarcated, and that advice on training and retraining for instructors in both on-the-job and off-the-job situations is generally in need of improvement. The main concern, however, is that all personnel in the training process – be they students, apprentices, managers or instructors – feel the need for guidance, and someone to talk to about their career.

It may be that wherever training is taking place, it will be necessary to appoint facilitators whose key role will be to act as learning and training specialists. Such persons are called 'learning facilitators'. Another type of facilitator, whose function would be to combine career aspirations with social needs, might also be needed in the future. This role is carried out by a person called a 'developmental facilitator', whose importance may grow with the need for workers in the future to be able to cope with change in their place of work and its effect on life outside it. This issue will be discussed further in the final section of the chapter.

Improved opportunities for research training and programme evaluation

The addition of research and research training to the list of aims of the new Singapore ITE is certainly a mark of the times. In company with other developments within higher education in the Republic eg, teacher education, economics, language and computer technology, ITE is in step with the drive for more time and money to be spent on research and development.

In Malaysia, there is also evidence that research and evaluation into technical and vocational education is beginning to be taken more seriously. These developments should be seen against the background of VOCTECH policy, for improving education and training within technical and vocational education.

There is a particular need to train key staff in the research methods used in social science and education. The training should include identification of relevant research problems in technical education, planning strategies for carrying out the research and a sound knowledge of statistical treatments and applications. Research is particularly needed in the fields of teaching methodology, evaluation of training, in exploring the use of computers in technical education training, student assessment and staff appraisal. Student selection into technical education and the long and short effects of certain types of training are also research priorities.

Organization, management and administration

The role of management in the organization, administration and support of technical education, is an issue which is receiving an increasing amount of attention (Fortuijn et al, 1987). The establishment of good management practice to ensure the effective implementation of the mission objectives of training institutions has a crucial role in the success of training for the school–work transition. There is clearly a need for training institutions to take action to train all the management staff as well as key administrative and teaching staff in modern management techniques. The application of effective and innovative management information systems and their use in planning and decision-making will need to become the norm in technical education.

Another area of concern is the mapping out of career pathways for not only the school leavers entering the workplace, but for on-the-job and off-the-job trainers. A related feature that needs to be addressed is the role incentives play in motivating staff; this emerged as a salient finding in the research carried on trainers by Kwong *et al* (1992) in Singapore. It is well known that at a certain point in the career of a well qualified technician, industry will give a higher level of remuneration than were he or she to become an instructor. Conditions of service, other than salary, are also factors which need to be taken into account. These would include the quality of the working environment and opportunities for upgrading. Career pathways will need to be planned alongside a realistic strategy which includes different types of incentives such as a salary commensurate with industry, a conducive working environment and opportunities for professional development. However, the provision of realistic and well thought out career pathways should not be seen as the sole preserve of the teaching and training staff: managers and administrators need to be fully included in any plans for improving staff development.

It is worth noting that VOCTECH not only pays attention to the training of teachers and lecturers of technical subjects, but also has courses in leadership and management practice for managers and administrators. This indicates that at the regional level, providing training for managers and administrators is perceived to be on a par with the need to update instructors. This reinforces the notion that much of the success of technical education should be equated with effective, efficient and innovative organizational and managerial support.

The challenge of change and the art of the possible

The fourth question posed in this chapter concerns the future, and particularly the future in the context of change. It is likely that Malaysia and Singapore will take their place amongst the ranks of OECD countries within the next decade or so. This may be sooner rather than later for Singapore. In the light of this prophecy, and in the terms of the present subject of this Yearbook, it is necessary to examine some of the possible challenges facing these two countries in their quest to transform their economies from ones that are 'emerging' to ones that have 'emerged' and so become 'developed'.

Faced with the inevitability of a considerable increase in the pace of social and economic development in these two countries, it is necessary to identify what type of challenges the education and training of school leavers for the world of work will meet in the next decade. Following from this, it is necessary to map out realistic strategies that need to be developed within formal and informal education to produce a workforce that is sufficiently skilled and adaptable to cope successfully with the challenges which change brings to the quality of life both in the workplace, and in the quality of one's leisure time.

How long will there be a manpower shortage and will not the nature of work change anyway?

Like many of the countries of the Pacific Rim, Malaysia and Singapore have chronic manpower shortages in most sectors of their economies and this is particularly serious in skilled and highly skilled jobs. It is evident from what has been discussed earlier in the chapter that both countries have embarked upon ambitious plans in the education and training of their school leavers to meet this challenge. They have borrowed ideas from North America, Western Europe and Japan relating to industrial training and the application of management and organizational principles to improve the quality of technical education. It must be recognized that these measures are necessary in the context of growth, but the problem arises when economic growth rates level off, resembling the less ebullient rates of developed countries, with the consequence that employment levels may have to be reduced.

While this situation may be some way off, it is necessary that curriculum planning should take a futuristic view, not only introducing new content areas and discarding unnecessary topics, but also engaging in a thorough analysis of general skills identification and their potential for transferability across tasks. In order for this to be realized, it is essential that research is carried out to identify these general skills and to decide how trainees are best able to apply them. Equally important is the extent to which instructors are able to communicate their knowledge and skills to the trainees. By identifying clusters of general and essential skills and having a knowledge about their transferability across tasks, the workforce would have the potential to adapt when the nature and availability of work changes.

How can education and training meet the challenge of technological change inflicting long-term environmental damage?

The impressive economic growth of Malaysia and Singapore, and the undoubted rise in the standard of living in these countries have not been without their price. Perhaps one of the most important challenges facing the governments of the two countries in the coming decade is to control the effects of industrialization, technological change and the contingent increase in urbanization. These changes are already having serious effects on the environment. In Singapore the effects are more in terms of increased levels of lead pollution in the atmosphere from cars, and noise pollution. In the tin-mining areas of Malaysia there are many unsightly waste dumps and effluent seeping into the sea, lakes and rivers. Alleged over-exploitation of timber reserves and the fragility of the rainforests are certainly challenging issues which will also need to be tackled in the next decade. Concern about environmental issues like these should be part of the general education and training of school leavers. This is especially relevant in the case of technical and vocational programmes which directly or indirectly affect everyday life through innumerable technological applications. Education and training programmes should not only tackle environmental issues at a general level of discourse, but should also include, where possible, the study of technologies that have been refined to protect the environment from pollution and damage such as the catalytic converter, anti-noise mechanisms and ways of cleaning up the environment.

Coming to terms with rising expectations

I have discussed elsewhere the issue of rising expectations in high population density states like Singapore (Thomas, 1992). The nature of the problem is still very much alive in Singapore and although Malaysia has a much larger land mass with a manageable population size at present, rising expectations of youth need to be placed at the top of the demographic agenda for the next decade. Even after channelling school leavers away from academic higher education to a technical and vocational career, the problem of high and unrealistic expectations is not eliminated but merely postponed for the future. I have argued in the case of Singapore that education and training alone cannot solve this problem. There has to be on the part of government the necessary will to take action in bringing together leaders of industry, finance, commerce, the professions (including teachers and teacher trainers) and members of the community (including parents) to map out a series of alternative national blueprints for the future. In Singapore the problem may be particularly acute, in view of the shortage of space and the population increase, which, although strictly monitored, is still likely to be a problem. From what has been discussed earlier in this section, the nature of work itself is likely to change and particularly the time that is spent doing it.

Rising expectations is also about changing values. In the schools of Malaysia and Singapore, there are determined attempts to retain the rich cultural, religious and aesthetic heritage of their diverse populations alongside the drive to prepare childrens' knowledge and skills after school (Thomas, 1994). One way of possibly neutralizing the expectations explosion in the next decade would be to strengthen the education of the school–work transition, by continuing the values emphasis of the school curriculum into further education, thereby promoting further the countries' rich cultural heritage through a sensitive and meaningful transmission of values during the training period. The result could be a mix in which the needs of employment are balanced with needs of an education, in which key values have an important place. The mix might be an antidote to unrealistic expectations of school leavers in the years ahead.

References

Chew, S B, Zulkifi, A M, Lee, K H and Noorshah, M S (1990) 'The transition from school to work: determinants of the demand for higher education', research report, Institute of Advanced Studies, University of Malaya.

Fortuijn, L, Hoppers, W and Morgan, B (1987) *Paving Pathways to Work; Comparative Perspectives on the Transition from School to Work*, The Hague: CESO.

ITE (1992) *Full Time Training Courses*, (Prospectus), Singapore: ITE.

Kwong, L W, Wong, M, Petzall, S, Yeo-Yoong, S and Hall, K. (1992) 'Factors affecting skills training of apprentices' Parts 1, 2 and 3, research report, Singapore: ITE.

Law, S S (1984) 'Trend of vocational training in Singapore', VITB paper 1, Singapore: VITB.

Law, S S (1985) 'The vocational training system — its development and challenges', VITB paper 4, Singapore: VITB.

Law, S S (1990) 'Vocational training in Singapore', VITB paper 6, Singapore:VITB.

Leong Y. C. *et al* (1990) 'Factors influencing the academic achievement of students in Malaysian schools', research report, Educational Planning and Research Division, MOE, Malaysia and World Bank.

MOE, Bahagian Pendidikan Teknik and Vokasidal (1992), Polyteknik Malaysia, Program Pencajian.

Thomas, E, (1990) 'Pupils' perceptions of parental influences on schooling', research report, University of London, Institute of Education.

Thomas, E (1992) Urbanisation and education in the nation city state of Singapore', in Coulby, D, and Jones, C (eds) *World Yearbook of Education: Urban Education*, London: Kogan Page, pp 87–96.

Thomas, E (1994) 'The state, teacher education and the transmission of values', paper presented at the BATROE Conference on Contemporary Crises in Teacher Education, 28–30 March, University of London, Institute of Education.

UNESCO (1983) 'The transition from technical and vocational schools to work', *Trends and Issues in Technical and Vocational Education*, **2**, Paris: UNESCO.

Ungku, A A, Chew, S B, Lee, K H and Bikas, S (1987) 'University education and employment in Malaysia', IIEP research report 66, Paris: IIEP/UNESCO.

VOCTECH (1993) *Information on the SEAMEO — VOCTECH Regional Centre*, Brunei Darussalam: VOCTECH.

Part 3: Curriculum and qualification reform in post-compulsory education and training

Introduction

Andy Green

Increasing global economic competition and rapid technological change put a premium on human resource development. At the same time, social aspirations are rising and growing numbers of young people seek the higher qualifications which will give them access to the most desirable jobs and lifestyles. It is no wonder then that governments throughout the world are increasingly concerned with the effectiveness of their systems of post-compulsory education and training, and invest much energy in efforts to reform them. These have focused, in particular, on three areas: institutional structures; standards and curricula; and qualification and assessment systems.

Institutional changes have been necessary to accommodate the growing and increasingly diverse range of students continuing in post-compulsory education and training. In some countries this has meant expanding and diversifying the traditional academic upper secondary institutions so that they can provide a broad range of general education courses to meet the needs of their students; in other countries it has meant creating new vocational institutions or new vocational tracks within existing institutions. In either case there has been pressure to increase the flexibility of provision; to improve possibilities for transfer and progression within different pathways; and to create greater parity between different types of provision. Inevitably there has been a continual tension between the pressures of diversification, on the one hand, and those of integration on the other.

The need to meet new challenges has also focused attention on the curriculum and the way in which curricula and standards should be developed. In most countries there have been conflicts between the competing claims of employers and higher education institutions and between the aspirations of individuals and the realities of the labour market. Whilst in most countries there are debates amongst experts around the relative merits of general education, vocational preparation and occupational training, the young people themselves have shown an increasing demand for the more academic programmes which give the best prospects of entering higher education and competing for a wide range of jobs. Academic drift and credential inflation have thus been the perennial unintended consequences of reform in many countries.

135

Qualifications form the main link between education and the labour market, and consequently the attention of reformers has also focused strongly on the systems of qualification and assessment in various countries. There have been concerns about the validity and reliability of qualifications and assessment systems; about the mechanisms for the setting of standards, and about the relationships between different types of qualification. In some countries vocational qualifications have been designed to match closely the competences required in particular occupations and this has often led to narrow vocational courses separated off from other general and academic ones; in other countries, the emphasis has been on providing a broad foundation of general and vocational education in preparation for uncertain and fluid future job roles, and this has generally been associated with efforts to create more integrated and unified qualification systems.

The chapters in this section deal with these issues from a variety of perspectives and in relation to different national contexts. Wolf analyses the patterns of qualification reform within a number of European states, emphasizing the common preoccupations with validity, reliability and flexibility. Keating examines the recent attempts to reform curricula and qualification systems in the Australian states as a response to the conflicting pressures of higher education and the labour market and notes the manifest tensions between federal and state policies.

Chapters 12 and 13 look at the issues as they arise in two contrasting national contexts: Inui and Hosogane examine the strengths and weaknesses of the Japanese system of general upper secondary education, whilst Unterhalter and Young assess the potential for creating a more integrated system of education and training in the new South Africa. The final chapter, by McCulloch, offers an historical perspective on the relation between academic and vocational learning and the articulation between education and work.

10. Vocational qualifications in Europe: the emergence of common assessment themes

Alison Wolf

Vocational education and training are of increasing concern and importance to all European governments, which share pressures generated by increasing participation rates in education and declining demand for unskilled labour. High levels of unemployment, a growing conviction that these are endemic in the current economic structure and worries about Europe's competitiveness in the world economy have led all governments to look to education and training as one of the key policy instruments at their disposal. In developing their policies there is, inevitably, a focus on assessment and qualifications. These are the currency which translate the achievements of formal education and training into labour market signals, and also channel information about labour market requirements back to teachers and candidates alike.

This chapter will be concerned with common themes in assessment and vocational qualifications. However, it is important to emphasize the enormous diversity in vocational education and qualification systems which continues to exist in Europe. This diversity is far greater than at elementary and secondary school levels, and reflects the growth, over time, not only of very different training institutions, but also of very different labour market structures. The largely unsuccessful attempts of the European Community to equate qualifications across member states, and the problems encountered by individual countries in reforming their systems, underscore how deeply vocational qualification systems are bound up with the wider economy.

There are three main varieties of vocational assessment system (and vocational training) in Europe. That of the UK is closest to English-speaking countries outside Europe and has, until recently, been highly decentralized and, indeed, unregulated, with vocational awards the concern of a multitude of more or less independent professional and craft level 'awarding bodies'. The Germanic tradition (Germany, Austria, Switzerland) is of a Dual System, whereby, at the end of compulsory schooling, most young people proceeded to apprenticeships, which combine workplace training with some time in formal education, all of this organized through agreed, occupation-wide training regulations. While the latter are developed in conjunction with the 'social partners', and very much industry-led in content, the state is a senior stakeholder with ultimate responsibility for maintaining the system. Most other countries in Europe have a school-based system of vocational education, involving more or less highly segmented institutions or syllabuses, and different qualifications and awards for vocational and academic pupils.

As noted above, in the last few years all these systems have encountered similar pressures – both in policy terms, as governments grapple with economic change and in demand terms, as they experience ever-increasing numbers staying on in full-time education and demanding access to higher education (see eg, Wolf, 1993; Parkes, 1993; Soskice, 1993.) This chapter focuses on developments in the specific area of assessment and qualification structures. However, these take place within the broader context of student and parental concerns that vocational awards will be seen as being of lower status, and a determination to remain in the academic 'competition' as long as possible. They are also affected by rates of economic and technological change that lead both industry and policy-makers to emphasize the growing importance of general skills, rather than specific ones which may soon be obsolete. Economic pressures and anxieties also increase the general concern to make vocational training and qualifications as closely tied to economic requirements and the provision of 'value added' as possible.

In this context, two major themes emerge: a concern for the validity of assessments, and a desire to increase the flexibility of the assessment and qualification system. The remainder of this chapter discusses these with particular reference to four European countries: England, representing the English-speaking approach; Germany, for the 'Dual System' countries; and France and the Netherlands, whose school-based systems are evolving in different fashions.

The validity of assessments

Everyone agrees that the validity of an assessment is tremendously important. However, no one has any very good ideas about how to measure or promote it (Wood, 1991). Validity is commonly defined as how far an assessment actually measures what is intended: for example, how far a driving test measures ability to drive safely and appropriately, or how far university final examinations measure whatever it is that the degree was meant to teach.

In some cases, this becomes circular. Many academic courses are effectively defined by their final examinations, so that asking about the validity of university finals papers in English and drama, or of exams for the Bac C (the high-prestige French maths baccalauréat), is less a question about assessment validity than about whether it might be better to teach, learn and test something different. In other cases, however, assessments are being used to generalize and draw conclusions of a quite specific sort. People make inferences and take actions which rest on the supposed validity of the measures: hiring someone as a long-distance lorry driver, deciding they have the appropriate personality for a salesperson, allowing them to use complex medical machinery unsupervised.

One of the factors affecting an award's validity is its reliability: whether the results are likely to be the same regardless of circumstance (and especially regardless of who carries out the assessment). Governments, in particular, tend to emphasize issues of reliability because they are aware of how much perceived 'fairness' and objectivity affect the credibility of awards, and the willingness of people to use them as evidence of relevant achievement. However, while reliability may be a precondition for validity, and one which it is relatively easy to address, it is not the same thing. A reliable assessment may not be very closely related to the skills one is interested in at all.

Validity is a particular concern for vocational assessments (whether one is discussing surgeons, accountants, butchers or motor mechanics) because it is not a circular concept, not something defined by the educational sector. However, it is also very difficult to find robust, feasible ways of checking validity, and the latter therefore tends, in practice, to be a matter of whether it 'looks right' to experts in the field. There are also a number of problems inherent in the way vocational education is delivered which further threaten the validity of its awards. It is almost inevitable that any educational institutions will lag behind developments in the workplace: machinery will be out of date, and replacement financially impossible, staff will themselves become out of touch, and there will also be internal pressures to maintain courses for which there is decreasing demand because staff and equipment are in place, and being paid for.

Added to this is increasing uncertainty about what exactly is being delivered even in a vocational course. In some craft areas, one can still think, meaningfully, in terms of clearly defined skills with a long 'shelf-life'. Such crafts are also the easiest to assess (though not to master). The medieval concept of a 'masterpiece', a single fine product on the basis of which one graduated from trainee or journeyman status, provided not only a valid but an economical measure in terms of the assessor's time, whether it was a goblet of gold or silver, or a fine pair of shoes or gloves.

Today, however, governments – and industry – are most concerned with the rapidly changing nature of the labour market, and the perceived need for higher levels of overall skill, flexibility, and a general ability to learn fast, 'problem-solve', and the like. Specific crafts, skills and skill shortages have not disappeared: but it is current concern over what vocational programmes should provide that is fuelling interest in the validity of current assessment procedures.

The notion of competence

Throughout Europe there is interest in the idea of 'competence', as a broad-based concept encompassing what current and future employers need, and what both vocational education and firm-based training should aim for. To date, however, it is only in the UK that this has been translated into a complete system of 'competence-based assessment' which is compulsory for any government-funded or subsidized vocational training scheme, and increasingly the basis for vocational awards delivered in full-time education.

Competence-based assessment of vocational skills is delivered through National Vocational Qualifications (NVQs). NVQs have now been developed to cover most sectors of employment. They derive from the activities of 'lead industry bodies' which represent a given sector of industry or employment. Each such body is responsible for drawing up detailed standards of occupational competence. No qualification will be recognized as an NVQ unless it is based on the standards issued by the lead industry body concerned: and government funding is tied to NVQ provision. The process of NVQ accreditation does not involve any formal discussion of curriculum (except insofar as it is implicit in the standards) or approval of learning programmes. The assumption is that use of the standards will ensure the latter's quality.

The purpose of the standards is to specify a set of outcomes; and to do so clearly enough for assessors, candidates and interested third parties to make objective judgements about whether these have been achieved. The system then certifies student progress on the basis of demonstrated achievement of these outcomes. Assessments are not tied to time served in formal educational settings, although many English NVQs are in fact delivered in educational institutions. Standards are based on analyses of actual occupational roles: 'functional analysis' is the official term for this process, reflecting an emphasis on the underlying general functions or purposes, rather than on specific, narrow tasks.

The occupational standards, and the statements of competence they embody, are meant to ensure that vocational assessment is valid. Gilbert Jessup, the main architect of the system, and deputy chief executive of the National Council for Vocational Qualifications, argues that:

> Validity ... implies comparison between the assessments and some external criterion, ie, that which one is trying to assess. Within the NVQ model of assessment one clearly has an external reference point for assessment – the statement of competence ... [T]he validity of assessments ... becomes a matter of comparing the judgements made on the evidence of competence collected, against the elements of competence. (Jessup, 1991, p 192)

The mode of 'assessment to standards' has also been emphasized as a major guarantor of validity. NVQs are meant to be delivered either (and ideally) by assessing in the workplace, or by creating workplace simulations in the school or college. The general assumption is that the closer the circumstances of the assessment are to those of the 'real world', the better – the more valid – the assessment and the resulting qualifications will be.

Unfortunately, the NVQ system, as implemented, has failed to fulfil all its promises. The concept of competence which was promulgated in early policy documents was a broad-based one, intended to provide training for the future, not merely to replicate the content of contemporary jobs. In practice, NVQs have become very atomistic and task based, heavily criticized by many educationalists for their neglect of general skills and their tendency simply to mirror current practice. The emphasis on 'performance evidence' further increases the tendency to deliver narrow tasks reflecting current practice rather than broad competences. There have been repeated criticisms of the reliability of NVQ assessment, with critics arguing that so decentralized a system, with no clear syllabus, or external assessments or examiners, cannot produce fair or consistent results. The system has also proven to be enormously time consuming, and therefore expensive, so that, especially for lower-level awards, the cost–benefit ratio is increasingly questioned (Smithers, 1993; Wolf, 1994).

The mixed reception given to NVQs by industry also reflects how problematic the pursuit of 'validity' can be. Industries are encouraged to use NVQs for in-house training of their workers, apprentices, and government-sponsored trainees, and can receive government subsidies for a good part of this activity. From the start, industry representatives pushed consistently for qualifications as close as possible to the very particular and short-term needs of their industry. The result was a proliferation of occupational standards and awards. Even so, the tension has not been resolved: one of the major retail chains in the UK, whose adoption of retail NVQs as the basis of their staff training was heralded as an example of the latter's utility, has abandoned them in favour of training more directly adapted to the company's in-house practice. The dilemma is a genuine one. Firms want flexible staff with broad skills because they know that jobs and markets will change. However, they do not know, any more than the rest of us, exactly how they will change: and in the meantime must concentrate on effective training within a much shorter time-horizon.

The Netherlands has also been attracted by the notion of competence – perhaps reflecting the fact that, like England, it has both a strong academic educational research community and a tradition of writing and research on assessment. The Dutch tradition is largely school based, like that of France, but with a relatively strong apprenticeship tradition. The school system itself is extremely hierarchical and structured, with divisions between programmes (and schools) starting at age 13 or 14. At that point there are no fewer than four alternatives, each with its own destination (university, higher vocational education, senior vocational education, apprenticeship).

Recent reforms (implemented in autumn 1993) are intended to bring the content and delivery of both apprenticeship and senior vocational education (which is school based) closer to the requirements of industry – to increase their validity. As the Dutch Ministry of Education and Science explains, the major element of the new legislation 'is the new relationship it establishes with the business world. The wishes of the business community are to be a decisive factor in shaping courses (both with regard to new courses and to changes in or abolition of existing courses)' (Netherlands Ministry of Education & Science, 1993, p 10).

Rather than examination syllabuses there are to be attainment targets developed by a partnership of employer organizations, trade unions, and government agencies, who will define the 'knowledge, skills and professional attitudes pupils should minimally attain' (van den Dool, 1993). The purpose is very similar to that behind the English reforms: to increase the validity of vocational programmes by making them much more directly a function of industrial and commercial requirements. However, there are also major differences in delivery. The groups which set the attainment targets represent a much wider range of organizations than in England, where lead bodies are employer-led and dominated. Moreover, while NVQs are based directly and entirely on the 'standards' which lead bodies produce, in the Netherlands, the targets will be translated into syllabuses (or 'standards') by the Ministry of Education. A similarity between the two systems is the delegation of the actual assessment process – both the devising of assessments and their marking – to those delivering the training.

The workplace as validator

French vocational education has been even more overwhelmingly school-based than that of the Netherlands. Although apprenticeships exist, they enjoy very low status: and attempts to encourage and enlarge the apprenticeship system (which is in the charge of the Ministry of Employment) have to date been largely unsuccessful. Moreover, the importance attached to including a major general education component in all vocational awards militates against expansion of apprenticeship. Apprentices have to pass exactly the same examinations as those in full-time institutions, yet they spend far less time in the classroom. Given the way the examinations are structured, their general superiority on practical skills is rarely enough in itself to outweigh their relative disadvantage on the 'educational' parts of the course.

Nonetheless, the French have also been concerned to increase the validity of their vocational qualifications. They have done so in part by increasing the role of industrial consultative committees in the development of new awards, and partly by adopting a language of 'objectives' which are not dissimilar in form (though generally far less specific and more wide-ranging) to the 'performance criteria' of English standards of competence. All awards (vocational and purely academic) are governed by detailed regulations. The syllabus – the *référentiel* – is expressed in objective terms: for example, carrying out a fault diagnosis, or drawing up a cutting list. However, far more detail is given than in England about the process of delivery, so that teachers not only have far more of a conventional syllabus to work from but also clear requirements and recommendations about how much time, for example, should be spent on each area.

Equally important, however, is the introduction of direct workplace experience. The requirement for such experience applies to every variety of *baccalauréat professionnel* (*bac pro*) – the vocational *baccalauréat*. This qualification is formally equivalent to the academic *baccalauréat* though designed for labour market entry rather than entry into higher education. It has grown rapidly since its introduction in the late 1980s: part of a general upsurge whereby young French people stay on in larger and larger numbers, faced with high youth unemployment, a spiralling qualification race and government policy which is devoted to increasing the educational level of school leavers.

A *bac pro* course lasts two years, and every student must spend 16 weeks in total (generally 8 weeks a year) in industry. These periods are governed by what is, in effect, a training contract with the host enterprise, laying out objectives. Without this workplace experience, the pupil cannot obtain their diploma.

However, whereas English NVQs demand extremely detailed assessment practices, and careful recording of exactly which performance criteria have been achieved, the French *bac pro* is far less prescriptive in what it demands of the employer. The regulations state quite explicitly that the activities which young people follow can be very varied (albeit within the general area of study). The purpose of their time in the workplace is to develop 'autonomy, a sense of responsibility, and creativity', for them to learn to work in a 'real-life situation', and to understand how enterprises operate. In some cases, work experience may be carefully structured by the school, in others rather less so. Either way, for the purposes of passing and obtaining their *bac*, it is still the final examinations that matter, not how students actually perform during their work experience. And while the examinations are clearly 'vocational' in that they may contain practical tests (and mathematics or French placed in the context of the relevant vocational area), the way they are marked, and their general tenor, remains emphatically that of the education system.

Since reform of vocational education, and vocational assessment, is the general pattern in Europe at present, it is important to note that the 'Dual System' countries are an exception to this rule. It would be misleading to describe the German system as unchanging: here, as elsewhere, more and more young people follow the academic stream through high school into higher education, and a large number of the more desirable apprenticeships are now taken up not by 16 or 17-year-olds, but by young people who have obtained their *Abitur* (ie, the high school leaving examination which provides entry into higher education). In the former East Germany the dearth of functioning businesses makes it very difficult to run an apprenticeship system. Over the last decade the academic demands of many apprenticeships have been increased, creating fears that they are becoming too demanding for a significant group of young people: and there is general worry about costs, and the unwillingness of young people to enter apprenticeships in manual occupations such as construction.

In general, however, stability is the notable feature of the system, deriving in large part from the way the dual system is intertwined with firms' hiring practices and their internal training and promotion systems (Rose and Wignanek, 1991). Equally important is the way that the system is organized and updated: a very slow but extremely consensus-based affair whereby the central government institute with responsibility for apprenticeships (the BIBB) consults with employers, unions and public agencies (the 'social partners') and develops joint proposals.

German apprenticeships involve formal examinations: but the format of these has changed little in recent years and they are, in any case, not the key determinant of what is learned – unlike the other countries discussed here, which are far more assessment-driven. Formal testing is the responsibility of the local chambers of commerce, and of committees (drawn from local employers) who take charge of particular vocational areas. Candidates take both practical and written tests – the former often occupying the better part of a day, the latter generally multiple-choice tests bought in from one of the specialized national agencies producing such papers. The tests – particularly the practical ones – are certainly demanding, but what is interesting is the pass rate: over 90 per cent in most occupations. Obviously, firms can generally be confident of bringing their apprentices up to the given standard before they take their exams.

They can do so not because the system is built around 'outcome statements', or centrally set examinations: but because it combines very detailed process regulations with long-established networks involving not only employers but over a million *Meisters*. The focus of apprenticeship reform or change in Germany is not the examinations but the training regulations, which lay down exactly what training an apprentice in a given occupation is to receive. Implementing these regulations is largely the responsibility of skilled workers who hold a *Meister* qualification and are therefore authorized as trainers. They are not assessors in any formal sense; and it is the process, not defined outcomes, to which they look.

Nonetheless, because of the tight networks that exist not only within a company, but across the area encompassed by a chamber of commerce, and because of the very intensive consultation that precedes any change, 'standards' are upheld successfully – as the final pass rates indicate. In this case, the validity of the qualifications is seen as inhering in and deriving from these processes. The stability of the German system, and its success in developing an extremely highly skilled workforce, underlines that there are alternatives to the competence or outcome-based perspective currently being adopted elsewhere.

The drive for flexibility

The second major theme in European vocational assessment and qualifications is the search for greater flexibility. This, in turn, is a response to general developments in the demand for schooling and for qualifications.

The traditional pattern for European education has been one of very marked segmentation. One academic route, often delivered in separate schools, led on to higher education and elite jobs. Children who were not admitted to this route by the age of about 14 were channelled into various types of vocational or lower-grade general education, but with no route back into the academic stream.

In recent years, there has been a huge increase in demand for academic education and for entry into university – fuelled partly by changing social patterns, producing a far larger middle class; partly by changing perceptions of the labour market, with higher long-term unemployment and lower demand for unskilled and semi-skilled labour; and partly by previous expansions in academic secondary and higher education. The more people who obtain higher level qualifications, the more are those who do not have them seen as inferior, lower-ability employees, and also the more attainable, and actively desired, does further and higher education become (see Dronkers, 1993).

The result throughout Europe has been a huge increase in the average number of years spent in full-time education, and a rejection by pupils and parents of traditional vocational education courses and qualifications. There are, of course, major differences between countries in the speed and degree with which this has occurred, just as there are differences in the pattern of provision for vocational awards. However, the general trend has been the same, as has been the response: to make it much easier, at least in formal terms, to move from a vocational stream over to extended technical and higher education.

We noted earlier that Germany has had the most stable form of provision in the vocational education and training area. However, these changes are also very evident here. Most German states retain a pattern of tripartite education for full time secondary schooling: the academic *Gymnasium*, the vocational *Hauptschule*, and, in the middle, the *Realschule*, which combines a fairly demanding academic curriculum with technical subjects. In the last 20 years, enrolments in the *Gymnasium* have increased markedly, with more and more pupils obtaining the *Abitur*: while enrolments in the *Realschule*, and numbers obtaining its final award, have grown even faster. The *Hauptschule*, the traditional entry point for apprenticeship, is increasingly rejected and stigmatized. Entry into choice apprenticeships is reserved for those with *Realschule* or *Gymnasium* backgrounds. Moreover, employers are finding that, to attract high quality apprentices, they must offer routes to further study and qualification. In manufacturing and technical areas, there is already a well-established sector of higher technical institutes, whose degrees are highly respected. However, now entrants into other sectors – banking, insurance – also want higher education, to the extent that these industries are developing their own higher institutions.

Germany has responded to the change without altering the underlying structure of the academic/vocational divide. Most other countries have chosen, instead, to attack the formal barriers. The French *baccalauréat professionnel* is a particularly clear example of this.

The French system has traditionally divided, irrevocably, at around age 15 or 16 (with three years of secondary education still to go). At that point, less-academic pupils would be channelled into vocational awards, in separate vocational high schools, and others would continue onto the *baccalauréat* programme. Obtaining the *bac* gave the automatic right of entry into higher education (although some faculties and institutions now operate *numerus clausus*: and the rest reduce their numbers drastically after the first or second year on the basis of examination results). The French employment market, with extremely high levels of youth unemployment, has produced a particularly rapid qualification spiral, as young people constantly try to position themselves strongly, and impress potential employers. Parents and students have increasingly resisted being 'counselled' into vocational schools, preferring instead to repeat years in the mainstream as often as allowed.

The *bac prof* was designed in part to break this log-jam in the secondary schools. It offers a progression route which previously did not exist. It is open to students who, after two years in vocational schools, pass their *BEP*

(*Brevet d'Etudes Professionnelles* — the vocational award with a fairly high proportion of general education). The latter can, in principle, go back into the regular academic high school too, and start a technical or general (academic) *bac* — and many do, though with higher failure rates than their mainstream colleagues. However, *bac pro* registrations have also grown very quickly, recruiting largely from the *BEP* but also from students who had remained in the academic stream up to this point. What remains unclear is whether this is a solution or merely a short-term holding operation. Although the *bac pro* was conceived as a labour market entry qualification, it does, formally, count for university entrance. Those who enter with it have extremely high failure rates: but as the proportion of the labour force with degrees also continues to rise, there may be pressures to create new pathways across from the vocational route.

The Netherlands, with its extremely hierarchical and segmented system, has felt similar pressures. There have, since the 1960s, been formal routes of progress from any one stream to the next. Those graduating from a particular stage with good results have the right to move over to the next 'highest' track — for example, from senior general secondary to pre-university secondary — although they must also repeat a year. However, the numbers involved are never large.

In recent years, there has been increasing pressure on enrolments for the pre-university and senior secondary streams. In response, from 1993, selection into streams will be postponed by use of a common core or curriculum, covering the first two or three years of secondary school. However, division into the preexisting streams may still continue as well: the decision is a local one.

There has been particularly strong resistance by pupils and parents to entry into the lower vocational track (LBO), which is seen as a dustbin. The percentage of pupils there has declined; many of those in the schools are the children of migrant workers. From 1992, in response, LBO has been replaced by VBO — pre-vocational education — covering the same four-year span. The main change was to reduce the vocational content of the courses, and continue with general education, thus increasing pupils' chances of being able to return to the mainstream. Under the new law, the first two years of pre-vocational education will now be aligned with the 'common core' of basic education.

The English government originally envisaged a post-16 sector with two sorts of qualifications: A-levels (Advanced Level General Certificate of Education — academic examinations used in university entrance) and NVQs. In so doing, they were ignoring an already established alternative route to higher education and the labour market. Qualifications offered in fulltime education by BTEC (the Business and Technician Education Council) had become pre-vocational rather than vocational in nature, with large amounts of general education: and were registering a far higher growth in demand than any other vocational pathway. During the early years of NVQ implementation, students continued to choose BTEC awards in preference to the very specifically vocational NVQs. In 1992, therefore, government recognized the strength of demand and introduced General National Vocational Qualifications delivered in full-time education. The

Advanced GNVQ has been given formal parity with A-levels, and policy emphasis has been on ensuring that it is acceptable to higher education. Although the latter has generally agreed that it meets their requirements, it is in a formal sense that they have done so: and the degree to which it actually offers HE entry (or how the promise is to be reconciled with current brakes on HE expansion) is unclear.

Accreditation of prior learning (APL)

Finally, mention should be made of policies which have been adopted by a number of European countries with the purpose of increasing flexibility and access to qualifications. Accreditation of prior learning is a system whereby adults who have acquired skills may obtain formal credit for them towards a qualification without having to take a course.

The approach has been envisaged by many advocates as opening up opportunities to large numbers of adults, and as likely to become a major part of the vocational assessment system. In fact, it has generally proven very difficult and cumbersome to implement (Crowley-Bainton and Wolf, 1994). In England, where APL has been most actively promoted by government, the idea is that people should bring evidence to assessors, who can then check this against the 'standards of competence' and award either the relevant credit or a full award. However, this is necessarily a highly individualized process: and, for quality control purposes, requires the amassing of comprehensive evidence that can be checked and validated. Many candidates do not have evidence of this sort to hand: and many find that they can only cover parts of an award. It is often as easy, or cheaper, to retest such candidates from scratch, or enrol them on a course. The one area in England where the approach seems to succeed and be cost-efficient is with office skills.

In France, *bilans de competence* are described as ways of certifying already-acquired skills, and a number of centres exist which specialize in preparing these records of competences with individual candidates. However, the documents have no legal or formal status, and cannot even give exemption from assessment on the UK pattern. They are, rather, part of the extensive network of support agencies and public employment programmes which currently serve France's large unemployed population.

Finally, the Dutch are actively exploring the possibility of new means to assess prior learning. The idea, in this case, would be to develop a range of tests and assessments, and a network of assessment centres – in other words, to decouple assessment from vocational courses. Compared with the English approach, a more formal system of assessment is envisaged, but the rationale is the same: to match the demand and supply of skills more closely, and also to encourage adults to start on a new 'learning pathway' (van den Dool, 1993, p 15). These aims, in fact, encompass the main thrust of recent assessment policy in European vocational education. What remains elusive is their achievement.

References

Crowley-Bainton, T and Wolf, A (1994) *The Access to Assessment Initiative*, Sheffield: Department of Employment.

Dronkers, J (1993) 'The precarious balance between general and vocational education in the Netherlands', in Wolf (1993).

Jessup, G (1991) *Outcomes: NVQs and the Emerging Model of Education and Training*, Lewes: Falmer.

Netherlands Ministry of Education and Science (1993) *The Changing Role of Vocational and Technical Education and Science*, report to the OECD VOTEC project, Paris: OECD.

Parkes, D (1993) 'Can parity between academic and vocational awards ever be achieved? Germany in European context,' in Wolf (1993).

Prais, S J (1991) 'Vocational qualifications in Britain and Europe: theory and practice', *National Institute Economic Review*, May.

Rose, R and Wignanek, G (1991) *Training Without Trainers? How Germany Avoids Britain's Supply-Side Bottleneck*, London: Anglo-German Foundation.

Smithers, A (1993) *All Our Futures: Britain's Educational Revolution*, a *Dispatches* report on education, London: Channel 4 Television.

Soskice, D (1993) 'Social skills from mass higher education: rethinking the company-based initial training paradigm', *Oxford Review of Economic Policy*, **9**, 3, 101–13.

van den Dool, P (1993) *New trends in VET and FET: policy issues for the late '90s in the Netherlands*, paper presented to the Workshop on New Trends in Training Policy, Geneva: ILO.

Wolf, A (ed) (1993) *Parity of Esteem: Can Vocational Awards Ever Achieve High Status?* London: International Centre for Research on Assessment, Institute of Education.

Wolf, A (1994) *Competence-based Assessment*, Buckingham: Open University Press.

Wood, R (1991) *Assessment and Testing*, Cambridge: Cambridge University Press.

11. Strategies for reforming post-compulsory education and training in the Australian states

Jack Keating

The federal settlement

The 1901 Australian Constitution, which created a federation of former British colonial states, divides power and authority for administration between the states and the federal government. Responsibility for education and training was left with the states, and unlike some other areas of administration, such as taxation and industrial relations, this settlement has not until recently been a point of significant tension between the states and the federal government.

The patterns of school education were settled through a series of education acts passed in the state parliaments in the 1870s which established systems of state schools alongside Catholic and independent schools. As in the UK, upper secondary education in Australia has been accessible to most young people only since the Second World War, and has emerged on a mass scale only in recent years. Before the 1950s upper secondary education was dominated by the independent schools, a small number of Catholic schools and mainly selective state high schools.

Post-school education was served by a small number of universities based upon English and Scottish models, with a second tier of colleges of advanced education, teachers' colleges and technical institutes. Industrial training was dominated by the craft-based apprenticeship system under the authority of state industrial training authorities, which in turn was closely tied to the respective industrial interests of unions and business and an industrial relations system based upon state and national craft awards. The Technical and Further Education (TAFE) colleges under the administration of state authorities grew as a major sector in the 1970s.

Although there were significant post-Second World War federal incursions into education in the form of increased funding for higher education and funding for non-government schools, they did not represent any major interventions into patterns of authority within post-compulsory education and training. Universities continued to maintain their considerable autonomy while gratefully receiving extra Commonwealth funds. Upper secondary schooling continued to be taken by a minority of the relevant age group, with a disproportionate number located in the independent schools. The curriculum was controlled by state government-appointed statutory awarding bodies which administered curriculum and awards and which, without exception, had primarily been designed to support preparation and selection for university education. Training remained craft based and bore no direct relationship to national economic policy.

The federal settlements thus entailed not only agreement over the divisions of government responsibilities, but acknowledgment, as in England, of the independence of both education and training from national macro- and microeconomic policy. Throughout the 1980s changes in the Australian economy provoked government action which has challenged and broken down this settlement in the 1990s.

Post-compulsory education – developments towards the 1990s

The catalyst for debate over post-compulsory education and training came from the sudden rise in unemployment amongst 16- to 24-year-olds in Australia in the late 1970s. The federal government and some elements of industry responded with an attempt to locate some of the problem in the failure of schools to develop transferable work skills in young people. This was similar to the criticism of British education by Prime Minister Callaghan at Ruskin College, Oxford, in 1976. No 'Great Debate' emerged, but with the publication of A Nation At Risk in the USA (National Commission on Excellence in Education, 1983) elements of the media supported by the emerging New Right joined the fray with wider-ranging and savage attacks on school education. Claims that progressivism in school education was undermining standards and in some cases was tantamount to indoctrination were widespread in the press, and were supported by some in the university sector.

High levels of youth employment have been endemic in the Australian social and economic landscape since the late 1970s. Federal governments and, to a lesser extent, state governments have responded with a range of labour market programmes.

School education

The increase in staying-on rates in post-compulsory schooling associated with youth unemployment led all state and territory authorities to reform their upper secondary awards during the early and mid 1980s. These awards are used for selection to higher education along with a tertiary entrance rank (TER) which is derived from year 12 subject scores. This is a dominant relationship: the raison d'être of post-compulsory schooling up to the late 1970s was university entrance. This was accompanied by the comparatively low staying-on rates. In some states there was a separate system of secondary technical education that extended to the end of the compulsory years and led to the labour market and entry level training. In general, there was a lack of post-school institutionally-based vocational and technical training options. The lack of recognition of institutionally-based vocational and technical qualifications within the labour market provided a disincentive for the development of these types of programmes.

Recently reformed upper secondary arrangements have been required to accommodate a more diverse cohort of students. Yet it has been clear to all states that they cannot afford to abandon the link between year 12 assessment and certification and university selection. Attempts to diversify the curriculum have mostly taken the form of alternative or vocational courses which do not result in a TER. The major difficulty with this approach has been that only a small minority of students have taken these courses (Russell, 1993). They are duly recognized as courses for the academic failures, and the currency of their awards is very low. Cognizant of this dilemma, the awards body in one state, Victoria, took a different approach. A common award was developed and all subjects (studies) were able to contribute to the TER. Reforms were enhanced through more flexible study designs and through progressive forms of assessment. Examinations still play a part, but they do not determine the award of the certificate.

This development in Victoria incited one of the most intense public debates on education ever experienced in Australia. The new arrangements were attacked by university and some school representatives. The ensuing debate has led to a powerful reassertion of university influence over post-compulsory schooling and further changes. The study designs for mathematics and English were changed; the grading scale was trebled; there is now a greater emphasis upon external examinations; a General Achievement Test has been introduced to provide the basis for the moderation of assessment tasks completed at the school level; and students who apply for higher education places will be ranked along a percentile constructed from the assessment scores.

These changes in upper secondary curriculum and assessment have taken place against a background of rapidly increasing staying-on rates to year 12. By 1992 the 'apparent retention rates' had nationally reached the level of 77 per cent, having risen from about 35 per cent in 1982 (AEC, 1993). These levels were well in advance of those predicted in the various reports commissioned by state governments to review upper secondary awards. They have brought increased pressure upon the upper secondary awards such that most are being revised, and in some cases face a fundamental restructuring. They have also brought a belated realization on the part of the school sector that they are a symptom of a fundamental restructuring in the Australian labour market which can no longer be ignored.

In the mid 1980s a federal Labour government increased funding to higher education and places increased from 341,390 in 1982 to 559,365 in 1992. A reformist federal education minister, John Dawkins, forced major changes in the sector. Working with predominantly sympathetic state Labour governments he was able to abolish the binary system of universities and colleges of advanced education and create a *unified national system* of higher education. Other changes have included the imposition of university fees (Higher Education Contribution Scheme – HECS) and the allocation of funding including research funds in a manner which meets 'national priorities'. Needless to say these changes have been controversial.

The federal government has also formulated its education and training, incomes, labour market, and benefits and allowances policies in a manner designed to encourage higher levels of participation in post-compulsory education and training. It would appear that this approach has been effective in that full time participation rates are now comparable with those of most other OECD countries.

Upper secondary school education – an academic culture

Historically, upper secondary education in Australia has been inextricably linked to higher education. Neither the emergence of selective entry into higher education in the 1950s nor the changes in upper secondary awards in the 1980s have seriously challenged this nexus.

The upper secondary certificates require a general and academic curriculum. Those awards which provide eligibility for entry into higher education have not included a broad range of vocational or technical studies as are common within the vocational lines or programmes within upper secondary awards in Europe. Group award provisions are minimal and are designed to achieve an academic balance rather than any vocational definition, and the patterns of studies which are taken by students are commonly confined to a narrow academic range (Ainley *et al.*, 1990).

The abolition of the binary system, while bringing the benefits of diversity to higher education, has also served to reinforce the academic culture within the upper secondary curriculum. Students now apply for all HE courses through a common selection system based upon the academic TER. More recently, applications for TAFE courses have been processed through the same system, thus further reinforcing the hegemony of the rank.

The massive expansion in the higher education system through the 1980s was not matched by a corresponding expansion in institutional provision for training. Within higher education, the growth in technological and engineering courses has been slow and continues to lag behind that of other OECD countries.

The growth in full-time first-cycle post-compulsory education and training in Australia has occurred almost entirely within the comprehensive school systems, with a focus upon a general academic curriculum. This is in contrast to most other OECD countries and, in particular, to England and Wales where the later growth in participation rates has occurred predominantly in the further education sector, and more recently within the general vocational curriculum. The Australian developments also contrast with those in Scotland where the 'comprehensive tradition' is strongly held, but where the vocational modules of the Scottish Vocational Education Council (SCOTVEC) have been taken up within secondary schools (Scottish Office, 1992).

The reasons for the concentration upon general secondary schooling within this stage are complex, yet fairly consistent. Only in New South Wales have the TAFE colleges enrolled any significant numbers amongst the 16 and 17-year-old cohort and this has not led to higher rates of participation in TAFE amongst 19-year-olds in this state (DEET, 1993c), suggesting that full-time training courses have provided a limited pathway. At a formal level, agreements were reached in some states between education and training authorities that schools would have the responsibility of providing for the first cycle of vocational training. But these agreements really endorsed trends which were well established and which have been associated with the poor image of technical education and training, the lack of recognition of training credentials in the labour market, and the fact that much of Australia's postwar skills needs had been met through migration. Changes in the youth labour market and greater pressure for post-compulsory qualifications led to a drift away from technical education at the school and immediate post-school level. Even the apprenticeship system, which historically has provided entry at the immediate post-compulsory level, has now moved upmarket so that many entrants have now completed the year 12 school certificate.

The TAFE system which had developed during the 1970s maintained a poor record in full-time courses, with high dropout and poor completion records. For school leavers, TAFE became a second-rate option, and its awards had little currency in the labour market. TAFE's share of enrolments, especially amongst 16- to 17-year-olds, actually fell up until 1992 (Australian Bureau of Statistics, 1993a) and together with the more recent decline in the apprenticeship system, this represented a substantial movement away from industrial training. Australia, which has always maintained a poor record in industrial training and intermediate skills formation, thus fell further behind other OECD countries.

The overall effect of these developments has been to bring almost the entire first cycle of post-compulsory education and training into an orbit dominated by the selection procedures for higher education and expressed in the single dimension of the academic TER. Most school students aspire to higher education (DEET, 1993a) and most apply (Russell, 1993). Unmet demand for higher education places has been estimated as 44,420 in 1991–2 (Russell, 1993). This compared with overall first-year enrolments from school leavers of about 65,600. Unmet demand has risen from between 9,000 to 14,000 in 1986.

The Australian economy and training – and the breakdown of the federalist settlement

Since the mid 1980s, another set of developments has taken place which relate to structural economic problems in Australia. Structural imbalances in the economy became apparent with a major fall in commodity prices. With an export market based mainly on commodities, Australia entered into a chronic balance of payments crisis and it became apparent to the federal government that radical restructuring of the Australian economy was needed. Measures were taken to increase competitiveness within the economy. They included financial deregulation and the lowering of protection for secondary industries. They also included deflationary measures which led in 1989 to a severe recession and an acceleration in the structural changes to the labour market, including the youth labour market.

But perhaps the most successful aspect of the Federal Labour government's economic policy has been its wages policy. When first elected in 1983 it reached an Accord with the Australian Council of Trade Unions (ACTU) which provided that the unions would limit their wage claims before the Federal Industrial Commission if the government would support rises in line with cost-of-living increases and the maintenance of the social wage. The Accord has actually led to a slight lowering of real wages over the past decade, but it has become a powerful instrument in government industry and economic policy, and training policy. It has been the basis of a tripartite or corporate approach to industrial policy and economic management, similar to those of a number of the Northern European countries.

In 1985, a joint ACTU/government team visited Europe and took a particular interest in those countries which had adopted the corporatist approach to economic management, industrial policy and training. A document followed, entitled 'Australia Reconstructed', which advocated a major reconstruction of Australian industries. Emphasis was put upon flexibility in both management and work practices and general measures to increase industrial productivity, including the restructuring of industrial awards. Under the persuasion of both the government and the ACTU, the Industrial Commission adopted the approach of awarding wage increases upon the basis of productivity tradeoffs. The ACTU, for its part, encouraged unions to amalgamate and to form industry-based rather than craft-based unions. The main business organizations and large corporations have in general also supported this approach to industrial restructuring, albeit with a tendency to concentrate upon the deregulation of wages.

Part of the report dealt with training. Observing the European approaches, it urged greater effort be put into industrial training, with an emphasis upon work-based learning. The craft-based apprenticeship system could not meet the needs of modern industry with its emphasis upon multi-skilling and flexible work practices and Australia needed to increase its training effort substantially, both institutional and work based. The federal government borrowed from the French and instituted a training guarantee in order to require medium-sized and large firms to provide appropriate training for their employees. Efforts were also made to have training built into industrial awards.

These developments have provided a catalyst for the breakdown in the federalist settlement, initially in the area of training. By the 1990s the federal government's corporatist approach had firmly tied a national training approach to national economic and industrial policy. This did not directly influence school and higher education, but the continuing structural problems in the economy and the corporatist approach are now having an impact on school education in particular.

The Australian training reform agenda

The weaknesses in the Australian industry training system had by the early 1990s become apparent not only to the federal government, the ACTU and the main business organizations but also to most state and territory governments. Responsibility for training, as with schooling, lies with state and territory governments. But, with some reluctance, state governments have conceded that there is a need for some elements of a national approach in the area. Governments have now reached agreement on a variety of measures which are loosely described as the National Training Reform Agenda. Elements of this agenda include:

- competency based training;
- the recognition of prior learning;
- industry-based rather than craft-based training;
- industry control of the training system, rather than provider or institutional control;
- national industry standards and industry training advisory bodies, controlled by industry;
- a national framework for the recognition of awards and standards, and the recognition of providers;
- an open training market;
- a national credentials framework.

This agenda largely embodies the corporatist approach of federal government. It is based upon national industry standards, with representative industry bodies, and it is tied to national industry policies. It has also a commitment on the part of the federal government to increase funding for training and agreement from state and territory governments to maintain funding. This has led to the establishment of an Australian National Training Authority (ANTA) with responsibility for overall national policy and the distribution of growth funds.

This agenda contrasts with that now followed by most state and territory governments, most of which are under Conservative control and which tend to follow free-market policies. While these policies have their most manifest form in the sale of public authorities and in measures to abolish or limit the scope of industrial awards, they have also affected school education policy, with reductions in funds for government schools and much rhetoric about diversity, competition and choice. At a national level they have included resistance to the development of national curriculum and learning outcome statements and more recently some concerted efforts to resist any Commonwealth role in schooling. It has involved a rejection of the tripartite or corporatist approach, with unions in particular being excluded from policy and development.

The intersection of a national corporatist economic approach with the federalist training structure has resulted in extremely complex and overburdened bureaucratic arrangements. The Australian training system is a confusing array of industrial training advisory bodies, conflicting patterns of responsibility and authority for course development and accreditation, complex procedural arrangements, and conflicting policy directions. The emerging national and state training systems have also been criticized for their overcentralized structures, including a national standards framework which has too many levels (eight) and which provides the framework for industry standards that are too rigidly defined (Sweet, 1993a).

In 1991, the federal government proposed a new federalist settlement which involved the Commonwealth taking full responsibility for higher education and training and its withdrawal from any role in school education. Although the two largest states, New South Wales and Victoria, were more receptive towards this proposal, the opposition from other states led to the compromise of the establishment of ANTA. This compromise settlement has left some major contradictions between national and state policies and has led to continuing crtiticism. Overall industry training arrangements have been criticized for bureaucracy and lack of industry participation and commitment (Sweet 1993).

The future role of TAFE colleges, which have so far maintained relative independence, is also uncertain. Should they continue to be providers of the off-the-job elements of the remaining entry level training programmes and labour market programmes, and providers of adult, hobby and short courses? Or should they attempt to move up market and provide advanced technical training?

Another issue is that of entry-level training. As in the UK, the number of apprenticeship places has fallen and traineeships modelled on the British Youth Training Scheme have never been able to provide the 70,000 places that were originally envisaged (Kirby, 1985). In 1992 there were only 7,334 places compared with 13,659 in 1988 (ABS, 1993a and b). Given the lack of industrial places, consideration has to be given to the type of initial vocational education and training which can be more broadly available in Australia. Part of this issue is which institutions (TAFE colleges, schools or other bodies) should act as providers. The states, and their various bureaucracies, have adopted different approaches towards this issue. The future of entry-level training is complicated not only by the changes in industrial structures and awards in Australia, but also by the changes in industrial relations practices. The federal government has supported a movement away from national craft-based and industrial awards towards enterprise level bargaining and awards. New entry-level arrangements will need to be able to accommodate these changes (Curtain, forthcoming).

Education – a corporate federalism?

The advent of a corporatist approach originating in national economic policies has some similarities with developments in the UK. There are also some obvious dissimilarities in that the initiatives of the federal government in Australia have not matched the intensity of the attacks by the Thatcher government upon what it saw as vested interests in schools, universities and Local Education Authorities (LEAs). Nor has the British government been eager to facilitate the participation of the unions in education and training matters. Yet the view which developed within

British government, post-Ruskin, that the 'secret garden' of the academic curriculum needed to be open to influences which more closely matched the reality of the workplace and working life, has been shared by the Australian government, which has utilized the corporatist approach in pursuing this view, largely because the federalist arrangements have limited alternative approaches.

Most of the state governments which administer the school systems have little attachment to corporatism and have been lukewarm about these developments. With three states changing to market-oriented Conservative governments in 1993, more open resistance has come from government and some university elements. Industry, however, remains strongly behind national developments. In a philosophical sense it is possible to describe this situation in Australia as the clash of two cultures: the education system's liberal academic tradition, with its syllabus and exam-based approaches; and the world of work and industry favouring competencies and modular approaches.

These differences should not be exaggerated. As Dale *et al* (1990) point out, the liberal academic ideal is held by almost nobody outside of schools and universities, and senior schooling and higher education is highly vocational in its intent. But in terms of the influences upon the curriculum, the free-market approach of Australian state governments is quite at ease with a mainstream academic school curriculum that delivers a conservatively conceived university entrance rank, but which in itself is highly vocationally directed. Just as the liberal ideal grew comfortably within the utilitarian goals of the emerging nineteenth-century British middle class, the general academic curriculum of liberal educationalists is less likely to be challenged by the free-market philosophies which have their more recent origins in the New Right movements of the 1970s and 80s, and their most recent hegemony in Conservative state governments. This is even more likely within a federalist settlement which has freed state governments from any significant macro- and microeconomic responsibilities.

Comparisons with the UK can be extended to the Technical and Vocational Education Initiative (TVEI) which represented a corporatist approach from the Manpower Services Commission and the Department of Employment. At the time it provided a challenge to the source and forms of the senior school curriculum. It has proven, ultimately, to be more decentralized and less authoritarian than the academic curriculum, and this may well prove to be the case in Australia. Like the corporatist approach in Australia, it has its origins in microeconomic policy. Thus the British government has been described as maintaining a contradictory approach to senior schooling as expressed bureaucratically through the Department for Education and the Department of Employment. In Australia the same contradiction is expressed through federalism, intensified through political circumstances. The irony for the liberal educationalists is their association with class interests.

Entry level training

A second major report (ESFC, 1992) with a potential impact upon post-compulsory arrangements came in 1992 from the Employment and Skills Formation Council (ESFC) of the National Board of Employment, Education and Training (NBEET). This is a body established by the federal government and as such its report into entry-level training, unlike the earlier Finn Review (AEC, 1991), is not directly influenced by state governments. The Council is chaired by Laurie Carmichael, a former trade unionist who, as the assistant secretary of the ACTU, had been the principal author of *Australia Reconstructed*.

Not surprisingly, the report, now known as the Carmichael Report, reflected the themes of *Australia Reconstructed*, including the corporatist approach to training. It recommended the establishment of a new system of entry-level training based upon a single national award, the Australian Vocational Certificate (AVC); competency based training; industrial rather than craft-based training, incorporating on-the-job training; and the establishment of a training wage based upon the principle of industry's capacity to pay.

While agreement could not be reached between the industrial parties on this last point the report gained qualified support from government (including most state governments), unions, major business organizations and some of the major corporations. The federal government has provided funds for a number of pilot projects, known as Australian Vocational Certificate Training System pilots, which operated in 1993, and further pilots in 1994. A national approach was endorsed through the establishment of the Australian National Training Authority.

The Carmichael Report has characteristically strayed well beyond its brief in ruminating on teaching practices in schools, proposing a year 13, and recommending structural changes to schools, but it was inevitable that a report which concerns the reestablishment of a mass system of entry level training should affect that sector where most of the potential participants in such a system are currently located. It should not be surprising, therefore, that almost half of the AVCTS pilot programmes involve schools, and that there is something of an emerging recognition that schools will be the principal institutional providers of the initial levels of the certificate. It is likely that this will become the official policy of at least one state: Queensland.

There are tensions in these developments. The curriculum, assessment and award arrangements for these trial entry-level programmes remain considerably different from those of the mainstream school certificates. The AVCTS is based upon national industry standards, is expressed in terms of competencies and requires periods of structured on-the-job learning and assessment. Furthermore, there is a range of other vocational education developments in schools which incorporate some or all of these features, and so far the state-based schools awards bodies have shown some reluctance in accommodating them.

Most vocational courses, including the AVCTS pilots, are taken by students who have achieved poor results at school, and as a consequence there are high dropout and low completion rates for these courses, a trend which has characterized full-time TAFE certificate level courses. This is of concern to industry, which is keen to attract the enthusiastic and successful students. The problem remains that the non-academic courses which do not lead to higher education courses are regarded by most students as second best. There are signs that this situation may be changing. Enrolments in TAFE courses have increased and unmet demand for university places is falling. Whether this is a sign of a change in preferences on the part of school leavers or reflects the fact that more students are facing up to the reality of the choices available to them remains to be seen.

There are advantages in locating initial vocational preparation within the schools. The bulk of the relevant cohort is currently located in schools and the geographical spread of schools makes them more accessible than TAFE colleges. School-age students can be placed in work locations in ways which avoid the industrial problems associated with apprentices, and which act as a disincentive for industry. Moreover, it appears that industry is more receptive to school students than might have been thought (see Lepani and Currie, 1993). From the student point of view, vocationally based courses can have incentives which are not only associated with changed styles of learning but which are created through structured pathways into post school education and training programmes and employment.

For school systems there would appear to be little choice in this matter. General academic courses cannot accommodate the almost 80 per cent of young people who stay on to year 12, and in the absence of more diverse and structured arrangements staying-on rates will fall, or other providers, including TAFE, will take their share of the market. In fact there are already signs that this is happening, and if this trend continues it will be tragic as its represents a great opportunity lost. Australia has enjoyed a rather unusual situation. It has managed to gain very high school staying-on rates without any significant restructuring of post-compulsory schooling. A falling away in these rates and the opening up of non-school vocational courses for the 16- to 17-year-old cohort will represent a return to the past, where these courses maintained very poor outcomes and were regarded as residual. Furthermore, it is likely that such programmes will articulate very poorly with both the labour market and TAFE programmes as the latter become more advanced and more valued by a wider range of the cohort.

In the same manner, vocational programmes in schools will need to shake off their image as low level and residual. To achieve this they will need to be substantially expanded, so that they reach middle-level students. Measures to ensure that students reach reasonably high and common standards at the end of the compulsory years, as is the case in a number of European countries, are also important if 'alternative' post-compulsory programmes are to be recognized as valuable and maintain strong currency within the labour market.

The European model that seems to be most attractive in the Australian situation is that of Sweden. The upper secondary curriculum, with a set of

2 theoretical and 14 vocational programmes with a common core of subjects, is not incompatible with the comprehensive approach adopted by most state authorities in Australia. Apprenticeships as variations of programmes in Sweden and the common work placements within the vocational lines would also match the arrangements for the first level of the Australian Vocational Certificate.

But it is highly unlikely that the federalist arrangements would allow such a consistent national approach in Australia. The approaches developed within some of the vocational programmes in France may offer more potential. The *baccalauréat professionel* in particular offers features which would meet both the constitutions and criticisms of the new entry-level training arrangements in Australia. It is incorporated within the *baccalauréat* award structure with a common core of subjects. It is industry based rather than craft based, with industry participation at local and regional levels. And it incorporates a moderate amount of work-based learning.

States such as Queensland are moving towards a recognition that schools will play a major role in initial vocational preparation and that they will become the major providers of the first and possibly further levels of the new Australian Vocational Certificate Training System. If schools should develop this role in Australia, the industry-based vocational *baccalauréat* may offer some useful lessons on how to bring together general and vocational curricula; the demands of state school authorities and a national training system; and the academic traditions of school education and the needs of industry.

But the substantial issue in Australia concerns the major transition phase from year 12 to post-school employment, education and training. The dominant university oriented paradigm and the hegemony of the tertiary entrance rank within upper secondary school education, will need to be challenged. The world of work, industry and the 'social partners' will need to claim the post-compulsory years as a legitimate sphere of influence. Whether this can be achieved through the vehicle of a national training system that represents a new and more productive federalist settlement remains to be seen.

References

Ainley, J, Jones, W, and Navaratran, K (1990) *Subject Choice in Senior Secondary Schools*, Canberra: Australian Government Publishing Service.

Australian Bureau of Statistics (1992) *Education and training in Australia*, Cat No 4224.0, Canberra: Australian Government Printing Service.

Australian Bureau of Statistics (1993a) 'Transition from education to work', Cat No 6227.0, unpublished table (reproduced in Sweet, 1993).

Australian Bureau of Statistics (1993b) *Labour Force Statistics and Educational Attainment in Australia*, Canberra: Australian Government Printing Service.

AEC (Australian Education Council) (1991) *Young People's Participation in Post Compulsory Education and Training*, report of the AEC Review Committee, Canberra: Australian Government Printing Office.

AEC (1993) *National Report on Schooling in Australia 1992: Statistical Index*, Melbourne: Curriculum Corporation.

Curtain, R (forthcoming) *Has the Apprenticeship System a Future?: The Impact of Labour*

Market Reforms on Structured Entry Level Training, report commissioned by the Department of Employment, Education and Training, Canberra: Department of Employment, Education and Training.

Dale, R et al (1990) *The TVEI Story*, London: Open University Press.

DEET (Department of Employment, Education and Training) (1993a) *New South Wales Year 10–12 Students' Attitudes to Post compulsory Education and Training*, Canberra: Australian Government Printing Service.

DEET (Higher Education Division) (1993b) *Entering Higher Education in the 1980s*, Canberra: Australian Government Printing Service.

DEET (1993c) *Education Participation Rates 1992*, Canberra: Australian Government Printing Service.

Employment Skills Formation Council [ESFC], National Board for Employment, Education and Training (1992) *The Australian Vocational Certificate Training System*, Canberra: Australian Government Printing Office.

Kirby, P (1985) *Report of the Committee of Inquiry into Labour Market Programs*, Canberra: Australian Government Printing Service.

Lepani, B, and Currie, J (1993) *Workplace Learning in NSW Senior Secondary Courses*, Sydney: Australian Centre for Innovation and International Competitiveness, University of Sydney.

National Commission on Excellence in Education (1983) *A Nation at Risk*, Washington, DC: US Department of Education.

Russell J (1993) *Patterns and pathways in post compulsory schooling: report to the Schools Council, National Board of Employment, Education and Training*, Unpublished.

Scottish Office (1992) *Statistical Bulletin*, Education Series edn/Et1992/6, Edinburgh: Government Statistical Service.

Sweet, R (1993) *A Client-Focused Vocational Education and Training System?* Sydney: Dusseldorp Skills Forum.

12. Education as a foundation for work? The efficiency and problems of the Japanese upper-secondary school

Akio Inui and Tsuneo Hosogane

The features of Japanese upper-secondary schools

The most remarkable characteristic of Japanese upper-secondary education is the domination of a particular style of general curriculum. This has far broader content than a British A-level curriculum, and is more academic than that found in many US high schools. It is provided not only to those who go on to university but also to many of those who enter the workforce directly. It does seem to prepare students for work: one reason for the competitiveness of Japanese industry seems to be that it produces a large, competent and homogeneous labour force. Some regard this upper secondary curriculum as a significant part of the excellence of the Japanese school system (HMI, 1991).

The Japanese upper-secondary education system has worked very well in supplying the labour force for the last few decades. However, this is not only because it is good in itself but also because it works as a sub-system of social competition. Strong competition dominated both schools and companies throughout the period of high economic growth that started in the sixties. This has compelled people to work hard in school as well as for the company. But it has also resulted in some serious problems, such as *karoshi* (death from overwork) among adults and *toko-kyohi* (neurotic school absenteeism) among young people. Therefore, we should look at the structure of social competition when we examine the labour market in relation to the performance of the education system, and should consider both the advantages and the disadvantages of the latter.

In this chapter, we concentrate on the upper secondary school system and the labour market as they existed from the sixties to the eighties. These patterns have been the most stable in postwar Japanese history, and vital to the growth of Japan's present-day economic power. Since the late eighties the school system has gradually changed, as has the structure of the labour market. We will refer to these changes in the last section.

Japanese upper-secondary education has some features that distinguish it from its counterparts in the other industrialized nations. First, although it is not compulsory, upper secondary education is virtually universal in Japan. The enrolment rate (at the age of 16) is over 95 per cent, and more than 90 per cent of the population graduate. Second, it is dominated by general courses. Three-quarters of upper-secondary students follow general courses, which are mostly academic and differ only slightly. Third, there is a strict streaming system among schools. Every upper-secondary school, including those that provide vocational courses, is graded according to difficulty of entrance, and the primary consideration for almost all applicants when applying is their own achievement level. Therefore, although more than 95 per cent of students go to public lower-secondary schools, each of which has a separate catchment area and no streaming, almost all pupils are confronted with streaming in the spring after their fifteenth birthday. Fourth, the high achievement is to some degree a mirage. For example, according to the IEA's international study of maths education, the achievement of Japanese students is the highest at 13 years old and second highest at the last year of secondary school (OECD, 1992). However, a look at the nature of this achievement reveals serious imbalances. Japanese students are good at memorization and calculation, but not at comprehension, analysis or application. Fifth, the Japanese system of post-compulsory education offers little vocational education and training before employment (Sako and Dore, 1988). At the upper-secondary stage, fewer than a quarter take vocational courses, and about half of a vocational curriculum is occupied by academic subjects. (The content of such subjects as maths and English is chosen less for immediate applicability than as a basis for university-level study.) Therefore, most young people enter the labour market without any particular vocational skill. Sixth, in spite of its general or academic character, it is closely linked with the labour market via a school placement system that efficiently supplies companies with hardworking employees.

These features partly date from the formation of the school system. As we shall show below, the school system was moulded by US-influenced postwar reform together with government policy (especially in the early sixties). However, the actual functions of the system have been defined in a social and particularly a corporate context. We shall therefore examine the function of social competition in section 3. Lastly we shall consider some contemporary problems.

Historical development since the war

The Japanese school system was reorganized in 1947, and the upper-secondary school system started in 1948. The new system of secondary education consists of a compulsory lower secondary school to age 15, and an optional upper-secondary school for three more years (*chugakko* and *kotogakko* respectively; also commonly referred to as junior high school and senior high school). Before the war, by contrast, only a few pupils (fewer than 20 per cent in the 1930s) went on to secondary school. A great number of pupils went to work directly after primary (age 6 to 12) or upper-primary school (age 12 to 14). There were three kinds of secondary schools, each with a selective examination: *chugakko* and *koto-jogakko* respectively were boys' and girls' schools with an academic curriculum, and *jitsugyo-gakko* were vocational schools.

The prewar system discriminated by sex and between general education on the one hand and vocational on the other. The most important part of postwar reform, therefore, was to unify and expand the secondary school system. The Ministry of Education intended to open upper-secondary education to all, and eventually to make it compulsory. Selective admission would continue only exceptionally, where the number of applicants exceeded that of places. They intended that every upper-secondary school would have a fairly comprehensive curriculum, be coeducational, and have a separate catchment area. The aim was to guarantee a unified upper-secondary school system.

The comprehensive curriculum consisted of general and vocational subjects and was available to all students, who were expected to study both compulsory general subjects and a large number of optional subjects, both general and vocational. A separate catchment area for each school was introduced in order to abolish school rank and to move in the direction of community schools. However, these principles were not implemented sufficiently.

In the mid 1950s, a change in government policy led to a change in the upper-secondary education system. The revision of the curriculum in 1955 led to general courses directed towards university entrance. Universities also specified subjects to be taken in upper-secondary school. As their demands centred on academic subjects, the status of vocational and non-academic subjects diminished. At the same time, business circles pleaded for better vocational education. As a result, many comprehensive schools came to provide either a general or a vocational course.

In the early sixties, there was another major change involving expansion and increased competition. The enrolment ratio of upper-secondary education had been rapidly increasing since the late fifties, and the baby-boom generation was entering upper-secondary school. The enrolment ratio, 51 per cent in 1955, increased to 62 per cent in 1960 and reached 71 per cent in 1965. However, this increase was not enough to cope with vastly increased numbers of teenagers, from families that increasingly had both the desire and the financial ability to have them educated. The number of 15-year-olds, 1,663,000 in 1955, reached a peak of 2,491,000 in 1965.

Government policy further stimulated competition. The Ministry of Education reversed its policy that had aimed at upper-secondary education for all, and introduced selective entrance examinations. It also enlarged the catchment areas for general courses at public upper-secondary schools. In most of Japan's prefectures, each catchment area has since included several schools. In 1952, 23 prefectures had separate catchment areas and 23 had joint catchment areas; by 1964, the former number had shrunk to three.

In the sixties, Japan needed a large increase in the number of upper-secondary schools. Partly because of government reluctance to increase the number of public schools, the eventual increase largely came from additional private schools. The number of students in private upper-secondary schools more than trebled in a decade, from 512,000 in 1955 to 1,665,000 in 1965. There are no limits to the catchment areas of private schools, most of which were and have remained ranked at or below the level of public schools.

Therefore, when upper-secondary education became universal, a selective and competitive entrance system did too. Students typically chose to apply to a few schools from several public ones and a larger number of private ones. As a result, all the upper-secondary schools in a given area were ranked and competition among students in lower-secondary school was universal. Rank was based on academic achievement as shown in the entrance examination. These tests were in five subjects: Japanese, mathematics, social studies, science and English. There was almost no room for personal preference.

Most of the features mentioned in section one came about in the sixties. From the late sixties to the mid seventies, the system was comparatively stable. The enrolment rate continued to increase, reaching 91 per cent in 1975. Any general course, no matter how low it was ranked, had an absolute advantage over any vocational course. Students and parents preferred general courses, and many new schools offering general courses were established, particularly in metropolitan areas. Most of these new schools were ranked low, and schools became ranked more strictly.

Since the mid seventies, another structural change has resulted from increasing pressure of competition on the upper-secondary school system. One reason was a halt in the increase of university enrolment. The university enrolment ratio, 17 per cent in 1960, increased to 34 per cent in 1975 but since then has stayed at around 30 per cent, partly due to government policy. Another reason was a sudden decrease in the demand for young workers in the mid seventies. We shall discuss this decrease further in the next section. These changes have virtually achieved a three-way division of upper-secondary schools according to their students' destination. Upper-ranked general courses have become more academic and more preparatory for university. Most vocational courses have gained in desirability because they can more easily lead to permanent employment than can lower-ranked general courses. These in turn have run into many difficulties, as they can secure neither university entrance nor desirable employment.

The increased competition has led to many conflicts, such as school disorder and low self-confidence among students. In the eighties, the government was forced to acknowledge these problems. For example, an April 1991 report of Chuo-Kyoiku-Shingikai (Central Council for Education) pointed to the 'ill effects of excessive competition for entrance', and recommended some reform to relieve this. Actually the Ministry of Education has been proposing a reorganization of upper-secondary schools since the early eighties. It has been propounding a 'new diversification' of upper-secondary education, centring on the diversification of general courses. Furthermore, it has been pushing for a complementary reform of upper-secondary school entrance examinations that would allow for more diversity in selection methods.

Upper-secondary school and the labour market

The upper-secondary school contributes to Japanese industry in two ways. First, it provides a broad academic foundation for what has been termed 'Japanese-style employment'. This encompasses the core workers of large companies, which recruit directly from school or university with little regard to specific abilities or skills, and thereafter continually train their employees in company-specific knowledge and skills (McCormick, 1991). Therefore, companies expect school and university to provide not specific abilities and skills but a broad foundation for further training. The generalist tendency of upper-secondary schools suits this.

Second and more important is the structure of competition. A unified structure of competition within school is synchronized with corporate competition. It works very well as a means of occupational selection, and also forms a student character that is amenable to the competitive style of labour management within the company.

A feature of the competitive structure that links school or university with the labour market is that those entering jobs not only at a higher but also at an intermediate or lower level enter a meritocracy (Kariya, 1992). School or university is combined with the labour market in a unified and closed articulation (Inui, 1993a); and in upper-secondary school, competition according to academic criteria also involves those who enter the workforce directly.

The wide compass of this meritocracy is an outcome of the school placement system combined with school ranking. The former means that the school handles job placement for its own students. Each school receives job-offer forms directly from companies, which select schools according to factors such as their ranking and the relationships formed through past recruitment. Students ordinarily choose jobs from these offerings, and apply through their schools. Therefore students' employment prospects differ between schools. Furthermore, the school greatly affects the students' choice and the employers' selection, mainly based on grades (Rosenbaum and Kariya, 1989).

The school placement system was prescribed by the Employment Stabilization Act of 1947, but it is only since the sixties, when the present corporate structure came about, that the system has worked adequately. Central to this corporate structure is the strong loyalty of employees to the company (Watanabe, 1990), which in turn depends on competition among the workers.

Japanese-style employment, despite its other names of 'lifelong employment' and 'the seniority system', actually involves a degree of competition. Core workers of a large company are recruited directly from school and university, and all start at a wage and rank determined by their educational career. They are evaluated every year, and the result affects their salary as well as their chances for training and promotion. Although they start as equals, the differences among them increase greatly as the years go by.

Evaluation involves not only achievement and specific abilities, but also competence for different jobs within the company and attitude, which involves company loyalty (Kumazawa, 1989). Career routes in a company tend to lead the worker through a very wide range of sections and jobs. This individual evaluation system also applies to blue-collar workers. The union has virtually no control over the evaluation.

It was in the sixties when this labour management system was established. From the late fifties, the government and Nikkeiren (Japan Federation of Employers Association) strived to reorganize labour management in order to catch up with the West. At first they tried to introduce the Western model, but eventually Nikkeiren broadened its application of the system of lifelong employment combined with competition, in part to retain workers' conformity and company loyalty. Until that time, large companies had offered lifelong employment to white-collar workers and a very small core of blue-collar workers; the system of recruiting new graduates did not yet exist, and recruitment of workers directly from school was unusual for large and small companies alike.

However, since the sixties, large companies have come to recruit new graduates, even for a wide range of blue-collar jobs. Moreover, a growing number of large companies have gained major influence in the youth labour market. Rapid industrialization starting in the late fifties increased the number of employees in the manufacturing sector enormously, and among them the percentage working for large companies also increased. Large companies wanted young workers who could adapt to new technology (see Table 12.1). This was a job market for which the school placement system worked well. Rapid industrialization also changed people's career prospects. In the early fifties nearly half of the working population was in farming. The ratio of employees, 41 per cent in 1955, reached 64 per cent in 1970. Company employment became a typical prospect even for the children of peasants, and entering upper-secondary school became the most reliable way to get a clerical or other lifetime job in a large company. The school placement system, which in 1956 covered only 47 per cent of those entering the workforce directly from lower-secondary school and 59 per cent from upper-secondary school, accounted for about 70 and 80 per cent respectively in the sixties.

In the early sixties, the government tried to reorganize the upper-

Table 12.1 *New graduate employees by company scale (Graduates of lower- and upper-secondary school)*

Year	Firms with more than 500 workers (%)		Firms with fewer than 99 workers (%)	
	Lower	Upper	Lower	Upper
1957	16.0	17.3	63.7	60.0
1960	23.6	22.9	49.8	48.1
1965	33.9	41.8	36.5	28.2
1970	37.0	44.6	35.5	25.4
1975	30.2	47.8	41.6	23.3

secondary system. The main purpose was diversification of upper-secondary schools to provide job-specific abilities and skills. This policy was combined with a Western-style modernization of labour management, a modernization that would end lifelong employment and the conventional seniority system, and organize an open labour market, link placement with specific skills and abilities, and pay according to the particular job and performance (Keizai-Shingi-Kai, 1963). However, and contrary to expectations, the labour market was not enthusiastic about a diversity of qualifications. Companies preferred graduates of higher-ranked general courses over graduates of technical or commercial courses because of the general competence and trainability of the former. Moreover, parents preferred general courses because of their wider career prospects and the possibility of entering university, and demanded an increase in general rather than vocational courses.

These objections modified the diversification policy. Diversity in upper-secondary courses did not help to form a job-specific labour force; rather, it worked almost exclusively to indicate the school's rank. General courses were ranked highest, then commercial, followed by technical and lastly by agricultural. The ratio of students taking general courses, below 60 per cent in the sixties, increased to 63 per cent in 1975 and 72 per cent in 1985. Furthermore, the schools providing each of these kinds of courses were strictly ranked according to the single yardstick of the achievement at lower-secondary school required for entry. The competitive structure spanning school and work was not diversified, but remained unified.

In the late seventies, when the Japanese economy experienced the oil crises and a subsequent recession, the social environment changed a little. The demand for labour fell rapidly and companies of all sizes decreased recruitment. Many jobs formerly done by the permanent workers of a large company were given to part-time or temporary workers or farmed out to smaller companies paying lower wages. Many middle-aged workers were transferred to smaller companies.

On the one hand such changes increased unemployment and the number of workers, especially young workers, who depended on a succession of short-term job contracts. On the other, they strongly stimulated competition both within the company and at school. Increased competition within the company reinforced loyalty and increased productivity (Watanabe, 1990). The productivity increase of Japanese industry from the late seventies was partly due to the swift introduction of new technology, and partly due to more demanding competition, which forced people to work harder.

The sudden decrease in job offers hurt upper secondary schools. Some lower-ranked schools could not attract sufficient job offers of any kind. More students wanted to go on to university and thereby improve their job prospects, and others decided to enter university or pursue some form of further education after failing to get a job. These trends were exacerbated by a competitive atmosphere in society as a whole and fuelled a further increase in competition across the educational system. There were more applicants for those private lower-secondary schools that were affiliated with upper-secondary schools successful at placing their graduates with prestigious universities. Evening and Sunday crammer schools attracted enormous numbers of pupils.

As a result of all this, and in addition to the *de facto* three-way division described above in section 2, severe problems afflict upper-secondary schools, particularly in those low-ranked schools offering general courses. These include low academic achievement, various kinds of disorder (even violence) and high dropout rates (Inui, 1993b). Thanks to institutional and cultural factors, the dropout rate in Japanese high schools was very low until the mid seventies; however, institutional factors have weakened since then, and in particular the school placement system has less effect as it can no longer secure enough long-term jobs. These conflicts and an excess of competition are the main causes of a series of attempts, starting in the eighties, at reforming the upper-secondary school system.

Conclusion and prospects

Japanese upper-secondary education was relaunched after the war as a comprehensive system and in the sixties moved toward a generalist or academic education. Japanese-style employment had a great influence on this, and interlocked with the school system as it evolved. The upper-secondary school system worked as an efficient selector and supplier of a well-educated and homogeneous labour force. The unified structure of societal competition, spanning school and company, involved almost all students, and compelled them to work hard. However, this competitive system now confronts some serious problems, and needs reform. The main problems are excessive competition *per se*, and the lack of public-sector vocational education and training.

Excess competition

The unified structure of competition, in school and at work, brings about excessive competition. Cramming schools are one symptom. According to the Ministry of Education, 16.5 per cent of primary school pupils and 44.5 per cent of lower secondary school students go to such schools. Third-year students of lower-secondary school (age 15) average 58 hours of study a week (NHK, 1986). This hard work leads to the high average academic achievement of Japanese students. However, a serious result is extremely low self-confidence. According to an IEA study, although Japanese students do well at maths, they find it harder to learn and like it less than do the students of any other nation (Robitaille and Garden, 1989). We see more evidence of a lack of self-confidence in a Japanese government study of 10 to 15-year-olds in six countries (USA, UK, France, Thailand, South Korea and Japan). In this study, only 37 per cent of Japanese children agreed with the statement 'I'm doing quite well at school', whereas 77 to 97 per cent of those in Western countries and 52 and 62 per cent in the other two Asian countries agreed (Sorifu Seishonen-Taisaku-Honbu, 1980).

Another serious result is a rapid increase in neurotic school absentees.

According to official statistics, there were recently 58,000 of these people in primary and lower-secondary school. They accounted for one per cent of lower-secondary students in 1992. The number has increased rapidly since the late seventies and is five times that of the mid seventies. We lack official statistics for upper-secondary school, but anecdotal evidence suggests about the same rate as at lower-secondary school.

The figures for absenteeism include truancy of the normal, 'delinquent' type. However, far commoner is a sort of obsessive neurosis, rare in the West. The students know they have to go to school, but cannot leave home, and tend to shut themselves in their rooms for a long time: sometimes for months, or more than a year. They feel guilty about this, but may also hold a grudge against their parents. While the causes of this syndrome may be complex, the main one is that they excessively conform with what school demands under the strong pressure of competition (Takeuchi, 1987). Both they and their parents are only too well aware of the need for success at school, and dread an inability to catch up with other students. A small failure at school hurts them and makes them fear school. The surveillant atmosphere of school is also a contributing factor.

Excessive competition leads to many conflicts in the workplace, too. A typical example is the increase of death from heart attacks and so forth linked to overwork; not surprising as the average number of working hours per year is hundreds more than in the West (National Defence Counsel for Victims of Karoshi, 1991). Therefore, control of competition is the most important social problem in the Japan of the nineties.

Lack of public-sector vocational education and training

Another problem is the lack of a publicly financed system for vocational education and training. The reorganization of the labour market since the late seventies has enlarged the external market, and the need for public vocational education and training has increased. However, little is publicly financed. Vocational courses account for fewer than a quarter of upper-secondary students and public vocational training institutes controlled by the Labour Ministry also provide for very few. Therefore, the reconstruction of a lifelong learning system connected to vocational training and retraining was one of the main issues for the *Ad Hoc* Council on Education of the Nakasone government (1984–7).

Increasing demands for vocational education and training have mainly been met by private bodies. Special training schools were recognized by the School Education Act of 1976, and the number of their students has rapidly increased. In 1991, 534,000 upper secondary graduates went to these schools: 30 per cent of all graduates (for graduates from general courses, 459,000 and 36 per cent). However, more than 90 per cent of students in post-secondary vocational education are in private schools, and the average fee paid by students or their families is 626,000 yen for the first year (Monbusho, 1990). This is too high for the average family.

One reason why so many students go to special training schools is the need for higher skills and knowledge. However, another reason, especially for students who have just graduated from general courses, is that they have not yet acquired any particular skill or career plans. Therefore, on the one hand we need more publicly financed and publicly accessible post-secondary vocational education, while on the other, we need to reorganize upper-secondary education so that it is less exclusively academic, by adding more vocational content.

Reform of general courses

As we mentioned in section 2, the reform of general courses in upper-secondary school has been a serious issue since the mid eighties. Central and local governments have been eager to introduce new types of courses, such as international communication, athletics and data processing. Most of these have been introduced as 'specialized general' courses. The reason is said to be response to the demands of society and students. However, the most important is the predicament of below-average schools offering general courses, of which very many have the serious problems discussed above.

Students choose these below-average schools, or are advised to enter them, only because their achievement is low. This demoralizes them. Although the curriculum is academic, their chances of entering university are low; and if they give up hope of entering university, they feel what they are taught is of little use. This is the background of school disorder and dropout. Although a healthy job market worked in the past as a reward for submissiveness, this has been lacking for the past two decades.

Therefore, the introduction of new types of courses aims at modifying and diversifying competition within the school system. It aims to change the criterion of choice of upper-secondary school from a single crude ranking to the provision of a desired *kind* of education. However, the resulting schools are still likely to be ranked on the old scale, because the linkage, if any, between upper secondary diversity and the various post-secondary options remains obscure.

If these new courses are to be viable, they will need some vocational elements to connect with post-secondary training and employment. Most of their students will eventually become employees in the external market. Schools have to provide their students with some basic work skills, ideas about work and life, and the skills and knowledge needed to protect their human rights in their jobs and outside life. This reform, with the establishment of a public vocational education and training system, will secure more recognition for them, and will protect them from the deleterious effects of the unified competition now spanning school and company.

Another needed reform is the introduction of more fundamental knowledge and skills for social interaction to the upper-secondary curriculum. Academic general education renders students unable to think or act on global issues, such as democracy and human rights, the environment and education, international understanding, sex and ethnic discrimination, and so on. A basic ability to deal with these issues would help to empower demoralized students. We need to encourage such an ability not only in one or two school subjects, but in all of them.

Acknowledgement

We would like to thank Professor Peter Evans for his great help in correcting and elaborating our English, and also for some useful comments on issues in this chapter.

References

Chuo-Kyoiku-Shingikai (Central Education Council) (1991) *Shingi Keika Hokoku*, interim report, Tokyo: Monbusho.

Her Majesty's Inspectorate (1991) *Aspects of Upper Secondary Education in Japan*, London: HMSO.

Inui, A (1990) *Nihon no Kyoiku to Kigyo-Shakai*, Tokyo: Otsuki-shoten.

Inui, A (1993a) 'The competitive structure of school and the labour market: Japan and Britain', *British Journal of Sociology of Education*, **14**, 3, 301–13.

Inui, A (1993b) 'Futsu-ka no bunretsu kaitai to koko-zo keisei no arata na kadai', *Koko no Hiroba*, **8**, 86–95.

Kariya, T (1992) *Gakko Shokugyo Senbatsu no Shakaigaku*, Tokyo: Daigaku Shuppankai.

Keizai-Shingi-Kai (Economic Deliberation Council) (1963) *Keizai-hatten ni okeru Jin-teki Noryoku Kaihatsu no Kadai to Taisaku*, Tokyo.

Kumazawa, M (1989) *Nihon-teki Keiei no Meian*, Tokyo: Chikuma-shobo.

McCormick, K (1991) 'Japanese engineers, lifetime employment and in-company training: continuity and change in the management of engineering manpower resources', in: Ryan, P (ed) *International Comparisons of Vocational Education and Training for Intermediate Skills*, London: Falmer.

Monbusho (Ministry of Education) (1989) *Gakko Kihon Chosa Tokei*, Tokyo.

Monbusho (Ministry of Education) (1990) *Senshu-Gakko ni kansuru Jittai-Chosa Hokoku-sho*, Tokyo.

National Defence Counsel for Victims of Karoshi (1990) *Karoshi: When the 'Corporate Warrior' Dies*, Tokyo: Mado-sha.

NHK (1986) *Nihon-jin no Seikatsu Jikan 1985*, Tokyo: Hoso Shuppan Kyokai.

OECD (1992) *Education at a Glance: OECD Indicators*, Paris: OECD.

Robitaille, D F and Garden, R A (1989) *The IEA Study of Mathematics II: Contexts and Outcome of School Mathematics*, Oxford: Pergamon Press.

Rosenbaum, J E and Kariya, T (1989) 'From high school to work: market and institutional mechanisms in Japan', *American Journal of Sociology*, **94**, 6, 1334–65.

Sako, M and Dore, R (1988) 'Teaching or training: the role of the state in Japan', *Oxford Review of Economic Policy*, **4**, 3, 72-81.

Sorifu Seishonen-Taisaku-Honbu (Department of Youth Affairs, the Prime Minister's Office) (1980) *Jido no Jittai tou ni Kansuru Kokusai Hikaku Chosa*, Tokyo.

Takeuchi, T (1987) *Kodomo no Jibun-kuzushi to Jibun-zukuri*, Tokyo: Daigaku Shuppankai.

Watanabe, O (1990) *'Yutaka na Shakai' Nippon no Kozo*, Tokyo: Rodo-Junpo-sha.

13. Human resource development in post-apartheid South Africa: some initial observations

Elaine Unterhalter and Michael Young

As a result of South Africa's first democratic election, held in May 1994, a government of national unity took office with the African National Congress (ANC) as the leading party. In its policy documents the ANC has committed this government to an ambitious programme of reconstruction and human resource development which is described in *The Reconstruction and Development Programme (RDP)* (ANC, 1994a).

This programme, which was produced by the ANC and its electoral allies (the Congress of South African Trade Unions (COSATU) and the South African Communist Party (SACP)), attempts to provide an integrated and sustainable programme that links reconstruction and human resource development, as the basis for meeting the basic needs of the people and enhancing the process of democratization and nation-building.

The RDP sets this task in the context of the ravages of apartheid that have divided the society on grounds of race, ethnicity, class and gender, and enormous differentials between rich and poor, leaving an intimidating legacy of economic, social, political, moral, cultural and environmental problems for a new government (ANC, 1994a, pp 2–3). A striking feature of the Reconstruction Programme is the way in which it seeks not only to overcome the grave problems the new government has inherited from the old regime, but to build on the positive legacy of the anti-apartheid struggle. An enormous achievement of the anti-apartheid movement was the mobilization of individuals and organizations of all kinds and from all sectors (trade unions, churches, women's groups, civic associations, cultural formations, sporting and artistic organizations). The Reconstruction and Development Programme maps out a strategy that entails drawing on and developing this mobilization in the building of a new society.

The ANC's education and training proposals are set out in greater detail in a policy framework document that was published at the beginning of 1994. (ANC, 1994b). These proposals adopt what might be described as a 'dual strategy' for overcoming the legacy of apartheid education. They recommend both a significant expansion and redistribution of formal

173

education, and the introduction of a national qualifications framework for education and training. The qualifications framework is designed to enable people to become qualified even if they do not have access to a school or college.

The framework has three objectives. First, it will enable those adults with skills, but no qualifications, to get them accredited; they will thus be provided with a basis both for progression to higher levels and new opportunities for promotion. Second, it will enable opportunities for lifelong learning to be encouraged in a wide range of contexts with educational potential, for example workplaces, cultural, religious and community organizations. Third, it is designed to provide an integrated multi-path system of qualifications, 'from sweeper to engineer', as one trade unionist put it, bringing together formal and informal learning as well as education and training. It is hoped that in this way educational opportunities will be provided for many people, especially adults and youth, who would be excluded from access to education and training for decades if they had to wait for sufficient new schools or colleges to be built.

This chapter is very much an initial assessment of these proposals and their possibilities in the situation that the newly elected South African government faces. It attempts to identify and assess those factors which will help to promote the implementation of the aims of the RDP and of the proposals for the expansion of opportunities for lifelong learning contained in the education and training policy framework proposals. It will also consider those factors that could retard this process. It begins by setting the discussion within the context of an analysis of the conditions in the economy and within the highly fragmented education and training systems, at the moment of transfer of power to a new government in May 1994.

Twin distinct but related strategies distinguish the RDP proposals and will be returned to at the end of this chapter. They are (i) the commitment to link mobilization, reconstruction and opportunities for lifelong learning within and beyond the formal education system, and (ii) the commitment to integrate education and training within a national qualifications framework. It is our view that as the basis of a model for human-centred economic growth, these strategies will have implications well beyond South Africa.

The economic and educational legacy of apartheid

The South African economy in the last decade of apartheid was in serious decline. Per capita economic growth was negative from 1982. The gap between the growing numbers of adults of employable age and the actual numbers employed grew. Employment was static between 1982 and 1992 and unemployment increased markedly in the 1990s. (Colclough and Pillay, 1994, p 55; MERG, 1994, pp 148–9). While there were no accurate ways of estimating unemployment, some dimensions of its extent were mapped. The South African Reserve Bank estimated in August 1993 that

46 per cent of the economically active population were not employed in the formal sector. The scale of the problem was confirmed by a countrywide survey of youth in 1993 which found that 52 per cent of the population aged between 16 and 30 were not employed (SAIRR, 1994, p 470).

The reasons for this economic decline involve a complex intermeshing of decreasing investment, partly (but not exclusively) because of the politics of apartheid and world recession, with low productivity, itself the partial outcome of a generally underskilled workforce. Public sector investments declined by 50 per cent between 1986 and 1992 (Colclough and Pillay, 1994, p 56). Private investment moved in parallel with government trends. Real gross domestic fixed investment declined by 23.5 per cent from the third quarter of 1989 to the second quarter of 1993 (MERG, 1994, p 5). When the interim constitution was agreed at the end of 1993 business confidence in South Africa was at an almost unprecedented low.

There have been some sectoral differences within this macroeconomic picture, but there are no marked differences from the general trend in those sectors that account for the largest output and employment. Thus employment in manufacturing was static between 1980 and 1990, and decreased by 7 per cent between 1991 and 1993. The size of aggregate capital stock in the industrial sector fell by 10 per cent between 1984 and 1990. The rate of productivity growth in manufacturing declined by 1.02 per cent per annum between 1970 and 1990 (Joffe et al, 1994, p 18).

Declining productivity is the result of complex processes. Its link to what has been described by Gelb as 'racialised Fordism' has been extensively analysed (Gelb, 1987; Kraak, 1991; NEPI, 1992a). Gelb describes racial Fordism as a phenomenon of postwar South Africa resulting from the combination of apartheid, industrialization and import substitution. Accumulation was based on increased mass production and mass consumption, though both processes had built-in racially inscribed restrictions. For example the wage rates of black workers were kept down through a web of official regulations.

The perpetuation of this form of work organization was linked in the 1980s and 1990s, when wage rates began to rise, to a decline in investment that might have enhanced technological capability. Business expenditure on R&D declined by 27 per cent between 1983/4 and 1989/90. There was a significant further decline between 1990 and 1993. The partially state funded system of science research councils did little to assist innovations in firms (MERG, 1994, p 231; Joffe et al, 1994, p 18). South African firms have relied heavily on the acquisition of technology from abroad, primarily through licensing argreements, which carry with them heavy levels of royalty payments, numerous restrictive clauses, particularly regarding exports, and minimal training provision.

Closely intermeshed with 'Fordist' forms of work organization and limits on technological development has been a divided and inequitable system of education and training in South Africa. These divisions have partly been the product of diversified sites of delivery, differing

Table 13.1 *Education level of 20–64-year-olds in 1991 by racial categorization (%)*

	African	Coloured	Indian	White	Total
Illiterate	41	24	11	1	30
Higher primary	16	20	10	1	13
Lower secondary	32	43	45	33	34
End of upper secondary	9	10	26	41	16
Tertiary	2	3	8	24	7

Source: CSS, 1991, Table 13.
Note: Data exclude the formerly nominally 'independent' areas of the Transkei, Bophuthatswana, Venda and Ciskei (TBVC), where approximately 20 per cent of the population live.

qualifications systems and a gendered and racially segmented labour market. In addition, apartheid-imposed racial categorizations of the population have sharply differentiated access to education and training. As Table 13.1 shows, people classified 'white' (although a minority of the population as a whole) were disproportionately represented in the section of the population with the highest level of education. The majority of people classified 'black', or African (who make up 80 per cent of the population), have had numerous legal and financial obstacles placed in the way of their access to education and training (Kraak, 1991; Unterhalter, 1991; Hartshorne, 1992).

Before the election of a new government in May 1994 there were 15 education departments in South Africa. Training provision was co-ordinated through the National Training Board (NTB) which was responsible to a separate Ministry of Manpower. It comprised of a complex web of training boards with responsibility for regional training centres, as well as public sector and local government provision, training for the unemployed and for the informal and small business sector. Separate training boards accredited some of the training carried out by private sector employers. The NTB did not operate a single system of certification. Outside the NTB remit, programmes of training were administered in the nominally independent homelands by their different ministries of labour. In addition throughout South Africa a large number of non-governmental organizations (NGOs) emerged in the 1980s, many with a particular training brief. While some undertook training for the community-based organizations which had led much of the opposition to the apartheid regime in the 1980s, many worked with employers in privately established training centres. (Muller, 1994; National Training Board, 1994, pp 37–41).

Education and training provision, therefore, has been fragmented because of differential, and racially inscribed forms of access, different modes of accreditation and separated administrative apparatuses. In addition, the quality of education and training has varied markedly. The examination (matric) which most 'white' pupils take at 17 (many black students take the exam when they are significantly older) is widely

Table 13.2 *Matriculation results according to racial categorization, 1990–3 (percentage of candidates passing at the higher level (matric exemption))*

	African	Coloured	Indian	White
1991	11	22	50	41
1992	10	21	49	42
1993	8	21	45	42

Source: SAIRR, 1994, p 713; Edusource, 1994, p 7.

Table 13.3 *Matriculation results according to racial categorization, 1990–3 (proportion of candidates passing only at the lower level (matric pass))*

	African	Coloured	Indian	White
1991	46	83	95	96
1992	44	86	95	98
1993	39	86	93	95

Source : as Table 13.2.

discredited because of the corruption surrounding its administration, the fact that standards vary according to the racial categorization of the schools, and its weakness as an indicator of potential for study at university or capacity to learn at work (Mathonsi, 1988; Cross and Chisholm, 1990). Nonetheless matric results are the only indicator of educational quality currently available across the different education departments and they indicate a very high rate of failure among black candidates (see Tables 13.2 and 13.3).

The fragmented education and training system in South Africa has also played a role in sustaining a highly segmented labour market, characterized by very marked racial and gender divisions. The report on human resources development for the National Education Policy Investigation (NEPI, 1992a) developed the following table to identify the characteristics of labour market segmentation in the formal sector in South Africa:

Table 13.4 *Labour market segmentation in the formal sector*

	Independent primary	Subordinate	Secondary
Job	Professional, semi-professional, skilled	Union-organized, secure operative	Unskilled, insecure, non-unionized
Race	Mostly whites; small black professional and managerial layer	Mostly black (African, Coloured and Indian); some poor whites	African
Gender	Mostly male; minority of white and black	Mostly male; small number black and white women	Mostly female women

Source: Adapted from NEPI (1992a) p 10.

The *independent primary* labour market, consists of managerial, professional and technical jobs offering reasonable job security, relatively high pay and opportunities for career and salary progression. Most employers relying on this labour are large local and multinational corporations, and most jobs require higher education. Most employees are white males. In the *subordinate primary* labour market most employers are also large corporations. Workers are increasingly unionized, and have over the past decade engaged in collective bargaining which has secured them better pay and working conditions than workers in the *secondary* labour market. Some have benefited from company training schemes leading to job upgrading. The majority of these workers are African males. In the secondary labour market most enterprises are small. Workers are poorly paid, unskilled and non-unionized. There are virtually no opportunities for career advancement. This sector comprises approximately half the workforce employed in the formal sector. A majority are African women. Mobility between the secondary and primary segments of the formal sector labour market is low (NEPI, 1992a, p11; see Table 13.4).

The informal sector, which grew rapidly in the 1980s as controls on black entrepreneurial activities were reduced, is estimated to employ between a quarter and a third of the workforce (MERG, 1994, p 147). African women predominate in most of the key service activities within this sector. Pay and skills are low (NEPI, 1992a, pp 11–12).

Each segment of the labour market has distinct processes of recruitment, skill formation and progression. These form barriers to the expansion of employment for African women, who form a majority of the most impoverished section of the workforce. In addition differences between rural and urban areas present enormous barriers to recruitment into the primary labour market. In rural areas limited health, housing, transport and any communications infrastructure for Africans mesh with very uneven provision of schooling and the legacy of the pass laws to further limit access to the labour market for a majority of rural African women and many men.

There are then two major elements in the situation facing the new South African government – the legacy that it inherits and the demands of the future. It inherits a declining economy, an underskilled labour force, high levels of unemployment and gross inequalities of educational opportunity between racial groups and between urban and rural communities. There is therefore a marked lack of available resources to expand education and training. However, all the predictions about a future basis for economic growth in South Africa suggest that it will only be possible if there is a massive upgrading of the qualifications of the present and future workforce (MERG, 1994, pp 157–60; Tucker and Scott, 1992, pp 141–5).

Furthermore, it is unlikely, in terms of existing wage levels in large corporations, that South Africa will attract the kind of investment that would provide the low-skill jobs that have been the source of at least initial economic growth in the South East Asian countries. Moreover the pitfalls inherent in an industrial policy oriented simply to the short-term creation of jobs by a handful of multinational corporations are evident. Such a policy would be unlikely to lead to a sustainable long-term expansion of countrywide employment; increases in productivity would eliminate the very jobs initially created (MERG, 1994, p 211).

On the other hand, investment in manufacturing and service industries oriented to technological capacity building and to the development of productive skills will not be attracted to South Africa with its present skill levels and its uneven provision of an infrastructure of healthcare, transport, housing, electrification and communication services. The Reconstruction and Development Programme was produced in order to address these problems in an integrated way.

The ANC policy for reconstruction and development

The Reconstruction and Development Programme (RDP), launched by the ANC Alliance in March 1994, sets out to integrate building the economy, meeting the basic needs of the mass of the population and encouraging human resource development. The programme seeks to draw on the experiences of the struggle against apartheid and mobilize the involvement of as many people, sectors and organizations as possible. It argues that the best way of ensuring that both economic growth and the distribution of its benefits are promoted is to ensure that the development of infrastructure (including electrification, water purification, communications, transport and health) is integrated with a human resource development strategy for upgrading the skills and qualifications of the population. It explicitly rejects any separation of growth and development. These are seen as people-driven processes, utilizing the energies and enhancing the knowledge of the mass of the population. The argument is that this approach to development will be both more effective and more equitable than when distribution is conceived as a passive form of 'trickle down' benefit.

The main elements of the human resource development strategy of the Reconstruction Programme can be summarized as follows:

- integration of the racially segregated administrative structures of education and training;
- 10 years of free compulsory schooling for all;
- a national pre-school (educare) policy;
- a qualifications framework to integrate education and training and provide access and progression for all through lifelong learning;
- a comprehensive approach to adult basic education and its integration with work-based training and distance education opportunities;
- developing skills and knowledge within the whole population through integration of education and training programmes with other facets of the infrastructural development programme.

The framework for implementation of the human resource development programme is explored in greater detail in the ANC Education Department's document *A Policy Framework for Education and Training* (ANC, 1994b). This considers the new structures and organizations that need to be put in place and how financial resources can be mobilized for a programme of educational reconstruction. The Policy Framework maps out a new policy for upgrading teachers, trainers and adult educators which will entail them playing key roles in curriculum development. It also considers the wide range of resources that will need to be built up in order to develop a society oriented to lifelong learning.

Both these documents seek to maintain a balance between development, growth and equity and to provide a framework for achieving this. The route they have mapped passes from needs to potential, to output, and crucially to capacity. The next five years will be a strenuous test of whether the programmes conceived in the moments of triumph at the end of minority rule can be implemented within a society deeply scarred by the long history of apartheid. The next two sections focus on some of the issues that the implementation process is likely to face, the resources and support that the new government can expect to draw on, and the barriers that will have to be overcome.

Implementing the Reconstruction and Development Programme: vision, possibilities and barriers

The RDP and its human resource strategy present a clear vision of the necessity of linking economic growth to the human development of the population as a whole and of involving as wide a section of the population as possible in the process. Within the approach to reconstruction, education and training provision have the potential to play an integrative role in a divided society and to build on the sense of unity that was achieved up to and through the election. Converting that vision and unity into quite specific policies for the creation of new institutions, and the reform of old ones is, however, another matter. It is not something that the RDP and the Education and Training Policy Framework document, which were essentially campaigning documents for an election, could be expected to tackle. The proposals are realistic in the sense that they do not depend on a massive injection of state funds. Furthermore they draw on a number of unique strengths and advantages that are specific to South Africa at this time. On the other hand they could be seen as over-optimistic about the possibilities of world economic growth and the democratizing potential of new technologies and so-called post-Fordist forms of work organization. They also play down the 'conservatism' of many educational institutions and the lack of capacity at all levels and of the system as a whole. This section assesses these factors and their possible implications.

Possibilities: the international context

South Africa has a number of unique advantages which have external and internal origins. Internationally, there are many positive indicators. With the world identification with the struggle against apartheid, the massive investment promised from the USA and Europe, and the hope on the part of the aid agencies that it might at last provide a model for success for the African continent, South Africa has a 'window of opportunity' that few other countries in similar situations have experienced. This is expressed in the allowances that have been made in the GATT agreement for the (short-term) continuation of trade tariffs, the acceptance by the African Development Bank that South Africa does not need to put up capital immediately, and the increase in aid from the UK, the USA and other countries. A less certain but possibly, in the longer term, more significant external factor is that South Africa will be embarking on its Reconstruction and Development Programme at a time when flexible forms of state intervention into the economy are being looked at more favourably as increasing numbers of countries look for alternatives to the failures of the market-oriented policies of the 1980s.

The internal context

A number of features of the moment of transition are likely to prove assets, if the government can find ways of incorporating them into its overall strategy. They are (i) the experience by individual institutions of participating in the struggle against apartheid, (ii) the emergence of trade unions with a strategic vision of their role, (iii) the development of civil society as a democratic force as expressed in the key role of non-government organizations (NGOs) and community based organizations (CBOs) and the establishment of consultative forums consisting of representatives of government, business and a wide range of organizations representing stakeholders.

Schools were, from 1976, one of the key sites of struggle against apartheid. Although the boycotts and other forms of resistance had a catastrophic effect on student learning, they also led to the establishment of unique forms of participatory organizations, the Parent/Teacher/Student/Associations (PTSAs),which are well placed, particularly in partnership with trade unions and civic associations, to play a key role in the transformation of the schools into self-governing high-achieving institutions. In this they have many potential allies in teachers, particularly those organized in the non-racial teachers union, SADTU, which has developed policy in relation to educational transformation and undertaken some key work in relation to local transformations of curriculum and forms of teacher assessment. However, for the PTSAs and SADTU to play a significant role in the implementation of the RDP, they too will have to undertake considerable changes in their approach to organization. Their stance will have to change from opposing an illegitimate regime, to working with a new administration in its tasks of reconstruction.

Much of the energy and many of the ideas underpinning the RDP and, in particular, key elements in its approach to human resource development (HRD), had their origins in COSATU (the Congress of South African Trade Unions) and a number of its affiliated unions. This partly reflects the outlook of trade unions that are based on broad sectors rather than crafts (though a craft basis still continues in the historically white unions). Two features of the strategic approach to training adopted by the unions will be crucial for the HRD strategy. First, they recognized in the early 1990s that they could improve the conditions of their members by collaborating with employers in developing a common training strategy. At the same time certain employers became aware of the benefits in improved productivity that would flow from a coordinated rather than a free-market approach to training. Key employers have thus developed a position of support for training strategies while unions have not been trapped into positions concerned only with confrontational wage bargaining.

Second, the unions understood that if they were going to promote employment opportunities for their members in whole sectors (such as engineering) they needed to demand curricula in training programmes based on broad generic skills and knowledge rather than narrow task-specific skills. They were able to build support for proposals on the integration of education and training among employers as well as among their own members. These proposals, set out in the National Training Board's Task Team proposals (National Training Board, 1994), represent a considerable victory for the strategic unionism of COSATU.

The lack of legitimacy of the previous regime gave rise to two organizational forms that could have an important role in furthering the aims of the Reconstruction and Development Programme. They are, first, the very large number of NGOs in the education and training field, especially in traditionally neglected areas such an INSET, adult literacy and early childhood education, and second, the emergence of consultative forums, specifically the Economic Forum (EF) and the National Education and Training Forum (NETF).

The importance of education and training provision by NGOs is not just that they fill some of the gaps in public provision, nor even that they continue to provide acceptable channels for private sector funding, but that because they are independent of state provision, they could provide important 'neutral' bridges that the government of national unity will need if it is to find ways of encouraging collaboration by those who voted against the ANC.

The future of the NETF is uncertain at the time of writing. However, during the previous regime, it succeeded in giving a voice in national policy discussions to a range of people and organizations that would not necessarily be consulted within a conventional parliamentary democracy.

There are, then, important positive features, both internationally and within the country, that the new government will be able to build on in developing the involvement and unity of purpose that will be necessary if the Reconstruction Programme is to be implemented. There is, however, a negative inheritance in the transition to democracy that will make achieving a consensus far from easy. A major dimension of this inheritance is a lack of capacity that the proposed reforms will need. The next section therefore turns to some of the barriers to implementing the programme and the possibilities of overcoming them.

The barriers: external and internal

The international context

Much of the analysis that informs the Reconstruction and Development Programme and which assumes a relatively favourable international context is informed by an optimistic version of what is widely known as a post-Fordist analysis. There is not the space here to go into the reservations about the relevance of post-Fordist analyses for South Africa; they are well discussed elsewhere (Kraak, 1993). However a number of points are worth making by way of cautions. The first is that the industrialized nations of the world have not yet come out of recession and there are still relatively high levels of unemployment in Europe. If this is added to the pressures to invest in Eastern Europe rather than South Africa, the rising investment scenario anticipated for South Africa is by no means certain.

Second, the generally optimistic accounts of the possibilities of flexible specialization for South Africa may need to be tempered in the light of experiences elsewhere in the world. South Africa is not equipped in terms of existing infrastructure or education and training levels to move to flexible modes of production except possibly in a very few areas. New forms of production are at best likely to be unevenly introduced in South Africa. In these circumstances, it may well be difficult for unions representing workers in specific firms or sectors to intervene on behalf of the mass of workers in low paid mass production or services. Such difficulties have confronted well-organized unions in countries like Brazil, where the high-tec industries remain largely insulated from the mass of workers in low-skill low-pay mass production (Lipietz, 1987).

The international context is not only global, but also regional. Economic growth in South Africa will probably involve the development of production for a mass market in the region in close collaboration with SADCC (Southern African Development Co-ordination Conference) countries (Bird and Lloyd, 1994). However regional cooperation cannot be assumed. It will have to be developed. The history of SADCC, which was established to overcome the dependence of other countries in the region on the old South Africa, may be a difficult legacy to overcome. Moreover the education and training systems in the SADCC countries, largely conceived in terms of a rigid academic and vocational divide, may prove difficult barriers to the integrated framework at the core of the RDP.

Internal barriers to reconstruction

The RDP and the education and training policy document both explicitly locate their approach to human resource development within an *integrated* administrative and qualifications framework. Such a strategy depends crucially on a national consensus on education and training policy. However, concessions, in the form of amendments to the interim constitution agreed at the end of 1993, devolved significant powers relating to education to the nine provincial parliaments. In the May 1994 general election, the ANC won a majority of seats in seven out of the nine regional parliaments. The National Party (NP) became the majority party in the Western Cape and the IFP (Inkatha Freedom Party) in Kwazulu-Natal. Both parties have long argued the case for a highly devolved form of federalism and a relatively weak role for central government. They might well use their regional power bases to undermine the integrated socio-economic approach that lies at the heart of the RDP. The extent to which the powers of the central government and the equality clauses contained in the Bill of Rights constrain their capacity to do this is yet to be tested. Much will depend on the ability of the new government to convince parties not involved in developing the RDP that it is a national rather than a party programme.

The proposals for integrating education and training which are integral to the RDP and the education and training policy framework documents are both highly ambitious and innovative. They will involve a massive transformation of the existing top-down bureaucratic system, in which curriculum development has consisted of instructions passed down to institutions to deliver. The new proposals will require new relationships between government departments and schools and colleges, and a wholly new set of authorities to develop and set standards for qualifications. Furthermore it will also depend on *individual* schools, colleges and training providers taking on responsibility for raising levels of achievement and for developing a view of the curriculum and its relation to the future of the economy that will be quite new for most South African teachers. If integration of education and training is to become a reality in South Africa, schools will need to develop partnerships with employers, trade unions and community organizations. At the same time, employers and others involved in training have to develop the commitment and capacity to deliver general education as well as occupationally specific skills. Given the traditional and 'conservative' view of their professionalism that characterizes all groups of teachers in South Africa, these partnerships will not be easy to establish. The links teachers built with communities during the anti-apartheid struggle were built on common political perceptions, not innovative approaches to teaching and learning. The challenge will be to build this sense of political commonality into rethinking teaching and learning and breaking down the barriers that have separated schools from productive life.

The so-called 'sunset' clauses in the interim constitution have guaranteed civil servants their posts for five years, which means that policy implementation will depend on existing staff. However, many of even the limited changes in education policy initiated by the former regime were frustrated by a civil service out of sympathy with moves towards a national rather than a racially divided system (Davies, 1984; NEPI, 1992c). The ability of the government of national unity to win support for its policies from key sections of the civil service will be crucial. This issue has two aspects. First, it is unclear whether it will be possible to transform white officials who were closely identified with the apartheid policies of the National Party into a professional civil service. Second, the government will need to gain the support and meet the aspirations of black civil servants who were given positions of relative superiority in the former homeland regimes, but not pay parity with whites in the central government.

Summary

In this section we have described the main features of the ANC Alliance's Reconstruction and Development Programme and indicated some aspects of the complex situation facing the South African government as it begins the task of implementing the programme. The positive and negative factors are, we assess, evenly balanced, though many are unpredictable and out of control of the government elected in May 1994. The time is short in relation to the extent of the changes needed. The government of national unity and the interim constitution have five years to run. If a government is to be elected in 1999 with the same commitment to democracy and to the economic betterment of the majority of the people as the ANC government of 1994, much will have to be achieved to convince a majority of people to maintain their faith in a multi-racial social democracy and a mixed economy.

Conclusion

This chapter can be no more than a preliminary assessment from two observers who are based in the UK, but who are deeply committed to the aims of the RDP and to the basis on which the ANC fought the election. At such an early stage, Gramsci's famous slogan linking 'pessimism of the intellect and optimism of the will' is probably the most appropriate stance, though because South Africa has surprised us before, more stress should be placed on the optimism.

In conclusion, we want to suggest that the South African case could be an important test for future international trends in education and training policy in a number of ways. There are a number of common features in the educational policies of most developing as well as developed countries. They can be summarized as follows:

- a concentration on expanding institutions (schools, colleges, and universities) geared to the provision of education and training for specific age groups rather than a strategy designed to encourage lifelong learning;
- maintaining academic (or general) education as separate from vocational education (or training); the former tends to be seen as largely independent of national economic aims or the occupational futures of individuals;
- placing the responsibility for educational provision in the hands of specialist administrators, accountable to national (and sometimes local) governments, but only intermittently, if at all, to a wider community of stakeholders.

These specialization trends in educational provision have hardly been debated, although there was some recognition of the issues in the deschooling literature of the 1970s (Illich, 1970; Reimer, 1970). In South Africa, where the majority have been excluded from formal education, there will remain strong popular pressures to follow traditional policies of educational expansion. However, in the policy documents we have considered in this chapter, there are elements of an alternative approach to educational development which have been referred to in passing. If educational developments are to benefit the majority of people who are unlikely to have access to more than a minimum of formal education, these alternatives might form the basis of a better model, especially for countries without large resources.

The alternatives are symbolized by (a) the proposal for a qualifications framework to encourage the educative potential of the *society as a whole*, and not just its specialist educational institutions and those involved in them, (b) the idea of integration which goes beyond overcoming the divisions that were specific to apartheid to those separating academic and vocational education and more broadly, theory and practice, and (c) the democratizing of educational provision beyond accountability to an elected parliament thus involving the democratic potential of civil society.

Each of these policies can be seen as attempts to make education and training less specialized activities and to bring them closer to the mainstream of everyday productive life. They are all underpinned by the notion that education should not be a form of welfare or social control (functions that have dominated the role of mass education in some industrialized countries), nor should it be something removed, as, for example, in the English grammar school tradition, from people's everyday needs. The policies that we have discussed here point to the need to reintegrate education with the political, economic, cultural and moral development of a society. In many ways the South African case is unique. Nonetheless it may provide the international community with some clues as to the feasibility of linking an integrated approach to education and training with a programme of reconstruction and development.

References

ANC (1994a) *The Reconstruction and Development Programme*, Johannesburg: Umanyano Publications.

ANC (1994b) *A Policy Framework for Education and Training*, Johannesburg: Education Department, African National Congress.

Bird, A and Lloyd, C (1994) 'South African labour market policy priorities: putting human resource development at the heart of regional reconstruction and development', paper presented at the United Nations/London School of Economics Joint Seminar, Sustainable Economic Growth and Development: Policy priorities for the Early Years of a Democratic Government, January.

Central Statistical Services [CSS] (1991) *Population Census. Report No. 03-01-01*, Pretoria: Government printer.

Colclough, C and Pillay, P (1994) 'Education in South Africa: present constraints and future challenges', *IDS Bulletin*, 25, 1.

Cross, M and Chisholm, L (1990) 'The roots of segregated schooling in twentieth century South Africa', in Nkomo, M (ed) *Pedagogy of Domination. Toward a Democratic Education* in *South Africa*, Trenton, NJ: Africa World Press.

Davies, J (1984) 'Capital, state and educational reform in South Africa,' in Kallaway, P, *Apartheid and Education*, Johannesburg: Ravan.

Edusource, (1994) *Edusource Data News*, March.

Gelb, S (1987) 'Making sense of the crisis', *Transformation*, **5**.

Hartshorne, K (1992) *Black Education, 1910–1990: Crisis and Challenge*, Cape Town: Oxford University Press.

Illich, I (1970) *Deschooling Society*, Harmondsworth: Penguin.

Joffe, A *et al* (1994) 'An industrial strategy for a post-apartheid South Africa', *IDS Bulletin*, **25**, 1, pp 17–23.

Kraak, A (1991) 'Post-Fordism and a future education and training system for South Africa', in Unterhalter, E *et al* (eds) *Education in a Future South Africa: Policy Issues for Transformation*, Oxford: Heinemann.

Kraak, A (1993) 'Free or co-ordinated markets? Education and training policy options for a future South Africa', PhD thesis, University of Western Cape, South Africa.

Lipietz, A (1987) *Mirages and Miracles: the Crises of Global Fordism*, London: Verso.

Macro-economic Research Group (MERG) (1994) *Making Democracy Work: A Framework for Macroeconomic Policy in South Africa*, Cape Town: Centre for Development Studies.

Mathonsi, E N (1988) *Black Matriculation Results: A Mechanism of Social Control*, Johannesburg: Skotaville.

Muller, J (1994) 'Development, reconstruction and education: a review for the Urban Foundation', unpublished paper.

National Training Board (1994) *National Training Strategy Initiative: A Concept for an Integrated Approach to Education and Training*, report by the National Task Team.

NEPI (National Education Policy Investigation) (1992a) *Human Resource Development*, Cape Town: Oxford University Press.

NEPI (1992b) *Post Secondary Education*, Cape Town: Oxford University Press.

NEPI (1992c) *Governance and Administration*, Cape Town: Oxford University Press.

Reimer, S (1970) *School is Dead*, Harmondsworth: Penguin.

SAIRR (South African Institute of Race Relations) (1994) *A Survey of Race Relations*, Cape Town: SAIRR.

Tucker, B and Scott, B R (1992) *South Africa: Prospects for Successful Transition*, Cape Town: Juta.

Unterhalter, E (1991) 'Changing aspects of reformism in Bantu education', in Unterhalter, E *et al* (eds) *Apartheid Education and Popular Struggles*, London: Zed Books.

14. From education to work: the case of technical schools

Gary McCulloch

To what extent and in what ways does education prepare young people for work? It has often been argued, most famously perhaps by Samuel Bowles and Herbert Gintis in the United States, that a close correspondence exists between education and work in a capitalist society (Bowles and Gintis, 1976). On the other hand, over the past decade it has become more common to argue that there is a close correlation between education and work in a very different sense. On this second view, it is the failure of the education system to prepare youth for the 'world of work' that is said to be directly responsible for the economic and industrial difficulties facing the UK. The further implication of this is that educational reform will lead directly to renewed economic and industrial growth. Both of these viewpoints share the basic premise that there is a 'tight fit', a relatively straightforward and direct correlation, between education and work. This chapter will inspect the grounds for this view by focusing on recent historical research in this area, first to discuss the different historical perspectives that have developed over the past decade, and then to examine in more detail the historical experience of technical schooling in Britain.

Educational policies in Britain since 1976 have increasingly reflected the view that education should be closely aligned with the demands of the work in order to encourage economic growth and industrial competitiveness. In the 1980s, the Manpower Services Commission, by encouraging innovations in the technical and vocational curriculum, sought to establish for itself 'an important role at the interface between education and work' (Young, 1982). City technology colleges were set up to promote parental choice and competition among schools, and help to improve the nation's economic and industrial productivity (eg, McCulloch, 1989a; Whitty, 1992). Such initiatives assumed that more practical, technical, and vocational curricula would correspond to the requirements of the workplace.

In the 1980s and early 1990s, it became commonplace to lament past failures to develop technical schools, and to relate these problems to Britain's long-term industrial and economic decline. However, the historical experience of technical schools suggests a rather more problematic relationship between this form of education and the world of work, than such a straightforward correlation would imply.

From education to work?

During the 1980s, as the Conservative government struggled with the consequences of economic decline and industrial conflict, the view gained ground that such problems were rooted in the character of the education system. The general outlines of this thesis were first sketched out by educational historians Gordon Roderick and Michael Stephens (1981, 1982) and also by Martin Wiener (1981) and Correlli Barnett (1986). These authors not only blamed past educational failures for current economic problems, but also suggested that a different type of education would transform the future prospects of the economy thus encouraging the 'modernizing' educational policies that were developed in the 1980s and 1990s.

Within this general interpretation, the failure of attempts to develop technical schools has been singled out as an important reason for the continuing problems of British industry. Secondary technical schools were promoted after the Second World War to enhance the links between education and industry and commerce. They were intended to cater for 'a minority of able children who are likely to make their best response when the curriculum is strongly coloured by these interests, both from the point of view of a career and because subject-matter of this kind appeals to them' (Ministry of Education, 1947, p 48). However, by the late 1950s, there were still fewer than 300 of these schools in England and Wales, and most of these were either closed or merged with other schools as comprehensive reorganization developed in the 1960s (McCulloch, 1989b).

The historian Michael Sanderson mourns the demise of the secondary technical schools, arguing that 'The failure to develop the junior technical and secondary technical schools is perhaps the greatest lost opportunity of twentieth century English education' (Sanderson, 1987, p 60). He relates this to the continuing dominance of the grammar schools, 'with their academic and pure science values', and the 'chronic shortage of skilled labour which British industry has suffered since 1945' (ibid, pp 60–1). The lesson for contemporary reforms is stated explicitly. While acknowledging that 'we cannot turn the clock back to recreate this form as an alternative for non-academic teenagers', Sanderson supports the development of city technology colleges and the Technical and Vocational Education Initiative (TVEI) (ibid, pp 6–7).

Despite the widespread influence of the Wiener–Barnett thesis, however, some historical research has questioned the validity of its central premise of a direct relation between education and work. W D Rubinstein, for example, has argued, against Wiener, that Britain's dominant values have always tended to be 'rational, moderate, and pro-capitalistic' (Rubinstein, 1993, p 24) and that the 'public schools simply did not produce a "haemorrhage of talent" away from business life in the sense continuously suggested by their critics' (ibid, pp 134–5). Keith Burgess has also found a much more complex relationship to be involved in his recent study of education policy and employment in the 1930s and 1940s (Burgess, 1993).

Elsewhere, other historical research also emphasizes the complexity of the relationship between education, youth and work. In Malta, for instance, Ronald Sultana argues that initiatives in technical and vocational education have appealed to political and educational leaders 'as a solution to a number of economic, educational, political and ideological problems', but that such schemes 'have generally failed either to arouse much interest in the population at large, or to attract an investment sustained over a sufficiently long period of time to generate a skilled pool of workers' (Sultana, 1992, pp 273–4). The nature of the relationship appears to have been no less problematic in the United States, where Kantor and Tyack have noted that vocationally oriented programmes have shown little evidence of actual results in terms of economic or industrial performance: 'Even allowing for the rhetorical oversell that usually accompanies educational reforms, the hopes for vocational education appear to have been misplaced' (Kantor and Tyack, 1982, p 2).

Indeed, whereas earlier American research conveyed a close link between vocational education and labour market structures, more recent discussions have indicated a looser relationship, 'with the connections mediated by political demands for solutions to the "youth problem" rather than labour problems' (Nelson-Rowe, 1991, p 29). Shan Nelson-Rowe suggests a need to examine 'the ways in which the interests and values of pupils and their families shaped the organization of vocational education and its impact on labour markets' (ibid, p 45). On this account, too, more 'process-oriented studies' are needed in order to complement the structural narratives of educational history that have tended to convey a tightly coupled and functional relationship between school and work (ibid, pp 45–6). Also in the United States, Herbert Kliebard emphasizes the symbolism as opposed to the material consequences of curriculum policies that have been designed to connect education with the workplace. They may therefore be interpreted at an ideological level, rather than in terms of their creation of job skills or their importance for industrial change (Kliebard, 1990).

In New Zealand, recent work also problematizes previous notions of the close relationship between education and work. Jones et al (1990) differentiate between 'instrumental' approaches, which have been dominant, and various kinds of 'non-instrumental' views of this relationship, whilst the perceptive social commentator, Roy Nash, points out that, 'schools can't make jobs'. In a situation of structural unemployment, argues Nash:

> the probability is that there is nothing the school can do: the schools do not create unemployment and they cannot create jobs. At the very most they can provide unemployed young people with structural ways of using their time. (Nash, 1983, p 25)

Technical schools developed in New Zealand particularly in the first half of the twentieth century. Although it was noted that 'few features of education in New Zealand have so interested and impressed visitors from overseas' (Hunter in Nicol, 1940, p ix), it was their 'ambiguity of purpose' (Beeby, 1937, p 11) that attracted special comment. As A E Campbell suggested in the early 1940s: 'The New Zealand technical high school is *sui generis*: it is, in effect, a secondary school strongly biased towards industry and commerce but much less specifically vocational than the term "technical" ordinarily implies' (Campbell, 1941, pp 122–3).

They did not give 'specific trade training' so much as 'a realistic education of a more general nature that was designed, so far as it looked to the vocational future, to produce adaptability and handiness and to give some insight into scientific principles' (*ibid*, p 124). Not only were these schools related to industry, commerce and work in only a haphazard and indistinct fashion, but they were also usually regarded both as socially inferior to secondary schools such as Auckland Grammar School and more limiting in their conception than the multilateral post-primary schools of the postwar era. This helps to explain their loss of popularity in the 1940s and 1950s (McCulloch, 1988, 1992).

Some historians have sought to emphasize the directly instrumental connotations of such schools (eg, Gordon, 1984), but it is the complex and contested nature of their curriculum and of their general role that seems of fundamental importance. Such discussions effectively challenge simple and straightforward assumptions about the relationship between educational change and the workplace. They remind us that this relationship has been complex rather than simple, and that it has been mediated and often contested among a range of rival ideologies and interests. They also tend to query the instrumental value of initiatives in technical and vocational schooling, suggesting that these kinds of initiatives often involve considerations that are tacit and unrecognized.

Prep schools of industry?

The historical experience of technical schools in the British context provides an opportunity to reflect upon this wider debate. The post-Second World War secondary technical schools attempted to develop a special relationship with industry and employers at a local and national level, to become indeed 'industry's prep schools' (*TES*, 1956). This was very much in the spirit of the Ministry of Education's advice in *The New Secondary Education* (1947). But industrialists and the organized labour movement alike were sceptical of such claims, preferring to look elsewhere for the focus of their educational activities. Technical school leavers, for all their presumed acquisition of vocational skills, came to be regarded with suspicion by both sides of industry.

Despite the general label of 'technical schools', it is important to recognize important differences in aims and curricula between the different types of school. Junior technical schools (JTSs), developed in the interwar period in the UK, were limited to a specific, clearly designated function, according to the Hadow Report of 1926 'to prepare pupils for domestic employment' (p 33). In such schools foreign language teaching was not encouraged except where it could be shown to be of 'direct vocational value' (Board of Education, 1937, p 20). There were no general examinations for JTS pupils, in order to maintain 'the individuality of the schools and the flexibility of their curricula and syllabuses' (*ibid*, p 35). More important as a guide to their efficiency, in the view of the Board of Education, was the 'actual performance' of their products in industry and business, to be judged by local employers 'in the cold light of industrial and commercial efficiency' (*ibid*, p 36). Indeed, throughout the 1930s the Board of Education resisted local pressures to broaden the curriculum and upgrade the status of JTSs, in order to maintain their role in training 'the British workman' (Board of Education, 1931). According to A Abbott, the Board of Education's Chief Inspector of Technical Schools, the JTS should be regarded as a 'school for training pupils who will eventually become foremen' (Abbott, 1934).

The secondary technical school, by contrast, was intended to provide a more general education within the changed educational context of 'secondary education for all'. It was therefore intended to develop a broader curriculum than the JTS had done, and to admit pupils at the age of 11 rather than 13. The possible implications of this development continued to worry Board officials. W Elliott, Chief Inspector of Technical Schools in the early 1940s, noted that although some generalization might be allowed in courses, 'this could not be carried too far without turning these schools into pale reflections of grammar schools and so losing their specific character which depended on close touch with industry'. He insisted that although some pupils might proceed to university, and a few technical schools might include sixth forms,

> their main objective was training for direct entry to industry, and he did not want the existing freedom of technical schools to adapt themselves quickly and accurately to local industry to be impaired by university requirements, such as matriculation, which would be of concern only to the very few. (Board of Education, 1942)

In practice, secondary technical schools as they developed in the 1940s and 1950s varied widely in their character. Many STSs continued to recruit their pupils at the age of 13, rather than at 11 (Weaver, 1955). Relatively few of the schools attained the objectives of the Ministry in terms of resources. In addition to this, the rationale of the schools, individually and collectively, remained persistently ambiguous and elusive. The growth of examination entries in some of the schools was an unexpected development that increased uncertainty about what made them distinctive.

Hence, wide differences existed between the ideals and realities of the secondary technical schools. These differences in turn tended to magnify the problems involved in relating such schools to the needs and interests of the workplace. It was difficult to predict with accuracy the value of this new kind of school for different industries. One senior Board official, H B Wallis of the technical branch, anticipated in 1941 that 'the aim of the technical schools should be to supply a continuously increasing proportion of the recruits to a higher grade of craftsmen, and of those who pass from the workshop, often through the drawing office, to positions of responsibility as foremen, sub-managers, and so on'. But he was conscious that industrial demand and conditions would change rapidly after the war, and that different localities would greatly vary in their demands. He reasoned, therefore, that the STS should seek to furnish the 'adaptable recruit to an industry' rather than to develop 'specialised skill' (Wallis, 1941). He was still doubtful about their long-term prospects and identity, however:

> In spite of arguments to the contrary, I retain my doubts about generalised technical schools and although there are differences in the extent to which industrial aims can be defined (this, for instance is easier at Wolverhampton than at Beckenham) I believe that the maximum definition possible should be aimed at, both to secure the specific virtues of the technical school and to distinguish its objects from those of the grammar and modern schools.

Even so, there was little notion of how these schools should attempt to do this.

Despite the vagueness of their role, the STSs did succeed in general terms in providing particular kinds of recruits for industry. A relatively high proportion of the pupils from these schools went on to enter industry, although evidence on this is much fuller in relation to boys than to girls. An occupational analysis of men registering for National Service in the last quarter of 1955 showed that as many as 36.2 per cent of male technical school leavers had gone into skilled engineering trades, with a further 10.8 per cent going into building trades. Meanwhile, male grammar school leavers tended to enter professional and administrative careers, and male modern school leavers generally went into various forms of skilled or unskilled manual work (Crowther Committee, 1956).

The extent to which such an approach could be applied to girls and women remained unclear. Several interested observers had suggested in the 1930s that STSs for girls would help to raise the status of 'domestic careers' (eg, Horniblow, 1934). Discussions within the Association of Teachers of Domestic Subjects indicated similar aspirations, but in fact domestic subjects continued to suffer from low status, in STSs as elsewhere (Purvis, 1985). So far as posts in industry were concerned, girls had poor prospects even if they had come through a secondary technical education. In the commercial field, too, opportunity was limited, and promotion to management level was unlikely (see McCulloch, 1989b, pp 83–4). The Chief Inspector of Technical Schools, A G Gooch, noted that while commercial courses were the most popular for girls, the 'educational content' of such courses was 'low', and 'the chances of advancement beyond the status of shorthand-typist are limited' (Gooch, 1954).

It is important to reflect, too, that many of the most prominent and successful of these STSs articulated their rationale only incidentally in terms of their relationship with the workplace. The key issue for such schools was their educational character, as opposed to their specifically work-related role. According to A J Jenkinson, an influential supporter of the STSs, 'the vocational or technical element in it is a means of educating boys and girls rather than of putting them into certain jobs'. The approach of such schools was in his view 'justifiable not because it produces engineers or plasterers, but because its realistic content and practical applications are well suited to stimulate and guide the development of adolescents' (Jenkinson, 1949, p 301). Many STS heads echoed this general line, and even sought to emphasize their hopes of developing a more 'liberal' curriculum. For example, John Kingsland, head of Cray Valley Technical High School for Boys in Kent, noted that his school aimed to provide 'a sound all-round education for boys from eleven to eighteen years', characterized by 'both practical activities and closely related book study' (Kingsland, 1965, p 342).

Moreover, if industry was only incidental to many STSs, the representatives of industry often regarded the STSs as being marginal to their concerns. The Trades Union Congress preferred to focus on the prospects of comprehensive schools for pupils of all abilities and aptitudes. Meanwhile, the Federation of British Industries was more interested in attracting boys from grammar schools and public schools into industrial management than in developing links with STSs. It could still be noted in 1958 that:

> The FBI has not given much consideration to technical schools as such, but has concentrated more on the numerically much larger sphere of the grammar school and the secondary modern. (Dore, 1958)

The STSs had little part in their plans. Many technical school leavers did enter industry, and most STSs had close contacts with technical colleges and industries at a local level, but in a sense it was the grammar schools rather than the STSs that were regarded as the authentic 'prep schools of industry'.

Conclusions

Closer study of the historical experience of the secondary technical schools seems, therefore, to favour a 'loose' rather than a 'tight' connection with the workplace. The simple and unproblematic relationship that has been depicted in many accounts over the past decade seems open to serious challenge in this regard. Further qualitative research into the aims of particular schools, how they related to their localities, and the nature of their pupils and curriculum, is needed in order to investigate more fully the significance of this form of technical education. Extended inquiry into interest groups and the role of the state is also necessary for a greater understanding of the politics of 'education, youth and work'. Greater recognition of the symbolic and ideological nature of such initiatives, along the lines of Kliebard's approach, may help to explain their potency and (retrospective) appeal.

Such a reassessment should also be of value in addressing other initiatives in technical and vocational education. For example, the junior technical schools of the interwar period, although they were conceived and developed more explicitly in terms of a close correspondence with the needs of the workplace, may be open to a similar kind of analysis that challenges the assumptions under which they operated.

More recent and contemporary initiatives in the UK, such as the TVEI and the city technology colleges (CTCs), certainly deserve more attention of this type. At its inception, the TVEI was rationalized as a scheme designed to provide the 'rebirth of technical education' that was essential if Britain was to compete successfully with its economic and industrial rivals (*The Times*, 1982). Within a few years, its tone and rationale had altered significantly, so that as well as reflecting 'a vision for the future taking account of changing patterns of occupations and employment and what they mean for education and training' (Young, 1984, p 449), it was also 'about educating people, about broadening the curriculum to give them new subjects to which to relate' (*ibid*, p 457). In practice, too, the TVEI proved to be 'very varied — so varied that there is no such thing as a TVEI stereotype' (Maclure, 1985). The aims of the city technology colleges, beneath the general rationalizations, were so broad and varied that parents at one flagship CTC assumed that such institutions represented 'the new grammar schools' (Walford and Miller, 1991, p 119).

The role of education in preparing youth for the labour market appears in the light of such evidence to be highly complex and anything but straightforward. As Mathieson and Bernbaum have argued, current drives for reform need to be placed 'in a context which treats the current prescriptions and recommendations as themselves problematic, and as being at risk precisely because the level of analysis from which they begin is inadequate' (Mathieson and Bernbaum, 1988, p 127). Awareness of the historical experience of technical and vocational education may help policy-makers at least to avoid 'reinventing the wheel', and perhaps even to appreciate the complexities and problems involved in curriculum reform.

References

Abbott, A (1934) Oral evidence to Board of Education consultative committee, 26 January, *Board of Education papers ED. 10/151*, London: Public Record Office.

Barnett, C (1986) *The Audit of War: The Illusion and Reality of Britain as a Great Nation*, London: Macmillan.

Beeby, C E (1937) *The Education of the Adolescent in New Zealand*, Wellington: NZCER.

Board of Education (1931) Note of meeting with deputation of Association of Directors and Secretaries, 6 November, *Board of Education papers ED. 12/419*, London: Public Record Office.

Board of Education (1937) *A Review of Junior Technical Schools in England*, London: HMSO.

Board of Education (1942) Minutes of 10th meeting of the Norwood Committee on the secondary school curriculum and examinations, 2–3 October 1942, addendum, Board of Education Papers ED. 12/478, London: Public Record Office.

Bowles, S and Gintis, H (1976) *Schooling in Capitalist America*, London: Routledge and Kegan Paul.

Burgess, K (1993) 'Education policy in relation to employment in Britain, 1935–45: a decade of "missed opportunities" ', *History of Education*, **22**, 4, 365–90.

Campbell, A E (1941) *Educating New Zealand*, Wellington: Department of Internal Affairs.

Crowther Committee (1956) Memo: The modern and technical school leaver (educational background and employment), Raybould Papers, Museum of History of Education, University of Leeds.

Dore, A J H (1958) Letter to Captain E C L Turner, 7 February, Federation of British Industries Papers 200/F/3/T2/1/8, University of Warwick.

Gooch, A G (1954) Memo: Secondary technical education, 28 December, Ministry of Education Papers ED147/207, London: Public Record Office.

Gordon, L (1984) 'Ideology and policy in the history of New Zealand technical education, 1900–1930', MA thesis, Massey University.

Hadow Report (1926) *The Education of the Adolescent*, London: HMSO.

Horniblow, E H (1934) Memo to Board of Education consultative committee, Board of Education Papers ED.10/222, London: Public Record Office.

Jenkinson, A J (1949) 'The slow progress of secondary technical education', *Vocational Aspect*, **1**, 93, 296–302.

Jones, A, McCulloch, G, Marshall, J, Smith, G and Smith, L (1990) *Myths and Realities: Schooling in New Zealand*, Palmerston North: Dunmore Press.

Kantor, H and Tyack, D (1982) 'Introduction: historical perspectives on vocationalism in American education', in Kantor, H, and Tyack, D (eds) *Work, Youth, and Schooling: Historical Perspectives on Vocationalism in American Education*, Stanford: Stanford University Press.

Kingsland, J C (1965) 'Cray Valley Technical High School for Boys (Kent)', in Gross, R E (ed) *British Secondary Education: Overview and Appraisal*, London: Oxford University Press, pp 335–68.

Kliebard, H (1990) 'Curriculum policy as symbolic action: connecting education with the workplace', in Haft, H and Hopmann, S (eds) *Case Studies in Curriculum Administration History*, London: Falmer, pp 148–58.

McCulloch, G (1988) 'Imperial and colonial designs: the case of Auckland Grammar School', *History of Education*, **17**, 4, 257–67.

McCulloch, G (1989a) 'City technology colleges: an old choice of school?', *British Journal of Educational Studies*, **37**, 1, 30–43.

McCulloch, G (1989b) *The Secondary Technical School: A Usable Past?* London: Falmer.

McCulloch, G (1992) 'Constructing the community: secondary schools and their neighbourhoods in 20th century Auckland', *Australian Journal of Education*, **36**, 2, 143–56.

Maclure, S (1985) 'Hands up for the enterprise culture?', *Times Educational Supplement*, 8 February.

Mathieson, M and Bernbaum, G (1988) 'The British disease: a British tradition?', *British Journal of Educational Studies*, **26**, 2, 126–74.

Ministry of Education (1947) *The New Secondary Education*, London: HMSO.

Nash, R (1983) *Schools Can't Make Jobs*, Palmerston North: Dunmore Press.

Nelson-Rowe, S (1991) 'Corporation schooling and the labour market at General Electric', *History of Education Quarterly*, **31**, 91, 27–46.

Nicol, J (1940) *The Technical Schools of New Zealand: An Historical Survey* (Foreword by Sir Thomas Hunter), Wellington: NZCER.

Purvis, J (1985) 'Domestic subjects since 1870', in Goodson, I (ed) *Social Histories Of The Secondary Curriculum*, London: Falmer, pp 145–76.

Roderick, G and Stephens, M (eds) (1981) *Where Did We Go Wrong? Industry, Education and Economy of Victorian Britain*, London: Falmer.

Roderick, G and Stephens, M (eds) (1982) *The British Malaise: Industrial Performance, Education and Training in Britain Today*, London: Falmer.

Rubinstein, W D (1993) *Capitalism, Culture, and Decline in Britain 1750–1990*, London: Routledge.

Sanderson, M (1987) *Educational Opportunity and Social Change in England*, London: Faber and Faber.

Sultana, R (1992) *Education and National Development: Historical and Critical Perspectives on Vocational Schooling in Malta*, Malta: Mireva Press.

Times, The (1982) 'Tebbit starts technical education scheme', 13 November.

Times Educational Supplement (1956) 'Industry's prep schools', 16 March.

Walford, G and Miller, H (1991) *City Technology Colleges*, Milton Keynes: Open University Press.

Wallis, H B (1941) Memo: Technical education: post-war policy and organisation, 15 October, Board of Education Papers ED. 136/296, London: Public Record Office.

Weaver, T R (1955) Note: Secondary technical schools, 14 January, Ministry of Education

Papers ED.147/207, London: Public Record Office.

Whitty, G (1992) 'Urban education in England and Wales', in Coulby, D. and Jones, C. (Eds.) *World Yearbook Of Education 1992: Urban Education*, London: Kogan Page, pp 39–53.

Wiener, M (1981) *English Culture And The Decline Of The Industrial Spirit, 1850–1980*, Cambridge: Cambridge University Press.

Young, D (1982) 'Helping the young help themselves', *Times Educational Supplement*, 26 November.

Young, D (1984) 'Coping with change: the New Training Initiative', *Journal of the Royal Society of Arts*, **5335**.

Part 4:   Youth, society and citizenship

Introduction

Leslie Bash

The chapters in this final section address some of the issues central to the lives of young people. There is a good deal of rhetoric concerning the need for young people to become full participants in their societies. Yet this frequently conflicts with a social order which disadvantages and discriminates against certain groups through the operation of its education/training arrangements. While the focus is, in the main, Western Europe and the United States, fundamental questions are explored in relation to integration into society at large against the backcloth of diversity and inequality, structures of power relations, and the capacity of state and inter-state machinery to aid the process of transition to full citizenship.

Chisholm's chapter looks at the European Union, focusing initially upon the transition of young people to 'social adulthood, political autonomy and economic independence'. This is followed by an analysis of the tension between education/training systems and 'the directions and the pace of economic and social change'. More specifically, the chapter by Watts examines careers guidance systems in the European Union, looking at the main differences between national systems as well as common trends and a possible emerging strategy. The last three chapters consider the prospects for particular groups: Heikkinen examines the fate of women and girls in the wake of the breakdown of the ideology of 'Nordic welfare-society'; Thomas and Moran's study concerns the peparation of urban African-American youth for citizenship; and Bash looks at the integration of young people from the Jewish community into UK society.

15. Youth transitions in the European union

Lynne Chisholm

Recent responses from British, Dutch and German students to the question of Europe's meaning for their lives included much anxiety about 'drowning in a United Europe', 'preservation of our cultural heritage' and lack of a personal sense of 'being European' — a seemingly unknown quantity (Chisholm, du Bois-Reymond and Coffield, 1994).

In practical terms, however, the past five years or so have seen a considerable upswing in transnational policy interest and applied research activity as European integration processes have gathered momentum, fuelled not only by the prospect of Maastricht but also by social and economic transformation in post-communist Europe. Youth studies has been no exception; in fact, it is a field that has derived considerable impetus from these developments. Youth issues are seldom a powerful political arena or policy portfolio on their own account, but they do become highly visible in certain circumstances, all of which are associated with periods of social change and political unrest. Quite simply, young people embody the hopes and fears of their elders for the future of their societies. But additionally, age/youth and generation consistently draw theoretical and empirical interest as social locations within which social change processes might somehow be observed and understood. /Describing and interpreting the social construction of youth transitions became the subject of intense attention during the 1980s in Western Europe as the pace of economic and social change began to suggest not only the close of the 'postwar era' but also macro-level transition to post-Fordist economies, post-industrial societies and post-modern cultures. The persistent lack of other than *ex negativo* definitions of the 'new age' reflects, on the one hand, continuing disagreement about the scale and implications of observed changes in life circumstances and value orientations. On the other hand, it suggests that economic, social and cultural complexity increasingly defies the attempt to construct overarching tableaux that catch the spirit of the age./

Both of these tendencies are reproduced in youth studies, communities, and discourses across Europe, which, on the whole, identify similar empirical trends but within and between which their significance is differently interpreted. This chapter is not the place to contribute to these debates. The first section offers an overview of young people's

circumstances and orientations as they make the transition towards social
adulthood, political autonomy and economic independence in the
countries of the European Union. The European Union is not Europe, of
course, but it is the nearest approximation to Western Europe for which a
base of information and analysis has become available across the past
decade. The Commission itself has only very hesitantly begun to engage
in social research as a distinct activity (although this is expected to change
in the near future), but has consistently invested in what would today be
termed policy research into social and educational questions, including
youth affairs (though almost exclusively into unemployment and training
issues). However, the very existence of the European Community has
undoubtedly contributed to providing a context in which communication
and interchange between discourses has accelerated more rapidly than it
might otherwise have done.

The second section of the chapter looks more specifically at education
and training issues within contemporary youth transitions. It neither
describes member states' education and training arrangements, nor does it
describe participation levels and patterns. This would simply duplicate
information now widely available elsewhere. Instead, the discussion
considers some of the tensions that arise as education and qualification
arrangements move out of synchronization with the directions and the
pace of economic and social change, and gives some examples of the
consequences for young people's options and actions. The closing section
then turns to an evaluative account of the directions in which Community
level policy on education, training and youth affairs is presently heading.
A major reorganization and rationalization of Community programmes is
due to be implemented from the beginning of 1995; these plans have been
accompanied by a shift of policy emphasis towards the creation of a Social
Europe alongside the Single Market. It may be useful to consider the
extent to which these developments offer scope for closer and more
positive response to the Union's young people themselves.

Youth transitions and social change in Western Europe

During the 1980s, the interdisciplinary youth studies literature across
Western Europe focused an increasing amount of theoretical and empirical
attention on the implications of contemporary social change processes for
the social construction of the youth phase (Cavalli and Galland, 1993;
Chisholm and Liebau, 1993; du Bois-Reymond and Oechsle, 1990). Since
the early 1990s, intensified transnational debate on these issues has
considered the extent to which the trends observed in individual Western
European societies are broadly similar across countries, and whether these
trends can be understood as representing broadly similar kinds of
macrosocial and economic change in Western Europe as a whole.

First, over the last 30 years or so (and accelerating in the past decade),
the life phase 'youth' has become more extended in duration and for
increasing proportions of the youth population. The youth phase has also
become less standardized, both in the sequencing of its interim 'milestones'

en route to social adulthood and citizenship and in the kinds of orientations and values represented by young people's ways of life and lifestyles. These trends can be usefully subsumed under the phrase 'extension, fragmentation and destandardization of the youth phase and youth transitions' (see Buchmann, 1989; Heinz, 1991). The changes to which these terms refer are multi-faceted and interrelated, and they can be observed in all spheres of social life: family, education, employment, leisure and social/political participation. Broadly speaking, the consequences of rising economic affluence and social reforms in post-1945 Western Europe set important elements of these changes in motion. The creeping return of austerity from the mid 1970s and, in particular, the ensuing collapse of youth labour markets, intensified their pace.

The patterns involved can be described, in outline form at least, very simply. More young people – and in particular, more young women – stay in education and training systems for longer and reach higher levels of qualification. Entry into the labour force consequently takes place later, but this is not simply (and for many, not primarily) a function of voluntary decisions in favour of continuing education and training beyond the minimum school leaving age. Not only have member states pursued policies of extending compulsory education and training participation, but they have also strongly encouraged post-compulsory participation too. Rising qualification demands in high-technology and service sector oriented economies are one reason, but an equally strong motivation during the 1980s has been to contain and dampen very high levels of youth unemployment and general problems of the socio-economic insertion of young people in the current economic circumstances. In other words, many young people are effectively obliged to spend longer in education and training – including in the palette of measures specifically designed for first job seekers and the young unemployed – whether they wish to do so or not, and regardless of whether such participation actually leads to improved labour market prospects or not. When young people do enter the labour force, they are increasingly likely to find part-time, temporary and precarious jobs. Only after some time, and for some never, do they find secure employment, which may bear a direct relationship neither to their qualifications and training experience nor to their personal interests and aptitudes.

Their circumstances in this respect dovetail with generalized labour market trends towards the flexibilization and deregulation of employment, by which increasing sections of the labour force are affected – including in higher qualified and professional occupations which have represented, until recently, the epitome of job and earnings security. Furthermore, the widespread instability and unpredictability of the education–employment transition also deconstructs its formerly unidirectional character, in which education and training preceded, once and for all, employment. Increasingly, young people move back and forth between all three and between combinations of these three elements. Once more, this fits into a more general trend towards a cyclical approach to learning and qualification, in which periods of alternation between education and paid work are envisaged to extend across the life cycle as a whole – as a consequence, in the first instance, of rapidly changing qualification requirements, although, in the second instance, such alternation might be viewed an an element of the strategy to combat general structural unemployment.

These changes in young people's circumstances as they make the transition between education, training and the labour force have a number of implications for other aspects of their lives, not the least of which is their acquisition of financial independence, and, alongside this, household autonomy. During the 1980s, young people's financial circumstances on the whole deteriorated. Fewer were earning regularly at a level that could adequately support autonomy from parents or from some form of public-purse income support. More were working part time to part-finance their education and training, in good measure due to the falling real value of allowances, grants and loans. Others were able – or obliged – to rely more heavily on their parents, whether to finance their studies or to replace or supplement their own earnings. Setting up an independent household, alone or as a part of family formation, has obviously become more difficult as a result – and this during a period of considerable change in lifestyle values in many (but not all) parts of Europe, which increasingly favour a period of being single and living either alone or with peers in shared housing. At the same time, housing markets across Europe have drifted into considerable imbalance: housing supply, in quantity, type, distribution and cost, has not kept up with changes in patterns of demand and affordability. Young people have been significantly affected by these imbalances during the 1980s, so that in many member states there has been both a rise in the young homeless and a decline in the proportions of young people living independently of their parental home. Accommodation problems are one (but by no means the only) reason why young people find it difficult, for example, to move to other towns and regions to take up training and employment opportunities.

The postwar decades in Western Europe brought not only a period of economic affluence (though not for all countries to similar extents and at the same time), but also a period of social and cultural change. Expansion of public educational provision and opportunity significantly changed the socialization contexts and institutional conditions under which young people make transitions to adulthood. Liberalization of values and lifestyles, together with the relaxation of rigid norms of behaviour, produced a 'flowering' of youth culture and youth sub-cultures as autonomous forms of cultural expression. Young people themselves were materially involved in initiating these processes (ie, they were not passive recipients of changes designed by their elders). The value shifts set in motion during this period and continuing in intensified form today can be described by the terms 'individualization', 'pluralization' and 'post-materialism' (see Beck, 1986; Zoll, 1992; in general: Giddens, 1991; Lash, 1990)

These characteristics of contemporary cultural patterns are also reflected in young people's ways of life. Broadly, relations between parents and children have become more open and relaxed, with a higher value placed upon respect for the rights and integrity of the individual family member, including its younger dependent members. In turn, more young people today have a greater sense of themselves as autonomous individuals who can — and moreover should — make their own plans and decisions about their lives. This necessarily brings a greater measure of individual responsibility for plans and decisions — and their consequences. Expanded chances for autonomous action bring increased risks of personally having to 'shoulder the blame' should things go wrong. But in terms of adopting ways of life and lifestyles, young people are also in a position to select from a wider range of potential alternatives, and to conclude that the views of others about the virtues or otherwise of doing so are not necessarily materially relevant to their own decisions and actions. The desire of rising numbers of young people to establish their own household — separately from their parents, perhaps also from their current partner, and not necessarily even with friends — is therefore unsurprising, even though much more difficult to realize today than 10 or 20 years ago.

Such changing value orientations are also implicated in changing patterns of marriage and family-building. On the whole, young people across Europe — from different starting-points — are waiting longer to marry and have children. The lack of an adequate economic basis to do so is a factor which, for many young people and in many parts of Europe, cannot be overlooked. But it is equally evident that changing values are contributing independently to these patterns — just as for the rising popularity of cohabitation and of single parenthood (at least for some young adult women making a conscious choice). Whilst the overwhelming majority of young people continue to value and to plan ultimately for a stable partnership with children, the recognition and acceptance of alternative patterns and of changing constellations across the life course is widespread in younger generations everywhere. In other words, the fluidity, cyclicality and reversibility of plans, decisions and ways of private and family life match similar trends in the spheres of education, training and employment.

Changing attitudes and practices in relation to gender roles and divisions of labour at home and in paid work are an important aspect of individualization and pluralization trends. The fundamental distribution of social and economic power between the sexes has changed relatively little (although it might be argued that here, too, we are on the brink of change), but there is no question that ever-increasing numbers of girls and young women aspire to and increasingly forcefully demand equality of opportunity, practice and outcome in all spheres. In the last 30 years, most progress has been achieved in educational participation and achievement, if not distribution across qualification sectors. Relatively much less progress has been achieved in equalizing participation in training, especially in terms of industrial and occupational sector distribution and in the labour market value of credentials and experience. As a partial consequence, little progress has been made in equalizing labour force distribution, both horizontal and vertical. However, the persistence of unequal gender relations in the family is at least as important in accounting for girls' and women's continued employment and career disadvantage. Equalizing women's and men's participation in and responsibility for housework and childcare is but one aspect of this problem; equally important is the question of the general valuation of such activities. Young women no longer apologize for their commitment to family life, but demand recognition of the necessity and the desirability of participation and responsibility in both family life and paid work, for both sexes. Young women construct 'dual life plans' which incorporate both elements as a matter of course, ie, of necessity *and* choice. It is young men who are lagging behind in this respect, although there is some evidence of change here, for some groups of young men in some contexts.

At the same time, the structuring of paid work itself and the persistence of traditional understandings of work and career patterns amongst employers and trainers hinder the realization of the potential for change that does exist amongst younger generations. A greater measure of flexibility and openness with respect to gender relations is one dimension of this potential for change. Another is the rise of what have been called post-material values in European societies, which have direct implications for young people's orientations towards education, training and employment themselves. Briefly, such values imply a distancing, first, from work as an activity to which individuals sacrifice themselves for the greater good or for the benefit of others and, second, from paid work as a purely instrumental activity for the purposes of financial support. Instead, such activities – paid or not – should be spheres of life in which, at least to some extent, individuals can find a sense of purpose, self-expression and self-actualization. This kind of orientation also implies that the definition of 'work' as a strongly bounded activity quite distinct from activities taking place in other everyday life contexts loses some of its logic and value-rationality. The boundaries between work, family, leisure and social participation themselves become more fluid and flexible, whereas the motivations for engaging in activities of all kinds become more individualized and open-ended in character.

There is a sharp dilemma in writing about youth and social change in Europe. In effect, it can be reasonably argued that such summaries paste over the gaping cracks of diversity in young people's life circumstances and prospects – not only between European societies but also within each of them. The only alternative, however, is a counsel of despair which denies the possibility of considering links at all between what are after all, in global terms, quite closely related economies, societies and cultures. This overview neither privileges (false) homogeneity nor discounts the significance of diversity, including the social and economic polarizations that European diversity inherently reflects. Rather, it proposes a mutual starting point from which to consider critically such diversity.

Education and training within contemporary youth transitions

The diversity of education and training systems together with widely varying participation and formal qualification rates and patterns across Europe are well documented. Nevertheless, during the 1980s, policy attention everywhere has focused upon measures directed both at raising overall participation and qualification levels and at improving the efficiency of provision in relatively simplistic cost–benefit terms. Policy emphases have variously focused on raising participation levels themselves (Portugal, France), on redirecting qualification profiles within the context of major 'root and branch' reforms (UK, Spain), on expanding vocational education and training programmes (most countries, in response to youth unemployment), or on cohort distribution imbalances across tracks, sectors and levels (FRG). At the beginning of the decade, the need to respond to youth unemployment – in practice, by inducing lengthier participation, whether as pupils/students or as trainees/apprentices – was the driving force behind education and training policy-making concerns. By the end of the decade, emphasis had shifted firmly onto the development of human resources as a vital and perhaps decisive element in, first, economic competition between the member states after the introduction of the Single Market post-1992 and, second, global competition between the EU and the Pacific Rim economies in the coming decades.

It is, therefore, economic rather than social concerns that have dominated educational and training policies in the 1980s, but national starting-points have been diverse and responses themselves have varied in their intensity. Accession to the Community generated strong pressures for the overall modernization of education, training and qualification systems in Spain and Portugal (though much less so in Greece). On the other hand, the UK and France (but much less so Italy), have been deeply concerned to maintain ground within the Community against the FRG, especially by the expansion and upgrading of vocational training and qualification routes. At the same time, education and training systems and qualification processes have *not* been the subject of significant reforms in the majority of member states at all. Rather, in response to changing patterns of economic and social chances and risks, young people's education and training *use patterns and motivations* have shifted. Existing structures and processes of provision are showing the strain: the pace of social change is outstripping the capacity for appropriate response under present arrangements. This is one reason for the urgency with which education and training policy is now hurtling to the top of the Community's economic and social policy agendas, to which we return in the third section of this chapter. But first: what kinds of fundamental tensions and contradictions can be pinpointed in the intersections between education/training and contemporary youth transitions?

Long-term restructuring of the modalities of social reproduction in modern Western societies towards stratification systems legitimated by achievement rather than ascription has placed education and training trajectories at the centre of the social construction of youth transitions. This restructuring can be seen in terms of the contemporary youth phase as an 'educational moratorium' rather than the 'transition moratorium' of earlier modernity. The two moratoria can be distinguished along two axes: dependence versus autonomy in relation to the 'adult world' and its institutions and organizations; and family- and work-centred versus education- and media/consumption-centred socialization and social control agents and processes. Insofar as social and economic changes loosen intergenerational and particularistic ties, gradually replacing these with intragenerational contexts and universalistic orientations, relationships between past, present and future are reshaped in the life perspectives of individual subjects. The 'present' of youth transitions is no longer so clearly prestructured by the 'past' of family and culture of origin, but is rather generationally self-referential and more directly implicated in constructing a social biographical 'future'. The 'present' has to 'do more work' in the practice of constructing and reconstructing subjectivity and social locations; this work takes place in and around education and training tracks and processes.

The result is a stretching out of the 'present' in which the long and winding road between origins and destinations becomes longer and more convoluted – but also lends wanderers at least the impression (and perhaps some degree of reality) that individual steps along the way are not necessarily irretrievable. In northwest European societies, we have now reached a point at which the road is up to 20 years long. Quite apart from the issue of long-term social and economic marginalization and non-integration occasioned by educational selection and underachievement, the tasks of educational/vocational qualification and occupational integration can take up some one-third of a standard 'employment life'. Only a quarter of a century ago, the majority of young people across Europe not only made the transition between education/training and employment (more accurately: production roles) much earlier than they do today, but they also typically made that transition quite cleanly and swiftly. This transition is turning into a drawn out and fragmentary sequence extending well into the third decade of life. Not only does this have consequences for young people's financial circumstances (as noted earlier), but it also transforms the context in which education and training takes place. This context is no longer obviously linear (education/training qualify for and precede paid work) and it is increasingly populated by young adults more able to assert *their* needs and demands of education and training (rather than the other way around). Given the parallel pressure to acquire as many formal qualifications as possible in order to secure a good foothold in a highly competitive labour market, tensions in the relationships between educators/trainers and learners must inevitably intensify.

Mass consumption of education and training over longer periods and to higher levels of qualification may have produced generational cleavages in values and lifestyles between those growing up before and after the era of educational expansion in the 1960s/1970s, but all the evidence indicates that relations of social inequality have remained stable. In Beck's (1986) analysis, expanded access to education and training may have encouraged individualistic strategies of betterment (which are not *prima facie* undesirable), but once labour market and career opportunities contract, education and qualification become little more than a defence against downward mobility. The effective demasking of the illusion of upward social mobility via educational achievement is especially precarious in the case of gender relations: young women across Europe are now at least as well-educated and well-qualified as are young men, but their equal integration into the labour market is blocked by structural under-employment and unemployment and by segmented labour markets. A return to traditional family-centred roles for women — however forcefully supported by governments' reprivatization policies — is simply no longer financially feasible for the majority of households and families, regardless of whether young women are prepared to relinquish their equal prioritization of family and paid work (and all the evidence underlines that they are not so prepared).

Shortage, redistribution and relativization of paid work have consequences for the rationale and use of education and training systems and contents. Where qualifications do not lead to jobs, the rationale of vocational education and training is weakened. Where young people do not *expect* their qualifications to lead to jobs, they take different kinds of decisions about what to do next. Increasingly, they sign up for more courses, but are decreasingly attached to their contents, whose ultimate utility appears highly questionable. The 1980s was a decade in which vocational education and training was promoted as the best defence against poor employment prospects and the best guarantee of 'real-life relevance' with the aim of raising young people's attachment to education. It was equally a decade whose policy-making — at national and at Community level — failed to ensure adequate opportunities for social and economic integration through paid work. The dual phenomenon of young people's detachment from and redefinition of education and training has emerged as a major consequence. Whilst the tasks of gaining formal qualifications are regarded as a necessary but senseless charade, the search for intrinsic meaning via education as self-development is more urgently pursued than ever.

This singular contradiction is, however, a singular privilege of the educationally successful. At the other end of the spectrum of youth transitions, credential inflation now means that unqualified young people have virtually no chance of securing social and economic integration; the lowest levels of qualification increasingly function as negative ascriptions rather than as evidence of positive achievement. In the European context, such polarization of chances and risks has a double dynamic: social polarizations are joined by regional polarizations between centres and peripheries. The modernization of education, training and qualifications systems acts here as a two-edged sword: both essential for economic development and competitiveness in the Single Market and constraining for the patterns of youth transitions, in which acquiring formal qualifications is the bottleneck through which all must pass en route to social and occupational integration (Machado Pais, 1993).

A set of recently completed studies on young people's needs and demands for vocational counselling and guidance in the EU offer many indications of these kinds of dislocations across education/training and employment transitions. Denmark's education system, for example, rests on universal participation in comprehensive *folkeskoler* through to the age of 16 (or 17, with the optional year followed by about half of each cohort). Early leavers — those who drop out before completing compulsory schooling — are very few indeed. The situation changes significantly in the 'youth education' (16–19 general or vocational upper secondary education and vocational training courses) and higher education sectors, where 'wastage rates' are viewed as high enough to warrant policy concern. Currently, some 15 per cent of those who register for courses in the youth education sector do not complete; in higher education, about two-fifths of those embarking upon a course either drop out or change track before completion. Overall, some three-fifths of the total extent of 'chopping and changing' in the education and training system arises from pre-completion discontinuation, the bulk of which occurs in the higher education sector. A further quarter is accounted for by 'double qualification': having success-fully completed one course, young people embark on a second, which leads to more qualifications at the same or at a lower level than those already held. The remainder of 'chopping and changing' is largely accounted for by non-completion of vocational training courses in the 16–19 sector.

From an economic viewpoint, high rates of 'chopping and changing' might be seen as wasteful of individual and public resources – and, indeed, are so viewed by Danish government policy. Educationalists and counsellors argue, on the other hand, that searching for the 'right' course and future occupation is a productive activity to be expected and, within reason, encouraged. Insofar as employers, young people and work tasks themselves converge towards higher demands for intrinsic commitment and personal identification with job and career, lengthier periods of search and experimentation are a logical consequence. Furthermore, non-completion does not necessarily indicate lack of application or interest on the part of students/trainees – instead (as Danish studies have demonstrated) they may well be expressing their dissatisfaction with course content, teaching/learning methods, and subsequent employment prospects. Finally, discontinuation/double qualification and unemployment rates have indeed been shown to be linked: when unemployment rates fall, discontinuation rates rise; whereas double qualification rates rise in the years following peaks in unemployment rates.

These patterns suggest that young people's decisions and behaviour are processes of negotiation and juggling between intrinsic and instrumental orientations to education and training in what have become, for most young people, complex and precarious transitions towards social and occupational integration. One important aspect of this complexity and pre-cariousness is the relatively weak link between type of qualification and type of employment which emerged, for example, in Belgian studies on education–employment transitions in the late 1980s. As elsewhere in Western Europe, post-compulsory education and training participation rates in Belgium have risen sharply across the 1980s. The reasons lie, first and foremost, in the scarcity of employment opportunities: labour market entry is consciously postponed and persistent efforts are made to gain qualifications in order to improve job chances. These efforts are reflected in the scales both of repeating the final year of compulsory schooling to gain a good leaving certificate (currently reaching up to a third of an age cohort) and of double qualification strategies in the upper secondary vocational education sector.

However, the qualifications young people obtain at this intermediate level are not a reliable guide to the kind of jobs they find. Graduates from the business studies track in upper level technical schools, whose training is intended to lead to white-collar employment in commerce and administration, are frequently subject to underemployment, ie, in jobs for which they are formally overqualified. Those young women who find jobs (and they are significantly more likely to be unemployed or employed on part-time and temporary contracts) do, for the most part, find white-collar office employment (but not necessarily at the appropriate level). Young men, on the other hand, are just as likely subsequently to be found in blue-collar as in white-collar employment. In some sectors – such as in the Belgian clothing industry – the link between qualification and job held remains close insofar as employers only recruit appropriately trained and qualified young people. But those who are so recruited constitute only a proportion of those young people who successfully finish their vocational education/training course: a year after completion, only a third of those who have gained the relevant qualification have found employment in the clothing industry.

Recruitment patterns differ between industrial and occupational sectors and young people themselves may decide not to seek employment in the sector for which they have qualified. But overall, it is clear that vocational education and training policies and practices – whether education-led, as in Belgium, or employer-led, as in the FRG's Dual System, or in mixed models for which the UK is now an example – do not subscribe to the principles that young people themselves are exhorted to pursue. They do not (and arguably cannot), in other words, respond effectively to labour market needs and demands. From young people's perspectives, it is only too plausible to conclude that qualifications have restricted intrinsic value in relation to occupational and work task relevance. Amassing qualifications *per se* offers a defence against labour market marginalization and exclusion, but the content of education and training is of ambiguous significance at best.

The only certainty is that minimum level qualifications or lack of qualifications offer very poor employment prospects: across Europe, it is these young people who are most vulnerable to long-term unemployment and who, where they do find jobs, are to be found in low-paid and precarious employment with no prospects of improvement. Level for level, young people of minority origin and young women find it more difficult to turn their qualifications into employment in general and into appropriate employment in particular. In some member states (for example, in Luxembourg and the FRG), educational marginalization and underachievement amongst minority groups remains high, so that these young people are highly overrepresented amongst the low-qualified and the unqualified. In other countries (for example, in the UK and the Netherlands), inadequate and discriminatory provision and response continues to play a significant role for the educational achievement of minority group young people but, at the same time, their commitment to education and qualification is high and, for specific groups, levels of formal achievement are well above average.

This is particularly so in the case of young minority group women (for example, see Safia Mirzah, 1992); and it is generally the case that young women are better qualified than are young men. Everywhere in the Community, they continue their education and education-led training for longer and to higher levels precisely because their employment and workplace-led training opportunities are poorer than those of young men at comparable stages of qualification. In turn, this means that it is young men who are overrepresented amongst the young unqualified. In regions where the traditional industrial or agricultural employment base has collapsed following large-scale economic restructuring (both national and in the European-wide context), such young people find themselves in a hopeless situation. This is the case, for example, on the Bilbao estuary in Spain's Basque country, where the steel and heavy industries that had originally grown up around shipbuilding have contracted dramatically since the mid 1970s, thus removing established channels of transition into training and employment for the large numbers of young men who left school at the minimum age (or indeed earlier). The disappearance of traditional training and employment prospects has inevitably left those young men behind who, for a variety of reasons, do not or cannot respond by developing higher levels of attachment to and success in formal schooling.

The consequences can be personally debilitating for those affected, expressed in withdrawal from (and not rejection of) active participation in social and economic life. Such young people are likely not to seek or to demand education, training and job opportunities at all: 'they are superfluous to requirements and they know it; their problem is that they are superfluous' (de Castro and de Elejabeitia, cited in Chisholm, 1994, p 96). It is unlikely that young people in these circumstances will have developed the self-confidence and personal resources to formulate and realize positive alternative life plans. In any event, their existence is a sharp reminder of the apparent inability of contemporary Western European societies and economies to foster potential and offer positive perspectives to their younger generations across the full range, as opposed to those who have proved themselves to be 'the brightest and the best' in highly individualized and competitive contexts. This brings the discussion back into the policy arena and the current concern at EU level for enhanced development of 'human resources'.

Community policies and youth affairs

Youth affairs remains a policy field for which the Commission has no explicit brief as such; paragraph 126 restricts Union involvement in education policy to that of encouraging cooperation between the member states and, if necessary, supporting and supplementing their actions; paragraph 127 allows wider involvement in vocational training policy, in which the Community is empowered to implement policies which support and supplement the actions of the member states.

Practically speaking, however, the scale of EU investment and involvement in education, training and (to a lesser extent) youth exchange and mobility programmes together with supporting infrastructures for information dissemination and exchange, language learning and curriculum development has steadily increased. Practitioners at local level throughout the EU would today find it difficult to imagine life without the many action programmes, even if criticism of obscure and long-winded procedures in meeting the criteria and securing adequate resources dominates immediate opinions. In some member states (such as Ireland, Portugal and Greece) nationally formulated reforms in education and training would be non-implementable without the transfer of Community resources. For the period 1995 to 1999, the Commission proposes to devote Ecu 1,005.6m to Socrates (planned to cover all education initiatives), Ecu 801.8m to Leonardo (vocational training) and Ecu 157m to Youth for Europe III (promotion of active citizenship). These are significant resources to be distributed; they imply significant *de facto* involvement in the face of *de jure* restrictions. In other words, the policy climate at Community level is not quite as insignificant as might be supposed (or wished).

The Community policy climate during the 1980s was increasingly dominated by the Single Market logic. In the case of youth affairs, for example, the core of Community involvement had, by the close of the decade, come to be interpreted for policy purposes in terms of exchange programmes and mobility. With the rising concern about the need to shape Europe into an economic force capable of competing successfully in the future with the Pacific Basin economies, the horizon of '1992' began to take on more significance. Social inclusion/exclusion comprised a secondary axis of policy concern, but the issues continued to be phrased in Single Market terms: Which groups of young people are in a position to take up the projected opportunities for greater interregional and transfrontier mobility in a positive context? Which groups, on the other hand, will either be less able to do so – or will find themselves unwillingly mobile? These kinds of questions became all the more pressing following the opening up of Eastern Europe after 1989, bringing the prospect of still more imbalanced standards of living and opportunity structures across Europe as a whole.

By the close of the 1980s, official Community policy documents and the realities of young people's lives were at considerable distance from each other. In recognition of this distance, a flurry of activity ensued, resulting in a series of Commission memoranda and proposals during 1990. Essentially, these confirmed the priority of raising skills and qualification levels in the Community's workforce in order to compete effectively on a global level, but introduced the 'European identity' anchored in citizenship rights, which could facilitate free movement throughout the Community whilst preserving regional-cultural diversity and socio-political harmony. The two themes of mobility and social cohesion became the key policy concepts informing Community level perspectives on youth affairs.

In the interim and in the light of the turbulence surrounding the ratification of the Maastricht Treaties and the impending accession of four new members (Norway, Sweden, Finland and Austria), the theme of social cohesion has gained ground and simplistic understandings of, and expectations for, mobility have been revised. During 1993/4 numerous policy documents have been published that place equal priority both on unemployment and its socially marginalizing consequences and on the need to upgrade workforce qualification levels in the context of rapidly changing labour force requirements. Up to a third of young people leaving school in the Community as a whole are inadequately formally qualified. This proportion includes those who leave school at or before the end of compulsory education with no diplomas (the unqualified); those whose general educational and/or vocational training qualifications are poor (the underqualified); those who do not proceed from general education into vocational education and training, and those whose education and training qualifications do not match labour force requirements in their home regions and perhaps further afield (the inappropriately qualified). The need for greater coherence in Community policy and practice is evident, which, in effect, demands greater cooperation and mutual effort on the part of the member states themselves.

The difficulty remains, *inter alia*, that there is no linear relationship between acquiring enhanced competences and improving young people's chances of securing (appropriate and satisfying) employment. So, for example, all other things being equal, those who have been on a placement abroad during their education and training may well be at an increasingly competitive advantage on the recruitment market. Unfortunately, all other things are not equal – partly because of credential inflation in tight labour markets, and partly because of increasingly complex patterns of inequalities of opportunity which, in turn, foster pernicious spirals of exclusion in the transition to adult life. From a Social Europe perspective, these are very worrying trends.

Whatever the precise mechanisms and processes are that lead to social and economic exclusion, inadequate access, participation and success in education and training are pivotal factors. They are pivotal factors not only because of the formal selection processes that accompany education and training as providers and arbiters of credentials themselves, which in turn open and close occupational routes and labour market opportunities. They are equally pivotal factors because education and training practices can either foster self-confidence and self-esteem by providing affirming experiences for individuals and groups, or they can, and frequently do, achieve precisely the reverse. Processes of exclusion and low self-esteem all too readily produce a vicious circle. In principle, the Youth for Europe programme, which is consciously detached from formal education and training contexts and which emphasizes creativity, self-initiative and solidarity within the framework of intercultural learning, could be a valuable means to combat personal and social negative spirals. In practice, the resources planned for the coming years fall far behind those allocated to education and vocational training.

In sum, the rising priority attached to youth affairs remains primarily informed by education and training policy concerns that are too narrowly formulated in terms of purely macroeconomic considerations. I might conclude by pointing out that effective economic policy presupposes effective and just social policy and practice. My preference, on this occasion, is to recall that youth transitions are about a good deal more than education and training. In this sense, young people's lives and education/training provision and practice are further apart than ever.

References

Beck, U (1986) *Risikogesellschaft. Auf dem Weg in eine andere Moderne*, Frankfurt am Main: Edition Suhrkamp.

Buchmann, M (1989) *The Script of Life in Modern Society. Entry into Adulthood in a Changing World*, Chicago/London: University of Chicago Press.

Cavalli, A and Galland, O (eds) (1993) *L'Allongement de la jeunesse*, Changement social en Europe occidentale 5, Paris/Poitiers: Actes Sud.

Chisholm, L (1994) *Young Europeans and Vocational Counselling: What Do Which Young People Need and Want?* Synthesis Report, project 081093, Berlin: CEDEFOP.

Chisholm, L, Büchner, P, du Bois-Reymond, M, Krüger, H-H and Hübner–Funk, S (eds) (1994) *Growing Up in Europe*, Berlin/New York: de Gruyter.

Chisholm, L, du Bois-Reymond, M and Coffield, F (1994) 'What does Europe mean to me? Dimensions of distance and disillusion amongst European students', in CYRCE (ed) *Handbook of Youth Policy and Youth Research*, Berlin/New York: de Gruyter.

Chisholm, L and Liebau, E (eds) (1993) 'Youth, social change and education: issues, problems, policies in post-1992 Europe', *Journal of Education Policy* (Special Issue), **8**, 1.

du Bois-Reymond, M and Oechsle, M (eds) (1990) *Neue Jugendbiographie? Zum Strukturwandel der Jugendphase*, Opladen: Leske and Budrich.

Giddens, A (1991) *Modernity and Self-Identity: Self and Society in the Late Modern Age*, Cambridge: Polity Press.

Heinz, W (ed) (1991) *Theoretical Advances in Life Course Research: Status Passages and the Life Course Vol I*, Weinheim: Deutscher Studienverlag.

Lash, S (1990) *Sociology of Postmodernism*, London/New York: Routledge.

Machado Pais, J (1993) 'Routes to adulthood in a changing society: the Portuguese experience', in Chisholm and Liebau, pp 9–16.

Safia Mirzah, H (1992) *Young, Female and Black*, London/New York: Routledge.

Zoll, R (ed) (1992) *Ein neues kulturelles Modell. Zum soziokulturellen Wandel in Gesellschaften Westeuropas und Nordamerikas*, Opladen: Westdeutscher Verlag.

16. Careers guidance systems in the European Community

A G Watts

Careers guidance services in the European Community vary a great deal in their nature, extent and quality. These services are currently receiving greater policy prominence within the Community. In part, this is based on the growing concern to reduce the high levels of unemployment stemming from the sustained recession of the early 1990s and from adaptation to technological and economic change; more positively, it is based on the greater recognition of the economic importance of improving skill levels and utilizing human resources to the full. It is also linked to increasing scepticism about the ability of planning approaches alone to attain such goals, and growing acknowledgement of the importance of activating the motivations of individuals if the goals are to be realized. Guidance is seen as a powerful policy tool in this respect.

This recognition is mirrored by, and reinforced by, the increased policy interest in guidance at Community level as a means of facilitating the mobility of students, trainees and workers. This is producing more networking between guidance services in the different member states, which in turn is encouraging more sharing of practices as well as a variety of collaborative initiatives (Banks *et al*, 1990; Plant, 1990; Watts, 1992a). The present chapter is based on a study carried out for the European Commission in 1992–3 of the educational and vocational guidance services for young people and adults within the EC member states (Watts *et al*, 1994). This updated an earlier study confined to guidance services for young people (Watts *et al*, 1988). Both studies were based on a series of country-studies commissioned from national experts within each of the member states, and on visits to each member state by a member of the central project team.

The chapter identifies the key features of the guidance systems in each of the twelve EC member states. It then analyses the main differences between the systems. Finally, it examines a number of common trends which cross-cut the national boundaries, and outlines a possible emerging strategy which can be discerned in some member states.

Key features

Because of their different administrative traditions and structures, the member states have very different guidance systems. In this section, the key features of each country's system will be outlined, in alphabetical sequence.

In *Belgium*, Psycho-Medico-Social (PMS) Centres offer educational and vocational as well as social and medical assessment and guidance up to the age of 21. Most of the centres serve a number of schools. No job-placement service is offered; there is some emphasis on tests; and the centres' counsellors participate in class councils making educational-choice decisions about pupils. In addition, Information, Guidance and Socio-Vocational Initiation Centres (CA/COISP) run short guidance-oriented courses for the unemployed, French-speaking community. There are also university guidance centres and youth information centres.

In *Denmark*, there are strong guidance services within educational institutions: in particular, teacher-counsellors working with classroom teachers in the *folkeskole*; and part-time educational counsellors in other institutions. The municipalities have to provide outreach educational and vocational guidance for all young people during the two years after they leave school, or until age 19. A Public Vocational Guidance Service based in the Public Employment Service offers an all-age guidance service. The trade unions are more involved in guidance than in most other member states.

In *France*, the main guidance service is provided by Information and Guidance Centres (CIO), which have a strong emphasis on education and training decisions (no job-placement services are offered), place a traditionally strong but declining emphasis on tests, and participate within schools in class councils making educational-choice decisions about pupils. There are also guidance services within Adult Vocational Training Centres under the Adult Vocational Training Association (AFPA); careers guidance service (mainly placement-focused) offered by the National Employment Agency (ANPE) under the labour ministry; local Advice, Information and Guidance Centres (PAIO) and *missions locales* for unemployed young people; a network of youth information centres; and a variety of voluntary-sector services, including 'Retravailler' ('Back to Work') for women returners and other groups. All employees and unemployed individuals now have access to Inter-Institutional Skills Assessment Centres (CIBC).

In *Germany*, vocational guidance can formally only be offered by the Federal Employment Institute (Bundesanstalt für Arbeit), which also runs vocational information centres in many areas. There are also curricular vocational guidance programmes (*arbeitslehre*) in schools, and educational guidance services in schools and universities based largely on school psychologists and guidance teachers (*beratungslehrer*) in secondary education, and on student advisers in universities. In addition, there are some voluntary-sector services, including initiatives run by churches and charitable organizations.

In *Greece*, careers education programmes have been officially established in schools, with careers teachers allocating about one-third of their teaching time to this. Responsibility for vocational guidance is allocated by the Ministry of Labour to the Manpower Employment Organization (OAED), but it has only a very limited number of vocational counsellors.

In *Ireland*, most careers guidance services are education-based and located within educational institutions. In schools, the guidance system is based largely on full-time guidance counsellors. Some guidance elements are also incorporated into FAS (Vocational Training and Employment Authority) training programmes.

In *Italy*, there is no national guidance system. School guidance services coordinators are being appointed in some school districts; and a new tutorial structure is being introduced in some universities, in conjunction with guidance coordinators. Guidance centres and youth information services are run by some regional, provincial and municipal authorities. There are more voluntary-sector (including trade-union) and private agencies than in most other member states.

In *Luxembourg*, the education-based services are broadly similar to the French model, with a strong emphasis on educational decisions and participation in class councils making educational-choice decisions about pupils. The vocational guidance service run by the Employment Administration is used extensively by those entering apprenticeships.

In the *Netherlands*, the main careers guidance services are provided within schools and higher education institutions by careers guidance teachers/officers (*dekanen*), often working with tutors (*mentors*) and other teachers. New Advisory Offices on Education and Employment (AOB) have recently been set up offering guidance services to individuals and also to schools, to the Manpower Services Organization and to employers on a contractual basis.

In *Portugal*, the guidance service in some schools is run by school-based guidance psychologists who are not teachers and are coordinated by regional units (*núcleos*); in others, it is based on an older system of careers advisers (*orientadores*) seconded from teaching; a more integrated structure has been agreed but has not yet been implemented. There is also a limited vocational guidance service provided by the Institute of Employment and Vocational Training, mainly for young people who have left full-time education.

In *Spain*, there is a guidance service in some schools, based mainly on a tutorial system and/or on external agents, though guidance specialists are now beginning to be appointed within schools. Some universities have limited Guidance and Job Information Centres (COIE), run by the National Employment Institute (INEM). In addition, INEM provides a limited vocational guidance service of its own, especially for unemployed people.

Finally, in the *United Kingdom*, careers education in schools and colleges is carried out by careers teachers and other teacher/lecturers; while the Careers Service, operated locally but answerable to the Department of Employment, offers a vocational guidance service, particularly for those attending or leaving educational institutions. In addition, universities and most other higher-education institutions have their own careers advisory services for their students; there are educational guidance services for adults in some areas; and there are more private-sector agencies than in most other member states.

Differences

In reviewing these systems, differences are evident in relation to six main factors: the *location* of guidance services, their *focus*, the range of guidance *activities*, the structure of *administrative control and financing*, the *professional identity and training* of guidance practitioners, and the *level of penetration* of guidance services.

Location. There are marked differences in the sectoral location of guidance services. In some cases (eg, Denmark, Greece, Ireland, Portugal) they are based mainly within *educational institutions*. In other cases (eg, Belgium, France, Italy, Luxembourg, Spain) they are based mainly in separate *agencies* which service educational institutions but which also have the capacity (or, at least, the potential) to provide support for those who have left the educational system. In further cases (eg, Germany) they are linked closely to the training system and based mainly within official *labour-market organizations*. These examples are not exclusive: several of these countries also have well-developed guidance services in other locations. Moreover, in some countries the main services clearly cover more than one location: in the Netherlands and the United Kingdom, for example, they are well developed both within educational institutions and in separate agencies.

Focus. A second set of differences relates to the extent to which the services are concerned with *educational* guidance – ie, guidance on choice of educational options, or on learning problems; and/or with *vocational* guidance – ie, guidance on choice of occupations and work roles; and/or with *personal* and *social* guidance – ie, guidance on personal and social issues (behavioural problems, emotional issues, accommodation, etc).

Different patterns are evident in different member states. In some cases (notably Germany) there is a clear-cut distinction between educational guidance and vocational guidance services, these being allocated to wholly separate agencies. In other cases (notably Belgium and Ireland) all three forms of guidance are brought together in one agency: in Belgium, through different roles based in one centre (the Psycho-Medico-Social Centre); in schools in Ireland, through a single role (guidance counsellor). In some countries (notably France, Germany, Luxembourg, Spain) the main emphasis of the education-based services tends to be on educational guidance, though in others they pay equal attention to vocational guidance. In all cases where services are based in labour-market organizations, their main and often exclusive focus is on vocational guidance.

Activities. A third set of differences relates to the guidance activities carried out by the services. Educational and vocational guidance can be defined in broad terms as referring to a range of activities through which people can be helped to make the decisions and transitions that determine the course of their educational and vocational development. A number of activities can be distinguished:

- *Information* – providing clients with objective and factual data.
- *Assessment* – making a diagnostic judgement about the client's suitability for certain options.
- *Advice* – making suggestions based on the helper's own knowledge and experience.
- *Counselling* – helping clients to explore their own thoughts and feelings about their present situation, about the options open to them, and about the consequences of each option.
- *Careers education* – providing a programme of planned experiences designed to develop in clients the skills, concepts and knowledge that will help them to make effective career choices and transitions.
- *Placement* – helping clients to achieve entry to a particular job or course.
- *Advocacy* – negotiating directly with institutions on behalf of particular individuals, especially those for whom there may be barriers to access.
- *Feedback* – feeding back unmet needs to opportunity providers.
- *Follow-up* – contacting former clients to see what has happened to them, and what further help they may need.

In these terms:

- Some countries (eg, Germany) are particularly well developed in terms of *information* services; in other countries (eg, Greece, Ireland, Italy, Portugal, Spain) such information is seen as an area of guidance services that needs to be strengthened.
- In some countries (eg, Belgium, France, Germany, Luxembourg, Spain), educational guidance in particular lays considerable stress on *assessment*, sometimes using psychometric and other tests for this purpose, and at times blurring the distinction which other countries establish more rigidly between assessment for *guidance* (ie, helping students to make their *own* decisions) and assessment for *selection* (ie, for making decisions *about* students) – though where guidance practitioners take part in selection decisions, it is usually clear that they act as *advocates* for clients.
- In some countries (eg, Belgium, France, Luxembourg) individual interviewing tends to be based mainly on *advice*-giving – ie, offering recommendations based on diagnostic judgements – whereas in others (eg, Denmark, Portugal, United Kingdom) there is more interest (in some agencies at least) in basing it on *counselling* – ie, facilitating the client's own decision-making in a non-directive way.
- Some countries (eg, Denmark, Germany, Greece, Portugal, United Kingdom) have made systematic attempts to build *careers education* into the curriculum of educational institutions; in some cases (notably Denmark, Germany, United Kingdom) this commonly includes programmes of work visits and work experience.

- In some countries (eg, Germany, Italy) job *placement* is the monopoly of one government ministry and is therefore not provided by other guidance services; in others too (eg, Belgium, France), job-placement services tend to be separate from other guidance services; but in some (eg, United Kingdom) a significant proportion of guidance agencies also carry out job placement.
- Some countries (eg, Denmark, France, United Kingdom) attach more importance than others to *advocacy* and *feedback*, especially in relation to services working with particular groups (eg, the young unemployed, adult learners).
- Some countries (eg, Denmark) have very systematic *follow-up* procedures, especially for school-leavers; in other cases such procedures tend to be more informal or are absent altogether.

Administrative control and financing. Fourth, guidance services in the member states can be distinguished in terms of their administrative and financial structures. Services based in labour-market agencies tend to be administered by central government, though in some cases (eg, Spain) they are being devolved to regional authorities; services based in the education system tend to be administered mainly by central government (France, Greece, Ireland, Luxembourg), by regional authorities (Belgium, Germany, Italy, Portugal, Spain), or by local authorities (Denmark, United Kingdom), depending on the administrative structure of the educational system in the country in question.

Most official services are free to the client, though in the United Kingdom some agencies are experimenting with fee-charging to some adult client groups. In most countries, private-sector and/or voluntary-sector agencies have built up a limited role for those who are dissatisfied with the official guidance services: private-sector agencies normally charge fees to clients. In Germany, on the other hand, individual vocational guidance is formally the sole and exclusive responsibility of a single public body, the Federal Employment Institute. In some countries (notably Italy) private and voluntary agencies are used to carry out some of the guidance functions within the public education system: these agencies tend to be partly grant-aided and partly supported by the payment of client fees.

In some member states, there are significant differences between guidance systems in different regions. In Italy, in particular, there is no national guidance system: most guidance services are organized at regional, provincial or municipal level; some regions have no services at all. Again, in the United Kingdom, the guidance systems in Scotland and Northern Ireland differ in important respects from those in England and Wales.

Professional identity and training. Fifth, the professional identity and training of those occupying guidance roles varies (Watts, 1992b). In some cases (eg, psychologists in Belgium and Luxembourg, school psychologists in Germany, guidance psychologists in France and Portugal) they are defined as *psychologists*, and their guidance training is regarded as being incorporated into, or supplementary to, their broad psychology training. In other cases (eg, careers teachers, teacher counsellors, school counsellors, etc in Denmark, Germany, Greece, Ireland, Luxembourg, Netherlands, Portugal and the United Kingdom) they are defined as *teachers* – indeed, they often continue to perform their guidance duties alongside broader teaching responsibilities – and their guidance training is regarded as being incorporated into, or supplementary to, their teacher training. In further cases (eg, vocational counsellors in Luxembourg) they are defined as *labour-market administrators*, and their guidance training is regarded as being incorporated into, or supplementary to, their administrative training. It is only in a residual number of cases (eg, vocational counsellors in Germany, Greece, and the Netherlands, careers officers in the United Kingdom) that they are defined as *guidance specialists*, and have their own specialist training.

The fact that in many cases guidance is a secondary adjunct to the individual's primary professional role explains why the guidance training is sometimes very limited (lasting a few weeks or even a few days), why it is sometimes on an in-service basis (rather than being required before undertaking any guidance practice), and also why it is sometimes optional (for example, some careers teachers in Greece and the United Kingdom, and some guidance teachers in Germany and Luxembourg, receive no guidance training at all). But this is not true in all cases: guidance counsellors in Ireland, for instance, receive a substantial one-year full-time course in guidance and counselling on top of their basic teacher training before assuming their guidance responsibilities. In general, the more substantial the supplementary training, the more guidance tends to take on the attributes of a sub-profession within the parent profession.

Level of penetration. Finally, the extent of guidance services and their accessibility to clients varies a great deal. This was indicated in a survey carried out by INRA (1991), which showed that guidance services in the northern member states achieved much higher levels of penetration than those in the southern member states (see Table 16.1).

Common trends

Alongside these differences, the study reported here endorses three common trends across the EC member states identified in the earlier study conducted in the mid-1980s (Watts *et al*, 1988):

- The view of guidance as a *continuous process*, which should start early in schools, should continue through the now often extended period of transition to adult and working life, and should then be accessible throughout adult and working life.
- The move towards a *more open professional model*, in which the concept of an expert guidance specialist working with individual clients in a psychological vacuum is replaced or supplemented by a more diffuse approach, in which a more varied range of interventions is used (eg, curriculum programmes, group work, computers and other media) and more attention is given to working with and through networks of other individuals and agencies (eg,

Table 16.1 *Agencies from which guidance related to career choices had been sought by young people aged 15–24 (by percentage)*

	Teachers and lecturers	Guidance services at school or university	Job centres, employment agencies	Information and guidance services outside school or university	Firms and companies	Information centres run by young people
Belgium	33	24	3	7	3	3
Denmark	22	41	6	3	5	1
France	27	28	6	10	4	2
Germany	16	20	26	13	13	3
Greece	11	4	1	3	2	1
Ireland	13	19	6	3	3	1
Italy	16	5	1	1	2	0
Luxembourg	15	17	4	5	4	0
Netherlands	26	44	11	5	6	1
Portugal	5	4	3	1	1	1
Spain	3	1	1	0	0	0
United Kingdom	15	15	8	6	4	1

supporting the guidance roles of teachers and supervisors, involving parents, providing feedback to opportunity providers).

- A greater emphasis on the *individual as an active agent*, rather than a passive recipient, within the guidance process.

To these should be added a fourth common trend: towards a greater awareness of the European dimension in guidance provision. This is currently being given considerable momentum by the PETRA II programme, which is the first Community action programme to include a separate funding strand for collaborative initiatives at national level in the guidance field.

While these trends remain valid, however, it is clear that difficulties continue to be experienced in converting the notion of guidance as a continuous process into reality. The general position at present is as follows:

- All member states agree that guidance should be available free of charge to young people while they are in full-time education and often for a period beyond that. All provide guidance services to such groups, though these services vary in their extent, nature and quality.
- For adults, the picture is more mixed. Many member states have committed themselves in principle to providing guidance services for individuals of all ages, but few have yet done so in practice. In some cases, services are not available at all for most adults; in others, they are so poorly publicized that they are able to run at a minimal level of provision.

In addition, continuity in guidance provision is still being undermined by lack of effective linkages between guidance services based in different sectors and addressed to different target-groups. Although efforts have been made to strengthen such linkages, they remain inadequate.

Where member states have developed or are developing a strategy to achieve an all-age guidance service, different approaches are being adopted. In some cases, the approach is based on strong centralized services; in some, on a more diffuse range of public-sector responses to specific needs; in some, on limiting the extent of services which are free to the client, and encouraging client payment where possible.

Linked to these varying approaches, four further trends can be identified. These are visible to a more limited extent, and tend to be concentrated in a number of member states rather than being evident − so far at least − across the European Community as a whole.

The fifth trend is a tendency towards *deregulation* and, in a few countries, towards some limited application of *market principles* in the delivery of guidance services. In Denmark and Spain, for example, the monopolies of job placement previously held by the public employment services have been broken up. In the Netherlands, the new Advisory Offices on Education and Employment (AOB) offer services to schools, to the Manpower Service Organization and to employers on a contractual basis: the contracts are guaranteed until 1995, but thereafter the AOBs may be exposed to more competitive pressures. In France, the new Inter-Institutional Skills Assessment Centres (CIBC) derive their income from the assessments they carry out, indicating explicit costing and the threat of closure if they fail to attract clients; moreover, some public organizations − eg, the National Employment Agency (ANPE) − are beginning to subcontract some of their guidance activities to voluntary associations or private bodies.

The moves to apply market principles have been particularly marked in the United Kingdom. New legislation has removed the Careers Service from the sole control of Local Education Authorities and permits a wider range of bodies to submit tenders to offer guidance services to statutory clients in particular areas. In addition, experiments are being introduced to issue guidance vouchers for specified target-groups to use, in theory with a choice of accredited guidance providers. In both cases there is an assumption that market forces will result in a reduction of cost and an improvement in quality of service; in the second case, there may be a further assumption that once the public (employers as well as individuals) have experienced the benefits of guidance, they will be willing to pay for all or part of it themselves. Both of these assumptions have still to be tested.

The sixth trend, again evident in several member states, is towards *decentralization*. In Belgium, there has been growing devolution from national level to the three communities (French-speaking, Dutch-speaking, German-speaking). In France, whereas only a few years ago almost all guidance organizations were run by the government and in particular the Ministries of Education and of Labour, a growing number of initiatives and services are now based on local structures or associations. In Spain, the autonomous communities are growing in importance, resulting in the diversification of guidance services; in particular, most services of the hitherto centralized National Employment Institute (INEM) are now being transferred to the control of the autonomous communities. In the United Kingdom, many responsibilities of the Employment Department in relation to training and guidance are being devolved to local Training and Enterprise Councils (TECs).

These fifth and sixth trends are closely linked to the seventh trend: an increasing concern for quality standards and for *evaluation*. If quality is to be sustained within more deregulated and/or market-oriented and/or decentralized structures, quality standards need to be defined more precisely and more explicitly. The issue of training standards for guidance practitioners is of particular importance here. Such attention to quality assurance is linked to evaluation efforts designed to measure the effectiveness of guidance in general or of specific guidance interventions in particular. In general, evaluation efforts to date have been patchy and diffuse.

A further complementary development is the eighth and final trend: the emergence in a number of member states of *national councils* designed to bring together the range of bodies involved in, and/or with 'stakeholder' interests in, the delivery of guidance. If guidance is to be viewed as a continuous process, available to individuals throughout their lives, but based on diversity of provision, then attention is needed to building stronger linkages which will assure continuity and progression, and to developing a national strategy which will enable roles and relationships to be clarified and gaps to be identified. A national council could provide this kind of strategic leadership, as well as supplying a useful focal point for Community-level contact.

An emerging strategy

Linked to the notion of strategic leadership, there are signs in some member states of an emerging strategy based on three complementary elements. The first is *careers education and guidance* as an integral part of all education provision, offering regular opportunities for students to explore the relationship between what they are learning and their career development. The second is *career development* as an integral part of all employment provision, offering trainees and employees regular opportunities to review their current work, their future aspirations, their skill requirements, and ways of meeting these requirements. The third is access to *neutral careers guidance* at points when individuals wish to review possibilities for movement between educational institutions, or between employers, or between the two, from a neutral base.

The potential advantages of guidance provision within education and within employment are that they have more continuous contact with the individuals based in their organization, and so are able to deliver more sustained guidance interventions than any external service could do; and that they may be in a stronger position to influence their organization to alter its opportunity structures in response to individuals' needs and demands, as revealed through the guidance process. On the other hand, many people spend significant parts of their lives outside education and employment structures — because they are unemployed, for example, or engaged in child-rearing; guidance services within particular organizations do not usually have a sufficiently broad view of opportunities outside that organization; and their organization can have vested interests in the outcomes of the client's decisions, which can make it difficult to provide guidance that is neutral.

It is therefore important that there should also be access to the broader and more impartial perspective which a neutral guidance service can bring. The emerging structure based on this three-pronged strategy is much more complex than the traditional structure, in which guidance has a very limited role to play at the transition between education and employment (Figure 16.1). It is linked to greater interchange between education and employment, and greater interaction between learning and working, throughout life; and to viewing 'career' not as progression within a particular occupation but as a process of lifelong personal development. Instead of being a kind of switch mechanism at the main transition point

The traditional structure

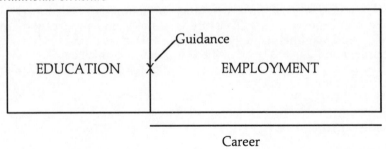

The emerging structure

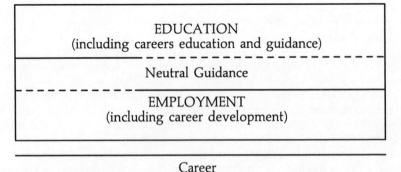

Figure 16.1 *Changing structures of guidance*

between education and employment, guidance becomes the lubricant that makes the individual's energies flow, and enables both education and employment systems to respond to, and draw from, those energies.

No member state has yet developed a sufficient range of services to deliver a strategy based on these principles. Across the Community as a whole, however, there are examples of all the elements that are needed. One of the aims of Community collaboration over the next few years could be to share such strategic visions, and also to share experiences of the provision required to deliver them.

References

Banks, J A G, Raban, A J and Watts, A G (1990) 'The Single European Market and its implications for educational and vocational guidance services', *International Journal for the Advancement of Counselling*, **13**, 4, 275–94.

INRA (1991) 'Young Europeans in 1990', *Eurobarometer* **34**, 2, Brussels: Commission of the European Communities.

Plant, P (1990) *Transnational Vocational Guidance and Training for Young People and Adults*, Berlin: CEDEFOP.

Watts, A G (1992a) 'Careers guidance services in a changing Europe', *International Journal for the Advancement of Counselling*, **15**, 4, 201–8.

Watts, A G (1992b) *Occupational Profiles of Vocational Counsellors in the European Community*, Berlin: CEDEFOP.

Watts, A G, Dartois, C, and Plant, P (1988) *Educational and Vocational Guidance Services for the 14–25 Age-Group in the European Community*, Maastricht: Presses Interuniversitaires Européennes.

Watts, A G, Guichard, J, Plant, P and Rodriguez, M L (1994) *Educational and Vocational Guidance in the European Community*, Brussels: Commission of the European Communities.

17. Risky futures for the daughters of the Nordic welfare state

Anja Heikkinen

This chapter reflects on some of the latest events in Nordic welfare states and education systems based on Finnish experience. The focus is on women and issues of gender, since they are at the centre of the idea and phenomenon of the welfare state. It also has a subjective bias: I grew up as a daughter of a young welfare state and raised my child while it was maturing. Now my daughter is finishing her *gymnasium* and leaving home, head full of dreams and heart filled with excitement. Do I feel proud, envious, frightened or sorry? The worldwide economic recession caused by financial speculation, overproduction and overinvestment and by the collapse of many socialist economies has strengthened neo-liberalist policy everywhere, including in the Nordic countries. In contrast to the UK where the educational system is blamed for shortcomings in national competitiveness, in Nordic countries the welfare state is the main target. Along with the proposals to join the European Union, political publicity and the media are filled with comparisons of labour costs, social service and public expenditure. Both at local and at national level, the scope and standards of public service are taken to be the key to a nation's competitiveness. Despite the phlegmatic temperament of its people, Finland is a nation of sudden turns. Among Nordic countries, reactions seem most extreme in Finland.

The chapter is divided into three sections. The first section contains information about females in the occupational and educational structures of Nordic countries and about the educational and social policy behind them. In the second section I describe some recent trends in social and educational policy in Finland, which have left girls and women deceived. In the last section I question whether these trends indicate an inevitable breakdown of the ideology – or delusion – of Nordic welfare-society. Is there any reason to hope for its survival and are there alternative utopias about a just and 'female-friendly' society?

A broken promise?

Although Finland never called itself 'Folkshem' like Sweden, it has nevertheless officially shared the ideals of equality, solidarity, collective responsibility for children, the old, the sick etc – as well as the commitment to promote these values globally and actively to resist aggression and militarism. This policy relied heavily on women, their social participation and valuation. Despite contradictions in reality, in political practice, industrial relations and family life, since the 1960s a generation of girls (and boys) grew up in a society which promised them equal partnership, open access to education and career, to social and political life, a commitment to peace, humanity and caring.

There are some occupational and educational differences between Nordic women. Table 17.1 gives a rough picture of female employment in the Nordic countries. Some of the differences are due to differences in industrial structure and to the use of immigrant workers in Sweden. One should note that because of the recession and reductions in public service, the situation is changing.

In all Nordic countries, the universalist welfare and educational system has provided labour and employment opportunities for women comparable to those of men. But whereas in other Nordic countries about 30–40 per cent of female wage-labour is part-time, in Finland about 90 per cent of employed women are full-time workers. This means that Finnish women are more dependent on public welfare provision both as a precondition and as a means of economic independence. In all Nordic countries, there are male-dominated branches like wood-processing and metalworking industries, construction and transport and female-dominated branches like community, social and personal services, retail trade, hotels and restaurants. A more detailed look at occupational tasks and organizational hierarchies would reveal a more gendered structure.

Compared with other Nordic countries, gender-based segmentation is even stronger in Finland. This seems, on the one hand, to be related to larger wage-differences between male and female occupations, but on the other, to wider professionalization of female tasks. It is also astonishing that Finnish legislation and regulations of gender equality as well as feminist activity have been minor compared with other Nordic countries. Norway, for instance, has for long been running a system of female quotas in public organizations. However, even without legislative support or radical feminist policy, Finnish women are quite well represented in parliamentary organizations both at local and at national level. It seems, however, that when women enter the field, either the centres of power change their location or – since women who are able to reach top positions fulfil their requirements too well – do not change their policies.

What about education compared with the employment structure? Again, despite similarities there are also differences between Nordic countries. The ideas of comprehensive schooling, equality of opportunity and the combination of national curricula and autonomy of schools and teachers are shared by all Nordic countries. They are also all committed to the promotion of equality between sexes in their legislation. Sweden has a long history of comprehensive schooling, which since the 1970s has been extended to a *gymnasieskola* for 16 to 19-year-olds, including academic and vocational tracks. Finland was the last Nordic country to introduce the

Table 17.1 *Percentage of female employees in industry, Nordic countries 1991*

Branches of industry according to ISIC 1968	Denmark[1]	Finland[2]	Norway[1]	Sweden[2]
1. Agriculture, hunting, forestry and fishing	25	36	26	27
2. Mining and quarrying	0	0	19	9
3. Manufacturing	33	34	26	28
31. Manufacture of food, beverages and tobacco	44	49	38	40
32. Textile, wearing apparel and leather industries	66	82	67	64
33. Manufacture of wood and wood products	29	27	23	19
34. Manufacture of paper and paper products, printing and publishing	35	34	32	33
35. Manufacture of chemicals and chemical products	36	35	25	36
36. Manufacture of non-metallic mineral products	19	19	20	19
37. Basic metal industries	11	14	16	21
38. Manufacture of machinery and equipment	21	24	15	22
39. Other manufacturing industries	50	43	25	43
4. Electricity, gas and water	15	21	24	16
5. Construction	11	9	8	8
6. Wholesale and retail trade, and restaurants and hotels	49	57	54	51
61. Wholesale trade	34	35	30	30
62. Retail trade	54	59	67	62
63. Restaurants and hotels	62	75	67	62
7. Transport, storage and communication	27	27	29	32
8. Financing, insurance, real estate and business services	45	55	44	45
9. Community, social and personal services	67	71	64	72
91. Public administration and defence	50	50	36	48
92. Sanitary and similar services	48	59	44	44
93. Social and related community services	76	81	75	80

Branches of industry according to ISIC 1968	Denmark[1]	Finland[2]	Norway[1]	Sweden[2]
94. Recreational and cultural services	49	55	50	47
95. Personal and household services	43	72	59	44
Activities not adequately defined	41	33	25	20
Total	46	48	45	48

Notes: [1] Including conscripts.
    [2] Excluding conscripts
Source: *Yearbook of Nordic Statistics 1993.*

comprehensive school and has maintained the traditional *gymnasium* with its encyclopedist curriculum. In Denmark the tradition of apprenticeship training is longest and strongest and options for private schooling more common. Compared with Finland, Norway and Sweden have more vocational and work-based courses and in Norway state-controlled apprenticeship training has remained a powerful option in vocational education (Mjelde, 1994). Pedagogically, Swedish education has been most student-centred, with minimal formal testing and selecting procedures. However, this has also led to blame for poor outcomes both in academic and in vocational education, especially in engineering. For instance, there have been compensatory programmes for university recruits to enable them to start their studies. Differences also exist between fields of study and their placement in educational levels. Industrial, engineering and natural-science programmes, medical and health programmes and teacher training programmes are more popular and have a higher status in Finland than in other Nordic countries. On a lesser scale, the same is true of agriculture, forestry and fishing, home economics and service trades. In commercial, business and social science programmes the situation has been the opposite.

Although a belief in the importance of education is shared by all Nordic countries, the explosion of schooling has been fastest in Finland. The proportion in an age-group graduating from university or vocational institute has risen during the last 20–25 years from 50 per cent to over 80 per cent. Among females the figures have increased from 40 per cent to over 85 per cent. The percentage of women taking matriculation is nearly 70 per cent and taking master's (or comparable) degrees over 20 per cent. However, women have continuously been underrepresented in higher education, compared with matriculations. Although already in the 1940s over 50 per cent of these were taken by women and the proportion is stabilizing at 60 per cent, the proportion of female students in universities has slowly risen from about 30 per cent to over 50 per cent. Despite the broad, academic syllabuses both in *gymnasial* and in university studies and difficulties in getting a place to study, the Finns seem to be most persistent in their studies. Combined with long programmes in both academic and vocational education, the academic drift makes people strive for double and triple education.

The gender-based segmentation is quite similar in all Nordic countries. Among Finnish women, medical and health programmes, home economics and service trade programmes and natural science and engineering programmes, to some extent, are more popular than in other Nordic countries. Besides, Finnish women study longest. For instance, in 1990 about 16 per cent of Finnish women continued their studies in full-time education when they were 25–29 years old, whereas the Swedish figure in 1991 was under 8 per cent. Along with gender-based divisions of labour, this means that Finnish women with higher education more often have to accept working in low positions in the organizational hierarchy and in occupational tasks not corresponding to their education. Table 17.2 features the streaming of females in vocational and university education in Finland. In making comparisons, one should note that according to international classifications 32 per cent of students in vocational fields actually study in higher education (five or six stages).

Since male students interrupt their studies more frequently, the female percentage of all students gaining leaving certificates was higher (about 58 per cent and 55 per cent, respectively). The segmentation of fields seems to parallel the employment structure. One can also distinguish the impact of organizational hierarchies in commerce, medicine and health, etc: the percentage of males is higher in university studies leading to managerial

Table 17.2 *Percentage of female students in different fields of study,*
Finland 1991

| | Students | |
Field of study	Vocational	University
Teacher education	83	74
Fine and applied arts	71	55
Humanities	87	75
Commerce and business administration	70	47
Mathematics and computer science	19	24
Medicine and health	92	66
Engineering	12	16
Agriculture, forestry and fishing	34	50
Home economics (domestic science)	98	88
Trade, craft and industrial programmes	17	–
Transport and communications	11	–
Service trades	75	–
Religion and theology	–	45
Social and behavioural science	–	61
Law and jurisprudence	–	47
Natural science	–	50
Architecture and town-planning	–	43
Other	48	43
Total	55	52

positions in these female-dominated fields. Generally, gender differences are most polarized at the lowest levels of education. The earlier the career choice is made, the more stereotypical it seems to be. Since most students at the lower school levels come from lower social and occupational strata, this also indicates a strong continuity in occupational stereotyping among them. It has also been found in all Nordic countries that, despite projects promoting more equal choice, the gender-divisions tend to reappear. In the Finnish case, this might indicate either the persistent prestige of certain educational fields and occupations among women themselves, or the impotence of the educational system against gender-stereotyping in families, media and the labour market.

How successful does the Nordic social and educational policy look from the Finnish perspective? In education, the attainments of Finnish pupils in compulsory comprehensive schools and *gymnasia* have generally improved, according to both national and international evaluations (IEA, 1992). An important characteristic has been the even distribution of educational opportunities and attainments between regions and social groups. Functional literacy, ie, the ability to understand and write various texts, is amongst the highest in the world. Comprehensive schooling seems to have had an empowering effect on Finnish young people – especially girls – who have traditionally shown low self-esteem in international comparisons. In vocational and higher education the most striking features are high participation-rates and relatively even access among regions and social groups based on a wide network of institutes and support for students. The teaching profession has also had quite high prestige. Public critique on education has, however, at all stages focused on the failure to promote excellence, on uniformity, on favouring girls and female values and on the high costs of a scattered network of small units. From a pedagogical point of view, the hasty and formal nature of structural reforms has raised doubts about genuine progress and caused stress among teachers. The time available for internal development of schools and for personal moral education has decreased. Thus, for example, in education for gender equality and solidarity, progress seems to have been limited. Despite formal goals the attitudes of most teachers, pupils and students have remained stereotypical (Näre and Lähteenmaa, 1992).

Both liberalism and security have increased in tandem in Finland during the last 20 years. Equality in sexual behaviour and freedom in choosing the mode of partnership and childcare have been legally encouraged by social subsidies and paid leave for caring for babies and sick children both for mothers and fathers and for single parents. The number of teenage pregnancies has been the lowest in Europe. The latest studies on Finns have shown increased tolerance towards various expressions of sexuality and modes of companionship (Haavio-Mannila and Kontula, 1993). Mutual satisfaction with sexual life had also increased. Until now pornography, prostitution and different modes of commercial sex have been marginal. However, the popularity of (American) mass culture has ensured that commercial gender-models with their myths of beauty and motherhood have continuously put a double burden on girls who try to do well in all areas of life. On the other hand, the stereotypical models of men have hindered the development of boys in the emotional and caring spheres which would correspond to equality in partnership and parental roles. The problems of emotional expression, alcohol and aggression remain among Finnish youngsters, too.

In the Finnish labour market, the number of female executives has continuously increased, especially in the public sector. According to follow-up studies, women are more inclined towards networking, flattening hierarchies and improving participatory practices in organizations. Teachers, even in elementary schools, enjoy a relatively high esteem. The salaries and influence of women in health and social occupations have improved together with rising levels of education. Compared with other European countries, female-dominated service trade and sanitary occupations are quite respectable and require specific education and training. Although later than in other Nordic countries, large projects were established a few years ago in order to study requirements in various jobs and to make proposals for more just payment. In politics, since 1990, women account for 40 per cent of members in parliament and nearly the same in local government. Among politial parties, women make up the majority of the Green Party and various environmental organizations.

Was the politics of equality of opportunity, of promoting female values and gender-equality a disaster for Finland? The most serious comparisons with Europe and with industry show that the collapse of the Finnish economy was not caused by inefficient, expensive and over-expanded educational, social and health system, but by irrational decisions of national and global trade and industry themselves (see Andersson et al, 1993; Allén et al, 1993). Although many achievements of the Finnish welfare state have been double-edged and incomplete, the expectations and attitudes of youth and their parents have been formed during a period where the political rhetoric was of equality and of consensual commitment to solidarity. It promoted career and economic independence for both boys and girls. It was based on expectations of improved status and greater demand of labour in education, social and health care; on a belief in the right of female self-definition of sexuality, on trust in collective responsibility for the children, the old and sick, the environment and peace.

Recent trends: threats and confusions

Similar neo-liberal trends in Nordic countries get their characteristics from various political and social contexts. There are right-wing governments in power both in Finland and in Sweden after a long period of social democratic (or social democratic–agrarian) hegemony, but much of current politics has its origin in earlier periods. Difficulties with the export industry, state subsidies for enterprises, deregulation of the money market, speculation and investment and bad debts caused similar problems in Finland, Norway and Sweden. Governmental efforts at saving the banking system have brought enormous levels of debt to all three. High standards of living and public services, high prices and salaries, all turned out to be based on speculation and cannot be afforded any more. The social and educational reforms which were planned during the days of economic boom are now put into practice in a way which differs from, or even opposes their original intentions. How do they look in Finnish society?

The biggest threat for the Finns is unemployment. It was only a few years ago when it was predicted both in Finland and in the rest of Europe that we would soon be facing a shortage of labour, especially of young people and in service and care occupations. The increasing recruitment of females to male-dominated areas was also thought to be necessary. The Finnish unemployment figures have, however, leapt to over 20 per cent during the last couple of years. Among young people and leavers from educational institutes, unemployment is above 40 per cent. It seems that only a third of employees will remain in permanent, lifelong employment. The majority will work on temporary contracts or move between short-term employment, vocational training and unemployment. The rest are permanently marginalized. Domestic production and consumption is frozen. After a collapse in the construction business, unemployment is growing fastest in office, service and welfare occupations. The subsidies for the collapsed banking system have run the state into unforeseen debts which accelerate cuts in social, health and educational services and benefits.

Many problems in Finnish society relate to those in the former Soviet states. Until now, Finnish people have accepted the sudden crash with astonishing calm and resignation. They are saving and avoiding taxes; the flea markets and black economy flourish. Whereas only a few projects from former Finnish–Soviet trade have remained, the chaotic and half-criminal trade with Russia and the Baltic together with prostitution and other sex-business have increased. The loss of moral plausibility of Finland's political and economic elite has had a wider demoralizing impact on the whole social and cultural climate. This includes attitudes towards women and relations between genders. Instead of equality and solidarity, we are witnessing growing income and status differences between young and old, men and women.

In industrial relations there has been a rapid change to local negotiations on wages and labour-conditions, to flexible use of the labour force, to the lowering of labour costs. The female-dominated fields lose in local negotiations. Incomes and security are improving in export industries and declining in domestic industry, retail, education, social work and healthcare. In 1994, the salaries of manufacturing and transport workers in export industry rose 3–5 per cent and the salaries of workers in communal and state service declined by 3–5 per cent. Finland has started the most advantageous capital-taxing and the strictest income-taxing in Europe. Whereas in successful industries flexibility may promote cooperative practices and the opportunity to adjust labour to personal life, in retail, banking and welfare service, flexibility has led to forced part-time work, short and uncertain labour contracts and a depressing working atmosphere. The cuts in public service are carried out in various ways: directly through part-time work and redundancies, indirectly by privatization. It is expected that in private enterprises the same personnel will offer service more cheaply to the local governments and citizens.

Benefits are given to the rest of the 'surplus' workers if they employ themselves in the private sector.

Despite very liberal sexual attitudes and behaviour among young people, Finnish society has been confronted with a rapid growth of the sex-business along with a black-market economy and criminality. It has been a shocking experience for most Finnish women. This is accompanied by arguments from the industrial and administrational elite of the importance of housewifery – not only for the good of the children and families, but for the good of women themselves, who are claimed to suffer from estrangement from their 'natural' dispositions. Simultaneously violence and rape have increased. This seems to correspond to the analysis of feminist researchers in USA and the UK (Faludi, 1992; Itzin, 1993). What is unpleasant for any woman to note is the ease with which the Finnish mass-media adopted the new attitudes towards women and female sexuality. Gone are the days when we did not have to look at images of naked women everywhere on television, in newspapers, pubs and restaurants. Though most of the sex-businesses were run by criminals and adventurers from ex-communist countries, Finnish entrepreneurs have collaborated and Finnish men consume the products. The attitudes among some politicians are alarming. The vice-governor of Helsinki, for instance, has repeatedly proposed public brothels in order to control the business, but primarily to make Helsinki 'a true metropolis' with a complete service for businessmen.

The originally liberal reform proposals in education have changed into neo-liberalist rationalization programmes. Finland's state and school-based, universalist system aiming at equality of opportunity is breaking down through reforms at all educational levels. In comprehensive, *gymnasial* and vocational education, the curricula are now constructed in individual schools in response to parental and pupil choice. In both upper-secondary and higher education, large amalgamations are created from former vocational schools and *gymnasia* and from vocational institutes. The upper secondary consists of three tracks preparing students with a vocational bias for working life, students with an academic bias for universities and the rest for vocational universities. New first degree programmes (bachelor's degree) have been introduced both into new vocational and traditional scientific universities; master's and post-graduate ('vocational' licentiate and doctoral) programmes have been shortened. Simultaneously small, separate educational units have been closed, causing regional inequality. Excellence is promoted by increasing accountability and competition among institutes, by privatizing, by increased streaming and selection. Courses and subjects promoting enterpreneurship – commerce, engineering, computer science, etc. – gain weight in syllabuses. Curricula are modularized and flexible, learning-times are shortened. There is more work-based, employer-led (but state-funded!) training, national and international testing and evaluation, 'league-tables', etc.

Hand in hand with cuts in regular educational supply under the Ministry of Education, there has been an expansion of substituting and compensating employment courses financed by the Ministry of Labour. According to the last governmental proposals, the state subsidy for a vocational student together with employment subsidy could be given straight to an enterprise taking an apprentice. If the proposals are implemented, the number of apprentices would increase five or six times and constitute more than a third of all foundation vocational students. Most apprentices would make a cheap, temporary labour force for small enterprises, which do not have the time, equipment or expertise for proper vocational training. A paternalist employer–employee relation would replace recent independence, which would surely increase conformity and authoritarianism in working life. In higher education the increase of shorter, cheaper alternatives will also further accelerate rationalization and cuts in universities.

There are new threats to the educational prospects of girls and women. Highly educated women seem to be a problem rather than a promise for the government. For example, the 'overeducated' women in social and health care are being replaced by private employees with shorter education or by relatives at home. Rationalization programmes for reducing educational supply and for increasing shorter and lower-level courses combining health and social care are proceeding at full speed. Besides raising general doubts about the high quality of Finnish education, the boom of the sex-business together with decreasing consumption has caused discrimination against qualified women in hotel and catering jobs. Generally, girls and young women are now facing contradictory requirements and confusion in education. They are challenged by degradation of female sexuality and jobs and by demands to take the traditional role in families. However, in order to survive, they are expected to develop an aggressive enterpreneuring and competitive character.

Farewell to the 'Nordic alternative' or new hopes?

Despite the large number of women in parliament and administration, it looks as if the parties and the state have cheated Finnish women. The Nordic 'third way' between market capitalism and communism appears to some to have been a chimera. Has there really been a Nordic alternative and on what grounds? Can there be a radical alternative or do we have to give up dreams of peaceful, cooperative, just societies? One might argue with Philip Wexler (1992; 1994) that, as in the USA, the core phenomenon in 'post-modern' societies is the disappearance of the *social* – as interaction, as society and as a medium for personal existence. In each institution and strata this occurs in its peculiar way. Are we not in Finland witnessing the disappearance of the basis of the Nordic welfare states, the social? And since it was mainly women who embodied, defended and were dependent on the social, which extended to all spheres of life, are there emerging new modes of coping with their risky futures among Finnish girls and women?

I have characterized earlier (Heikkinen, 1991) contemporary trends in Finnish society on the basis of gendered moral segmentation. I defined as (ideal-typical) opposite poles a trend towards making (intimate) love and caring 'like labour' – a prerequisite for its status – and a trend towards 'lovelikeness' of (objectified) industrial or productive labour. Against women and promotion of 'female' values, these trends were taken to function in a contradictory way. On the one hand, they could indicate increasing solidarity and justice in society; on the other they might be precursors of the total instrumentalization of human existence. In the current situation, some corrections are necessary — again through simplifications. Set in a broader perspective and compared with recent feminist ethical studies, the gendered moral segmentation in Finland seems to deviate from many other countries. If we call the gendered moral traditions 'ethics of care' and 'ethics of justice' (Larrabee, 1993), then the West-European model has primarily been to divide them into the private (home, family, woman) and the public (politics, industry, wage-labour, man) spheres of life. In Finland, however, the moral segmentation has occurred through gendered vocationalization or professionalization of care. This seems to be related to analogous differences in the feminist movement. In most West-European countries the feminist movement functions as a self-organized, often extra-parliamentary resistance to the suppression of women. It is expressed in individual choices in lifestyle (alternatives in housing, clothing, resistance against the beauty-myth, etc) and in internal support (childcare and therapeutic groups, networking, counselling). On the other hand, in former socialist countries the gender problem was denied. The self-evidence of the 'double-burden' of women with wage-labour and household duties, of public childcare and healthcare disappeared with socialism. The chaotic model of market capitalism with no tradition of female self-organization or self-defence has led many women to poverty, social insecurity, or to a confused sexual identity ('popularity' of housewifery, prostitution, beauty myth, etc).

The Finnish case looks rather different. Throughout history, the role of women has been important in managing the conflicts and opposition among peasant groups, between the Swedish-speaking elite and the Finnish nationalists, against the Russian oppressors, between the labour movement and industrial capitalism. Thus the state as a 'meta-collective' has come to represent responsibility for collective care, consensus, national interests. This has required recognition of the needs and aims of women and their work. Simultaneously the needs of industry have been satisfied in a rational and cost-effective way. The employers have been able to delegate the commitment and attention to family affairs and social policy to the state. The state also aided in maintaining consensus between male executives and labourers in export industry and female workers in public service. The lack of a strong, self-organized feminist movement is, however, a disadvantage in the current situation. It seems that the universalist ideals of full-time jobs, economic independence, individual careers, equality in partnership, collective social responsibility for children and the elderly and for environmental and global problems are mainly 'female' values. It seems that the policies of resisting the trend to 'labourlike' love and caring, of returning collective responsibility to women and promoting economic and social insecurity and dependence of women are mainly propounded by leading male politicians, industrialists and trade unionists.

But is it possible to turn back the wheel of welfare society in Finland?

For one thing, the competitiveness of industry and the political strength of Finland among nations is not possible without women. The survival of Finnish culture relies heavily on educated females as artists, professionals and enlightened consumers. In all national and international contacts, client-centredness, cultural sensibility, empathy and flexibility are becoming increasingly important. The communicative, social and cultural skills and knowledge of Finnish women are much ahead of the old boy networks in economy, politics and industry, which are still dominated by defensive and aggressive strategies and narrow technical expertise. As environmental and ethical issues have become crucial for the Finnish export industry – especially in wood-processing – female values and ethics gain strategic importance.

Second, Finnish women do not seem to accept the 'backlash' against them. Since women have actively and consciously defined the meanings of Finnish welfare society, they can also critically reflect the contradictions between its rhetoric and practices and possibilities for correction. Girls and women are aware of the connection between the degradation of female sexuality and the blaming of women for our social and economic problems. Neither the proposals of some leading male politicians and industrialists that most women could become dependent on their spouses or work like housemaids for wealthy people for pocket-money, nor their support of the sex-business, suit women's image of normal female biography. Women's organizations, for instance, made the public employment offices stop offering jobs in the sex-business to unemployed women. Individual women have forced newspapers to remove pornographic illustrations and advertising. Pressure on politicians – especially female politicians – consumer boycotts, etc are increasing. The 'industrial' model of collective care in our welfare state seems to be changing through emerging local survival strategies, mostly carried by women. The welfare aspect has also labelled categories like knowledge, competence and skills with images of humanism and reciprocity instead of mere competition, aggressive enterpreneurship or promotion of egoistic interests. In a wider perspective, we are forced to change our profit and consumption oriented lifestyle towards a more reasonable simplicity and collaboration. Local survival experiments may constitute new models for the welfare system in such a society.

Third, the future of the welfare society depends heavily on Finnish men. We have seen that the gendered segmentation of morals, labour market and education has led Finland into trouble. There is no guarantee of a representative, 'female-friendly' state if there is no direct organization and promotion of 'female' values among people themselves. A crucial question is whether the welfare state already means something for the majority of Finnish boys and men which they cannot or no longer want to lose. On the one hand, it is pure economic realism: Finnish families can afford a male 'family-wage' no more than the Finnish nation can. On the other hand, it is a question of a chance for a new male identity: a more balanced personality and life with equal and intimate relations with partner and relatives, which not only includes sharing various domestic duties but also brings out new dimensions of human existence and ways of participation in public affairs.

The 'backlash' against Nordic women belongs to a complex of worldwide economic, moral and political endeavours. Women are blamed for the uncompetitiveness of European economies, for the bureau-cratization of public administration, for increased unemployment, for poor educational achievement, for unentrepreneurial spirit, etc. The preference is given to countries with a low-paid female labour force, with scant welfare services, with female oppression. There are two future options for highly educated Finnish females. They may use their virtues as a competitive advantage in European and global economic competition, making them superior to other men and women. But they can also use them as a resource to increase collective responsibility for survival and human dignity, against nationalist or continentalist, racist or sexist oppression in the name of economic and technological superiority. I believe that the daughters (and sons) of the Finnish welfare state understand – despite much of its hollow rhetoric – the value of its tradition of solidarity and collaboration and realize the faults of its industrialized and anonymous mode and its gendered segmenting of values, labour and education. The strength of our school-based education, aiming at social and regional equality and promoting 'female values', should not be lost just because a few geniuses are promoted for international economic competition. The Nordic traditions of solidarity and mutuality cannot materialize without an educational system committed to both its ideals and its practices. The original meaning of education is more relevant than ever: the challenges we face are truly vocational, but concern ethics more than technology.

References

Allén, T, Heinonen, V, and Pantzar, M (1993) *Täyskäännös?:taloutemme valintojenedessä*, Helsinki: Gaudeamus.

Andersson, J and Kosonen, P and Vartiainen, J (1993) *The Finnish Model of Economic Social Policy from Emulation to Crash*, Åbo: Åbo Akademi.

Faludi, S (1992) *Backlash*, Reading: Vintage.

Haavio-Mannila, E and Kontula, O (1993) *Suomalaisten seksielämä*, Helsinki: VAPK.

Heikkinen, A (1991) *Lessons from the Periphery: Some features of Finnish Vocational Education*, London: Post 16-education Centre. European Series. University of London.

IEA Study of Written Composition (1992) *Education and Performance in Fourteen Countries*, Oxford: Pergamon Press.

Itzin, C (ed) (1993) *Pornography: Women, Violence and Civil Liberties*, Oxford: Oxford University Press.

Larrabee, M J (1993) *An Ethic of Care*, London: Routledge.

Mjelde, L (1994) 'Will the Twain Meet?', in Heikkinen.

Näre, S and Lähteenmaa, J (1992) *Letit liehumaan. Tyttökulttuurimurroksessa*, Tampere: SKS.

Wexler, P (1992) *Becoming Somebody: Toward a Social Psychology of School*, London: Falmer.

Wexler, P (1994) 'Schichtspezifisches Selbst und soziale Interaktion in der Schule', in Sünker, H, Timmermann, D and Kolbe, F-U (eds) *Bildung, Gesellschaft, soziale Ungleichheit*, Frankfurt am Main: Suhrkamp.

Yearbook of Nordic Statistics 1993.

18. Teacher–student estrangement and the schooling of urban youth for citizenship

William B Thomas and Kevin J Moran

As a study of a predominantly African-American school district similar to other urban public schools and their communities throughout the United States, this chapter provides systematic insights about important issues affecting the preparation of urban youth for participatory citizenship in the twenty-first century.

From 1991 to the present, we observed the effects of rapid changes in this community. Our interactions have uncovered a mixture of scepticism, defensiveness, and self-doubt on the part of students. They harbour apprehensions in the face of some school and public perceptions that Wilson High School students are not bright and that they have no future. Students counter that they are 'just as smart as any white person'. Discussing the declining status of the school and future employment goals, one student asked: 'What will employers think of us when they find out that we are from Wilson Township?'

Previously tacit citizen groups have openly expressed dissatisfaction with inefficiency and lack of educational quality in their high school. They point to emerging gang activity and violence in the community as signs that schools are failing to prepare youth for purposeful citizenship. They are critical of seemingly unemployable graduates. One resident described the value of the high school diploma as 'a certificate to stand on the street corner and lean against a lamp post'.

Problem statement

This study highlights the interactions between teachers and students in this school and documents a growing sense of alienation from the perspectives of these stakeholders. It considers what happens in public schools when there is, according to Philip Wexler (1992), 'a patterned withdrawal of people's energies from organized public life ... [and] an erosion of the institutional mechanisms and processes that build social commitment' (pp 155–56). Alienated teachers seem resigned to their inability to affect the lives of their students in positive ways. They withdraw from new challenges to their profession and, in many cases, are reluctant to go beyond the measured mile in the interest of reconnecting with the next generation of youth. Reciprocally, disaffected students also have withdrawn, appearing to have lost an optimistic view of their futures, faith in their teachers' willingness to help them succeed, and confidence in their own resolve to achieve. As we will see, mutual withdrawal and the concomitant erosion of social relations between teachers and their students are symptomatic of a general uncoupling of people's responsibilities to each other in a distressed community.

Community and school demographics

Demographic changes occurring over the last 20 years have transformed this suburban community. They have brought social and economic problems similar to those that impinge upon inner cities throughout the United States. Among these are white flight; spiralling welfare rolls; increases in the numbers of ageing citizens and single-parent families; the exodus of manufacturing jobs; a regressive tax structure, with soaring expenses to pay for truncated public services; increases in the numbers of absentee landlords whose rental properties are falling into disrepair; deteriorated and abandoned family homes on delinquent tax rolls, which become havens for drug users; and rising juvenile crime, substance abuse, and random violence. Rival gang shootings and competition for drug trade have had chilling effects upon all segments of the community. Law enforcement officials describe the current situation in terms such as: 'This is a more violent generation, but it is not their fault'; 'Life is taken for granted'; and 'Kids do not believe that they will live beyond ages of 23–24 years'.

In 1980, Wilson Township was a community of 23,669 residents, 61 per cent of which were white and 37 per cent African-American. By 1990, there was an 11 per cent decrease in its total population, with a 32 per cent decrease in its white and a 27 per cent increase in its African-American residents. The results of these demographic shifts over the decade were a population comprising 46 per cent whites and 53 per cent African-Americans. In addition, patterns of emigration contributed to a housing vacancy rate of 13 per cent, with 56 per cent of these residences having been built before 1939 (Health and Welfare Planning Association, 1983; University Microfilms, 1993).

Contradictory demographic patterns conceal the immediacy of a crisis in this community. On the one hand, the percentages of residents employed as professionals and managers increased between 1980 and 1990 from 27 per cent to 32 per cent, while those in skilled and semi-skilled positions decreased from 8 per cent to 5 per cent and 11 per cent to 8 per cent, respectively. As the region underwent shifts in its production, dramatic changes occurred in the percentages of residents employed in manufacturing industries, dropping from 19 per cent to 9 per cent. Levels of educational attainment rose concurrently. The percentages of residents 25 years and older with a high school education increased from 71 per cent to 81 per cent, as the percentages of college graduates increased from 19 per cent to 23 per cent.

On the other hand, the township's level of poverty is 50–65 per cent above the average for its county, rising from 14 per cent in 1980 to 17 per cent in 1990. Police records show that juvenile crime increased by 22 per cent from 1991 to 1993, averaging 22.7 offences monthly. Given the opportunity to improve frayed relations between youth and the police, 'the township', according to one state legislator, 'could not raise $25 to pay a police officer overtime to talk to kids who may be shooting at them next week'.

As members of the numerical majority in this community, African-American children comprise 96 per cent of the public-school population. United States census shows that in 1990 there were 19 per cent of school-age children who had opted out of the public schools to attend private institutions. By 1992, this number had risen to 23 per cent. The consequent siphoning of human capital from the public school denotes a decline in public confidence in its schools. When asked in a survey about reasons for not sending their children to the high school, one resident sardonically responded: 'They want their children to read'.

Pawn shops, second-hand clothing stores and quick cheque-cashing establishments have replaced longstanding family businesses. White flight has left the school district with a 51 per cent pupil population that receives Aid for Dependent Children, in contrast with an 8 per cent state average. The cost per pupil in this district is $7,368, which places it in the highest 20 per cent of the 501 districts in the state. The local district bears responsibility for paying 55 per cent of school costs, underwritten with property taxes. An eroding tax base, resulting from some citizens' failure to pay their taxes, deserted properties, and state cutbacks on special education allotments, places an inordinate strain on limited resources. For the 1992–3 school year, citizens faced and vehemently opposed a 14.5 per cent tax increase to pay, in large part, for rising teacher salaries and benefits.

Administrator–teacher characteristics

In the high school, female teachers comprise 38 per cent of the faculty. Only nine (13 per cent) of its 67 teachers reside in the community. The teaching staff is a veteran faculty, averaging 24 years of teaching. Although the superintendent, principal, and vice-principal are African-American males, in a high school that is 93 per cent African-American, only 5 per cent of the teachers are so. All teachers of academic subjects are white, while African-American faculty teach either special education or art.

For their services, teachers of Wilson Township earn nearly twice the median income of the average township household. In 1990, US census reported the median household income in this community as $22,709. In the same year, the teacher union struck against the school board and won a 21 per cent salary increase over a three-year period. In 1991–2, the median teacher salary in this community's high school was $41,401. Under these terms, the median salary rose by over $9,000 in the next two years.

Internal impediments to achievement and citizenship

There are few differences in pedagogic relations in this school and in two of the three schools which Wexler (1992) studied in upstate New York. The picture in Wilson High School, however, is bleak when viewed in the context of its demographics and daily interactions. Not surprisingly, the school population reflects many of the social and economic patterns of its community. Statistics (Pennsylvania System of School Assessment, 1993) report that of the students who graduated in 1993, there were only 21 per cent enrolled in an academic track. In contrast, 62 per cent were in a general curricular track, 7 per cent in a vocational-technical track, and 10 per cent were in special education.

From 1982 to 1992, the high school experienced a 38 per cent decrease in the 7th to 12th-grade student enrolment. Two decades earlier, the high school had graduated 370 seniors, but recently graduated only 54 students. As the public looks with hope to its schools to help revitalize the community by transmitting useful knowledge, skills, and social values to its youth, academic failure rates soar. Typically, during a nine-week grading period in 1991–2, 45 per cent of the faculty failed 20 per cent or more of their pupils. A teacher explained glibly that 'failure is also instructional'. Standardized reading and mathematics test scores for that year show that at least 55 per cent of the student body scored below the national average. Seventy-nine per cent of ninth graders scored below the national average in mathematics.

Students' acts of defiance appear to be rampant. During the first 12 weeks of school in 1993, high school teachers referred 1,301 cases to the principal, enough referrals for each pupil to have been cited twice during the three-month period. The majority of referrals report high incidences of classroom disruption (297), tardiness (271), cutting class (197), insubordination (188) and disorderly conduct (156). The most serious offences included 49 fights and 20 verbal attacks on and threats to adults in authority. School climate is such that many teachers close their doors and lock them while they teach. They have adopted this measure to deter students wandering into their classrooms to speak to their friends without authorization. Responding to the rash of discipline referrals, administrators remanded 538 cases to after-school detention. There were 323 in-school suspensions and 164 out-of-school suspensions.

Although there are many external factors which contribute to lowered school success, interactions and relationships internal to the school also impinge upon these outcomes. They include problems in the knowledge content and transmission process; and estrangement in teacher–administrator, teacher–student, and teacher–teacher relationships.

Problems in pedagogy and knowledge content

One internal factor relates to problems occurring in classrooms. Students complain of boring and uninspiring lessons. Yet, there is an unwillingness by some veteran teachers to adjust their pedagogy and to upgrade their professional knowledge of how to fit their teaching to learning styles of contemporary pupils' needs and daily experiences. Moreover, the content and transmission of knowledge may be less relevant to the needs and life experiences of contemporary students than they were to white upper-middle-class students in years when many of the teachers began their careers. One teacher noted: 'Teachers must learn to truly evaluate themselves and their teaching and change their methods and content'.

All teachers realize obvious changes in the student composition; but, some are reluctant to come to terms with its full implications for their teaching. A teacher reported: 'Many of the teachers here now were here 20 years ago when we did not have problems like we have now. Something is different, and it is not the teachers'. Others are critical of co-workers' negative attitudes about changes in student composition and 'staff's unwillingness to change with time'. They perceive a need for 'teachers to become more involved in the school and to have an investment in teaching the students ... A lot of apathy is seen'. Teachers charge that some 'come only to "work" because it's their job – not because they want to do everything they can to reach the kids'.

From the first week of school, we observed classes in world history on an ongoing basis. Classroom interactions illustrate the disconnectedness between teacher pedagogy and the learning of their students. First, there was an emphasis on rote memorization and the completion of worksheets. Frequently inattentive students either slept during the class or were engaged in off-task activities, such as repeatedly asking to go to the toilet. One female pupil continually stretched and yawned aloud, as the teacher, with arms folded and perched on the edge of the desk, futilely attempted to engage students in a lecture on Mesopotamia. During class, there was a paucity of positive reinforcement from the teacher to attentive students. The homework assignment consisted of students answering questions at the end of each chapter in the textbook and preparing for an end-of-the-week test on 20 definitions. Interestingly, only when the teacher veered briefly from the text to relate its content to his childhood and working-class background did the entire class take a studied interest in his comments. When he returned to the text, student attention drifted once again.

Study-hall activities were often filled with academically meaningless experiences. At mid-year, we observed well-behaved students in a study hall engaged in mindless activities of playing low-level computer games in a classroom stocked with state of the art computer hardware. In another study hall, students sat in small groups engaged in no academic learning activities, as the teacher ordered students to open their books and study. One 12th-grader, ignoring the teacher, drummed idly on his desk.

There is no singularly focused course taught in either African-American history or literature. Students continue to graduate with little knowledge of their past as a racial group. Given the current climate of teacher-student wariness and the racial composition of the academic faculty, teachers may be wary about attempting to teach these subjects as separate, semester-long offerings. There does not appear to be an articulated faculty concern about the absence of these courses in the curriculum, despite secondary school accreditation association recommendations that the school teach these courses (Middle States Association of Colleges and Schools, 1991). A long absence has spawned debate among community members about whether to offer them, and if so, what should be their orientation. Some teachers reason tautologically that students need to 'stick to the classics because they need to know the classics'. Others point to their lack of preparation to teach African-American history and literature, yet make no attempt to study the field in an effort to fill this cultural void. During African-American history month in February, students receive a dose of concentrated instruction in their heritage, at times from some teachers who are reported to be contemptuous of the subject and of their students' unfamiliarity with African-American history. Students cited teachers' insensitivity when they relayed some of their teachers' quips: 'Since this is black history month, I'm going to work you like slaves'.

Teacher–administrator relationships

Suspicions and resulting tensions between teachers and administrators have confounded instructional supervision, the primary role of the principal in effective schools. Some teachers perceive that when they speak openly and critically of administrative decisions, they are vulnerable to retaliatory acts. A teacher reported: 'If a teacher complains about something wrong, he/she is harassed by extra class observations. You name it, the administration will do [it] to make your life hell'. Other teachers perceive that: 'Our teachers feel that "nobody tells me what to do", or they cry grievance.' To remediate conflicts, some teachers have called for administrators 'to become more sensitive to the needs of the faculty; to become more personal and friendly; and to build positive, professional relationships with faculty'.

When the high school principal resigned in mid-year, some teachers hoped for improved relationships with the new administration. Others pessimistically contended that 'some adults cannot work with any other adults in this building in a peaceful, professional manner – and that's a sad state of affairs'. The succeeding principal set into motion new discipline policies. Contrary to a policy of 'getting tough with the kids', which many teachers had sought in a new administration, he called for 'child-centred' relationships between teachers and their students. He reasoned that 'closeness' to the child is a prerequisite to the application of any disciplinary actions. From his perspective, some teachers may not wish to become emotionally invested in their students' lives, which requires risk-taking on their part and much time beyond contracted school hours. The principal explained that respect for teacher authority was earned, not mandated. Also, a caring and nurturing relationship could not be contracted.

No administrative policy seems to have disillusioned teachers more than these ideas. This policy did not allay some teachers' 'frustration of having to deal with disruptive students over and over without expulsion procedures being initiated'. His critics perceive that the principal allows some students to 'get away with murder'. His open-door policy has led to teacher complaints that 'he is too close to students', which undercuts his effectiveness as a disciplinarian. Seeking instant and more authoritarian responses to their disciplinary referrals, one teacher maintains: 'This society only functions effectively in areas of strict, sure or certain punishment. This is the reason society is in such a mess.' In frustration with the child-centredness approach, a teacher union official exclaimed: 'I am tired of hearing that the kids of this school are the bottom line!'

Offering a contrasting view of past practices in the administration of student justice, another teacher posited:

> These children are suspended for some of the most stupid reasons. We have teachers who get in students' faces, follow them around, yell at them, curse at them, and lower the children's self-esteem. Teachers need to be dealt with instead of the attitude being 'the teacher is always right'. The teacher is not always right.

Teacher–student relationships

A third internal factor mitigating student achievement and citizenship is a loss of emotional and physical connections between teachers and their students. With a student–teacher ratio of 11:1, teachers highlight the fact that there were 28 per cent of the student population absent on any given day in 1992–3. Teachers attribute excessive absenteeism to their belief that 'parents allow their children to miss school for any reason'. High transiency rates exacerbate average daily attendance figures; 27 per cent of students enrolled transferred out of the district before the end of the school year.

Despite grim pupil attendance statistics, many teachers overlook Wexler's observation that '... the interaction between teacher and student is the quintessential social relation'; that in some schools 'there is a lack of the emotional commitment and caring that is required for the relation – teaching and learning – to be successful'. He notes that the 'recognition by students and teachers of this lack ... is indicated by the simple phrase: 'nobody cares' (p 35).

This loss of an emotional connection between teachers and their students in Wilson High is reflected in numerous interactions. A 1992 survey asking teachers about their greatest concerns in school showed that a consistent worry within the teaching corps was the lack of uniform enforcement of disciplinary policies. Responses included their perceptions that 'administrators are not effective in punishing, suspending, or expelling students that are consistently a threat to the educational environment as well as safety and well being of other students and staff'.

At times, teachers are critical of inconsistent signals students receive from within the institution. Confounding messages are evident in the simultaneous operation of an alternative school within the high school. Misbehaving youth who are at risk of dropping out are remanded there for special counselling, instruction and general support to remain in school. In turn, they receive prizes as incentives for doing well in school work and deportment. Classes begin later and end earlier than those in the regular high school. These and other motivational perks have bred some envy among teachers and students of the larger student body, who perceive that the only way to be recognized and rewarded is to 'act up'.

Without doubt, breakdowns in school discipline and inconsistencies in managing disciplinary cases have contributed in no small measure to lowered teacher morale. Several teachers describe co-worker morale in terms such as: 'It would take a ten-foot ladder to kiss a worm's hind end'; 'Morale is low!' This is because of a sense that the school is 'out of control'; and 'Struggling to motivate students and to control behavior so that I can teach is the most unsatisfactory part of my job.' One indication of an estranged faculty has been teacher withdrawal, whereby teachers report 'giv[ing] up monitoring and disciplining', and retreating to their classrooms.

The 1992 survey of teachers called for more respect for teacher authority. However, the student survey showed discordance between students' needs for nurturing and meaningful educational experiences and their teachers' needs for discipline and control. The dominant perceptions among students in grades 7 to 11 was that there is a lack of teacher care, encouragement, and concern for them. Twelfth-graders highlighted the need for more interesting classes, relevant to their future careers. In addition, there was consistent agreement among students that they needed more opportunities for extracurricular activities and hands-on learning experiences.

In 1993, a cross-section of 50 students representing high, middle, and low achievers, gang members, and student leaders described to us the behaviours of a 'caring teacher'. Students agreed that caring teachers acknowledge and interact with their students outside of school, such as on the street and in shopping malls; they are friends to their students; they go out of their way to listen to and to help students with their problems; they do not use sarcasm against their students; they praise them; and they allow students opportunities to express themselves so as to learn what problems students are having outside the classroom. At the end of their meeting, students learned that teachers and administrators would meet in the afternoon to discuss student concerns. They directed us to 'tell those teachers that they will get no respect from students until they show some caring for us'.

When 25 representatives from the faculty and administration met to share perceptions of caring teachers' behaviours, their list included many items characterizing the ideal teacher their students sought. They noted that caring teachers volunteer for extracurricular activities that involve time and effort without compensation; mentor students for academic and emotional needs; show mutual respect for students by speaking respectfully and never making deprecating comments about them; encourage self-esteem and praise their students; provide 'a shoulder' for students and listen to students talk about their personal problems; refuse to accept students' failure, and tell students directly that they care for them; ask students how they feel; and put themselves in students' shoes to empathize with them.

During follow-up discussions with teachers, many agreed with, but some discounted, student concerns on the grounds that students failed to recognize that teacher caring consisted of prompting students to do their school work. One veteran teacher, responding to his students' allegation that he lacked a caring attitude, retorted: 'When I stop prodding students to complete their assignments, then they will know that I no longer care about them.' Another teacher asked his students 'Do you expect me to be your friend or your teacher?'

Students called for, and teachers realized the need for, an emotional attachment which, for students, could best be achieved through informal interactions that bring teachers and students into closer proximity. Despite some congruence between teacher and student perceptions of caring teachers, the two groups continue to withdraw from each other. Teacher union leaders cite community threats to close the high school as a factor which undermines their commitment to a caring relationship with their students. One activist asserted that teachers would show no caring until community members and administrators began to show more sensitivity for them and their needs for job security.

Indeed, withdrawal of emotional risk-taking is best illustrated by some teacher reticence to reach out to their pupils through any form of physical contact. Teachers cite charges of sexual harassment and physical assault as factors giving rise to their reluctance to give students a 'pat on the back' to recognize good work. James Kennelly (1994) characterizes this nationwide 'no-touch' policy as 'the big chill at school' that is 'freezing teacher–student relations'. He reports that students perceive the 'no-touch' policy as an indication that teachers are afraid of their pupils or that there is something unsafe about them. In Wilson High, local union leaders have been advised by their attorney to caution the membership against any kind of physical contact with students.

The effects of teacher–student estrangement are most evident when economic crises in the district forced managers to retrench funding for most after-school and extracurricular activities. Wexler illustrates how students use extracurricular activities as their 'identity anchor' to compensate for the loss of caring interpersonal relations. Withdrawal of extracurricular activities as supports with which students identify thwart students developing a sense of belonging. To fill the void, some students may have resorted to gang membership or to antisocial behaviour, of which the community is most fearful. Many high school sponsors of student activities refuse to direct them without compensation. Simultaneously, student interest in activities has waned, implying to teachers student apathy. One teacher remarked: 'Students do not stay after school for activities or practice. As a result, functions and student organizations have been terminated.'

Some teachers do volunteer their services with some success. For example, the graduating class of 1993 had no yearbook as a remembrance of their high school years. This outcome was due to student refusal to go to a studio located in another community to sit for photo sessions. The next year, two teachers volunteered their time and held the photo sessions at the school. When asked how they got a 95 per cent student participation rate, one sponsor replied: 'We brought the mountain to Mohammed.'

When a journalist from a nearby university learned that students had lost their newspaper owing to a teacher transfer, he volunteered to help them publish their paper. Before his arrival though, a union representative made it patently clear that if he discovered the journalist was being paid for his efforts, he would use his authority to stop his involvement on grounds of 'unfair labor practice'. Students have enthusiastically rallied around the effort to revitalize the tabloid as an organ for their heretofore unheard voices. Their first edition devoted considerable space to criticisms of 'uncaring teachers'. One contributor, titling her poem 'Teachers', wrote:

> Teachers can be mean. A teacher can be nice, but our teachers are just mean and grumpy
> Teachers can be nice and sweet, but our teachers can be nice if they wanted to be
> Teachers can be loud or quiet, but our teachers are just loud and annoying.

This poem and an editorial on uncaring teachers provoked some teacher remonstrance that they are being unfairly judged.

Teacher—teacher relationships

Strained relations within the rank and file are a fourth internal barrier to school success. Given declining standardized test scores and pupil academic achievement, and rising tides of student resistance, too few adults, in and out of school, seem willing to share in the responsibility for school outcomes. The tendency has been to shift the locus of control to others. Taxpayers of the community who have been detached from the high school blame the superintendent. Elected school managers blame school site administrators, who then impute teachers, further straining relationships between the two groups. One teacher remarked: 'Those of us who try are being beaten down by administrative and board accusations.'

Occasionally, culpability turns inwardly when teachers reflect upon the behaviours and attitudes of co-workers toward their work. Secondary school teachers blame elementary teachers for the poor academic preparation of some pupils entering high school. Others note that 'teachers feel defeated, perhaps because of student apathy, partially due to the teachers' lack of ability to change'; and that 'if teachers took a more positive outlook and attitude, this would help the staff and student body'. Some teachers attribute student failure to the likelihood that 'Students aren't given a challenge. They are set up for failure.' Co-workers are critical also of the fact that:

> Many teachers do care and work very hard, but there are many who do not get involved. They do not fairly assess the students. They do not work with other faculty members. Their attitude is totally negative. They spend time complaining, but when asked to help

change things, they are too busy. Many teachers spend more time out of classrooms at meetings and [being] 'ill' than in classrooms.

At times, teachers' reluctance to go beyond the measured mile stems from fears of peer coercion. They worry about 'putting pressure on others to follow' or 'making the others look mediocre'. These attitudes are not limited to the high school. To address students' low achievement, a permanent substitute teacher in one of the elementary schools organized an after-school tutorial programme, involving parents, high school and university students, and professors. In this school, that is a tributary to the high school, 72.1 per cent of 6th graders performed below the 1993 national average in reading; 67.5 per cent fell below this mark in mathematics. These scores reflect a regressive trend in the academic performance of elementary pupils in this 99 per cent African-American school. Yet, co-workers of this African-American teacher have openly refused to render one hour per week to assist in this educational endeavour, which attempts to bridge the gap between teachers and parents and to bring school and community resources to bear upon an important problem. Moreover, the teacher is forbidden to ask for teacher volunteers, because any voluntarism would put undue pressure upon teachers who chose not to assist, and their refusal would cast unwilling teachers in an embarrassingly negative light. As she continues this work, some of her co-workers have elected to ostracize her.

A failure to attenuate teacher–student disengagement

To fill the gap between community expectations and student outcomes, school managers negotiated in 1991 with the local teachers' union for a programme which might help alleviate problems of teacher–student estrangement. In exchange for a 21 per cent salary increase and other negotiated benefits over a three-year period, the union endorsed student–teacher instructional conference (STIC). The programme provided for three additional 30-minute instructional periods per week for students needing more intensive academic interaction. School managers believed that STIC was the most significant negotiated item in the new contract. In a spirit of teacher empowerment, they reasoned that if teachers designed the programme, the school district could be assured its success. Teachers agreed to study and then recommend strategies for its implementation. However, in a district already financially strapped, there were few additional funds available for needed supplies in an extracurricular component to be included in STIC. Therefore, in the second year, the board changed the emphasis from extracurricular activities to academic enrichment and remediation, requiring few additional resources, save teacher time, creativity, emotional commitment and a willingness to invest totally in attaining a mutual goal of student success.

Students favourable to STIC viewed it in much the same light as school managers; ie, as an opportunity to talk with their teachers about careers, their problems, and academics. Some students benefited from this learning experience. One 10th-grader stated: 'Kids don't think STIC is important and act bad. You learn more in STIC, though. If you have trouble in math, [the teacher] always helps you'. Other students reported experiencing more individualized attention during STIC than in their regular class periods. One student, offering a favourable response noted: 'In class, the teacher is at the board. In STIC, the teacher sits at the desk and helps you'. Another reported: '[STIC] is the only time the teacher sits down one-on-one'. Students highlighted their relationships with teachers as important contributors to their success.

These positive experiences, however, were exceptions to an overwhelming aversion for the programme. After two years, teachers and students, when polled, rejected the continuation of the concept. Foreshadowing its doom in the high school, the teaching corps never accepted full ownership of the programme. Teachers and students recalled few enrichment activities during the conference period, and even less one-to-one teacher–student interaction. Teachers complained of student indifference to the programme and characterized it as 'a valuable waste of time!' Ironically, students who were tardy or absent during STIC were also the very ones who most needed teacher counselling, teachers' caring interaction and remediation. Students reported: 'The teacher talks during class; he sits during STIC and works on his grade book. It's a waste of time.' Students reported and teachers verified that for the most part, the time was spent on make-up work or as a study period.

Although students highly valued a personal interaction, this relationship seemed to have been the most difficult to garner from their teachers. A student noted: 'I don't understand some stuff. Sometimes you tell [the teacher]; she's mean sometimes. She says she can't help me.' A white student, transferring out of Wilson High at the end of the year, reported:

> The teacher is the problem, not STIC. The teachers think that you do not want to learn, so they won't listen. Certain students get along with the teacher. Those who need help don't get along and don't get help. All teachers are friendly, but don't show it. They want total control … in social studies, I wait for the teacher to tell me what to do. Half the time he doesn't tell me. It's a waste of time. Now I have to make up this course when I move to another high school.

A 9th-grader, so much in need of more positive engagement with his teachers, expressed total detachment from the concept and its goals. When asked what he liked best about the programme, he retorted: 'nothing got dammit … I don't like a dame thing … If I was to change something it would be the holl dame thing [sic]'.

Analysis

Alienation, broadly defined, occurs when there is deterioration in a shared system of values. Destabilization of traditional social values and depersonalization in human relationships may follow rapid social change and may be related to one's inability to adjust to change or to realize one's goals.

Teachers in Wilson have experienced changes in standards and relationships to which they once subscribed. Two decades ago Wilson Township was an upper-middle-class suburban community in which parental and teacher social values of achievement were in sync. Today, this community has undergone dramatic change in its demographics, in the characteristics of its schools, and in the social values of the community. Owing to rapid changes in the community, to destabilization of community values, and to depersonalization in human relationships, estrangement abounds between teachers and administrators, teachers and students, and teachers and their co-workers.

In response to the uncertainties which teachers have experienced in the face of change, they have retreated into the security of their union. Mark Ginsburg (1988, p 9) points to the contradictions in the status of teachers. He contends that although some teachers may perceive themselves as professionals, others have learned that they do not own or control the means of educational production and are little more than labourers who work for a wage. In a region with a long history of estrangement between workers and owners, teachers demonstrate that they have successfully learned to sell their labour for wages when they are treated as workers. Vulnerable to supervision of their work, to community pressures for accountability, and to retrenchment when enrolments decrease, they have embraced the security of the contract and adopted the language and strategies of labour. They charge administrators with 'unfair labour practices,' inundate them with grievances, and at times withhold their labour from their students.

Some teachers express concern that community members have not forgiven their union for a bitter selective strike that it waged in the last set of contract negotiations. The estrangement that results from adversarial labour-management relationships have mitigated attempts to reform education in Wilson High School. Innovations are often met with disenchantment and a crippling cynicism within the teacher corps and student body. Discouraged teachers report that new programmes have come and gone. They comment that 'no one can enact change'; and 'it did not work then, and it won't work now'.

Strained labour-management relations notwithstanding, challenges which African-American youth pose for their teachers are immense. In this school, the chances of these demands being met so that youth realize the goals of productive, participatory citizenship seem uncertain. Ambivalence stems in part from the alienating terms under which some students and their teachers interact and the emotional disengagement which has followed.

In this community, there is open contestation between social values of youth and traditional institutional roles of adults. Seasoned teachers perceive respect for their authority as an institutionally sanctioned entitlement. Meanwhile, students demand a nurturing relationship with their teachers as a precondition for giving their respect. In the failure of one group to acquiesce to the demands of the other, both have emotionally withdrawn. In the resulting estrangement, it appears that too many teachers now avoid the risk of an emotional investment in 'defiant adolescents' that would require teachers going beyond the measured mile in reaching out to them. The consequent detachment is apparent in a time when there are pressing social needs for teacher willingness personally and caringly to counsel alienated students as an imperative to educating them. Instead, subject-oriented teachers hold expectations of transmitting the knowledge of their disciplines using pedagogy acquired decades ago. While they call for a 'more personal and friendly ... positive professional relationship' with administrators, they seem not to perceive an emotional attachment to their students as essential to their work.

There is institutional condemnation of the social values which students now bring to school from their community. Unstable family life and community withdrawal of social commitment to the lives of some youth signify an altered system of values. Yet, the traditional institutional structure of schools, based on deference to teacher authority, continues to exist, even though the community culture has changed. Youth values are not in sync with those of the school. Some teachers believe that the loss of respect for their constituted authority is rooted in child-rearing practices of the family. They are concerned that 'the responsibility of the student and the parents to achieve a quality education for the student has been entirely forgotten. It seems to be everybody's responsibility except theirs.' Teacher perceptions that 'the beliefs we preach contradict what is practised at home' signal the breakdown in articulation between traditional institutional values of the school and those of a community culture.

Given these beliefs, there appears to be little common ground between teachers and the parents of their students. Parents reciprocate teacher accusations in their claims that some teachers are aloof. Their perceptions of social distance are exacerbated by teacher residency. They charge that teachers have no stake in the community in which they work. Although there is no residence requirement for public employees of the district, community groups are sceptical of teacher allegiance to the community when they live outside it. Indeed, the extent to which teachers do not live in communities in which they teach is a loss of human and social capital to that community. It curtails out-of-school contacts with their pupils, parents, and other community members, resulting in greater detachment between teachers and the homes of their students. This detachment also fuels community misperceptions that teachers have neither a stake in community politics nor empathy for economic crises when they arise. Residency, coupled with a 'no-touch' policy between teachers and their students, are issues which tragically highlight the community's loss of faith in allegiances and the wholesome character of its teachers. Consequently, conflict-ridden relationships among parents, students and their teachers have laid a tenuous foundation for achievement and productive community citizenship. The resulting distant relationships between groups give alienated students few reasons to invest in their teachers' concerns, their own education, and their uncertain futures.

Conclusion

Despite its dissatisfaction with current outcomes, the community will continue to rely on the skills and knowledge of its teachers to foster social commitment within its young citizenry. Therefore, it is imperative that educators recognize the long-term effects of contentious and mistrusting relationships in classrooms and corridors. They will likely carry over into adulthood, when this generation seeks their niche in a highly competitive society, or when many of these same teachers must interact with former students who will enrol their children in Wilson High. Alienation, rooted in student perceptions of uncaring adults, will surely sour the intellectual appetites of these young citizens as lifelong learners. The new challenges in this community are for educators to forge future citizens in whom some teachers may have little emotional investment. It is their willingness to build a nurturing environment for urban youth today that will in large measure determine the quality of community living and citizenship for their pupils, wherever their destinies may lead them.

Acknowledgements

The authors wish to acknowledge the Pittsburgh Plate Glass Foundation's financial support of this research. We thank Dean Kenneth F Metz, Professors Wilma Smith and Joseph Werlinich of the School of Education, University of Pittsburgh, Pittsburgh, PA for their invaluable participation in this collaborative project. We also thank our colleague Rolland Paulston for his critical comments in the preparation of this chapter.

References

Ginsburg, M (1988) *Contradictions in Teacher Education and Society*, Lewes: Falmer.
Health and Welfare Planning Association (1983) *1984 Community Profile*, Pittsburgh, PA: Health and Welfare Planning Association.
Kennelly, J (1994) 'The big chill at school', *USA Weekend*, 14–16 January, p 18.
Middle States Association of Colleges and Schools (1991) *Report of Visiting Committee*, Philadelphia: Commission on Secondary Schools.
Pennsylvania System of School Assessment (1993) *School Profile*, Harrisburg, PA: Pennsylvania Department of Education.
University Microfilms (1993) *1990 Census of Population and Housing*, Summary tape file on CD–ROM.
Wexler, P (1992) *Becoming Somebody: Toward a Social Psychology of School*, London: Falmer.

19. The integration of young people into UK society with particular reference to the Jewish community

Leslie Bash

The challenge to successive UK governments has been to effect the successful integration of youth into the adult community. Adolescence has conventionally been defined, in Western industrialized societies, in social psychological/biological terms with the accent upon maturation, period of transition, search for independence, and so on. Such a view is encapsulated by Friedenburg (1959):

> Adolescence is the period during which a young person learns who he is, and what he really feels. It is a time in which he differentiates himself from the culture, though on the culture's terms. It is the age at which, by becoming a person in his own right, he becomes capable of deeply felt relationships to other individuals, perceived clearly as such.

During the course of this century Western conceptions of youth crystallized into a model of an individual, much as Friedenburg has described. Education was a significant aspect of this, based upon an implicit notion of development from infancy, through childhood, adolescence, to adulthood. The ghosts of Piaget, Freud, and other icons of the developmental psychological tradition were clearly present throughout much of this discourse.

It might be noted, however, that, notwithstanding the conventional use of the masculine pronoun before an era of gender awareness, the emphasis for most writers on adolescence was generally, although not exclusively, male. Moreover, there had also been a tendency to view the phenomenon as a period of potentially deviant behaviour. There was a fixed image of the street 'hooligan' portrayed as a threat to social order, especially in the late nineteenth century city (Pearson, 1983, Chapter 5). According to this version of social reality, there was a need to control/channel the urges and energy of (male) youth into desirable, if not worthy, activities. The institutionalization, if not the demonization, of adolescence rapidly took root and youth (saving) movements mushroomed at the turn of the century: the Boy Scouts, the Boys' Brigade, youth settlements, etc. Such movements had a clear mission to rescue and protect young males in order that they should make the successful transition to being responsible members of society.

Youth culture

However, the postwar period in the UK, and elsewhere in the West, gave rise to a slightly different view – a view which seemed to suggest that adolescence had a degree of integrity, that it was not merely a staging post en route to adulthood. So, despite serious objections to its usage, the assumption of a 'youth culture' has prevailed for some decades and the more popular media have sought to maintain the 'sex, drugs and rock and roll' image of the teenager. Long since perceived as a metropolitan phenomenon, the 'problem' of youth is increasingly viewed within a broader geographical context with even the small town and village unable to escape the ravages of the rampant young.

The sensationalist approach to young people has, no doubt, been far more attractive than a calm appraisal of the social complexities which characterize an age category whose boundaries are far from clear. Age stratification has always held out the expectation that society would neatly divide into well-defined groups, each of whose behaviour, norms and values could be identified with some ease. A number of commentators on postwar UK society have focused on the young, with an attempt to demonstrate the rise of a distinct, coherent youth culture, founded on the achievement of a degree of financial independence during the 'boom' years of the 1950s and 1960s. Rock and roll was seen as merely the outward manifestation of the integrity of this culture, while the supposed new freedoms related to sex and drugs underlined the significance of the 'generation gap'.

There have been a diversity of responses to this apparent phenomenon. The inevitable moralistic approach which bemoans the waywardness of youth and its decadence was observed in a heightened form when confronted with 'extreme' behaviour: delinquent activity, teddy boy gangs, mods and rockers, etc. Cohen's (1972) well-known description of the amplification process in the creation of moral panics showed how public opinion could be garnered to express outrage at the failure of young people to abide by the norms and values of 'adult' society. Even so, the mods and rockers portrayed by Cohen in time became socially and economically integrated, no doubt spending holidays with their partners and their children on the beach at the seaside in time-honoured fashion, instead of providing the challenge of the motorbike and scooter. Some years later, Willis's (1977) study of working-class boys attempted to explain how the values and behaviour characteristic of a counter-school 'subculture' paradoxically eased the passage into male, adult working-class life, thus contributing to social reproduction. Neither of these studies suggests a picture of a monolithic youth culture reflecting a great divide between adults and the young. On the other hand, others, especially students, were perceived to be politically radical, if not revolutionary in outlook, and seemingly posed a rather different threat to establishment values. Public perceptions in the 1960s suggested a potent mix of left-wing ideas, sexual licence, drug influenced behaviour and general abandon, such that a number of politicians in the 1990s were able to blame this period for the supposed decline in moral and educational standards.

All this, however, masks a rather more complex reality demanding a consideration of class, race, and gender and the general structure of power relations in UK society (see Brake, 1980). This requires rather more careful deliberation with the likely outcome that few if any categorical statements are able to be made about the nature of youth as such. The notion of 'integration into society' remains somewhat problematic in any case and, at the very least, may indicate distinct notions of cultural integration, social integration, economic integration and political integration. Cynically, it may be that it is important to ensure the cultural integration of all young people while maintaining hierarchical divisions regarding the economy and the polity: a pool of unemployed and disenfrachised youth might be acceptable if they continued to adhere to established norms of behaviour.

Such a Durkheimian view of societal reproduction might be relatively unproblematic where there is a basic assumption of homogeneity. The presence of self-defined minority groups suggests at the very least some resistance to the idea of complete social integration and, accordingly, a rather more complex view of the entire process. That social/cultural homogeneity and heterogeneity are social constructs is accepted; the criteria are often ideological in character (for example, the nature of Englishness). Yet, despite their social construction, it is difficult to dismiss the reality of minority groups and the issues revolving around the integration of the young.

Young people in the Jewish community

Thus, a consideration of the integration of young people in the context of UK minority cultural communities might serve to illustrate some of the larger issues. In particular, the intention is to focus on the situation of young people in the Jewish community, a group which is itself characterized by diversity and contradiction as a consequence of differential patterns of subcultural behaviour, religious adherence and ethnic attachment. Moreover – and central to the thrust of the chapter – the Jews provide an example of a minority group in UK society which has evolved over a period of centuries and which has presented a complex and sometimes contradictory picture to the gentile world. The Jews, on the one hand, are seen as an integral part of European history and, thus, of the development of European cultural traditions, and, yet, on the other, as the perpetual outsiders, as archetypal aliens. It may not be surprising, then, to find the situation of Jewish populations throught Europe, including the UK, to be considered as problematic, not least by the Jewish communities themselves.

Historically, it might be possible, albeit in a somewhat crude manner, to represent the cultural dynamic characterizing the Jewish population as

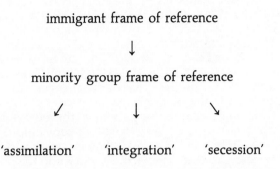

Figure 19.1 *Cultural dynamic of the Jewish population*

shown in Figure 19.1. However the reality is not that clear-cut. While the majority of Jews in Britain at the turn of the century possessed immigrant status (Ashkenazim, of Central/Eastern European origin), a significant minority were descended from earlier settlers – mainly Sephardim (Spanish/Portuguese in origin). These latter had already undergone a degree of assimilation, differing only from the population at large in terms of religious practice – and, even then, frequently displaying a good deal of laxity in observance. On the other hand, such were the prevailing atttitudes of much of the gentile population that even the most Anglicized of Jews experienced a degree of alienation from the dominant culture which, in turn, prompted calls for the establishment of schools and youth organizations which would be committed to the process of assimilation. Hence the creation of such entities as the Jews' Free School in London, one of the largest elementary schools of the nineteenth century, and the Jewish Lads Brigade, a youth movement modelled on the Boys Brigade, a church-based organization.

A basic issue for adults in the mainstream UK Jewish community has been the reconciliation of the desire for assimilation with the need to ensure the continuation of endogamy in an effort to maintain the cohesiveness of religious tradition and surface cultural norms. Until the Second World War the problem was relatively small since, for the most part, the community was located within well-defined geographical limits. Thus, the East End of London had been home to a population which enjoyed different degrees of involvement in Jewish affairs, from the strictly religious to the atheistic, often avowedly political and well to the left; but for all that, social life among most of the young was centred upon the community and marriage with non-Jews was rare.

The 1990s, however, are witness to a significantly changed position regarding the UK Jewish community in general and Jewish youth in particular. First of all, apart from the relatively few refugees from prewar central Europe, some survivors of the Holocaust, and recent immigrants, the community is second, third, and even fourth-generation UK born. Second, the individual outward manifestations of religious Jewish identity

– distinctive clothing, beards, etc – have disappeared except for a minority of the strictly observant. Third, the community is not as concentrated geographically as it was at the turn of the century: the East End is no longer a Jewish area and nor are similar inner-city areas in other UK cities such as Manchester or Leeds; dispersal to the suburban and exurban areas has meant a decline in the traditional tight-knit homogeneity of the 'ghetto'. Fourth, as a corollary to these changes, there has been a significant alteration in the economic circumstances of the majority of the community including wider participation in the employment structure. While there are clearly some Jews who are in conventional working-class occupations (though less so with the decline in such industries as printing, cabinet-making and garment manufacture), entry into the professions (both modern and traditional) and the service sector has been an important factor in shaping contemporary values and attitudes.

Jewish young people in the UK are accordingly at a crossroads. A minority group frame of reference now predominates along with a diversity of responses. The strictly orthodox, Hasidic minority might be considered as the least problematic, having rejected cultural assimilation/ integration in favour of secession (see above). Even on the economic and political fronts there is a tendency for somewhat limited participation, with the emphasis on male employment, often in family concerns, while women – often from their teenage years – concentrate on child-rearing and tending to the domestic needs of their partners. The Hasidim comprise a range of groupings – from those who have sought to preserve, at least outwardly, the traditional lifestyle of the eighteenth- and nineteenth-century Polish *shtetl* (Jewish village), to the more 'modernist' Lubavitch with its penchant for the use of the mass media and information technology. Children from within this collection of sects tend to grow up with a tightly defined set of values and norms of behaviour. For many, the Hasidic culture of Stamford Hill and Golders Green remains hermetically sealed from the outside world, with children frequently raised with Yiddish as their first language and a prohibition on secular media (newspapers, television, radio, etc). Of vital importance is an emphasis upon religious study for males and preparation for domesticity for females, and, to complete the process, arranged marriage using the services of the *shadchan* (traditional matchmaker).

The secessionist approach adopted by the strictly orthodox community has meant that it has been able to reproduce a system of social and cultural relations amongst the young which has held reasonably tight. Insofar as the label of Jewishness may be viewed within a framework of 'stigmatization' (see Goffman, 1968) the Hasidim have sought to manage their 'spoiled identity' in a highly visible manner, thus reinforcing the tendency towards a segregated social and cultural life amongst the young – including a marked gender separation as a consequence of a rigid code of sexual relations. Of course, the reproductive process can never be totally successful and, like every close-knit group, the Hasidim have experienced a degree of disaffection and demands for integration with the broader Jewish community and the world at large.

At the other end of the spectrum, the process of assimilation has continued unabated. Here, young people, while perhaps acknowledging their Jewish identity, or at least viewing themselves as being of Jewish descent, have few if any ties with the community as such. To those born of parents with a conscious Jewish identity, whether observant or not, and with some connection with Judaism in an institutionalized form, a particular kind of tension is frequently experienced. Sometimes this is in the context of nostalgia or guilt on the part of such parents, that they have a responsibility to ensure that their children continue to maintain some sort of relationship with the organized community and, most importantly, that they marry within. The conflicts with the demands of the secular world as well as with the considerable complexities of sexual relations are apparent, not least with current issues concerning homosexuality.

These last points do not relate merely to those who have ceased to be Jewish in all but name but also to the vast majority of Jewish youth who, either through family ties or through a conscious decision, have maintained a connection with the organized community. The social and geographical mobility which entailed a move to the suburbs and exurbs coincided with the emergence of a more 'privatized' mode of living, in comparison with the traditional, more 'community-based' life of the East End. In line with changes in general family structures, there has been the trend towards the conjugal, nuclear family (although less pronounced within the Jewish community). It could be argued that the suburban experience has tended, therefore, to result in a fragmentation of life for the Jewish community (as with the non-Jewish community). The synagogue remains as some kind of focal point, but, for many, merely serves its purpose for the three high holy days of the year. This contrasts with Jewish life in the East End, as it was at the turn of the century, where synagogue permeated every activity, where for young boys in particular, attendance was required every day.

Secularism and Jewish youth

Associated with this change in the situation of the community at large is the role of education. Arguably today this has come to be viewed in largely secular terms. Schools are no longer seen as a focus for Jewish identity, but remain as a perceived avenue for social mobility and, perhaps, a means by which social position is consolidated. It is therefore not surprising that for those Jewish young people educated in secular, maintained schools the reference group is likely to be of a more inclusive, universalistic kind than exclusive and particularistic. While, for example, the influence of a traditional, Jewish, gender-based culture may persist, there is a greater likelihood that the young will take their cue from the broader context; likewise with tastes in fashion and music.

On the other hand, the Jewish community continues to be in a state of flux with 'neo-orthodoxy' in religion reemerging throughout the last hundred years or so in Western Europe as a response to secularization, and making itself felt in the UK. Here, established Jewish religious values are often perceived to be under threat from competing secular cultures and from alternative sects and cults, against which measures have been taken to attempt to counter their 'influence'. It is these perceived threats to Jewish existence which have possibly helped give rise to increased pressures for the establishment of Jewish day schools during the course of this century (Bash, 1993).

However, these pressures were also partly the consequence of an increased standard of living among the Jewish community and a fair degree of geographical mobility, seen especially in the context of London, by far the largest centre of Jewish population in the UK. As with other minority groups (for example, those of Cypriot origin) there has been a tendency for Jews to move in groups in order to preserve a sense of community and provide some kind of security. A significant aspect of this movement to the suburbs of London was their physical growth during the early part of this century. The rise of the suburbs was associated with the development of an urban public transport system (trams, the Underground, buses) and the increasing part played by property developers. Interestingly, twentieth-century Jewish migration to suburban London occurred in quite specific directions. Before the Second World War, for example, families began to settle in the Golders Green area, which was a convenient neighbourhood for workplaces in London. Settlement spread to nearby Hendon, so that by 1939 there was a well-established community, reinforced by refugees from Nazi Europe. The result was that today, these areas, plus Edgware, have made what is now the London Borough of Barnet a major locus of Jewish communal life in London. In the main, those who settled in these northern and north-western (in contrast to the eastern) suburbs of London tended to be from the more affluent sections of the community.

Not surprisingly, the move to the suburbs, particularly in the northern and eastern sectors of the capital, resulted in the fragmentation of the community and thus sparked fears that Judaism would disappear altogether. Schooling, however, which was controlled by the religious authorities was perceived by some to offer a counter to the assimilationary tendencies associated with suburbanism and the acquisition of wealth.

Jewish ethnicism

It was clear at the beginning of the century that Jewish children, whether they had attended a voluntary or maintained school, were beginning to be assimilated to a large degree. In response, a section of orthodoxy began to press for the establishment of a Jewish secondary school which would combine a secular education to university entrance level with what they saw as a sound religious education. The impetus came from the strictly orthodox Adath Yisrael congregation, whose rabbi became the first headmaster of the new Jewish Secondary School in north London in 1929. The school also admitted girls in 1933, but, owing to traditional notions of gender segregation, as soon as it was viable (1936), girls were housed in a separate building, under a female head teacher.

In the midst of this confused situation, community leaders have continued to voice concerns about Jewish youth. For those who have been raised, even minimally, to participate at an institutional level there has been the experience of supplementary education in synagogue-based religion classes which have catered for children at least until the age of 13. In the mainstream orthodox tradition this has had possibly greater meaning for boys as they prepare to become bar mitzvah, ie, attaining the age of religious majority; while in the progressive (reform/liberal) tradition, this has equal significance for both sexes (with bar/bat mitzvah). Thus, the young are frequently kept within 'the fold' until this stage of initiation into the adult community, but, soon afterwards, except for a minority, begin to drift away.

The fear of 'losing' the young has increased with each successive generation born in the UK. In the Anglicized Jewish community of the 1990s – both orthodox and progressive – the youth 'problem' remains, and a multiplicity of organizational initiatives have emerged over the years as potential solutions. As with youth work at large, the aims have been diverse. On the one hand, some importance has been placed on the necessity to continue the general socialization process, with the aim of enabling young people to become 'good' citizens. On the other, the Jewish youth club has traditionally existed to provide an opportunity for early encounters between the sexes, and for courtship in a relatively secure environment, which has acted as a means of resistance to the attractions of the gentile world. As far as the latter is concerned, the entertainment function of youth work has been of greater importance than any particular educative aspect and, from the prewar years up until the 1960s, Jewish youth clubs based upon this premise were able to hold considerable sway over the social lives of young people.

However, competition from the secular world has become increasingly harder to withstand. For some Jews, especially since the creation of the Israeli state, a non-religious focus for the young arose in an effort to counter assimilation – that of Zionism. Until the postwar period, it held little attraction for the bulk of the affiliated Jewish population, and indeed was long resisted by the strictly orthodox. However, one consequence of the Holocaust was the conversion of most Jews in the UK and elsewhere to the establishment of a Jewish nation-state. Many young Jews in the UK, while not actually taking the step of emigrating to Israel, have nonetheless participated in Zionist-oriented youth groups. These groups have been characterized both by particularistic aspects of Judaism and Zionism and by the more universalistic aspects of social and moral responsibility, as well as general camaraderie manifested in weekends together and summer camps. The question arises, however, as to the extent to which this fosters integration within UK society or whether, given the appeal to an alleged ethnic identity, it is likely to encourage secession – a question which resonates through other minority groups facing the 'problem' of youth.

The argument so far has tended, apart from a recognition of the consequences of religious differences within the community, to homogenize Jewish youth. This flies in the face of earlier comments on youth culture and its inabilty to take into account such aspects as gender, class and race. There is an impression that girls are under less pressure to conform to the stereotype of Jewish wife, mother and matriarch, compared with a generation or two ago. In line with changes outside the community, this would even appear to be the case amongst the more religiously observant, although rather less so. Whether this will have the consequence of changing the 'ethnic' identity of the Jewish community is a matter for continuing enquiry, but there is the question of the maintenance of the structure of the orthodox family and its function within the religious community. The traditional gender division of labour has tended to be rationalized and played out along the following lines: the wife/mother is deemed to to be in charge of the household, certainly as far as child-rearing and other domestic responsibilities (including religious observance in the home) are concerned, while the husband/father is required not to question the manner in which these are carried out. On the other hand, the husband/father is central to the functioning of the synagogue – indeed, women are perceived as no more than onlookers, physically separated from men during services. Yet, in recent times, challenges to 'tradition' are being felt in mainstream orthodox circles as a partial consequence of the impact of feminist perspectives.

As far as race is concerned, it is difficult to examine the situation of Jewish young people in the UK without a consideration of the impact of the Holocaust and the ideology which gave rise to it. Conventionally, in the UK, race as a socially defined category has played a comparatively minor role in the fortunes of the Jewish population; visible differences in skin colour have not generally been perceived and Nazi-style anti-semitism failed to make its impact (even when fascism gained a degree of popularity in the 1930s). That is, except in the case of the 'ethnic' Jewish *self*-identity. Arguably, the state of Israel would not ultimately have achieved concrete reality had it not been for the Final Solution and, quite apart from the Zionist-oriented youth movements previously mentioned, a (re-)awakening of an identity based upon a perception of common ancestry has emerged among the young. In part, this is a consequence both of secularization and of the general rise of 'ethnicism', ie, ethnicity as an ideological tool. With the movement away from religious observance and affiliation on the part of a considerable number of Jews, the perpetuation of Jewish identity demanded an alternative basis – and an ethnic identity appeared to provide this.

A conclusion from this brief analysis is that the integration of Jewish youth into UK society is relatively unproblematic. From an economic standpoint, most young Jews face a situation at least as advantageous as the population as a whole: further/higher education and career prospects are probably somewhat better than for many other minority groups – and similarly with income levels. Against the backcloth of a modernist perspective on society, Jewish youth would appear to stand very little chance, in the long run, of a collective existence: assimilation apparently is both painless and inevitable. Yet, as events in Europe have unfolded in the final two decades of the twentieth century, the old certainties have tumbled and nothing remains inevitable. Anti-semitism, while never having disappeared from many countries, is now beginning to be taken seriously again in the UK (Runnymede Commission on Antisemitism,

1994) where, for most of the postwar period, the emphasis has been, correctly, mainly upon racism in the context of people of Afrocaribbean and Asian descent. Perhaps, for this reason, and, for all the adherence to the general prevailing cultural norms and practices of the day, there are a significant number of Jewish young people who will continue to retain a degree of separateness.

From this study of Jewish youth, we may judge that the integration of the young into society as a whole remains as interesting as ever. Marxist perspectives (archetypally, Bowles and Gintis, 1976) have generally tended towards a reproductive view; that in the absence of radical social, economic and political change, the likelihood is that the process of schooling will result in the reproduction of the relations of production and that minority groups will simply be incorporated into the social hierarchy. This kind of interpretation is often no more than a mirror image of a rather dated assimilationary approach, an approach which is belied by the persistence, even after generations of settled existence, of identifiable ethnic groups whose presence is not defined solely by superficial aspects of 'culture'. Until the advent of a more equitable social structure, ethnicity will continue to have currency for those whose place in society seems rather more precarious than the majority's. On the basis of the historical experience of the Jewish population, young people from other minority groups might well find that ethnicity may function, paradoxically, both to ease the process of integration and to provide a mode of resistance and protection when times are difficult.

References

Bash, L (1993) 'Collective identity and urban schooling: the case of the London Jewish community', paper presented at a symposium on International Perspectives on Culture and Schooling, Institute of Education, University of London.

Bowles, S and Gintis H (1976) *Schooling in Capitalist America*, London: Routledge and Kegan Paul.

Brake, M (1980) *The Sociology of Youth Culture and Youth Subcultures*, London: Routledge.

Cohen, S (1972) *Folk Devils and Moral Panics*, London: MacGibbon & Kee.

Friedenburg, E (1959) *The Vanishing Adolescent*, Boston: Beacon Press.

Goffman, E (1968) *Stigma*, Harmondsworth: Penguin.

Pearson, G (1983) *Hooligan: A History of Respectable Fears*, London: Macmillan.

Runnymede Commission on Antisemitism (1994) *A Very Light Sleeper*, London: Runnymede Trust.

Willis, P (1977) *Learning to Labour*, Farnborough: Saxon House.

Biographical notes on contributors

Leslie Bash is currently Principal Lecturer in Education at Anglia Polytechnic University. He has specific interests in urban, multi-cultural and policy issues in education and is the co-author of *Urban Schooling* (1985, with Coulby and Jones); *The Education Reform Act: Competition and Control* (1989, with Coulby); *Conflict and Contradiction: the 1988 Education Act in Action* (1991, with Coulby); and has edited a collection of papers: *Comparative Urban Education* (1987).

Phil Brown is a Lecturer in Sociology at the University of Kent at Canterbury, England. He has written, co-authored and co-edited a number of books including *Schooling Ordinary Kids* (1987); *Education for Economic Survival* (1992, with Hugh Lauder) and *Higher Education and Corporate Realities* (1994, with Richard Scase).

Lynne Chisholm is Acting Professor at the University of Marburg Institute of Education. She has formerly taught at universities in England, Ireland, Canada and in the United States. She directed the ESRC-funded *Girls and Occupational Choice* project and has published widely in the fields of gender, education and the labour market. Her current interests include the development of European research and policy perspectives on youth transitions and she is currently coordinating a Task Force project on women returners' training and counselling needs.

Jane Gaskell is a Professor in the Faculty of Education at the University of British Columbia. She has written on the sociology of secondary education, feminist approaches to education and vocational education.

Andy Green is Senior Lecturer in vocational education at the Post-16 Education Centre in London University Institute of Education. He has published widely on the historical and comparative aspects of education. His books include *Education and State Formation* (1990); *Education Limited* (1991, with Birmingham Cultural Studies Education Group); and *Changing the Future* (1992, with others in the HillCole Group).

Anja Heikkinen has worked as a teacher of science, a school inspector and in educational planning. She is lecturing in vocational education in the Department of Education at University of Tampere, Finland, and finishing her doctorate. She has published on philosophy and history of education.

Tsuneo Hosogane is an associate Professor in Education at the University of Waseda. He has widely researched secondary education, and is a co-editor of *Koko-Nyushi-seido no Kaikaku* (*Reform of Entrance Examination of Upper-Secondary school*) (Rodo-Junpo-sha, 1988).

Akio Inui is a Professor in Education at Hosei University. He has researched secondary education, especially the relation between secondary education and the youth labour market. His previous publications include *The Competitive Structure of School and the Labour Market: Japan and Britain* (BJSE, 1993), *Nihon no Kyoiku to Kigyo-Shakai* (*Education and Corporate Society in Japan*) (Otsuki-shoten, 1990).

Jack Keating works for the Curriculum Corporation in Melbourne and is currently completing his doctorate at London University. His research interests lie in vocational education and training and labour markets and he has published a number of articles and reports on VET in Australia and Europe.

Hugh Lauder is Professor of Education at Victoria University of Wellington, New Zealand. He has co-edited *Education: In Search of a Future* (1988, with Phil Brown); *Towards Successful Schooling* (1990, with Cathy Wylie), and published many papers on educational inequality and on the economics of education.

Gary McCulloch is Professor of Education at Sheffield University. His work has focused on aspects of the social history of education policy. His publications include: *The Secondary Technical School: A Usable Past?* (1989) and *Educational Reconstruction: The 1944 Act and the 21st Century* (1994).

Martin McLean has been a member of the Comparative Education area at the Institute of Education, London University since 1980. His work in recent years has focused on education in Europe with particular reference to issues of curriculum and political cultures.

David Marsden is Reader in Industrial Relations, London School of Economics and Political Science. His current research interests include the integration of European labour markets and industrial relations, public sector pay reforms, and the effect of industrial relations and management practices on unemployment. His recent books are: *Pay and Employment in the New Europe* (editor) (1993) and *Marchés du travail: limites sociales des nouvelles théories (1990).*

Kevin J Moran is currently an Adjunct Assistant Professor and a Post-doctoral Fellow at the School of Education, University of Pittsburgh, where he is conducting research on a grant underwritten by the National Science Foundation. His research appears in *Journal of Social History, Paedagogica Historica, American Educational Research Journal, Journal of Urban History, Journal of Education, Urban Education,* and in the *World Yearbook of Education 1992.*

Jeroen Onstenk works as an Educational Researcher at the Centre for Educational Research/Kohnstamm Institute of the University of Amsterdam. Recent research has included apprenticeship in senior vocational education, company training for poorly educated adults, and a survey of concepts and practices of learning on the job in six countries. He is currently preparing a doctoral thesis on the acquisition of key qualifications through learning on the job.

Paul Ryan is Lecturer in the Faculty of Economics and Politics and Fellow of King's College at the University of Cambridge. He is editor and contributor to *International Comparisons of Education and Training for Intermediate Skills* (1991) and *The Problem of Youth: The Regulation of Youth Employment and Training in Advanced Economies* (with P Garonna and Richard C Edwards, 1991). He is currently writing a book on the economic history of apprenticeship in twentieth-century engineering.

Elwyn Thomas is Senior Lecturer in, and formerly Chairperson of, the Department of International and Comparative Education at the Institute of Education, University of London. His current research interests include cross-cultural influences on schooling, the transition from school to work and assessing the effectiveness of training in education and the world of work. He was head of biological education at the University of Malawi for two years and spent a further five years as an educational psychologist working for the government of the Republic of Singapore.

William B Thomas teaches history and sociology of education at the University of Pittsburgh. He has published in journals such as the *American Sociologist, Journal of Social History, Paedagogica Historica, American Educational Research Journal, American Journal of Education, Journal of Urban History, Teachers College Record, Journal of Education, Journal of*

Negro Education, Urban Education, Phi Delta Kappan, and *Phylon.* Other works have appeared in *Education and the Rise of the New South, Black Communities and Urban Race Relations in American History,* and in the *World Yearbook of Education 1992.*

Janusz Tomiak was a Senior Lecturer in Comparative and Eastern European Education in the University of London Institute of Education and School of Slavonic and East European Studies until his retirement in 1988. He is the author/editor of five books on comparative and eastern European education and numerous articles and chapters in books published in this field of study.

Elaine Unterhalter is Director of the RESA (Research in Education Policy in Southern Africa) project based in the Post-16 Education Centre, Institute of Education, University of London. She has written/edited a number of books on the transformation of apartheid education including (with Harold Wolpe and Thozamile Botha) *Education in a Future South Africa* (Heinemann). Her main research interest is in the impact of the current South African transformation on the pattern of gender inequalities.

Eva Voncken works as an Educational Researcher at the Centre for Educational Research/ Kohnstamm Institute of the University of Amsterdam. Recent research has included early school leaving, educational and vocational guidance, apprenticeship and minimum qualifications for school leavers.

Tony Watts is Director at the National Institute for Careers Education and Counselling (NICEC), which is sponsored by the Careers Research and Advisory Centre (CRAC) in Cambridge. He was joint-founder of CRAC, has published many books and articles on careers guidance and related topics, and is editor of the *British Journal of Guidance and Counselling.* He has acted as a consultant to a number of government departments and international organizations, including the European Commission.

Bruce W Wilson is currently the Director of the Union Research Centre on Organisation and Technology. He has taught extensively in sociology and education in Education at the University of Melbourne, and was the Director of its Youth Research Centre from 1988 to 1991. He has co-authored two books, *Confronting School and Work* and *Shaping Futures,* and was co-editor of *For Your Own Good: Young People and State Intervention in Australia* and of *Pink Collar Blues: Work, Gender and Technology*

Alison Wolf is Reader in Education and co-director of the International Centre of Research on Assessment (ICRA) at the Institute of Education, London University. She has worked extensively for the Employment Department in the UK on issues relating to vocational education and assessment. She has also conducted comparative work on French and English education. Her recent publications include *Competence-Based Assessment* (1994) and *Parity of Esteem?* (1993).

Roger R Woock is currently Head of the Department of Social and Educational Studies at the University of Melbourne. He has held senior academic positions in Canada and the USA and has written widely on the sociology and political economy of education, including co-authorship of *Confronting School and Work.*

Michael Young has been Head of the Post-16 Education Centre at the London University Institute of Education since it was established in 1985. He was a lecturer in sociology of education and edited/wrote a number of influential books in the field including *Knowledge and Control: New Directions for the Sociology of Education* (Collier Macmillan). He was one of the authors of the influential report *A British Baccalauréat,* published in 1990 by the Institute for Public Policy Research, and in 1991 was Specialist Advisor on 16–19 Education to the House of Commons Select Committee on Education.

The series editors

David Coulby is Professor of Education and Dean of Education and Human Sciences at Bath College of Higher Education. His current research interest concerns post-modernism and European curricular systems, on which he is authoring a book with Crispin Jones.

Crispin Jones is a Senior Lecturer in Education at the University of London Institute of Education. He works in the Department of International and Comparative Education and the Centre for Multicultural Education. His main research interest is the study of diversity in inner city schools and the consequences for education of late modernity.

Bibliography

Abbott, A (1934) Oral evidence to Board of Education consultative committee, 26 January, *Board of Education Papers*, ED.10/151 London: Public Record Office

Acker, J (1988) 'Class, Gender and the Relations of Distribution', *Signs*, **13**, 3, 473–97

ACTU/Trade Development Council (1987) *Australia Reconstructed*, Melbourne

Ainley J, Jones W and Navaratran K (1990) *Subject Choice in Senior Secondary Schools*, Canberra: Australian Government Publishing Service

Ainley, P and Corney, M (1990) *Training for the Future: The Rise and Fall of the Manpower Services Commission*, London: Cassell

Ainley, P and Vickerstaff, S (1993) 'Transitions from corporatism: the privatisation of policy failure', *Contemporary Record*, **7**, 3, 541–56

Alyokhina, M (1992) 'Some practical aspects of transition to market economy', paper presented to the Educational Leadership International, held in Oslo in November, Moscow: MGPU

Amann, R (1994) 'What is to be done?', *Times Higher Education Supplement*, 11 February, pp 14–15

Applebaum, D (1994) 'Education: unions fail to learn their lessons', *Financial Times*, 18 March, p 7

Ardagh, J (1973) *The New France 1945–1973*, Harmondsworth: Penguin

Ashton, D N, Maguire, M and Spilsbury, M (1990) *Restructuring the Labour Market: The Implications for Youth*, London: Macmillan.

Australian Bureau of Statistics (1992) 'Education and training in Australia', Cat No 4224.0, Canberra: Australian Government Printing Service

Australian Bureau of Statistics (1993a) 'Transition from education to work', Cat No 6227.0, unpublished table, Canberra: Australian Government Printing Service

Australian Bureau of Statistics (1993b) *Labour Force Statistics and Educational Attainment in Australia*, Canberra: Australian Government Printing Service

Australian Education Council (AEC) (1991) 'Young people's participation in post compulsory education and training', report of the AEC Review Committee, July, Canberra: Australian Government Printing Office

Australian Education Council (AEC) (1993) *National Report on Schooling in Australia 1992: Statistical Index*, Melbourne: Curriculum Corporation

Bailey, B (1990), 'Technical education and secondary schooling, 1905–1945', in Summerfield, P and Evans, E (eds) *Technical Education and the State Since 1950*, Manchester: Manchester University Press

Ball, C (1991) *Learning Pays*, London: Royal Society of Arts

Ball, S (1990) *Education, Inequality and School Reform: Values in Crisis*, London: Centre for Educational Studies, King's College

Banks, J A G, Raban, A J and Watts, A G (1990) 'The Single European Market and its implications for educational and vocational guidance services', *International Journal for the Advancement of Counselling*, **13**, 4, 275–94

Barnett, C (1986) *The Audit of War: The Illusion and Reality of Britain as a Great Nation*, London: Macmillan

Bash L (1993) 'Collective identity and urban schooling: the case of the London Jewish Community', paper presented at a symposium on International Perspectives on Culture and Schooling, Institute of Education, University of London, May.

Bates, I, Cohen, P, Finn, D and Willis, P (1984) *Schooling for the Dole? The New Vocationalism*, London, Macmillan

Bathory, Z (1992) 'Some consequences of the change of regime in Hungarian public education', in Mitter *et al*, pp 27–39

Becker, J R (1987) 'Sex equity programs which work', *School Science and Mathematics*, **87**, 3, 223–32

Beeby, C E (1937) *The Education of the Adolescent in New Zealand*, Wellington: NZCER

Benet, M K (1972) *Secretarial Ghetto*, New York: McGraw Hill

Bennett, R J, Wicks, P and McCoshan, A (1994) *Local Empowerment and Business Services: Britain's Experiment with Training and Enterprise Councils*, London: UCL Press

Bennis, W (1972) 'The Decline of Bureaucracy and Organisations of the Future', in Shepard J M (ed) *Organizational Issues in Industrial Society*, Englewood Cliffs: Prentice-Hall

Bernstein, B (1975) *Class, Codes and Control*, Vol 3, London: Routledge

Bessant, B (1992) 'Managerialism, economic rationalism and higher education', paper delivered at a conference on The Governance and Funding of Australian Education, Federalism Research Centre, Research School of Social Sciences, Australian National University, February

Best, M (1990) *The New Competition: Institutions of Industrial Restructuring*, Cambridge, MA: Harvard University Press

Blaug, M. (1976) 'The empirical status of human capital theory: a slightly jaundiced survey', *Journal of Economic Literature*, **14**, 827–55

Block, F (1990) *Postindustrial Possibilities: A critique of Economic Discourse*, Berkeley: University of California Press

BMW (1993) *Apprentice Training for the 90s*, Bracknell: BMW (GB) Technicians' Institute

Board of Education (1931) Note of meeting with deputation of Association of Directors and Secretaries, 6 November, Board of Education papers, ED.12/419, London: Public Record Office

Board of Education (1937) *A Review of Junior Technical Schools in England*, London: HMSO

Board of Education (1942) minutes of 10th meeting of Norwood Committee on the secondary school curriculum and examinations, 2–3 October 1942, addendum, Board of Education papers, ED.12/478, London: Public Record Office

Bowles, S and Gintis, H (1976) *Schooling In Capitalist America*, London: Routledge and Kegan Paul

Boyd, W and Cibulka, J (eds) (1989) *Private Schools and Public Policy*, London: Falmer

Brake, M (1980) *The Sociology of Youth Culture and Youth Subcultures*, London: Routledge

Braverman, H (1974) *Labour and Monopoly Capitalism*, New York: Monthly Review Press

Briggs, A (1968) *Victorian Cities*, Harmondsworth: Penguin

British Columbia Ministry of Education (1990) *Gender Equity: Distribution of Females and Males in the British Columbia School System*, Victoria: BCME

Brown, P (1990) 'The "third wave": education and the ideology of parentocracy', *British Journal of Sociology of Education*, **11**, 65–85

Brown, P and Lauder, H (1992) 'Education, economy and society: an introduction to a new agenda', in Brown, P and Lauder, H (eds) *Education for Economic Survival: From Fordism to PostFordism?*, London: Routledge

Brown, P and Scase, R (1994) *Higher Education and Corporate Realities*, London: UCL Press

Brzezinski, Z (1989) *The Grand Failure: The Birth and Death of Communism in the Twentieth Century*, New York: Scribner

Brzezinski, Z (1993) *Out of Control: Global Turmoil on the Eve of the 21st Century*, New York: Scribner

Burgess, K (1993) 'Education policy in relation to employment in Britain, 1935–45: a decade of "missed opportunities" ', *History of Education*, **22**, 4, 365–90

Burton, L (ed) (1986) *Girls into Maths Can Go*, London: Holt, Rinehart & Winston

Campbell, A E (1941) *Educating New Zealand*, Wellington: Department of Internal Affairs

Canadian Advisory Committee on the Status of Women (1985) *What Will Tomorrow Bring? A Study of the Aspirations of Adolescent Women*, Ottawa: Government Printer

Canadian Teachers' Federation (1990) *A Capella: A Report of the Realities, Concerns, Expectations and Barriers Experienced by Adolescent Women in Canada*, Ottawa: Canadian Teachers' Federation

Carnoy, M, Levin, H M and King, K (1980) *Education, Work and Employment*, Vol 2, Paris: UNESCO

Casey, B (1990) *Recent Developments in West Germany's Apprenticeship System*, London: Policy Studies Institute

Castles, S and Wustenberg, W (1979) *The Education of the Future*, London: Pluto

CEDEFOP (1987) *The Role of the Social Partners in Vocational Training and Further Training in the Federal Republic of Germany*, Berlin: CEDEFOP

CEDEFOP (1992) *The Role of the State and the Social Partners; Mechanisms and Spheres of Influence: Vocational Training*, Berlin: CEDEFOP

Charmasson, T *et al* (1987) *L'Enseignement technique de la revolution a nos jours*, Vol 1, Paris: Economica

Chesnais, F (1993) 'Globalisation, world oligopoly and some of their implications', in Humbert, M (ed) *The Impact of Globalisation on Europe's Firms and Industries*, London: Pinter

Chew, S B, Zulkifi, A M, Lee, K H and Noorshah, M S (1990) 'The transition from school to work: determinants of the demand for higher education', research report, Institute of Advanced Studies, University of Malaya

Chitty, C (1991) 'Introduction', in Chitty, C (ed) *Post-sixteen Education: Studies in Access and Achievement*, London: Kogan Page

Chuo-Kyoiku-Shingikai (the Central Education Council) (1991) *Shingi Keika Hokoku*, (interim report) Tokyo: Monbusho

Clapham, J H (1961) *The Economic Development of France and Germany 1815–1914*, Cambridge: Cambridge University Press

Clifford, G (1982) 'Marry, stitch, die, or do worse: educating women for work', in Kantor and Tyack

Coffield, F (1992) 'Training and Enterprise Councils: the last throw of voluntarism', *Policy Studies*, **13**, 4, 11–31

Cohen, M (1991) 'Restructuring of women's employment opportunities: policy implications for feminist organizing', occasional paper, Toronto: OISE

Cohen, S (1972) *Folk Devils and Moral Panics*, London: MacGibbon and Kee

Collins, R (1979) *The Credential Society*, New York: Academic Press

Coulby, D, Jones, C and Harris, D (eds) (1992) *World Yearbook of Education: Urban Education*, London: Kogan Page, pp 87–96

Council of Europe (1992) *Standing Conference on University Problems, Legislative Reform in Higher Education, Russia*, Strasbourg: Council of Europe, Directorate of Education, Culture and Sport

Crowley-Bainton, T and Wolf, A (1994) *The Access to Assessment Initiative*, Sheffield: Department of Employment

Crowther Committee (1956) Memo: The modern and technical school leaver (educational background and employment), *Raybould papers*, Leeds: Museum of History of Education, University of Leeds

Crozier, M (1964) *The Bureaucratic Phenomenon*, Chicago: University of Chicago Press

Curtain R (forthcoming) *Has the Apprenticeship System a Future: the Impact of Labour Market Reforms on Structured Entry Level Training*, report commissioned by the Department of Employment, Education and Training, Canberra: Department of Employment, Education and Training

Dale R *et al*, (1990) *The TVEI Story*, London: Open University Press

Day, C R (1987) *Education and the Industrial World: The Ecole d'Arts et Métiers and the Rise of French Industrial Engineering*, Cambridge, MA: MIT Press

Deakin, S and Wilkinson, F (1991) 'Social policy and economic efficiency: the deregulation of the labour market in Britain', *Critical Social Policy*, **11**, 3, 40–61

Department of Employment (1988) *Employment for the 1990s*, London: HMSO

Department of Employment (1992) *People, Jobs and Opportunity*, London: HMSO

DEET (Department of Employment, Education and Training) (1993a) *New South Wales Year 10–12 Students' Attitudes to Post-compulsory Education and Training*, Canberra: Australian Government Printing Service

DEET, (Higher Education Division) (1993b) *Entering Higher Education in the 1980s*, Canberra: Australian Government Printing Service

DEET (1993c) *Education Participation Rates 1992*, Canberra: Australian Government Printing Service

DEET, Higher Education Division (1993d) *Recent Trends and Current Issues in Australian Higher Education*, Canberra: Australian Government Printing Service

Dench, S (1993) 'Why Do Employers Train?', working paper 5, London: Department of Employment, Social Science Research Branch

Devereaux, MS (1984) *One in Every Five: A Survey of Adult Education in Canada*, Ottawa: Supply and Services, Canada

Dewey, J (1916) *Democracy and Education*, New York: Free Press

Dicken, P (1992) *Global Shift: The Internationalisation of Economic Activity*, London: Paul Chapman

Dolton, P J (1993) 'The economics of youth training in Britain', *Economic Journal*, **420**, 1261–78

Dore, A J H (1958) letter to Captain E C L Turner, 7 February, Federation of British Industries papers, 200/F/3/T2/1/8 University of Warwick

Drexel, I (1980) Die Krise der Anlernung im Arbeitsprozess, *Soziale Welt*, **31**, 3, 368–95

Drexel, I (1994) 'The relationship between education and employment as seen by Germany', paper presented to CNRS Colloquium on Education and Work, Paris, March

Dronkers, J (1993) 'The precarious balance between general and vocational education in the Netherlands', in Wolf, A (ed) *Parity of Esteem: Can Vocational Awards Ever Achieve High Status?*, London: International Centre for Research on Assessment, Institute of Education.

Dunning, J H (1988) *Multinationals, Technology and Competitiveness*, London: Unwin Hyman

Dunning, J H (1993) *The Globalisation of Business*, London: Routledge

Economic Council of Canada (1990) *Good Jobs, Bad Jobs*, Ottawa: Economic Council

Economic Planning Advisory Council (1986) *Human Capital and Productivity Growth*, council paper 15, Canberra

The Economist (1992) 'A Survey of Russia', supplement, 5 December, pp 3–30

The Economist (1993) 'A Survey of Eastern Europe', supplement, 13 March pp 3–22

The Economist (1994a) 'Russia: the road to ruin', 29 January, pp 27–9

The Economist (1994b) 'Russia's bankruptcy bears', business section, 19 March, pp 83–7

The Economist (1994c) 'Russian privatisation – not the real thing yet', 12 December, p 46

Eklof, B and Dneprov, E (eds) (1993) *Democracy in the Russian School: The Reform Movement in Education Since 1984*, Boulder: Westview Press

Employment Skills Formation Council (1992) *The Australian Vocational Certificate Training System*, Canberra: Australian Government Printing Office

England, P (1982) 'The failure of human capital theory to explain occupational sex segregation', *Journal of Human Resources*, **17**, 4, 358–70

England, P, Chassic, M and McConnock, L (1982) 'Skill demands and earnings in female and male occupations', *Sociology and Social Research*, **66**, 147–68

England, P G, Farkas, B, Kilbourne, B, and Dau, T (1988) 'Explaining sex segregation and wages: findings from a model with fixed effects', *American Sociological Review*, **53**, 4, 544–58

England, P and Norris, B (1985) 'Comparable worth: a new doctrine of sex discrimination', *Social Science Quarterly*, **66**, 627–43

Fauconnier, P (1992) 'Les grandes écoles dans les collimateur', *Le Nouvelle Observateur*, **1437**, 24, 14–28

Felstead, A (1993) 'Putting individuals in charge, leaving skills behind? UK training policy in the 1990s', discussion paper in Sociology S93 (7) University of Leicester

Finegold, D (1993) 'Making apprenticeships work', RAND issue paper 1, Santa Monica: RAND Corporation

Finegold, D and Soskice, S (1988) 'The failure of training in Britain: analysis and prescription', *Oxford Review of Economic Policy*, **4**, 3, 21–53

Finn, B (1991) *Young People's Participation in Postcompulsory Education and Training*, report of the AEC Review Committee, Canberra: AGPS

Ford, B (1986) 'Learning from Japan: the concept of skill formation', *Australian Bulletin of Labor*, **12**, 2

Fortuijn, L, Hoppers, W and Morgan, B, (1987) *Paving Pathways to Work; Comparative Perspectives on the Transition from School to Work*, The Hague: CESO

Fox, A (1974) *Beyond Contract: Work, Politics and Trust Relations*, London: Faber & Faber

Friedenburg, E (1959) *The Vanishing Adolescent*, Boston: Beacon Press

Fukuyama, F (1991) *The End of History and the Last Man*, London: Hamish Hamilton
Gariboldo, F (1989) 'The crisis of the "demanding model" and the search for an alternative in the experiences of the metal workers union in Emilia Romagna', paper delivered at meeting at Bielefeld University
Garonna, P and Ryan, P (1991) 'The regulation and deregulation of youth activity', in Ryan (1991)
Gaskell, J (1990) 'What counts as skill?' in Fudge, J and McDermott, P (eds) *Just Wages: The Politics of Pay Equity*, Toronto: University of Toronto Press, pp 141–59
Gaskell, J (1992) *Gender Matters from School to Work*, Milton Keynes: Open University Press
GB DE (1994) *Modern Apprenticeship*, Sheffield: Department of Employment
GB HMI (1991) (Her Majesty's Inspectorate), *Aspects of Vocational Education and Training in the Federal Republic of Germany*, London: HMSO
Géhin J-P, and Méhaut, P (1993) *Apprentissage ou formation continue? Strategies éducatives des entreprises en Allemagne et en France*, Paris: L'Hartmann
Gerschunskij, B (1994) 'Russland: Bildung und die Zukuft', in Mitter, W (ed) *Curricula in der Schule: Russland 1992*, Deutsches Institut fur Internationale Pedogogische Forschung, Cologne, Weimar, Vienna, Böhlau, pp 13–38
Gilligan, C, Lyons, N, and Hanmer, T (1990) *Making Connections: The Relational Worlds of Adolescent Girls at Emma Willard School*, Cambridge, MA: Harvard University Press
Goffman, E (1968) *Stigma*, Harmondsworth: Penguin
Gonon, P (1993) Georg Kerschensteiner Lecture, University of London, Institute of Education, June
Gooch, A G (1954) Memo: Secondary technical education, 28 December *Ministry of Education papers*, ED147/207, London: Public Record Office
Goodson, I and Dowbiggan, I (1991) 'Subject status and curriculum change: commercial education in London Ontario 1920–1940', *Paedagogia Historia*, **29**, 2
Gorbachev, M (1987) *Perestroika: New Thinking for our Country and the World*, London: Collins
Gordon, L (1984) 'Ideology and policy in the history of New Zealand technical education, 1900–1930', MA thesis, Massey University
Gramsci, A (1971) *Selections from Prison Notebooks*, London: Lawrence and Wishart
Grant, G, Elbow, P, Ewens, T, Gamson, Z, Kohli, W, Neumann, W, Olesen, V and Riesman, D (1979) *On Competence: A Critical Analysis of Competence-Based Reforms in Higher Education*, San Francisco: Jossey-Bass
Green, A (1991) *Education and State Formation: The Rise of Education Systems in England, France and the USA*, London: Macmillan
Green, A and Mace, J (1994) *Funding Training Outcomes*, post–16 working paper, University of London, Institute of Education
Green, A, Mace, J and Steedman, H (1993) *Training for Work Funding Pilots Study: Internation Comparisons*, report to Employment Department, London: National Institute of Economic and Social Research.
Green, A and Steedman, H (1993) *Educational Provision, Educational Attainment and the Needs of Industry: A Review of the Research for Germany, France, Japan, the USA and Britain*, report series 5, London: National Institute of Economic and Social Research
Grew, R and Harrigan, P (1991) *Schools, State and Society: The Growth of Elementary Schooling in the Nineteenth Century*, Ann Arbor: University of Michigan Press
Hacham, T F (1992) *A quoi sert le plan? Un regard sur le system educatif*, Paris: Economica
Hadow Report (1926) *The Education of the Adolescent*, London: HMSO
Halsey, AH, Heath, A and Ridge, J (1980) *Origins and Destinations*, Oxford: Clarendon
Halstead, M (ed) (1994) *Parental Choice and Education*, London: Kogan Page
Harlan, S and Steinberg, R (1989) *Job Training for Women: The Promise and Limits of Public Policies*, Philadelphia: Temple University Press
Harvey, D (1989) *The Conditions of Postmodernity*, Oxford: Blackwell
Hayes, C (1984) *Competence and Competition*, London: IMS/NEDO
Hepple, B A and O'Higgins, P (1981) *Employment Law*, London: Sweet & Maxwell
Her Majesty's Inspectorate (1991) *Aspects of Upper Secondary Education in Japan*, London: HMSO
Heyneman, S (1991) 'Revolution in the East: the educational lessons', paper presented to the Oxford International Round Table on Educational Policy, 5 September, New York

HM Government (1994), 'Competitiveness: Helping business to win', Cm 2563 HMSO: London

Hooks, B (1984) *Feminist Theory: From Margin to Center*, Boston: South End Press

Horniblow, E H (1934) Memo to Board of Education consultative committee, Board of Education papers, ED.10/222, London: Public Record Office

Hosking, G (1993) 'Watching the big brother', *Times Higher Education Supplement*, 19 November, p 17

Huber, B and Lang, K (1993) 'Tarifreform 2000: Forderungskonzepte und Verhandlungs- stande im Bereich der Metalindustrie', *WSI Mitteilungen*, **12**, 789–97

Hughes, J (1992) 'For sale – Russia's best brains', *Guardian*, 15 September, p 23

INRA (1991) 'Young Europeans in 1990', *Eurobarometer*, **34**, 2, Brussels: Commission of the European Communities

Inui, A (1990) *Nihon no Kyoiku to Kigyo-Shakai*, Tokyo: Otsuki-shoten

Inui, A (1993a) 'The competitive structure of school and the labour market: Japan and Britain', *British Journal of Sociology of Education*, **14**, 3, 301–13

Inui, A (1993b) 'Futsu-ka no Bunretsu Kaitai to Koko-zo Keisei no Arata na Kadai', *Koko no Hiroba*, **8**, 86–95

ITE (1992) *Full Time Training Courses* (Prospectus), Singapore

Jackson, N (1991) 'Skill training in transition: implications for women', in Gaskell, J and McLaren, A (eds), *Women and Education*, Calgary: Detselig

Jackson, N and Gaskell, J (1987) 'White collar vocationalism: the rise of commercial education in Ontario and BC', *Curriculum Inquiry*, **17**, 2, 77–201

Jenkinson, A J (1949) 'The slow progress of secondary technical education', *Vocational Aspect*, **1**, 93, 296–302

Jessup, G (1991) *Outcomes: NVQs and the Emerging Model of Education and Training*, Lewes: Falmer

Jones A, McCulloch, G, Marshall, J, Smith, G and Smith, L (1990) *Myths and Realities: Schooling in New Zealand*, Palmerston North: Dunmore Press

Jones, C (1994) 'Fewer students completing year 12', *The Australian*, 13 January

Kaletsky, A (1994) 'Why Russians mustn't be slaves to the free market', *Sunday Telegraph*, 6 February, p 6

Kampfner, J (1994) 'A farewell to Russia', *Daily Telegraph*, 10 January, p 10

Kanter, R (1984) *The Change Masters*, London: Unwin

Kanter, R (1989) *When Giants Learn to Dance*, London: Unwin

Kantor, H and Tyack, D (1982) 'Introduction: historical perspectives on vocationalism in American education', in Kantor and Tyack, pp 1–13

Kantor, H and Tyack, D (eds) (1982) *Youth, Work and Schooling*, Stanford: Stanford University Press

Karakovsky, V (1993) 'Russia's schools today and tomorrow', *The Study Group Bulletin of Education in Russia, The Independent States and Eastern Europe*, **2**, 1, pp 18–24

Kariya, T (1992) *Gakko Shokugyo Senbatsu no Shakaigaku*, Tokyo: Daigaku Shuppankai

Karlov, M and Merkuriev, S (1992) *Education and the Economy in Russia*, Paris: OECD

Keay, J (1992) 'Czechoslovakia – the art of falling apart', *Business Europa*, August/ September, pp 7–12

Keay, J (1993) 'Much pain, little gain', *Business Europa*, January/February, pp 6–9

Keizai-Shingi-Kai (Economic Deliberation Council) (1963) *Keizai-hatten ni okeru Jin-teki Noryoku Kaihatsu no Kadai to Taisaku*, Tokyo

Kicinski, K (1993) *Wizjeszkoly w spoleczenstwiepost-totalitarnym* (Visions of schools in a post-totalitarian society), Warsaw: OPEN

Kingsland, J C (1965) 'Cray Valley Technical High School for Boys (Kent)', in Gross, R E (ed), *British Secondary Education: Overview and Appraisal*, London: Oxford University Press, pp 335–68

Kinoshita, H and Kokumin-Kyoiku-Kenkyujo (1981) *Koko-Nyushi-seido no Kaikaku*, Tokyo: Rodo-Junpo-sha

Kirby P (1985) *Report of the Committee of Inquiry into Labour Market Programs*, Canberra: Australian Government Printing Service

Kitaev, I (1992) *Labour Markets and Educational Systems in the Former Soviet Union*, Paris: IIEP

Kliebard, H (1990) 'Curriculum policy as symbolic action: connecting education with the workplace', in Haft, H and Hopmann, S (eds) *Case Studies in Curriculum Administration History*, London: Falmer, pp 143–58

Kohn, M and Schooler, C (1983) *Work and Personality: An Inquiry into the Impact of Social Stratification*, New Jersey: Ablex

Kopp, B von (1993) 'Global changes and the context of education, democracy and development in Eastern Europe', in Mitter and Schäfer, pp 85–98

Kornilov, V (1992) 'Transition to Market Economy and its Effect on the System of Education in Russia', paper presented to the Educational Leadership International, held in Oslo in November, Moscow: MGPU, pp 1–11

Kuebart, F (1986) 'Vocational training in the 1980s', in Tomiak, J J (ed) *Western Perspectives on Soviet Education in the 1980s*, London: Macmillan, pp 138–59

Kumazawa, M (1989) *Nihon-teki Keiei no Meian*, Tokyo: Chikuma-shobo

Kwong, L W, Wong, M, Petzall, S, Yeo-Yoong, S and Hall, K (1992) 'Factors affecting skills training of apprentices, parts 1, 2 and 3', research report, Singapore: ITE

Labour Canada (1986) *When I grow up ... Career Expectations and Aspirations of Canadian School Children*, Ottawa: Labour Canada

Lacey, C (1988) 'The idea of a socialist education', in Lauder, H and Brown, P (eds) *Education in Search of a Future*, Lewes: Falmer

Lane, C (1989) *Management and Labour in Europe*, Aldershot: Edward Elgar

Lauder, H (1987) 'The New Right and educational policy in New Zealand', *New Zealand Journal of Educational Studies*, **22**, 3–23

Lauder, H and Hughes, D (1990) 'Social inequalities and differences in school outcomes', *New Zealand Journal of Educational Studies*, **23**, 37–60

Lauder, H et al (1994) *The Creation of Market Competition for Education in New Zealand*, Wellington: Ministry of Education

Lauglo, J (1993) *Vocational Training: Analysis of Policy and Modes, Case Studies of Sweden, Germany and Japan*, Paris: IIEP

Lauwerys, J A (1967) *General Education in a Changing World*, Berlin: CESE

Law, S S (1984) 'Trend of vocational training in Singapore', VITB paper 1, Singapore: VITB

Law, S S (1985) 'The vocational training system – its development and challenges', VITB paper 4, Singapore: VITB

Law, S S (1990) 'Vocational training in Singapore', VITB paper 6, Singapore: VITB

Leong, Y C et al (1990) 'Factors influencing the academic achievement of students in Malysian schools', research report, Educational Planning and Research Division, MOE, Malaysia and World Bank

Lepani, B and Currie, J (1993) *Workplace Learning in NSW Senior Secondary Courses*, Sydney: Australian Centre for Innovation and International Competitiveness, University of Sydney

Levin, H (1984) 'Improving productivity through education and technology', working paper, Stanford University

Levy, M (1992) 'The Baltics: bridge over roubled waters', *Business Europa*, August/September pp 13–17

Liebrand, C G M (1991) 'Recent developments in the Dutch system of vocational qualifications', *European Journal of Education*, **26**, 1

Lloyd, J (1994) 'Beware of the sickly Russian bear', *Financial Times*, 20 March, Section II, pp i and x

Mace, J (1979) 'Internal labour markets for engineers in British industry', *British Journal of Industrial Relations*, **17**, 1, 50–63

MacKeracher, D (1990) *Women's on the Job Procedural Knowing*, Proceedings of the Canadian Association for the Study of Adult Education, Victoria

Maclure, S (1985) 'Hands up for the enterprise culture?' *Times Educational Supplement*, 8 February

Marginson, S (1993) *Education and Education Policy in Australia*, Cambridge: Cambridge University Press

Marklund, S (1987) 'Integration of school and the world of work in Sweden', in Lauglo, J and Lillis, K (eds) *Vocationalizing Education: An International Perspective*, Oxford, Pergamon, pp 181–6

Marsden, D W (1982) 'Career structures and training in internal labour markets in Britain and West Germany', *Manpower Studies*, Spring, 4, 10–17

Marsden, D W (1990) 'Institutions and labour mobility: occupational and internal labour markets in Britain, France, Italy and West Germany', in Brunetta, R and Dell'Arringa, C (eds) *Labour Relations and Economic Performance*, London: Macmillan, pp 414–38

Marsden, D W (1994) 'Industrial change, "competencies", and labour markets', *Vocational Training* (forthcoming)

Marsden, D W and Ryan, P (1990) 'Institutional aspects of youth employment and training policy in Britain', *British Journal of Industrial Relations*, **28**, 3, 35–70

Marsden, D W and Ryan, P (1991) 'Initial training, labour market structure and public policy: intermediate skills in British and German industry', in Ryan (ed), 251–85

Martin, J R (1985) *Reclaiming a Conversation*, New Haven: Yale University Press

Mathews, J (1989) *Tools for Change: New Technology and the Democratisation of Work*, Sydney: Pluto

Mathieson, M and Bernbaum, G (1988) 'The British disease: a British tradition?', *British Journal of Educational Studies*, **26**, 2, 126–74

Mayer E (1992) *Report on Employment Related Key Competencies for Post-Compulsory Education and Training*, Melbourne: Australian Education Council and Ministers for Vocational Education Employment and Training

McCormick, K (1991) 'Japanese engineers, lifetime employment and in-company training: continuity and change in the management of engineering manpower resources', in Ryan (ed)

McCulloch, G (1988) 'Imperial and colonial designs: the case of Auckland Grammar School', *History of Education*, **17**, 4, 257–67

McCulloch, G (1989a) 'City technology colleges: an old choice of school?', *British Journal of Educational Studies*, **37**, 1, 30–43

McCulloch, G (1989b) *The Secondary Technical School: A Usable Past?* London: Falmer

McCulloch, G (1992) 'Constructing the community: secondary schools and their neighbourhoods in 20th century Auckland', *Australian Journal of Education*, **36**, 2, 143–56

McKenzie, D (1992) 'The technical curriculum: second class knowledge?' in McCulloch, G (ed) *The School Curriculum In New Zealand: History, Theory, Policy And Practice*, Palmerston North: Dunmore Press, pp 29–39

McLean, M (1990) *Britain and a Single Market Europe: Prospects for a Common School Curriculum*, London: Kogan Page

Meager, N (1990) 'TECs: a revolution in training and enterprise, or old wine in new bottles?' *Local Economy*

Meijer, K (1991) 'Reforms in vocational education and training in Italy, Spain and Portugal', *European Journal of Education*, **26**, 1, 13–27

Mieszalski, S and Kupisiewicz, C (1992) 'The present state and recent trends in Polish education', in Mitter *et al*, pp 69–81

Millard, F (1994) *The Anatomy of the New Poland: Post-Communist Politics in its First Phase*, Aldershot: Edward Elgar

Millward, N (1994) *The New Industrial Relations?*, London: Policy Studies Institute

Ministry of Education (1947) *The New Secondary Education*, London: HMSO

Ministry of Education of the Russian Federation (1992) *Development of Education in Russia*, national report for the 43rd Session, International Conference on Education in Geneva, Moscow

Mitter, W (1992) 'Education in Eastern Europe and the Soviet Union in a period of revolutionary change', in Mitter *et al*, pp 121–36

Mitter, W (1993) Education, democracy and development in a period of revolutionary change', in Mitter and Schäfer, pp 1–2

Mitter, W and Schäfer, U (eds) (1993) *Upheaval and Change in Education*, Frankfurt am Main: German Institute for International Educational Research

Mitter, W *et al* (eds) (1992) *Recent Trends in Eastern European Education*, Frankfurt am Main: German Institute for International Eductional Research

MOE, Bahagian Pendidikan Teknik and Vokasidal (1992), Polyteknik Malaysia, Program Pencajian

Monbusho (Ministry of Education) (1989) *Gakko Kihon Chosa Tokei*, Tokyo

Monbusho (Ministry of Education) (1990) *Senshu-Gakko ni kansuru Jittai-Chosa Hokoku-sho*, Tokyo

Motyl, A (1993) *Dilemmas of Independence: Ukraine after Totalitarianism*, New York: Council of Foreign Relations Press

Nagy, M (1992) 'A transition to market economy and changes in the education system in

Hungary', paper presented to the Educational Leadership International, held in Oslo in November, Budapest: National Institute of Public Education

Nash, R (1983) *Schools Can't Make Jobs*, Palmerston North: Dunmore Press

National Commission on Excellence in Education (1983) *A Nation at Risk: The Imperative for Educational Reform*, Washington DC: US Government Printing Office

National Defence Counsel for Victims of Karoshi (1991) *Karoshi: When the 'Corporate Warrior' Dies*, Tokyo: Mado-sha

National Economic Development Office/Manpower Services Commission (1984) *Competence and Competition: Training and Education in the Federal Republic of Germany, the United States and Japan*, London: NEDO

Nelson-Rowe, S (1991) 'Corporation schooling and the labour market at General Electric', *History of Education Quarterly*, **31**, 91, 27–46

Netherlands Ministry of Education and Science (1993) *The Changing Role of Vocational and Technical Education and Science*, report to the OECD VOTEC project, Paris: OECD

NHK (1986) *Nihon-jin no Seikatsu Jikan 1985*, Tokyo: Nihon Hoso Shuppan Kyokai

Nicol, J (1940) *The Technical Schools of New Zealand: An Historical Survey*, (foreword by Sir Thomas Hunter) Wellington: NZCER

O'Donnell, C (1984) *The Basis of the Bargain*, Sydney: Allen and Unwin

OECD (1985) 'Changes in work patterns: implications for education', *Innovation in Education*, Paris: OECD

OECD (1988) *New Technologies in the 1990s: a Socio-economic Strategy*, Paris: OECD

OECD (1989) *Education and the Economy in a Changing World*, Paris: OECD

OECD (1992a) *Education at a Glance: OECD Indicators*, Paris: OECD

OECD (1992b) *Report on Education and Training in Poland during the Transformation of the Socio-Economic System*, Paris: OECD

Parkes, D (1993) 'Can parity between academic and vocational awards ever be achieved? Germany in European context', in Wolf

Paul, J-J (1985) 'Basic concepts and methods used in forecasting skilled manpower requirements in France', in Youdi and Hinchcliffe, pp 35–56

Pearson, G (1983) *Hooligan: A History of Respectable Fears*, London: Macmillan

Penington D (1993) 'Education and its relevance to the development of Australia', address to the Institute for Public Affairs seminar, A culture for Full Employment, Sydney, December

Perry, P J C (1976) *The Evolution of British Manpower Policy*, London: BACIE

Phillips, A and Taylor, B (1980) 'Sex and skill: notes toward a feminist economics', *Feminist Review*, **79**, 79–88

Pickard, J (1994) 'The future of apprenticeships', *Personnel Management Plus*, February, 24–5

Pinson, K S (1966) *Modern Germany*, New York: Macmillan

Piore, M and Sabel, C (1984) *The Second Industrial Divide: Possibilities for Prosperity*, New York: Basic Books

Pipes, R (1992) 'Starting from scratch', *Independent*, 19 August, p 17

Pipes, R (1993) 'Yeltsin's move: the struggle to achieve stable and effective government in Russia', *Times Literary Supplement*, 18 October, p 15

Plant, P (1990) *Transnational Vocational Guidance and Training for Young People and Adults*, Berlin: CEDEFOP

Prais, S J (1981) 'Some practical aspects of human capital investment: training standards in five occupations in Britain and Germany', *National Institute Economic Review*, **98**, 47–59

Prais, S J (1991) 'Vocational qualifications in Britain and Europe: theory and practice', *National Institute Economic Review*, May

Prais, S J and Beadle, E (1991) *Pre-vocational Schooling in Europe Today*, report series 1, London: National Institute of Economic and Social Research

Prais, S J, Jarvis, V and Wagner, K (1991) *Productivity and vocational skills in services in Britain and Germany*, in Ryan (ed) pp 119–45

Prais, S J, and Wagner, K (1983) 'Some practical aspects of human capital investment: training standards in five occupations in Britain and Germany', *National Institute Economic Review*, **105**, August, 46–65

Pringle, R (1988) *Secretaries Talk: Sexuality, Power and Work*, London: Verso

Prost, A (1992) *Education, societe et politiques: une histoire de l'enseignement en france de 1945 a nos jours*, Paris: Editions Seuil

Prucha, J (1992) 'Trends in Czechoslovak education', in Mitter *et al*, pp 83–102

Purvis, J (1985) 'Domestic subjects since 1870', in Goodson, I (ed) *Social Histories Of The Secondary Curriculum*, London: Falmer, pp 145–76

Raffe D (1990) *Beyond The Mixed Model: Social Research and The Case for Reform of 16–18 Education in Britain*, Edinburgh: Centre for Educational Sociology, University of Edinburgh

Rainbird, H (1991) *Training Matters: Union Perspectives on Industrial Restructuring and Training*, Oxford: Blackwell

Razumovskij, V (1992) 'Education in the Soviet school today and tomorrow', in Mitter *et al*, pp 57–68

Reich, R (1991) *The Work of Nations*, London: Simon and Schuster

Robitaille, D F and Garden, R A (1989) *The IEA Study of Mathematics II: Contexts and Outcome of School Mathematics*, Oxford: Pergamon

Roderick, G and Stephens, M (eds) (1981) *Where Did We Go Wrong? Industry, Education and Economy of Victorian Britain*, London: Falmer

Roderick, G and Stephens, M (eds) (1982) *The British Malaise: Industrial Performance, Education and Training in Britain Today*, London: Falmer

Rose, R and Wignanek, G (1991) *Training Without Trainers? How Germany Avoids Britain's Supply-Side Bottleneck*, London: Anglo-German Foundation

Rosenbaum, J E and Kariya, T (1989) 'From high school to work: market and institutional mechanisms in Japan', *American Journal of Sociology*, **94**, 6, 1334–65

Rosenberg, R (1982) *Beyond Separate Spheres: Intellectual Roots of Modern Feminism*, New Haven: Yale University Press

Royal Society (1991) *Beyond GCSE*, London: Royal Society

Rubinstein, W D (1993) *Capitalism, Culture, and Decline in Britain 1750–1990*, London: Routledge

Runnymede Commission on Antisemitism (1994) *A Very Light Sleeper*, London: Runnymede Trust

Russell J (1993) 'Patterns and Pathways in post compulsory schooling: report to the Schools Council, National Board of Employment Education and Training, (Unpublished)

Ryan, P (ed) (1991) *International Comparison of Vocational Education and Training for Intermediate Skills*, Lewes: Falmer

Ryan, P (1995) 'The institutional setting of investment in human resources in the UK', in Buechtemann, C and Soloff, D (eds) *Human Capital Investment and Economic Performance*, New York: Russell Sage

Sabel, C F (1982) *Work and Politics*, Cambridge University Press

Sachs, J (1993) *Poland's Jump to the Market Economy*, Cambridge, MA, and London: MIT Press

Sako, M and Dore, R (1988) 'Teaching or training: the role of the state in Japan', *Oxford Review of Economic Policy*, **4**, 3, 72–81

Samuelson, P (1954) 'The pure theory of public expenditure', *Review of Economics and Statistics*, **36**, 4, pp 387–9

Sanderson, M (1987) *Educational Opportunity and Social Change in England*, London: Faber and Faber

Sanderson, M (1994) *The Missing Stratum:Technical School Education in England, 1900–1990s*, London: Athlone Press

Sasaki, S (1976) *Koko-Kyoiku-ron*, Tokyo: Otsuki-shoten

Scase, R and Goffee, R (1989) *Reluctant Managers*, London: Unwin Hyman

Science Council of Canada (1982) *Who Turns the Wheel?* Ottawa: proceedings of a workshop on the science education of women in Canada

Scottish Office (1992) *Statistical Bulletin*, Education Series edn/ET1992/6, Edinburgh: Government Statistical Service

Sellin, B (1983) 'The development of alternance training for young people in the European Community', *Vocational Training*, **12**, September 73–83

Setenyi, J (1993) 'Regional human resource development and the modernisation of the non-university sector in Hungary', paper presented to the annual meeting of the Study Group on Education in Russia, the Independent States and Eastern Europe in November, 1993, in London, Budapest: Hungarian Institute for Educational Research

Sheldrake, J and Vickerstaff, S (1987) *The History of Industrial Training in Britain*, Aldershot: Avebury

Shephard, J (1992) Speech to the TEC Conference, Birmingham 9 July

Simons, D (1966) *Georg Kerschensteiner*, London: Methuen

Skatkin, M (1963) 'Marxist–Leninist ideas on polytechnical education', in Shapovalenko, S (ed) *Polytechnical Education in the USSR*, Paris: UNESCO

Smith, A (1977) [1776] *The Wealth of Nations*, Harmondsworth: Penguin

Smithers, A (1993) *All Our Futures: Britain's Educational Revolution*, a *Dispatches* report on education, Channel 4 Television

Sorifu Seishonen-Taisaku-Honbu (Department of Youth Affairs, the Prime Minister's Office) (1980) *Jido no Jittai tou ni Kansuru Kokusai Hikaku Chosa*, Tokyo

Soskice, D W (1993) 'Social skills from mass higher education: rethinking the company-based initial training paradigm', *Oxford Review of Economic Policy*, **9**, 3, 101–13

Stanglin, D et al (1992) 'The wreck of Russia', *US News and World Report*, **7**, December, pp 40–55

Statistics Canada (1991) *Women in Canada*, (2nd edn) Ottawa: Statistics Canada

Steedman, H (1992) 'Mathematics in vocational youth training for the building trades in Britain, France and Germany', discussion paper 9, London: National Institute of Economic and Social Research

Steinberg, R (1990) 'Social construction of skill: gender power and comparable worth', in *Work and Occupations*, Beverley Hills: Sage

Streeck, W (1989) 'Skills and the limits of neo-liberalism: the enterprise of the future as a place of learning', *Work, Employment and Society*, **3**, 1, 89–104

Streeck, W (1992) *Social Institutions and Economic Performance*, London: Sage

Streeck, W, Hilber, J, van Kevalaer, K, Maier, F and Weber, H (1987) *The Role of the Social Partners in Vocational Education and Training in the FRG*, Berlin: CEDEFOP

Sultana, R (1992) *Education and National Development: Historical and Critical Perspectives on Vocational Schooling in Malta*, Malta: Mireva Press

Sweet R (1993a) *A Client-Focused Vocational Education and Training System?*, Sydney: Dusseldorp Skills Forum

Sweet R (1993b) 'Vocational education and training: beyond the federalist settlement', paper presented to the Third National Workshop on Vocational Teacher Education, Sydney, October

Takeuchi, T (1987) *Kodomo no Jibun-kuzushi to Jibun-zukuri*, Tokyo: Daigaku Shuppankai

Tanguy, L (1991) *L'Enseignement professionel en France: des ouvriers aux techniciens*, Paris: Presse Universitaires de France

Thomas, E (1990) 'Pupils' perceptions of parental influences on schooling', *Research report*, University of London, Institute of Education.

Thomas, E, (1992) 'Urbanisation and education in the nation city state of Singapore', in Coulby et al, pp 87–96

Thomas, E (1994) 'The state, teacher education and the transmission of values', paper presented at the BATROE Conference on Contemporary Crises in Teacher Education, 28–30 March 1994, University of London, Institute of Education

Thompson, S (1879) *Apprentice Schools in France*, London

Thurow, L (1975) *Generating Inequality*, New York: Basic Books

Times Educational Supplement, (1956) 'Industry's prep schools', 16 March

Tjeldvoll, A (1992) 'Ideological changes and educational consequences – Eastern Europe after 1989', in *Educational Leadership International Education in East/Central Europe, 1991*, report from a Seminar held in the University of Oslo, 28–30 November 1991, University of Oslo, pp 29–38

Toffler, A (1990) *Powershift*, New York: Bantam

Tomiak, J (1986) 'Education and vocationalism in Eastern Europe', *Secondary Education Journal*, **16**, 2, pp 7–9

Tomiak, J (1986) 'Poland', in Kurian, G (ed) *World Education Encyclopedia*, Vol 2, New York and Oxford: Facts on File, pp 1006–20

Tomiak, J (1992a) 'Education in the Baltic States, Ukraine, Belarus and Russia', *Comparative Education*, **28**, 1, pp 33–44

Tomiak, J (1992b) 'General trends in Eastern Europe in West European perspective', in Mitter et al, pp 137–55

Tomiak, J (1992c) 'Implications of political change in Eastern Europe for educational policy development', *Journal of Educational Finance*, **17**, 3, pp 19–34

Tomiak, J (1993) 'Erziehung, kulturelle Identität und nationale Loyalität. Die Fälle Ukraine und Belarus' (Education, cultural identity and national loyalty. The cases of Ukraine and Belarus), *Bildung und Erziehung*, Cologne, Weimar, Vienna, Bohlau, **46**, 4, pp 393–409

Touraine, A (1989) 'Is sociology still the study of society?' *Thesis Eleven*, **23**

Tyack, D and Elizabeth, H (1990) *Learning Together: A History of Coeducation in Public Schools*, New Haven: Yale University Press

UNESCO (1983) 'The transition from technical and vocational schools to work', *Trends and Issues in Technical and Vocational Education*, **2**, Paris: UNESCO

Ungku, A A, Chew, S B Lee, K H and Bikas, S (1987) 'University education and employment in Malaysia', IIEP Research report 66, Paris: IIEP/UNESCO

Vaizey, J (1962) *The Economics of Education*, London: Faber and Faber

van den Dool, P (1993) 'New trends in VET and FET: policy issues for the late '90s in the Netherlands', paper presented to the Workshop on New Trends in Training Policy, Geneva: ILO

Vickers M (1991) 'Building a national system for school-to-work transition: lessons from Britain and Australia', paper presented at 'Jobs for the Future' conference, Somerville, Oxford, August

Vickerstaff, S (1992) 'Training for economic survival', in Brown and Lauder

VOCTECH (1993) *Information on the SEAMEO – VOCTECH Regional Centre*, Brunei Darussalam: VOCTECH

Walford, G and Miller, H (1991) *City Technology Colleges*, Milton Keynes: Open University Press

Wallis, H B (1941) Memo; Technical education: post-war policy and organisation, 15 October, Board of Education papers, ED.136/296, London: Public Record Office

Walsh, J (1993) 'Internalisation v decentralisation: an analysis of recent developments in pay bargaining', *British Journal of Industrial Relations*, **31**, 3, 409–32

Watanabe, O (1990) *Yutaka na Shakai' Nippon no Kozo*, Tokyo: Rodo-Junpo-sha

Watts, A (1983) *Education, Unemployment and the Future of Work*, Milton Keynes: Open University Press

Watts, AG (1992a) 'Careers guidance services in a changing Europe', *International Journal for the Advancement of Counselling*, **15**, 4, 201–8

Watts, AG (1992b) *Occupational Profiles of Vocational Counsellors in the European Community*, Berlin: CEDEFOP

Watts, AG, Dartois, C, and Plant, P (1988) *Educational and Vocational Guidance Services for the 14–25 Age-Group in the European Community*, Maastricht: Presses Interuniversitaires Européennes

Watts, A G, Guichard, J, Plant, P and Rodriguez, M L (1994) *Educational and Vocational Guidance in the European Community*, Brussels: Commission of the European Communities

Weaver, T R (1955) Note: Secondary technical schools, 14 January, Ministry of Education Papers, ED.147/207, London: Public Record Office

Weiss, J H (1982) *The Making of Technological Man: The Social Origins of French Engineering Education*, Cambridge, MA: MIT Press

Whitty, G (1992) 'Urban education in England and Wales', in Coulby *et al*, pp 39–53

Wiener, M (1985) *English Culture and the Decline of the Industrial Spirit, 1850–1980*, Penguin: Harmondsworth

Willis, P (1977) *Learning to Labour*, Farnborough: Saxon House

Willms, J and Echols, F (1992) 'Alert and inert clients: the Scottish experience of parental choice of schools', *Economics of Education Review*, **11**, 339–50

Winterton, J and Winterton, R (1994) *Collective Bargaining and Consultation over Continuing Vocational Training*, London: Department of Employment

Wolf, A (1993a) *Assessment Issues and Problems in a Criterion-Based System*, London: Further Education Unit

Wolf, A (ed) (1993b) *Parity of Esteem: Can Vocational Awards Ever Achieve High Status?*, London: International Centre for Research on Assessment, Institute of Education

Wolf, A (1994) *Competence-based Assessment*, Buckingham: Open University Press

Wolf, A and Rapiau, M T (1993) 'The academic achievement of craft apprentices in France and England: contrasting systems and common dilemmas', *Comparative Education*, **29**, 1, 29–43

Wood, R (1991) *Assessment and Testing*, Cambridge: Cambridge University Press

Youdi, R V and Hinchcliffe, K (eds) (1985) *Forecasting Skilled Manpower Needs: The Experience of Eleven Countries*, Paris: UNESCO/IIEP

Young, D (1982) 'Helping the young help themselves', *Times Educational Supplement*, 26
    November
Young, D (1984) 'Coping with change: the New Training Initiative', *Journal of the Royal
    Society of Arts*, **5335**
Zinberg, D (1993) 'Russia's hard frontier', *Times Higher Education Supplement*, 5 November,
    p 12
Zuboff, S (1988) *In the Age of the Smart Machine: The Future of Work and Power*, New York:
    Basic Books

Index

Abbott, A. 192
academic education 30
  Germany 43
accreditation of prior learning (APL) 147
African-American school district study
    243–57
African National Congress *see* ANC
A-levels 146
ANC 179, 184
apprentice relative pay 72
apprenticeship 40–41, 94, 95
  Australia 15
  Denmark 233
  France 142
  Germany 26, 74, 75, 143–4
  intermediate skills 72
  neglect of 67
  Netherlands 110
  Norway 233
  quality of training 69
  Sweden 233
  UK 67, 70, 74, 77–8
Astier Law 37
Australia
  apprenticeship 15
  corporatist approach 156–7
  education and training arrangements
      14–16
  education, training and economic
      expansion 12–14
  entry level training 158–60
  federalist settlement 149–50
    breakdown in 154
  industrial restructuring 154
  industrial training 154
  post-compulsory education 150
  school education 150-2
  structural economic problems 153–54
  TAFE courses 159
  training centres 15
  training reform agenda 155–6
  upper secondary school education 152–3
  vocational programmes in schools 159
  wages policy 154

Australia Reconstructed 154
Australian Council of Trade Unions
    (ACTU) 154
Australian National Training Authority
    (ANTA) 155
Australian Vocational Certificate Training
    System (AVCTS) 158, 160
automation 29
award restructuring 12, 15

baccalauréat professionnel 38
Balcerowicz, Leszek 53
Balcerowicz Plan 53
Barnett, Correlli 189
Belarus 50
Belgium, careers guidance systems 219
Bessant, Bob 10
Blaug, Mark 9
BTEC 146
bureaucracy, and education 22–3
bureaucratic organizations 19

Canada, school–work transition 80–91
career pathways 129
careers development 227
careers guidance systems 127–8
  activities carried out by 221–3
  administrative control 223
  as continuous process 224
  as open professional model 224
  Belgium 219
  common trends 224–7
  decentralization 226
  Denmark 219
  deregulation 226
  emerging strategy 227–9
  European Community 218–29
  evaluation 227
  financing 223
  focus differences 221
  France 219
  Germany 219
  Greece 219
  Ireland 220

Italy 220
level of penetration 224
location differences 221
Luxembourg 220
market principles 226
Netherlands 220
Portugal 220
professional identity and training 223–4
Spain 220
traditional structure 228
United Kingdom 220
Carmichael, Laurie 158
Carmichael Report 158
Central-Eastern Europe 49–61
economic restructuring 55–6
end of one-party rule 51–2
new opportunities for employment 55–6
polytechnic education 57–8
preparation for work 57–8
reforming and restructuring education
56–7
transforming the economy 52–3
transition from central planning to open
market economy 53–4
Certificat d'Aptitude Professionnel (CAP) 37,
38
change
challenge of 129–30
in nature and availability of work 130
City and Guilds 102
city technology colleges (CTCs) 189, 195
clerical work 87
collective bargaining 73
collective intelligence 27
from individual to 28–9
COMECON 54
competence, notion of 139–42
COSATU 181, 182
craft courses 38
craft occupations 42–3
cultural patterns 206
cultural revolution 16–17
Czech Republic 50

decision-making process 29
Denmark
apprenticeship 233
careers guidance systems 219
developing countries 9
Dewey, John 40
Dix 12

Eastern Europe 49–61
economic restructuring 55–6
end of one-party rule 51–2
new opportunities for employment 55–6
polytechnic education 57–8
preparation for work 57–8
reforming and restructuring education
56–7

transforming the economy 52–3
transition from central planning to open
market economy 53–4
economic objectives and educational policy
11
economic rationalism 10–11
economic theories about education 8–11
education and training
and the economy 35
corporatist function 42
economic theories about 8–11
Europe 33–48
integrated approach 29
within youth transitions 208–14
see also vocational education and training
(VET)
educational and vocational guidance see
careers guidance systems
educational cultures, and vocational
education 39–40
educational policy, and economic
objectives 11
Elliott, W. 192
employers' interests 26
employment, gender discrimination in 239
Employment and Training Act 1973 97
Employment Training Act 1981 98
encyclopedism 40
environmental damage and technological
change 130–31
Estonia 50
ethnic minorities 24
Europe
education and training 33–48
vocational assessment systems 137
vocational qualifications 137–48
European Bank for Reconstruction and
Development 55
European Community
careers guidance services 218–29
policies and youth affairs 214–17
European Union (EU) 92, 93
youth transitions 203–17
excellence in education 29–30
externalities 11

family-building patterns 207
Federal Institute of Vocational Training
(BIBB) 104
Federal Vocational Training Institute 75
female issues
employment
in Finland 231
in Nordic countries 231
executives in Finland 236
sexuality in Finland 238, 239
students in Finland 234
see also gender; women
feminist movement in Finland 240–42
Finland 230

backlash against women 241–2
female employment 231
female executives 236
female sexuality 238, 239
female students 234
feminist movement 240–42
gender-based segmentation 231
gendered moral segmentation 239–40
industrial relations 237
liberalism and security 235
sex-businesses in 238
unemployment in 237
vocational education 238
welfare policy 230–31
flexible accumulation 6, 8, 20
Fordism 19, 20
and bureaucracy and education 22–3
and national development 22
see also neo-Fordism; post-Fordism
France
apprenticeship 142
careers guidance systems 219
validity of vocational qualifications 142
vocational education and training 145–6
further education as preparation for world
of work 122–4

gender-based culture, Jewish community
263
gender-based segmentation
Finland 231
in education and training 85
in Nordic countries 234
gender differences
and school–work transition 80–91
in course enrolments 84
in education and training 214
gender discrimination in employment 239
gender equity in job training 84
gender issues
in distribution of work and learning
82–6
in vocational education 86–9
Nordic welfare states 230–42
see also female issues; women
gender roles, changing attitudes and
practices in 207
gender-specific occupational preferences 30
Germany
academic education 43
apprenticeships 26, 74, 75, 143–4
careers guidance systems 219
Dual System 40-41, 105, 143
educational cultures 43–5
vocational education and training 103–6,
145
global issues 6–7, 21, 33
globalization 34
Gooch, A.G. 193
Greece, careers guidance systems 219

Green Party 236

Holland see Netherlands
Holland, Geoffrey 98
human ability and motivation 28
human capital theory 8–9
humanism 40
Hungary 50

ideology of meritocracy 27
Individual Action Planning 100
individualization 206, 207
industrial relations, Finland 237
Industrial Training Act 1964 72, 96
Industrial Training Boards (ITBs) 71, 75,
96–7
Industry Lead Bodies (ILBs) 102–3
Industry Training Organisations 71, 75, 98
information and information technology 7,
21, 29
Institute of Technical Education (ITE) 123–4
institutional linkages 125–6
intermediate skills 72
apprenticeship 72
training for 67
internal structures 71
international capitalism 5
international economic instability 5
International Monetary Fund 55, 56
international pressures 5–6
interpersonal work 88
Ireland, careers guidance systems 220
Italy, careers guidance systems 220

Japan 162–72
diversification policy 168
excessive competition 169–70
historical development since the war
163–5
reform of general courses 171–72
school placement system 166
upper-secondary schools 162–3, 165,
168–9, 171
and labour market 166–9
vocational education and training 46–7,
170–71
Jenkinson, A.J. 193
Jessup, Gilbert 140
Jewish community 258–67
cultural dynamic 260–61
ethnicism in education 264–7
gender-based culture 263
integration of young people in 260–63
UK society 266–7
role of education 263–4
secessionist approach 262
secularism in 263–5
junior technical schools (JTSs) 191–2

Kerschensteiner, Georg 44

Kingsland, John 194
Kirby Committee of Inquiry into Labour
    Market Programs 14
knowledge 21

labour market
    Dutch 109–11
    segmentation 177–8
    structures and vocational training 67–74
labour relations 6
Latvia 50
learning 21
Lithuania 50
Local Enterprise Councils 100
Luxembourg, careers guidance systems 220

Maastricht Treaty 25, 93, 203, 215
Malaysia 119–32
    coming to terms with rising expectations
        131
    further education and training as
        preparation for world of work
        122–4
    issues for future success 124–9
    schooling as preparation for world of
        work 121–2
    vocational education 123
Manpower Services Commission (MSC)
    96, 97
manpower shortages 130
market economy 53–4
market reform 23–6
marriage patterns 207
Martin, Jane Roland 88
Mathews, J. 12
Mill, John Stuart 8
Modern Apprenticeship initiative 67, 70,
    74, 77–8
Moldova 50
Morris, William 44–5
motivation and human ability 28
multinational companies 25, 34

National Education and Training Forum
    (NETF) 182
national pay structures 73
National Vocational Qualifications (NVQs)
    74, 76–8, 100, 101, 140–42, 146–7
neo-Fordism 20, 21
Netherlands
    careers guidance systems 220
    early school leaving 115–16
    labour market 109–11
        perspectives for school leavers 110
    labour organization and new
        organizational model 110
    notion of competence 141
    trends in educational participation
        111–15
    vocational education and training 45,

109–18, 146
networking 125–6
New Right 22, 23, 25, 26
new technology 7–8, 29
newly industrializing nations (NICs) 20, 25
Nordic countries
    female employment in 231
    gender issues 230–42
    neo-liberal trends 236
Norway, apprenticeship 233

occupational markets 68, 70
occupational structures 71
OECD 8, 9, 14
organizational efficiency 23

pay equity schemes 89
PETRA II programme 225
pluralization 206, 207
Poland 50, 52–3
political interests 7, 23–6
political–social cultures of work and
        vocational education 41–3
polytechnicalism 40
Portugal, careers guidance systems 220
post-Fordism 19–32
    education system 27–9
post-materialism 206
private goods 10
Private Industry Councils (PICs) 99–100
public goods 10–11

racist practices 30
recruitment patterns 213
research and research training 128
Roderick, Gordon 189
Rubinstein, W.D. 189
Russia 50

Sachs, Jeffrey 52
SADTU 181
Samuelson, Paul 10
Sanderson, Michael 189
school–work transition 189–90
    and gender 80–91
    Canada 80–91
    United States 80-91
schooling as preparation for world of work
    121–2
schools
    parental choice and competition among
        24
    social class and ethnic polarization 24
secondary technical schools 192–4
secretarial work 87
self-esteem 42
sex-businesses in Finland 238
sexist practices 30
sexual harassment 85
Singapore 119–32

coming to terms with rising expectations 131
further education and training as preparation for world of work 122–4
issues for future success 124–9
schooling as preparation for world of work 121–2
vocational education 123–4
Single European Market 34, 204, 209
skills
and control requirements 11
and efficiency 11
certification 74–7
concept in education and work 86
designations 87
formation 15
specification 87
taxonomies 35
Skills For Australia 13
Slovakia 50
Smith, Adam 8
Social change, Western Europe 204–8
social class 24
social conflicts 7
social context 6–7
social partnership in vocational education and training 106–7
social status 42
social technology 23
South Africa 173–87
education level by racial categorization 176
internal barriers to reconstruction 183–5
internal context 181–2
international context 180-81, 183
labour market segmentation 177–8
legacy of apartheid 174–9
matriculation results according to racial categorization 177
national qualifications framework 174
Reconstruction and Development Programme (RDP) 173, 179–85
Soviet Union 50
Spain, careers guidance systems 220
Spranger, Eduard 44
Stephens, Michael 189
student–teacher instructional conference (STIC) 253–4
Sultana, Ronald 190
Sweden, apprenticeship 233

teacher–administrator relationships 248–9
teacher–student relationships 243–57
teacher–teacher relationships 252–3
teamwork 12, 30
Technical and Vocational Education Initiative (TVEI) 157, 189, 195
technical baccalauréat 38
technical change 74–7

and environmental damage 130–31
technical competence 21
technical education
evolution of 94
organization, management and administration 128–9
technical schools 188–97
as prep schools of industry 191–4
see also city technical colleges (CTCs)
technological context 6–7
Third World 9
Thompson, Sylvanus 94
trade unions 102–3
Trades Union Congress 194
trainers, education and training 126
training see education and training
Training and Enterprise Councils (TECs) 74, 76, 99–102
Training Credits 100
Training Guarantee Scheme 15
Training Opportunities Programmes 97

Ukraine 50
unemployment in Finland 237
United Kingdom
apprenticeship 67, 70, 74, 77–8
careers guidance systems 220
competence-based assessment 139–41
vocational qualifications 146–7
youth culture 259–60
United States
school–work transition 80–91
vocational education 46–7

Vaizey, Sir John 9
Vocational and Industrial Training Board (VITB) 123
vocational assessment systems
Europe 137
flexibility in 144–7
validity of 138–9
vocational education and training (VET) 30, 35–45, 65–6, 92–108
and educational cultures 39–40
and labour market structures 67–74
and political–administrative cultures 37
and political–social cultures of work 41–3
central government intervention 98–9
centralized administration 38
continental systems 103
corporatist–statist political culture 38
curriculum development 126-7
England and Wales 93–101
evolution of 95
extra-European perspectives 46–7
Finland 238
France 145–6
gender issues in 86–9
Germany 43–5, 103–6, 145

Japan 46-7, 170–71
limits of voluntarism 101–3
Malaysia 123
Netherlands 45, 109–18, 146
programme evaluation 128
return to voluntarist principles
    99–101
Singapore 123–4
social partnership in 106–7
state-school 36–7
transition period 98–9
United States 46–7
work-employer based 40–41
vocational qualifications
    and workplace experience 142
    UK 146–7
    validity of 142
Vocational Training Act 72
VOCTECH 127–9

Wallis, H.B. 192
Western Europe
    social change 204–8
    youth transitions 204–8
Wexler, Philip 239, 243
Wiener, Martin 189
Wilson High School 243–57
    internal impediments to achievement
        and citizenship 246
    problems in pedagogy and knowledge
        content 246–8

teacher–administrator relationships
    248–9
teacher–student relationships 243–57
teacher–teacher relationships 252–3
Wilson Township 243–57
    administrator-teacher characteristics 245
    demographics 244–5
    poverty level 245
women
    association with interpersonal relational
        work 88–9
    in traditionally male areas 86
    occupational aspirations 85
    preferences in course enrolments 85
    see also female issues; gender
workplace organization 7–8
World Bank 56

Young, David 98
youth affairs and European Community
        policies 214–17
youth culture in UK 259–60
Youth for Europe programme 216
youth training initiatives 69
Youth Training Scheme 99
youth transitions
    education and training within 208–14
    European Union 203–17
    Western Europe 204–8
youth unemployment 115
Youth Work Plan 115